HANDBOOK FOR CLASSICAL RESEARCH

One of the glories of the Greco-Roman classics is the opportunity that they give us to consider a great culture in its entirety; but our ability to do that depends on our ability to work comfortably with very varied fields of scholarship. The *Handbook for Classical Research* offers guidance to students needing to learn more about the different fields and subfields of classical research, and its methods and resources.

The book is divided into 7 parts: The Basics, Language, The Traditional Fields, The Physical Remains, The Written Word, The Classics and Related Disciplines, and The Classics since Antiquity. Topics covered range from history and literature, lexicography and linguistics, epigraphy and palaeography, to archaeology and numismatics, and the study and reception of the classics.

Guidance is given not only on how to read, for example, an archaeological or papyrological report, but also on how to find such sources when they are relevant to research. Concentrating on "how-to" topics, the *Handbook for Classical Research* is a much needed resource for both teachers and students.

David M. Schaps, Associate Professor of Classical Studies at Bar Ilan University, is the author of *Economic Rights of Women in Ancient Greece*, *The Invention of Coinage and the Monetization of Ancient Greece*, *The Beauty of Japheth* (a primer of ancient Greek for speakers of modern Hebrew), and dozens of articles on classical topics covering ancient history, economics, tragedy, metrics, lexicography, epigraphy, palaeography, and classical reception.

HANDBOOK FOR CLASSICAL RESEARCH

David M. Schaps

Routledge
Taylor & Francis Group

LONDON AND NEW YORK

First published 2011
by Routledge
2 Park Square, Milton Park, Abingdon, Oxon, OX14 4RN

Simultaneously published in the USA and Canada
by Routledge
711 Third Avenue, New York, NY 10017

Routledge is an imprint of the Taylor & Francis Group, an informa business

© 2011 David M. Schaps

Typeset in Joanna and Scala Sans by
Swales & Willis Ltd, Exeter, Devon
Printed and bound in Great Britain by
CPI Antony Rowe, Chippenham, Wiltshire

British Library Cataloguing in Publication Data
A catalogue record for this book is available from the British Library

Library of Congress Cataloging in Publication Data
A catalog record for this book has been requested

ISBN 13: 978–0–415–42522–3 (hbk)
ISBN 13: 978–0–415–42523–0 (pbk)
ISBN 13: 978–0–203–84437–3 (ebk)

From my teachers and my students
For my students and their students

Contents

PART IV: THE PHYSICAL REMAINS

PART V: THE WRITTEN WORD

PART VI: THE CLASSICS AND RELATED DISCIPLINES

PART VII: THE CLASSICS SINCE ANTIQUITY

Figures

PREFACE

WHY THIS BOOK WAS WRITTEN

Cassius Severus, a noted speaker in the Roman law-courts, once walked into a school of oratory where Lucius Cestius Pius was holding forth. "If I were a gladiator," said Cestius, "I would be Fusius.[1] If I were a mime, I would be Bathyllus; if I were a horse, I would be Melissio." "If you were a sewer," added Severus dryly, "you would be the *cloaca maxima*."[2] My achievements have never allowed me the illusion that I really was Fusius or Bathyllus, much less Alexander or Demosthenes; but when I was younger I indeed harbored the ambition[3] to excel in all fields to which I might put my hand, and the advice of Peleus to Achilles[4] was the blessing of my beloved teacher, Martin Ostwald, when I finished my under-graduate study. This did not make me the greatest scholar of my genera-tion, nor even the greatest classicist of my generation, but it left me uncomfortable with the super-specialization that would have offered an

---

[1] Apparently an eminent one; such is the nature of fame that Severus and Cestius are little known today, Bathyllus hardly more, Fusius and the horse Melissio not at all.

[2] Si cloaca esses, maxima esses: Sen. Contr. 3.17.

[3] This delusion of grandeur was perhaps more common in my generation than in others. I was fourteen years old when John F. Kennedy, in his inaugural address, promised a struggle against "tyranny, poverty, disease, and war itself." Kennedy was sober enough to realize that those goals would not be realized quickly, "nor even perhaps in our lifetime on this planet"; but they were goals that offered our generation a heroic view of the tasks before us, and of the importance of our own efforts.

[4] αἰὲν ἀριστεύειν, καὶ ὑπείροχον ἔμμεναι ἄλλων, μηδὲ γένος πατέρων αἰσχυνέμεν, Hom. Il. 6.208–9.

easy excuse for ignorance of all matters not relevant to the subject of my doctoral dissertation. Hence this book, which is intended, in the first instance, to form the basis for a graduate course offering a survey of classical research, its subfields, research methods and resources.

Because the remains of Greco-Roman antiquity, however impressive, are relatively few, we cannot afford to ignore any of them if we wish to understand the works themselves and the people who produced them. The books and manuscripts that contain, or claim to contain, their words; the languages in which they expressed their thoughts; the ruins of their monumental buildings and of their humble homesteads; their marble statuary and their clay pots; their official inscriptions and their graffiti, the scraps of their papyri, their coins, their pictures, and the reflections of scholars, heirs and imitators who have collected, pondered and used the thoughts that they themselves thought or that later generations have derived from them—all of these contribute to the understanding of antiquity.

Until relatively recently the training of classicists was almost entirely linguistic. The essential skills required were a thorough understanding of Greek and Latin and careful reading of the ancient texts. Interested students arrived at the university after a good number of years spent studying the languages, and with some familiarity with basic texts. A person pursuing postgraduate studies would be expected to have a good knowledge of the major texts, and graduate training consisted of honing critical skills and exercising them for new critical research. Ancient art and ancient ruins were there to be seen and ancient history was a tale told by ancient historians; the philologically trained scholar could be expected to approach them with the same critical faculties that were applied to texts.

By the middle of the twentieth century it was becoming obvious that philological training alone would not suffice, and in the intervening half-century that conclusion has become ever more inescapable. Linguistics, archaeology, epigraphy and even literary criticism have developed a life of their own. What there is to know about the ancient economy is vastly more than can be gleaned by an untrained eye surveying Trajan's Forum; the first lines of an Athenian decree reveal much more than mere knowledge of the language will tell; the vocabulary of Thucydides or of Plautus can tell us more about those authors, their works and their societies than we can find in a dictionary. A classicist today needs a reasonable acquaintance with a whole arsenal of critical tools.

It is dismaying, though in our overspecialized, research-project-driven universities perhaps not surprising, that, although most graduate departments require their students to take a course in these subjects, no book exists in English that can serve as the basis for such a course. Martin McGuire's mimeographed text,[5] the only one there was, is mostly a list of books and is now half a century old; the series of pamphlets published by Routledge under the title *Approaching the Ancient World* includes some excellent introductory works but makes no pretense of covering the field, being very much slanted toward historical research. A comprehensive introduction to classical research has been needed for fifty years, but no scholar has been presumptuous enough to attempt one.

WHY I HAVE WRITTEN THIS BOOK

The naive reader, on leafing through the table of contents, may draw the not unreasonable conclusion that its author is familiar, or pretends to be familiar, with all the various fields discussed in it. Quite the contrary is the case. Were I more familiar with each of these fields, I would not be so acutely aware of the difficulties encountered by an outsider trying to deal with them. I have, in the course of a career which I fear is much more than half-completed, had to deal with many of these fields in the course of my reading, my research or my teaching. It is my hope that this handbook will help its readers start at age twenty-five or thirty at the point that I have reached as I pass sixty, and carry on from there.

But why have I done this alone, rather than appointing myself editor and requesting articles from specialists in all the various subfields discussed? I am not an archaeologist, nor a philosopher, nor a papyrologist; so why did I not ask those who are to write the appropriate chapters? The answer is that I feared that a book so produced, though undoubtedly more authoritative than the one before you, would inevitably suffer from such wide varieties of approach that it would be next to useless as the basis for a course; no editorial hand is so firm that it can produce a clear and useful progression from chapter to chapter, with unity of approach, tone and all the other essentials that make a book readable and usable. The same reasoning, applied to the classroom, makes most university departments entrust the teaching of their survey course to a single lecturer, rather than having each department member give a single lecture on what that member knows best. Collections of essays have many important uses, but they do not generally make good textbooks.

Even though they are all the work of a single author, the chapters of this book are not uniform. Some are long and some are short; some devote a

---

[5] McGuire, *Introduction to Classical Scholarship*.

number of pages to the major scholarly resources, some only a paragraph or two, some nothing at all. In two cases—literature and history, the two chief components of most classical curricula—I have made no effort to discuss the subject matter itself, with which I expect my readers to be familiar, but have restricted myself to a discussion of various approaches that have been or can be taken towards the subject.

I have no doubt that some reviewers will say that the time has passed when a single person could write a book encompassing the whole study of the ancient world, and if this book were designed to be a *Summa Totius Antiquitatis* I would surely agree; the great Augustus Böckh planned such a study for Greece alone a century and a half ago, and even he never accomplished it. But this is not a *Summa*, but a handbook; nor was it designed, like the *Handbuch der Altertumswissenschaft*,[6] to offer a handy guide to all available knowledge, but to offer an orientation that will allow the interested student to progress further independently. The undisputed fact that nobody can conquer all of the realms so briefly outlined here should not prevent a person from entering them. I do not think that it is necessary or desirable for classicists to entrench ourselves within the confines of our specialty, fearing to venture beyond them for fear of breaking the illusion of omniscience that we can project in the subjects we have studied closely. On the contrary, I think that in allowing ourselves to become specialists rather than generalists we have renounced the ability at least to consider a society in its entirety, one of the great advantages that the study of antiquity offers to the modern world. I want, by this book, to encourage classicists to think that they may indeed dare to venture beyond the bounds of their specialty. I hope that my book will be a welcome research aid not only to beginners, but to those whose work has already taken them far down some of the many roads that lead from Greece and Rome.

For all that, as work on this book has progressed, it has become increasingly apparent that it is likely to demolish whatever reputation I may have had as a scholar. I take it for granted that there is no professional classicist who does not know something of importance that I do not know, and it follows that each one is likely at some point to say, shocked by my ignorance, "He doesn't even know *that*! And I had thought he was a serious scholar!" Even if the scholarly world should be generous enough to welcome the book for what it has, it will undoubtedly age quickly, and a new generation, frustrated by trying to follow my out-of-date instructions, will mention my name, if at all, with a sigh or a sneer. Nevertheless

---

[6]   On which see below, p. 36.

I have persevered, chiefly out of a desire to help the many teachers and students for whom some book of this sort, however imperfect, can save hours, weeks, months or years of discovering what other people know.

HOW THIS BOOK WAS WRITTEN

This is not a "companion to classical studies," many of which already exist: it does not offer a background to Greek and Roman history and literature, but presumes that you already have at least the beginnings of such a background. It is not a style manual of how to write scholarly articles: if you have not taken a course in expository writing, many books exist to help you with the style, and *The Chicago Manual of Style* will tell you more than you want to know about the formatting. The book you are holding does offer some bibliographical help, but Jenkins, *Classical Studies: A Guide to the Reference Literature* will give you fuller guidance in that field. Lastly, it is not a researcher's manual in any of the subfields of classics: it will not tell you how to organize an archaeological dig, how to recognize the age of a manuscript or an inscription from the letter forms, or which emperor bore the titles PIVS · ARAB · ADIAB · PARTH · MAX · BRITT · MAX, though it will tell you where such information can be found.

"The intelligent newcomer's next questions," Richard Talbert has written to me,[7] "are,"

> So, if I'm interested, what background preparation is best? Then where should I plan to study, and who are the experts from among whom I should seek one or more potential advisers? What have been the field's main approaches and controversies over the past 20 years? What has proven productive, *and what hasn't*, and why? In this context, what themes/areas are currently looking interesting and remain unexplored or underexplored or clearly ripe for rethinking?

These are the questions that lead beyond the realm of a handbook to classical research and into the world of specialization. Some of them are addressed by more specialized books, of which a selection, by no means exhaustive or authoritative, is given in the guides to resources appended to most of the chapters in this book. Others can only be judged by speaking to others in the field and by doing your own reading and evaluation:

---

[7] He was commenting on an earlier draft of this book.

no book will tell you in print that Professor X is a nasty curmudgeon, or that Professor Y hasn't had an original thought in thirty years, or that Professor Z may steal your ideas and pretend to have invented them, or—to take a more sanguine tack—that Professor A is particularly helpful, Professor B exacting but fair, Professor C a well-connected scholar who will introduce you to the most important people in the field.

Looked at from two millennia later, the world of the Greeks and the world of the Romans tend to blend into a single thing that scholars sometimes call "Greco-Roman antiquity," and we indeed try to be *periti utriusque linguae*; but life is short, the world of Vergil was very different from the world of Homer, and classicists tend to divide into Hellenists and Latinists. More significantly, generalizations that are made about Greece do not necessarily hold for Rome, and vice versa. Nevertheless, at the risk of speaking *grosso modo* about things that are not really comparable in their details, I have tried throughout this book to address both the dominant cultures of classical antiquity and to draw my examples from both. One of my goals, after all, is to encourage all of us to broaden our scholarly horizons.

Obviously any research handbook that does not deal with internet resources is living in an earlier age; but the resources available there change so often and so rapidly that anyone looking for an internet resource should look on the web itself, where there are well-maintained websites that offer portals to other resources, though none, so far, attempts to catalogue everything the way the great bibliographical journals do.[8]

"The subject of Renaissance literature," said Professor Scintillating in a student-written play of my undergraduate days,[9] "is a difficult and subtle one, that can only be understood through a series of vapid generalizations, which I will attempt to deliver in as scintillating a manner as possible." The real Professor Scintillating—we all knew who was being parodied—was in fact an excellent and beloved teacher, whose students have gone on to be among the greatest literary and cultural scholars of my generation. There is not a chapter in this book that cannot be seen as a series of vapid generalizations. Part of the reason is space—I am, after all, trying to summarize a subject that fills many research libraries—but the major reason is that I am not writing to show you what you must do, but to give you a general view that will allow you, like the real Professor

---

8   Below, pp. 36–8.
9   I was not the student who wrote it, and I quote from memory, probably inaccurately. The author, Lawrence E. Arnstein, tells me that he, too, now knows the scene only from memory.

Scintillating's students, to get your own idea of what fields are available and what can be done with them. Others will guide you in your chosen direction; my job has been to show you the lay of the land so that you can pick out your road with discernment, and always be aware of what other realms are out there, available to you when you need them.

Acknowledgements

As the academic year of 2005–06 approached and the presence of some new graduate students in our department made it necessary to schedule the course Introduction to Classical Philology that we require of them, I realized that the time had come, ten years after his retirement, to allow Professor David Sohlberg to feel that someone else in the department he had created would be capable of teaching the course. It was my student Yevgeniy Zingerman, a student not of classics but of biblical studies, who defined for me what he wanted to get from the course: "I want to be able, if the need should arise, to deal with material from the classics without sounding immediately like someone who knows nothing about them." This handbook, which was prepared as a textbook for that course, has arisen from a belief that most students, and indeed most researchers, share Yevgeniy's feeling that there is a good deal of material in the classics for which their intellect is sufficient but their background is not; and my first thanks have to go to Professor Sohlberg for pioneering the course, and to Yevgeniy for defining its purpose.

It was Richard Stoneman to whom I first broached the idea of this project, and his encouragement was what turned a passing idea into a practical plan; he and his assistant Amy Laurens and their successors at Routledge, Matthew Gibbons and Lalle Pursglove, deserve credit for seeing the book through to completion. If the new editors can reproduce the energy, wide horizons and openness to new ideas that Richard Stoneman always combined with accuracy and attractive packaging, they will undoubtedly be, as he has been throughout his career, among the lions of classical publishing. It is Lalle Pursglove who has dealt with the manuscript directly. If she really speaks about me as gently as she writes to me, she is a woman of great patience. If not, she is a woman of great diplomacy. Caroline Watson of

Swales & Willis has managed the physical production of the book courteously, efficiently, and professionally.

The chapters were shared with the members of my department, whose suggestions and criticisms were so helpful that each must be thanked by name: David Sohlberg, Ranon Katzoff, Daniela Dueck, Gabriel Danzig, Lisa Maurice and Hava Bracha Korzakova. Some of my students had the temerity to add their own criticisms, for which I owe them thanks; particular mention must be made of the many useful comments of Tal Relles-Shorer and David Merhav, and, although Tikva Kronman offered only one suggestion, it was a particularly good one. The assistance and generosity of the staff of the Wurzweiler Library at Bar-Ilan University, the Elias Sourasky Library at Tel Aviv University, the Van Pelt Dietrich Library at the University of Pennsylvania and the Sackler Library at Oxford have been essential to the preparation of this book, as to many others.

The students' comments helped assure that the handbook would be of use to those who need it; the comments of scholars, some of whom had never met me but agreed to review my work on the shortest of notice, reduced the number of blunders, once much more numerous, to what you see before you. Particular thanks go to David Adan-Bayewitz, Sheila Ager, Roger Bagnall, Drora Baharal, George H. Brown, Werner Eck, Moshe Fischer, Richard Hamilton, Orna Harari, Steven Harvey, David Konstan, John Kroll, Avshalom Laniado, Polly Low, Alexander Nehamas, Daniel Riaño Rufilanchas, Israel Roll, Cynthia Shelmerdine, Miriam Shlesinger, Bernard Spolsky and Dan Tompkins, and especially Malcolm Heath, David Sansone and Richard Talbert, who read and commented on (but are not guilty of) the entire manuscript. Most of the criticisms were quite accurate—including the suspicion of those who judged the original proposal, that it would take longer than I had allotted for it. The greatest thanks go to the harshest critics, since criticism was what I needed. Errors, of course, are my own, as are all translations unless otherwise stated.

A special acknowledgement goes to the Israel Society for the Promotion of Classical Studies, whose annual conferences, too small to have parallel sessions and too interesting to skip, expose me year by year to research in every area of the classics, and have a lot to do with my belief that it would be helpful to all of us to have a better background in the sort of work others are doing. The years I spent as an editor of the *Scripta Classica Israelica* only strengthened that belief.

My wife recognized immediately the size of this undertaking, and the professional cost it would exact. She has nevertheless taken it with good grace, as she has regularly taken my tendency—quixotic, she calls it—to take on myself projects that are overly ambitious. I wonder if I would do anything without her help and appreciation.

REPRODUCTION PERMISSIONS

The following were reproduced with kind permission. While every effort has been made to trace copyright holders and obtain permission, this may not have been possible in all cases. Any omissions brought to our attention will be remedied in future editions.

Figure 9.1: Public domain.
Figure 17.1: Walter de Gruyter GmbH & Co. Reproduced by permission.
Figure 17.2: Photograph by the author.
Figure 17.3: Photograph by PRA at http://en.wikipedia.org/wiki/ File:Crete_-_law_of_Gortyn_-_boustrophedon.JPG, access date 3 March 2010. Available under the GNU Free Documentation License.
Figure 17.4: Photograph by Μαρσύας at http://en.wikipedia.org/ wiki/File:EPMA-6794-IGI(3)48-Sacred_law-3.JPG, access date 3 March 2010. Available under the GNU Free Documentation License.
Figure 18.1: Courtesy of the Egypt Exploration Society.
Chapter 19: All figures from Thompson, *An Introduction to Greek and Latin Palaeography*. Public domain.
Figure 21.1: Penn Museum object E17527, image #31345. Reproduced by permission.
Figure 21.2: Photograph from http://www.greek-thesaurus.gr/ Museum_of_Delphi.html, access date 3 March 2010. Courtesy of Theodoros Koletsis.
Figure 21.3: Photograph by Fikret Yegul at http://commons. wikimedia.org/wiki/File:Trajan's_Column_(Roman_Soldiers_ Building_a_Fortress).png, access date 3 March 2010. Available under the GNU Free Documentation License.
Figure 21.4: Photograph by Marie-Lan Nguyen at http://commons. wikimedia.org/wiki/File:Herakles_tripod_Louvre_F341.jpg, access date 3 March 2010. Public domain.
Figure 21.5: © bpk / Antikensammlung, Staatliche Museen zu Berlin. Photo: Johannes Laurentius. Reproduced by permission.
Figure 21.6: Photograph by Gunnar Bach Pedersen at http://commons. wikimedia.org/wiki/File:Fra-titusbuen.jpg, access date 3 March 2010. Public domain.

Figure 21.7: Photograph © by Yossi Zeliger. Reproduced by permission.
Figure 21.8: Photograph © by Ken Fuller. Reproduced by permission.

Thanks also to the Trustees of the British Museum/Bibliothèque Nationale
de France, for permission to reproduce text from *Roman Provincial Coinage* by
Andrew Burnett, Michel Amandry and Pere Pau Ripollès (British Museum
Press/Bibliothèque Nationale, London/Paris 1992–).

PART I

THE BASICS

1

THE NATURE OF THE FIELD

WHY DO WE PURSUE RESEARCH IN THE HUMANITIES?

There are many open questions in the humanities: whether the poems of Homer were written by one person, two or many; whether the works of John Cage can properly be called music and those of Jackson Pollock art; whether it was Richard III, Henry VII or someone else who was responsible for the death of the last legitimate Yorkist heir to the throne of England. I suppose that there have been people who were attracted to the study of the humanities by the hope of solving these and similar questions. I doubt that there have been many. Most of us who study and teach the humanities do so from a fascination—perhaps love, perhaps curiosity, perhaps even hate[1]—of the works, the people and the periods that we study, and our interest in the subject is not dependent upon its further development by research.[2] A student generally falls in love with

---

[1] Love of the subject matter is not the only possible reason for undertaking a career in the humanities. Many people study Nazism not out of a love of history or of the period when it flourished but out of a desire to understand how that nightmarish tyranny arose, and how it can be prevented from ever raising its head again. For people like these the reasons for pursuing research are self-evident.

[2] Exceptions to this are those fields of the humanities that have achieved some semblance of scientific structure: archaeology, for example, or psycholinguistics (for the distinction, see Schaps, *Invention of Coinage*, 333–9). These fields may indeed attract students by the promise of new and exciting discoveries; for that very reason they are exceptional among the humanities.

Homer, not with the Homeric Question; with music, not with its classification or description; with history, not with this or that party to an ancient conflict. We would rather be Homer than Wilamowitz, rather Beethoven than any of his biographers. Why, then, do most of us spend a good deal of our lives researching the humanities rather than simply enjoying and sharing them?

A cynic's answer would be that many of us are employed by universities that, dominated by a paradigm more appropriate to the natural sciences, pay us in proportion to the number and quality of our research articles; but that cannot be the entire answer. Scholars were researching the humanities, and arguing about them vituperatively, before anyone dreamed of paying them for it.[3] Why did they do it? Why do we?

Probably each researcher will have a personal answer, but in the general case I think it can be said that anyone who is fascinated by a subject will think about it, will ask questions about it and will want to know more about it. On first looking into Homer we may be spellbound; on the second or third reading we start to notice things we hadn't noticed before, and to wonder about matters that had not at first commanded our attention. As long as we keep our questions and opinions to ourselves, we may be satisfied with them; but the moment we reveal them to others, we discover that they may see things otherwise. What seemed self-evident to us may seem nonsensical to them. At this point we start looking for an argument that will demonstrate that we are right; and that is the point where passive enjoyment has ended and research has begun.

There is, in fact, a practically unlimited variety of ways in which to read a book, to hear a symphony or to imagine a historical event. Some of these ways are more enlightened, more enlightening or simply more correct than others. It is the intention of this book to put before classical scholars a brief account of the resources and methods that are available to us to help us delve more deeply into the things that interest us.

TEACHING AND RESEARCH

I will admit at the outset that the relationship between teaching and research in the humanities is fundamentally different from that in the natural sciences. Teaching in the sciences is the handmaiden of research:

---

[3]   Long before the advent of the research university, Jonathan Swift's *Battle of the Books* and George Eliot's *Middlemarch* parodied scholars who, whatever their faults, were passionately devoted to scholarship that brought them no monetary reward.

we train biologists and physicists by the thousands because we hope for further progress and need a new generation of researchers to carry our knowledge forward. Most students of the natural sciences will not become researchers, but it is only by training large numbers that we will produce the leaders whose solutions to the outstanding questions in the sciences are likely to have momentous consequences for us all, hopefully for the better. It is certainly a great public benefit to disseminate broadly the scientific knowledge that is so essential a part of our lives, and it could be wished that our electorates and decision makers had more such knowledge; but few university departments of natural science take the broad dissemination of scientific knowledge as their central purpose.

In the humanities the situation is somewhat different. Few lives will be changed by solving the question of whether the Iliad and Odyssey were written by a single author, or why Cleopatra's ships fled at the battle of Actium; but we do think that almost anyone's life will be made richer by knowing the Iliad, almost anyone's political understanding and judgment about public affairs deepened by reading Thucydides or Cicero. We certainly do research; it is a superficial reader who can read widely without asking questions, and a singularly incurious questioner who does not look for an answer to the questions that arise. But research does not occupy as central a position in the humanities as it does in the sciences—surely not in the classics, a discipline whose essence is not so much the invention of new knowledge as the preservation of old knowledge for the use of the future. Our research output is neither the only nor the essential justification for teaching the classics in universities. This point is often lost sight of in universities built on a research-oriented model whose basis is in the natural sciences.[4]

Another important point that a classicist must always keep in mind is that nobody can be a good classicist who does not know the classics. A modern research university is built not only around research but around research projects, planned in advance with defined questions, methods and research goals, and often—very importantly for the continued existence of the university and its departments—outside funding to support the research. Many such projects are quite valuable; but they are not a substitute for a thorough knowledge of the classics, which means reading and rereading the texts, visiting the sites, and looking at the

---

[4]   It will not be helpful to the Anglophone reader, but courtesy requires me to state that the previous two paragraphs are based on an article by Professor Ben-Ami Shillony entitled *Maddaei HaRuach b'chavlei HaMadda* ("The Humanities in the Chains of Science") that appeared in Hebrew in 1994 in the Israeli daily *Haaretz*.

artworks and artifacts on which our knowledge of the ancient world is based. Unless you are exceptionally fortunate, nobody will pay you for sitting down with Plato, Plautus or Plutarch just to read them and think about them; on the contrary, your employers may consider it a waste of time. Their opinion must be taken into account, since they pay for your bread and butter; but it is precisely wide reading and thinking, broadened and deepened over the years, that produces the great classicist that your employers, too, want you to be. Somehow time must be made for constant and undirected reading, observing and exploring if you are ever to get from the classics what they have to offer.

THE CHANGING SIGNIFICANCE OF ANTIQUITY

The Distinctive Position of Greco-Roman Culture

The study of Greco-Roman antiquity has meant different things to different people over the ages, and its place in the totality of culture has varied widely. That we study the past is unremarkable; every generation learns from its predecessors, and it would be foolhardy not to do so. That we study the past in greater depth and in greater detail than most people also needs no apology: if the past is worth knowing, it is worth knowing accurately. What is peculiar about our field is the privileged position it gives to two societies of the past, skipping over others closer to us in place and in time, and treating one particular area and one particular period as being of exceptional importance—as being classical.

It is not unreasonable to ask why Greece and Rome should hold this privileged position, and whether it is still worth our while to study them. Readers of this book, no doubt, have already made that decision; but it is worth noting that the answers to these two questions have varied considerably; and the way the subject is approached will depend quite a bit on the answers that we ourselves give to them.

The simplest explanation for the special regard given to Greece and Rome is one that classicists are loath to put forward: force of arms and institutional power. Greek culture was spread from the Indus to Ethiopia by the conquests of Alexander, and became part of the culture of the Romans when they, in their turn, spread their rule from Britain to the Euphrates. Although their dominion eventually fell, the religion that they had adopted remained, and so the Roman Empire (and before it classical Greece) was always seen as the ancestor of the Catholic church, which indeed continued to speak the language of the Romans until 1963.

According to this understanding, which parallels the way non-Europeans tend to see the current ascendancy of European and American culture, the prestige of Greco-Roman culture is merely a consequence of the military success of the Greeks and Romans and the institutional success of the church, unrelated to any intrinsic value that their culture may or may not have. This argument has a good deal of force, particularly in a post-imperialist age, and it is almost certainly part of the answer; but it is not the entire story, for people of different ages have had widely varying reasons for studying the Greco-Roman classics.

How the Particular Became Classical

Discussion of past events and of great literature in classical Athens was not qualitatively different from any society's interest in its own past; the activities of Hellenistic scholars in the Museum of Alexandria were remarkable but understandable, an effort to maintain what the conquerors saw as their superior culture in a sea of barbarity. That the Greeks considered their culture to be superior to others was only natural;[5] if anything, the Greeks were exceptional in their willingness to admit that other nations had cultures worthy of study, or at least of description.

It was in Rome that Greek civilization became classical. Many influential Romans accepted the Greeks' estimation of Rome as a barbarous or semi-barbarous state, and set out to learn true culture from the Greeks. From the third to the first pre-Christian centuries, Rome underwent a period of conscious and even extreme Hellenization, in which its literature, its artwork and its architecture refashioned themselves on Greek models. During this period, the study of Greek culture was, for those who pursued it, the study of culture itself: one studied Homer or Theognis in order to learn how to write poetry, the works of Phidias to learn sculpture, Demosthenes to learn to speak persuasively. Cultured Romans spoke Greek, and, to study the arts in which the Greeks excelled, Roman nobles might travel to Athens or import Greek teachers to Rome. It is perhaps to this age that we owe the impression that Greek culture and the culture that the Romans built upon it are in a sense the only real culture that there is.

Not every Roman thought that way. Cato, who dismissed the entire study of rhetoric (at which he excelled) with the formula *rem tene, verba*

---

[5]   And equally natural was the fact that the Egyptians thought the opposite: cf., for example, Herodotus 2.143 or Plato *Timaeus* 22–3.

sequentur,[6] and Sulla, who told the Athenian ambassadors who pled for mercy on the grounds of their city's illustrious past that he had been sent not to enjoy learning but to defeat rebels,[7] expressed as well as any modern Philistine the opinion that the world could get along quite well without the study of the classics. But once we have learned something, we may accept it or reject it, but we cannot think it away and return to the state we were in before we knew it. However uneasy it may have made some of them, the Romans had become what we can only see as Greco-Romans.

To the Greeks, in the meantime, it became bitterly obvious that the days of their greatness were over, and there developed a cultural nostalgia that expressed itself in an effort to restore the forms of ancient Greek life and literature, and even their language.[8] This was the first clear sign of an inevitable and fateful development, the increasing distance between the language of the classics and the spoken language. In the west, the dominance of Latin written on classical models was so complete that it is almost impossible to trace the early development of the modern Romance languages; by the time they were written at all, they had become entirely different languages, not merely Latin dialects. In the Latin-speaking areas, Latin had become a foreign language by the early Middle Ages, its use confined to certain classes of people and certain religious, social or institutional contexts. The Greeks do not quite admit that ancient Greek is a foreign language[9]—there exists a modern dictionary of all Greek from Homer to today,[10] and one could hardly imagine a single dictionary of everything written in Rome from Livius Andronicus to *Il Corriere della Sera*— but it is not intelligible to modern Greeks unless they study it in school, just as foreigners must.[11] The classics have become irrevocably bound up

---

6   Iulius Victor, *Ars Rhetorica* I (p. 374 in Halm, ed. *Rhetores Latini Minores*).

7   ἐγὼ γὰρ οὐ φιλομαθήσων εἰς Ἀθήνας ὑπὸ Ῥωμαίων ἐπέμφθην, ἀλλὰ τοὺς ἀφισταμένους καταστρεψόμενος, Plut. Sulla 13.4.

8   This was not the only reason for the Atticizing movement that began in the first century CE; see the brief and striking description of this development in Browning, *Medieval and Modern Greek*, 44–50, and Kazazis, "Atticism."

9   For this reason the speech of educated Greeks traditionally used an intentionally archaizing dialect, a practice that was finally abolished from the schools only in 1976.

10   Dimitrakos, *Mega Lexikon*.

11   Well before the nationalist movement that produced modern Greek, the expression Ἑλληνικὴ γλῶσσα referred to ancient Greek, and ancient works might be translated into the modern tongue; the moderns, until the nineteenth century, tended to call themselves Ῥωμαῖοι. See Liakos, "'From Greek into Our Common Language.'"

with the study of dead languages, a study that on the one hand places enormous difficulties in the learner's path and has often offered, on the other hand, significant prestige to those who overcome the difficulties and can express opinions on works that most people cannot read.

The conversion of the Roman Empire to Christianity did not mean the entire overthrow of classical culture, but it did mark a new cultural era in at least one sense: the works of the ancient Greeks and Romans had now become problematical, because their authors and their ideologies were pagan. The controversy about the proper place of Homer, Aristotle, Cicero and Vergil in a Christian empire and a Christian education was long-standing and wide-ranging, but the debate itself shows that at least to some extent, for Christians, the pagan authors were no longer entirely "our" authors in the way that they had been for earlier generations. History now began with Jesus; what came before was not far different from what we think of as prehistory—time that undoubtedly existed, and about which a good deal is known, but time in which the essentials of our existence were not yet there. Yet more, the prehistory of Christendom was less that of Greece and Rome than that of Israel: Abraham, Moses and the prophets loomed larger than Alexander or Caesar. For the first time but not the last, the classics had to justify their place in education.

No less fateful for the classical tradition was the division of the Empire, and after it of the church, into two halves, one speaking Latin and one speaking Greek.[12] In the western part of the Empire, the Greek language was almost entirely forgotten; in the east the same happened to Latin. For a long period of time people of one church could know the works of the other language only in translation; when the Renaissance revived the ideal of a person *peritus utriusque linguae*, neither the ancient Greek nor the Latin language was anybody's mother tongue any longer.

And yet the culture of the ancients did not die with their languages. If both Hellenic culture and Roman civilization had originally been spread by the force of arms, they asserted themselves in later ages by their intellectual and artistic qualities, without and to a large extent in spite of institutional efforts. The first appearance of this anomaly was the success, already mentioned, of Greek forms in superseding and indeed

---

[12] Both empires, of course, were huge polyglot assemblages of peoples speaking any number of languages, but the language of empire—that is, the language of administration—was Latin in the west, Greek in the east. In the west, Latin supplanted most of the local languages, and much of what was the western empire today speaks Romance languages; in the east, on the other hand, where the caliphs ceased to use Greek, it has retreated to more or less its classical boundaries.

condemning to almost total oblivion the native cultural forms of the Romans; but it was not a phenomenon that happened only once. Saint Jerome was at first unable to control himself from reading Cicero and Plautus.[13] Both Christians and Jews of the twelfth century found the philosophy of Aristotle so compelling that they thought it necessary to rethink their entire religious philosophy in his terms,[14] and people of a more literary bent found Ovid so compelling that they felt it necessary to recast him in a more moral light.[15] The humanists of the Renaissance scoured the monasteries and offered princely sums for copies of classical works. The very lively theatrical forms of the late Middle Ages, the morality plays and the biblical cycle plays, were swept off the boards in the Renaissance by tragedy and comedy that were heavily influenced by classical models. In our own days, a soldier in a bombed-out building may turn at random to a passage of Vergil and find that "these lines, written some thirty years before the birth of Christ, expressed, more directly and passionately than any modern statement I knew of, the reality of the world I was living in."[16] Every modern teacher of the classics who teaches long enough and well enough will have students who will come up and say: *this passage* expresses what I have always felt and never been able to say; *this author* has defined for me the question that has been bothering me, and that I have not been able to identify on my own; *this work of art* shows an aspect of existence that I have seen nowhere else. The classics, as long as people still read and experience them, continue to assert themselves even when the dominant culture ignores or even opposes them.

For centuries after the Renaissance, the Greco-Roman classics were considered the apogee of culture; but by the end of the seventeenth century, in the famous "Quarrel of the Ancients and the Moderns," voices began to be heard claiming that modern culture had nothing to be ashamed of in the comparison with the ancients. And although the ancients did not lose their place quickly or entirely—not only the classicists of the eighteenth century but also the romantics of the nineteenth were heavily

---

[13] Hier. Ep. 22.30. Later, in the wake of the famous nightmare in which he was accused *Ciceronianus es, non Christianus*, he succeeded in weaning himself from the pagan authors.

[14] For the Christians, it was the scholastics who incorporated Aristotle; for the Jews it was chiefly Maimonides, particularly in *The Guide for the Perplexed*. They did their job so well that, when later generations rejected Aristotelian physics, many considered that to be a rejection or a disproof of religion.

[15] The culmination of this was the famous fourteenth-century *Ovide moralisé*, making Ovid not only acceptable but a downright moral authority.

[16] Knox, *Essays Ancient and Modern*, xxxi.

influenced by classical models—they have ceased to be the defining form of culture. When we speak of Homer and Vergil nowadays we speak not of epic but of Greek epic or Roman epic; when we speak of Plato and Aristotle we speak not of philosophy but of Greek philosophy. In some areas, notably science, medicine and engineering, the moderns have progressed so far beyond the ancients that classical authors are of antiquarian interest only. Much of what the ancients had to say has become outmoded, and much has been absorbed into the general culture. With the advent of Christianity, the classics faced attack as something decadent and pagan; now they face competition from cultures that began as their own imitators.

In retrospect it is remarkable how long the Latin language managed to maintain its position. The Renaissance, for all its classicism, had brought about a flowering of vernacular literature, and after the Reformation it was only in the Catholic countries that Latin remained the language of religion. But it retained the cachet of an international language, and so much of scholarship continued to be written in Latin that fluency in that language remained for long a requirement for all fields of study; university classes were conducted in Latin until well into the nineteenth century, and schoolchildren were required to work and even to play in that language.[17] Competence in Latin, whether real or pretended, could be a sign of either intellectual accomplishment or social class—an aspect that has not entirely disappeared even today. As it was displaced, it retained certain niches, sometimes precisely because it could serve as a secret language unavailable to the vulgar: it was long convenient for physicians to write prescriptions in Latin, and words too impolite to be written in a language everyone could understand could be printed with impunity in Latin.

The Broadening of the Field

Whether or not it was a result of the new competition, the study of Greco-Roman antiquity underwent a fundamental change in the nineteenth century. The study of antiquity was broadened not only to include the study of the texts themselves for the pleasure or instruction they could afford us, but to attempt a complete picture of the society that had

---

[17] On the varying cultural significances of Latin see Waquet, *Latin, or, The Empire of a Sign*; on its use among English schoolboys in the Elizabethan era see Baldwin, *Small Latine and Lesse Greeke*.

produced them: in Wilamowitz' words, "Graeco-Roman civilization in its essence and in every facet of its existence."[18] This was not a fundamentally new departure—ever since the Renaissance, scholars had dealt with problems both textual and historical—but in the nineteenth century it came to the fore as the main point of academic study. In this environment such subjects as epigraphy, archaeology and art history ceased to be matters for dilettantes and were put on a more scientific footing, important components of what on the continent was still called "philology." New ways of looking at antiquity produced new approaches. Karl Marx saw a history of Rome in which the passage from Republic to Empire was a sideshow, the Struggle of the Orders the main event; Nietzsche, a professor of classics, denied the detached rationality that had long been taken for the hallmark of Greek thought; and Freud's use of classical mythology is well known. The study of the Greco-Roman classics had become the study of Greco-Roman antiquity, broader in its subject matter, more restricted in its audience, and a fertile field from which new social sciences grew.

In the latter half of the twentieth century, with an enormous numerical contraction of the field as the ancient languages ceased to be an essential part of the school and university curriculum, the influence began to move in the opposite direction: classical studies tended less to produce new approaches to literature and society and more to apply approaches developed elsewhere to throw new light on the classics: feminism, structuralism, postmodernism, narratology, and even psychoanalysis and Marxism, long since separated from their classical roots, were approaches brought in from other fields to serve the classics. Much interesting work has been done in this way, but it has been of interest chiefly to those already involved in the study of antiquity; it has not served to return the classics to the center of the scholarly world, much less to an influential position in society. Some classicists have held the opinion that this more modest position is more appropriate for the field; but others continue to think that the works of antiquity still have much to teach us. It is not likely that we have heard the last word from the ancients, nor seen the last way from which their study may be approached.

The broadening of the subject in the nineteenth century and its incorporation of other fields and approaches in the twentieth have transferred what was once essentially the study of two great literatures into a deeply interdisciplinary field. History, literature, art history, archaeology,

---

[18] Wilamowitz-Möllendorff, *History of Classical Scholarship*, 1.

philosophy, psychology, sociology and many others today form part of the study of classical antiquity.

Our education has not kept up with this broadening. On the contrary, the increasing specialization of the individual fields has coincided with an increasing specialization of disciplines. Each of the areas just mentioned has its own university department; others that are still considered sub-fields—epigraphy, numismatics, papyrology—nevertheless offer their practitioners a specialized education of which outsiders know little. As the field of classical studies has broadened, we have grown narrower, less and less able to offer our students, much less the world, a broad and deep understanding of what the classics still have to teach us.

It is often asserted that nobody today can encompass all of these fields, and in a sense that is undoubtedly true; but we can do much better than we have been doing. It is the goal of this book not merely to offer a smorgasbord from which a beginner can taste before choosing a specialty, but to help produce less departmentalized classicists, better able to appreciate the wealth of knowledge available to us, to incorporate it into our understanding, and to apply it to the world in which we all live.

THE VARIOUS NATIONAL TRADITIONS OF CLASSICAL STUDIES

Ideally, a classicist should be able to read any important work of scholarship, whatever its language, and among the upper reaches of classical scholarship, a pretense is kept up that we are all proficient in, at least, the major scholarly languages; international conventions in classics sometimes offer talks in English, French, German and Italian—at least—with no simultaneous translation. In fact, very few people reach such polyglot proficiency that they are equally at home in all of these languages, to say nothing of Spanish and modern Greek or even Dutch, Swedish and Japanese. The preference of scholars for their native language is so pronounced[19] that each linguistic community tends to have its own scholarly tradition, with borders often crossed but never obliterated. The German tradition has tended to be heavily based in *realia* and close reading

---

[19] This phenomenon has recently been given a name ("own-language preference") and has become the subject of studies in information science; see, for example, Egghe, Rousseau and Yitzhaki, "The 'Own-Language Preference,'" and Bookstein and Yitzhaki, "'Own-Language Preference,'" which deal, however, with sociology, not classics.

of the sources, the French have tended more to abstraction, the English to a form of historical and literary criticism that has eschewed, until recently, heavy theorizing. The attitudes of Italians and Greeks are undoubtedly influenced by the fact that the Romans and the ancient Greeks are their ancestors;[20] the imperial English long tended to identify with the imperial Romans, while the politically fragmented but culturally developed Germans identified with the Greeks. Even those Jews who know nothing about antiquity still celebrate their liberation from the Seleucid Empire, and the observant among them still mourn the destruction of their temple by Titus. For Americans the ancient world is the cradle of democracy; for Arabs it was the birthplace of philosophy. Every one of these general-izations is so sweeping as to be almost a caricature, but the fact remains that each of us comes to the classics from a national or local tradition that emphasizes certain aspects of antiquity and tends to ignore, deny or explain away other aspects, and it is inevitably from this tradition that we bloom or within this tradition that we wither. All of that may make you feel less guilty about the fact that you do not speak other languages with perfect fluency; but it only emphasizes the importance of developing a good reading knowledge. What is going on among German or Italian or French scholars is not simply more of the same things the English and Americans are doing; their interests, their point of view and their abilities are different, and they have things to say that you will not get in English. If your eyes are open for what is being said and thought in other nations and other languages, you will have a much broader view of the subject than you could ever have gotten within the confines of your mother tongue.

---

[20] Or at least their cultural ancestors; many ethnic groups have gone into the making of modern Greece and Italy.

2

THE STAGES OF RESEARCH

CONFRONTING OUR IGNORANCE

We are born ignorant, but for many years we inhabit a world where ignorance is a failing that is not shared by everyone. We presume that our parents, our teachers and even our older siblings or friends have the answers to the questions that puzzle us. In this situation—a situation that usually persists through primary, secondary and even undergraduate education—we look to our elders and our betters to enlighten us, and we demonstrate our own worth by showing that we, too, are now masters of what we once held for mysteries. Any remaining ignorance is to be hidden, and children quickly learn the tricks for doing so: steering the subject to matters more familiar; quoting an authority, whether real or imagined; brazening it out in the hope that we will reach the goal safely without revealing our ignorance; spreading around words that knowledgeable people use and ignorant people do not, whether or not we know what they mean. Small children use these tricks on their parents and on each other; undergraduates and, alas, adults use them, often at only a slightly higher level of sophistication, on their teachers, on each other and on themselves.

The truth—and as we get closer and closer to adulthood we see more and more indications of it—is that adults, too, inhabit a world that they understand very imperfectly; but in the adult world, ignorance is universal. Questions to which we once thought adults knew the answers (Is

Nation X our friend or our enemy? Should we support the poor generously or should we encourage them to help themselves?) turn out to be
subjects for bitter and inconclusive debate. Even matters that were once
presented to us as simple and clear cut (Why do we wear clothing? Is milk
healthy?) turn out to be complex or downright unknowable, the explanations we were given imprecise or entirely wrong. It will no longer do just
to ask our teachers or to look it up in a book or on the internet: the answer
may not be there, or we may not find it if it is, or the answer that is there
may not be right.

   We are at sea, but we are not without a compass. If ultimate truth is
beyond the limits of the human mind, there are nevertheless many
methods and resources that allow us to answer those questions that are
answerable, and to see what the possibilities are for many of those that are
not. As children, we overcame our ignorance by asking others, and did our
best to hide it in those situations where it was important to appear
knowledgeable. As adults, we can overcome our ignorance only by
confronting it and by using the best strategies we can learn or can devise
for finding out the truth. This approach, when successful, is not only
much more satisfying than simply asking our teachers or parents; it also
holds the possibility of discovering truth that they themselves do not
know, or that nobody knows, or even truth that nobody else has ever
known. Ignorance, for an adult, is not something to be denied or hidden;
it is the necessary predecessor of understanding. We can never find a solution until we know we have a problem.

DEFINING THE PROBLEM

The first step in research is to know what it is that we do not know.
Usually this is a trivial matter: if my problem is that I don't know what a
particular word means, I am generally aware of the fact, and a dictionary
will usually solve my problem.[1] Grammatical difficulties often are harder
to define: we may look blankly at a sentence for some time before we
realize what our problem is with it. Here, too, the problem can probably
be solved easily if properly phrased.

---

[1]   Sometimes even this may take a while to recognize: in the famous trick-sentence *Mea
mater, mea pater, filium vestrum lupus est*, even people who know Latin do not notice
immediately that they have not understood the words *mea* and *est*.

Other problems may be more intractable. Why did Pericles reject the Spartans' embassy on the eve of the Peloponnesian War?[2] Why does Aeneas leave the underworld by the gate of ivory, the gateway of false dreams?[3] Here, too, defining the question points the road to an answer, and suggests secondary questions that may help us deal with the main one. What else do we know about Pericles' policies? What would accepting the Spartan offer have involved? Who else spoke of the gate of ivory? What was the Romans' attitude to dreams? Does Vergil mention them elsewhere?

Defining a problem is the first step to a solution, but it is not always a trivial step. Many apparent problems can be defined in different ways, and, if a given definition can point out a path of research, it can also close off some paths that might have been of interest. When we ask, for example, why Pericles chose to refuse the Spartans' offer, we omit the question of why the Athenians followed his opinion. Sometimes we discover, in the course of research, that our problem has to be rephrased in order to accommodate the relevant material. A person who wants to find the truth should not be afraid to redefine the search even in the last stages; but it is obviously better to try to think the problem through, at least on the theoretical level, at the very beginning, and to formulate it in a way that will be both clear and comprehensive. Often the best research is done by someone who asks a question where others had seen none, or who asks it in a way that others had not thought to ask it.

Not every research project is organized around a specific question. A translation, a commentary on a text, or an archaeological excavation may perhaps ask nothing more specific than "What is written here? What is buried under this mound?" In general, however, even this kind of project must have some question behind it. A person translating a text that has already been translated does so because of a sense that the translations available do not put across aspects of the texts that could be made clear by a different translation; a commentator hopes to point up aspects of the text not known, or not available, to unaided readers; an excavator does not bring the spade to a site that does not seem likely to hold under its surface information that will deepen our understanding of subjects or people in whom we are interested. Behind even the most broadly defined project

---

[2] Thuc. 1.139.3–145. Thucydides puts in Pericles' mouth a clear statement of his reasons, but that has not prevented people, from his day (cf. Ar. *Ach.* 526–34) to ours, from suspecting that he may have had other things in mind.

[3] Verg. *Aen.* 6.898.

lies a question, or at least a curiosity, that is not entirely satisfied. If we cannot identify the question then we do not know what we are looking for, and in that case it is not likely that we shall ever find it.

ASSEMBLING A BIBLIOGRAPHY

Once the problem has been defined, the next step is to find written material relevant to it. This is essential for two reasons: for one, your question may already have been asked and answered; for another, even if your particular question has not been answered (or has not been answered to your satisfaction), there may be published material available that can throw light on it or, alternatively, that has obscured the question so thoroughly that it must be addressed and challenged before the question can be dealt with more profitably. How to go about assembling a bibliography is a subject in itself, and we shall deal with it in the next chapter. For now it suffices to point out that there is hardly a question in the humanities that has not at some point been dealt with by somebody; and even when the question is entirely new, there will be items in the literature that can help, or sometimes hinder, its solution.[4]

Our field is a bookish one, and the background one needs for research is normally a list of books; but books are not the only source that can be used. If the question being researched involves a work of art, it will probably be necessary to visit a museum to see it; if a battle, you are more likely to get a good idea of what happened if you have seen the battlefield; if a question involving agriculture, it will probably be worthwhile to familiarize yourself with farming and farmers, despite the great differences between ancient and modern practices. Even background that you have picked up outside academia may be relevant: I don't advise fighting

---

[4]   Even if a researcher were to stumble upon a subject to which nothing ever written was relevant, the fact would be so surprising that it would be necessary to discuss previous research in order to demonstrate its irrelevance. This is why no student of humanities is likely to have the happy experience that my wife, a mathematician, once had: working on the first draft of the introduction to her doctoral thesis, she thought of a good way to generalize a theorem that she had proven for two dimensions to any number of dimensions. She asked her advisor whether that was good enough for a doctorate, and, on receiving a positive answer, she wrote up her proof and had her thesis—only fifty-seven pages long—approved within two months.

a battle as part of a research project, but the experience of battle may well provide insights that the armchair historian does not have.[5]

READING THE MATERIAL

It will be either a very meager or a very original research topic about which so little has been written that you can read it all. Scholars have been writing about Homer and his fellows for more than two thousand years, and, unlike our colleagues in the natural sciences, we cannot presume that what was written hundreds of years ago is not worthy of our attention. Once the bibliography is assembled, it is necessary to choose what to read carefully, what to read selectively, what to scan and what to skip. I know of no really scholarly way to make this judgment: granted that one shouldn't judge a book by its cover, by what criterion *should* one judge whether a book is worth reading? Reviews and chapter-headings of books and abstracts of articles, where available, can help, but until one reads it one never knows what revolutionary observation or what essential piece of information may be buried in note 7 on page 142. Nevertheless, the judgment must be made as well as possible, taking into account considerations like time available, resources and language.

None of these books or articles is saying quite what you want to say; if you should find one that is, you will have to abandon your project, because it has already been done. Most of them are not even writing directly about your topic. You are interested in drawing out of them whatever is relevant to your topic, and whatever else may be helpful to you as background. Of course, every item you learn is likely to raise new questions: here, too, you must exercise some judgment to know when you are being drawn too far from your subject. Too narrow a focus on your topic will probably cause you to make egregious errors in matters of background; too broad an area will lead you into a boundless ocean of

---

[5] Twice in my undergraduate career I used my own experience as part of a term paper: once, in a paper in political science, I drew some of my observations from what it had been like, a year earlier, working in my teacher's husband's losing campaign for local office; again, in a paper on the classical tradition, I compared quasi-demonic figures from Greek mythology with stories from Jewish legend that I had culled from books on my father's bookshelf. In both cases I thought I was somehow cheating by using knowledge that I had not achieved by sitting in the college library; in both cases my teachers expressed disappointment that I had not told them more about my own special knowledge.

reading material. A line must be drawn somewhere, perhaps with the hope of getting back some day to one of the interesting questions that you could not follow up this time.

FOLLOWING UP REFERENCES

As long as we thought that our teachers were the possessors of knowledge, we could rely on what we read in our textbooks. Now that the secret is out, and we know that our teachers may themselves be as full of doubts, uncertainties and simple ignorance as we are, we cannot place too much faith in what they tell us, or in what we find written in books. It is not just that a book may have a mistake in it somewhere: every book written by a human being has mistakes in it, and many books have quite a large number of them. And mistakes are only the beginning of the problem: many statements that are not quite mistakes are nevertheless uncertain, tendentious, unclear, meaningless or misleading. A book's entire thesis may be mistaken; even odder, a book whose entire thesis is mistaken is not necessarily worthless. Nobody today believes the hypothesis of Samuel Butler[6] that the *Odyssey* was written by a young unmarried Sicilian woman, but many people find much in his book that is illuminating.

This being the case, it is always necessary to ask the questions "What exactly is the author saying?" and "How does the author know it?" The answer to the first question can generally be gotten from the context; for the second, the authors of scholarly books offer footnotes in which they tell the reader on which sources they are relying for their statements.

A casual reader will ignore these footnotes; in most books designed for a non-scholarly audience they will be omitted completely, lest the reader be frightened off by the book's overly learned appearance. For the researcher, on the other hand, they are essential: if an article on Plato claims that Plato believed thus and such, it is the footnote that will reveal to us where the evidence is that Plato really thought that.

Unfortunately, footnotes are no less likely than any other part of the book to be mistaken, uncertain, tendentious, unclear, meaningless or misleading. A person who simply presumes that the footnote can be trusted to support the statement it seems to be supporting will eventually have the unpleasant experience that I had of being told by a more careful

---

[6]   Butler, *The Authoress of the Odyssey*.

scholar, "You copied that footnote, and you copied it from so-and-so's article."[7] Checking the footnote indeed revealed to me that it did not say what I had thought it said, and why my teacher could tell at a glance which article had misled me.

It is not usually possible to check all the footnotes in a book or an article that you read, nor would it be worthwhile doing so. For items that are important to you, however—and doubly so for items that you will actually use in your own publication—you had better check the source mentioned in the footnote. Often you will have to go further and check the source's source and so on to the original, primary source. Sometimes you will come out of this experience no wiser than you were before. More commonly, if my own experience is any guide, you will have discovered by the end many things about your topic that you would not have learned from the book with which you began. You may also discover that things you learned from highly regarded books and professors are no longer tenable, or perhaps never were.

A CRITICAL APPROACH AND AUTHORITY

Attitudes towards authority have varied from time to time and from place to place. In medieval Europe, the authority of Aristotle in philosophy and of Galen in medicine was all but absolute: *ipse dixit*, "[Aristotle] himself said it," could put an end to the discussion. Modern students of medicine marvel at the fact that medieval doctors, some of whom performed dissections, could continue to repeat palpable errors about anatomy, but that was the case: the authority of Galen was stronger than the authority of their own eyes.[8]

The modern approach is to encourage the student to question authority and to make independent judgments. The reader will have noticed that this very chapter advises you to do exactly that, and warns against blind

---

[7]   The scholar was Professor Ernst Badian, and he was perfectly correct.

[8]   The idea is not dead in some cultures. Once a student of non-western background complained to me about a failing mark on a plagiarized paper. "But I copied it out of the book," he said. "What could be wrong with it?" When I explained to him that copying out of the book was not what was required, he countered: "If I were to learn the entire book by heart, what mark would you give me?" When I told him that if he could merely repeat the book without thinking about it I would fail him, the discussion, as far as he was concerned, was at an end. It had apparently been his misfortune to fall into the hands of a teacher for whom perfection was not enough.

acceptance of authority. That said, it must be admitted that all of us accept authority to a considerable extent, and it is good that we do: we would be inarticulate, illiterate and insufferable if we had never adopted any behavior or opinions before being persuaded for ourselves.

We all approach new problems in the context of a body of knowledge that we have built up over many years, most of it accepted unquestioningly on the authority of someone more knowledgeable. For most such knowledge, we no longer remember how or where we learned it. I have had the embarrassing experience of realizing, when challenged, that I believed something to be true because my sister had told me so when she was seven and I was three and a half.[9] Not every authority we once accepted is worthy of our continued confidence; but to deny every authority would return us, as Descartes at first discovered, to total ignorance.[10] In practice, we always retain a good deal of received opinion.

Much of that received opinion is wrong,[11] but only careful inspection will tell us what is wrong, and what it is that is wrong about it. It is not irrational to presume that others who have studied a question, an author or an era knew more about it by the time they wrote their book than we do when we begin our research. It may be surprising that medieval doctors should have trusted Galen more than their own eyes, but our own behavior is not that much different. If an organ the textbook says should be there is not, we, too, would be more likely to suspect that we had botched the dissection than that the textbook had it wrong; nor would that suspicion be unreasonable. Authority has some place in the humanities as well, but its weight cannot be decisive on its own. As time

[9]   Similar experiences may occur even with quite respectable sources. David Sansone points out to me that the oft-repeated story that the Romans in 146 BCE sowed the site of Carthage with salt apparently has no ancient source whatsoever: it appeared first in CAH[1] 8:484 in 1930, and passed from historian to historian until R. T. Ridley, "To Be Taken with a Pinch of Salt" finally exposed the invention half a century later.

[10] Descartes himself continued past this state to an entire philosophy built, he thought, only upon reason. True skeptics continue to hold that it is possible to build a coherent world-view without accepting any authority at all, and for a sympathetic treatment I refer the reader to Spolsky, *Satisfying Skepticism*, by the same sister, still—for all my efforts—three and a half years older than I.

[11] Dr. Stockmann, in Ibsen's *An Enemy of the People*, famously held that "the majority never has right on its side"; but he based that belief on the fact that most people are not very intelligent, so that the (presumably more correct, though that, too, is arguable) opinions of the intelligent will always be minority opinions. The same argument can be applied to scholars' opinions only by a reader who thinks that most scholars are not as intelligent as the reader.

goes on, and as we check more and more footnotes, we get a clearer opinion as to who is worthy of our confidence, and to what extent. Even the best of guides will sometimes fail us: no mortal is entirely reliable.

DEDUCTION VS. INDUCTION

Simply to record the information we have discovered in our research will rarely interest anyone: for a work of scholarship to be valuable, it should be more than a mere rearrangement of known material. There are two basic ways by which new knowledge is derived from old: deduction, whereby a set of known facts forces us by purely logical operations to a previously unknown conclusion, and induction, whereby a set of known facts suggests to us a pattern that we think can be generalized to previously unknown cases. In most of the humanities, induction is the dominant mode of thought. We read many tragedies and we start to develop generalizations about how tragedy is written, how it was performed and what it means; we look at many pieces of pottery and we start to generalize about what kinds of pots were made where, at what time and by whom.

Deduction is generally more convincing than induction. If all men are mortal, and Socrates is a man, then Socrates is mortal: that is deduction, and once we have granted the original premises (that all men are mortal and that Socrates is a man) it is hard to argue with the conclusion. Induction, on the other hand, is always open to debate, because another person may see a different pattern, or may simply refuse to believe that the pattern is really universal. Are all men really mortal? It is true that billions of men have been born into the world and practically all of them have died; but some are still alive, after all, and who can say for certain that all of them will die? Who can say, for that matter, that there has not been some case in the past of a person who never died? Many hypotheses that were once held on the basis of induction were eventually proven by deduction (Euclidean geometry is the most famous example), and at that point discussion on the matter has generally ceased, at least until a more sophisticated approach to the subject suggested that the matters proved might not be the entire story. In the humanities, few hypotheses ever reach this level of proof.

Behind both induction and deduction, moreover, lies an essentially unscientific phase of imagination. The most pedantically designed scientific project comes about only after the researcher has developed a hypothesis: that some previously unknown principle or item of information is or is not the case. Nobody, to my knowledge, has ever offered an entirely satisfactory explanation of how the human intelligence makes this leap,[12] but we do it all the time, and, without it, we would have none but the most mundane of questions to answer.

WRITING AND PUBLICATION

Research that is not imparted to others is research wasted—sometimes even worse than wasted, since some forms of research (such as archaeological excavation) permanently change the matter being researched: once I have dug up the site, it is not there to be dug up again, and, if I die before writing my report, my work has destroyed information without preserving it.

Since ignorance is a universal state, the results of your research have probably given you knowledge that nobody else (or hardly anybody else) has. Passing on that knowledge, however, is not a trivial matter. A good deal of thought has to be given to the questions: What have I learned? What are the central points, and what matters are secondary? What kind of background will other people need to understand what I have to say? Why did I care about this subject? Why should they?

This is the point for an outline that will lay out before you the stages in which you can present your work. It may be a lecture, an article, a book or a series of books. Perhaps another medium entirely is appropriate: John S. Morrison and his co-workers, for example, decided that the best way to test and to demonstrate their ideas about the construction of an ancient Athenian trireme was to build one themselves.[13] Usually, scholarship is made available either in journal articles or in books.

When you have an outline, you have reduced the task of writing to manageable proportions: a project that may have been bigger than anything you had ever undertaken has now been broken down into pieces of a size you can deal with. How to organize your book or article, how to write clearly, where to cite your sources, and all the other things that come under the heading of "expository writing" are matters that are regularly

---

[12] It was some years ago the subject of a best-selling book, Gardner, *Aha! Insight*, and since then various intriguing studies, none of which are the subject of the current book, have occasionally made headlines, but, to my knowledge, no comprehensive theory exists.

[13] Morrison, Coates and Rankov, *The Athenian Trireme*; see below, p. 377.

taught in universities, and there are good guidebooks available for those who have not learned it, and websites like *The Writing Site* and websites of various university writing courses, if your own university does not teach the subject. Writing well is not the subject of this handbook; but, without it, most of what you learn in this book will ultimately be of little use to anyone but yourself.

3

ASSEMBLING A BIBLIOGRAPHY

WHERE TO START

When I realized one day that I was about to start writing my doctoral thesis in the classics without having learned a thing about the life of Greek women,[1] I walked into Smyth Classical Library and asked whether anybody there knew anything about women in Greece. "I think de Ste. Croix has something about it in the latest *Classical Review*," said one student; I picked up the *Classical Review* from the magazine stand in the library, and, sure enough, there were a few "very inconclusive" pages on the subject, "offered mainly in the hope of stimulating a thorough inquiry into the whole subject."[2] Sensing a promising thesis topic (and not being very happy with the one that had been suggested to me), I walked down to the Widener Library stacks to look for some of the books mentioned in the article, and once I got there I glanced around in the same area to find other books on the subject. I checked them out, placed them in my carrel, and had the beginnings of my doctoral bibliography.

That is the advantage of working at a major research university with colleagues who are abreast of the material, a library that has been

---

[1] A gross exaggeration, I now realize, for I had read epic, tragedy and comedy, and had surely read a good deal about women there; but many good ideas begin from misapprehensions.

[2] de Ste. Croix, "Property Rights of Athenian Women," 273.

collecting classical books for hundreds of years and a budget large enough to order everything of importance as it comes out. Anyone who has had the experience of working at such an institution will know how much faster and deeper research can go when everything is easily available, and seasoned researchers compete among themselves for the privilege of spending a term or two at such a place. For the rest of us, assembling a bibliography requires some more effort.

Usually we are not utterly clueless when we first approach a project. The person who asks why Pericles rejected the Spartans' embassy could not ask the question without knowing something about the Peloponnesian War; the person who asks about the gate of ivory has at least some notion of what is in the Aeneid. Not every researcher begins with even this much background. Sometimes, as in my case, a question may intrigue us precisely because we know nothing about it; sometimes we may find ourselves involved in a question raised by somebody else, for which we have no background at all. If nobody has given me any hints, where should I start?

A good first idea is one of the classical encyclopedias: the *Oxford Classical Dictionary* (OCD[3]), *Brill's New Pauly* (BNP), or one of the encyclopedias of the various subfields of classics. Here it will generally be possible to find a bit of background on something sufficiently close to your question to give you a start on locating other work, and the end of each article will offer a few references for further reading. This isn't a bibliography, but it is a start. If the smaller encyclopedias fail there is always Pauly-Wissowa (RE), if the subject is sufficiently "real" to merit inclusion there. Although the secondary bibliography offered in RE will necessarily be at least a few decades out of date, and sometimes, depending on when your subject was dealt with, a good deal more, the textually based slant of RE means that its articles age well, since generally all the relevant ancient sources are cited and discussed there.

Even better than a classical encyclopedia is one of the many "companions" that are now becoming available. In the past two decades a number of publishers have undertaken companions to a plethora of subjects: *The Cambridge Companion to the Aegean Bronze Age*, *to Virgil*, *to Plotinus*; *Blackwell's Companion to Ancient History*, *to Ovid*, *to the Roman Army*; *Brill's Companion to Thucydides*, *to Hellenistic Epigram*, *to Alexander the Great*; *The Oxford Handbook of Hellenic Studies*, *of Byzantine Studies*, *of Papyrology*, for a small sampling.[3] These companions are collections of essays, each of them by a

---

[3]   The titles chosen are not necessarily the best or the most important; I have intentionally given examples of the broadest and of the narrowest. The total number will be longer by the time this book is printed.

specialist in the subject discussed, and their purpose is to introduce the reader to the major scholarly issues and debates about the subject discussed. As such they offer, when well conceived and well executed, a natural continuation to the barebones introductions offered in this book.

Another possible starting-point is a web search. It sometimes takes a bit of trial and error to find a useful set of words: many classical phrases are so commonly used that few of the references found will have anything to do with the classics; others have been hijacked for commercial or scientific use; still others may have homonyms so common that they swamp the references for which you are looking. If you use only the English term (or spelling), you will miss articles in other languages. In almost any case, however, a bit of perseverance will turn up something of interest.

Web searches need not be restricted to searching after web pages; one may go after the books themselves in their home territory, the world's major research libraries. The catalogues of the British Library, the Library of Congress and the libraries of the major research universities are today generally available online—some for a fee, many for free—and a search of keywords will turn up many items that may have been unknown to you and to your home library. Even better, many of these books, and particularly the old, out-of-print ones, may themselves be available online. Not every one of them will be worth tracking down, but almost certainly some of them will. For now, put them onto your list.

Not everything—often not anything—that is relevant to your question has been the subject of an entire book. Articles can be found by searching *L'année philologique* (APh) and/or the *Gnomon Bibliographische Datenbank* (GBD); the authors and titles of the most recent ones will be at the *TOCS-IN* site.[4] Articles published in non-classical journals (and you are likely to need them more often than you might think) can be found through *Periodicals Index Online*. Since books usually deal with broad trends and articles with points of detail, it will often be articles that will give you the clearest picture, and the best leads to further reading. Many of these articles may be available online, particularly if you are connected to a library that subscribes to some of the major internet archives of scholarly articles: JSTOR, Project MUSE, EBSCO MegaFILE and, for French periodicals, *Persée*, where access, bless them, is free to all.

Lastly, there are websites that are themselves rich sources of information. First of all, there are meta-websites that are themselves lists of other sites, with links to the various scholarly resources available; a good

---

[4]   On these three sources see below, pp. 37–8.

one in English is Maria Pantelia's *Electronic Resources for Classicists*, and in French *AgoraClass*. Of particular interest for classicists is *Perseus*, an online database offering a good selection of searchable classical texts in Greek and Latin, each with a linked English translation and various aids to independent translation; an ample art gallery; a collection of secondary literature; and much more that can be found by wandering around the site. There are also websites devoted to particular subjects: some of these will be mentioned in coming chapters, others can be found by a search engine, and still more are forming in people's minds or on their computers at this very time.

BROADER AND MORE FOCUSED

A good bibliography should not begin the way it is likely to end, as an alphabetical list of a few dozen or a few hundred books and articles. Such a list is not very helpful to the person beginning a research project. There is no way to tell what is relevant and what is not, and reading through the books from A to Z—in the unlikely event that you really succeed in reading them, rather than quitting scholarship forever or falling into a twenty-year sleep—will mostly be time wasted: most of the things you will read will have little to do with the topic you are researching.

A good bibliography grows piece by piece: one begins with a few items, picking out of them what is relevant; these items will make clearer to you what sort of background information you are going to need, and where you are likely to find it, so that each item leads you on to more. Of course this should not go on forever. As soon as possible you should try to write up an outline of what your eventual paper or book will look like: this will help you define your subtopics, and keep you from straying too far.

FOLLOWING FOOTNOTES

A person reading along in an interesting book is not generally interested in having the text cluttered with side issues. Footnotes often, endnotes almost always, will be ignored entirely. Even a person who reads footnotes is not likely to pay much attention to a footnote that is merely a source-citation: "Hom. Il. 18:323" does not say much to people who do not have the text of the Iliad on the tip of their tongue.

We already mentioned[5] the usefulness of footnotes for checking the accuracy of an author's assertions; the footnotes are no less useful as an aid to building your bibliography. It is hard to make any constructive use of a mere alphabetical list of books, but, if you find the section of the book relevant to your topic, see what the author has to say, and track down the books, articles or ancient sources with which the author's assertions are supported, you will start making up your own list of sources that are appropriate to your topic, and you will find out, on the way, what matters are certain (or are thought to be certain) and what assertions are controversial. Note, however, that this applies only to books of scholarly research, where the footnotes are offered to support the author's arguments. In books designed for a general audience that is expected to rely on the author's expertise, including encyclopedia articles and such, footnotes and bibliographies, where they exist, merely refer the reader to books that offer more background. Following up footnotes like these may never get you to the sources.

For a bibliography compiled by following up footnotes, it is important to start from as up-to-date a source as possible, following the article's sources, and then its sources' sources, until you feel you have got to the bottom of things—to all the relevant information. If for one reason or another you have started from a publication now decades old, a citation index can be helpful: the *Web of Science* maintains the *Arts & Humanities Citation Index*, a large database of publications including a list of all the earlier works cited in the bibliography. This database can then be searched in the other direction, producing a list of later works that refer to the one you have in hand. This is an exceedingly valuable tool, and would be even more valuable if it were complete; unfortunately, it does not come near recording all the publications that appear, so that it alone cannot offer you a guarantee that you have found all the important recent scholarship.

Probably, indeed nothing can; but there is one more resource that can be quite precious, and that is the human being. Every published article and book was written by a flesh-and-blood person; many of them were written by people who are still alive, and of these a not insignificant number will answer a letter of inquiry. You should not expect them to do your work for you, but some of them may be very helpful in giving you ideas about what sort of questions to ask and where to look for the answers.

---

[5]   Above, pp. 20–1.

FINDING THE CLASSICAL SOURCES

In the end, most classical research is based upon the texts left to us from the classical world. For some projects, you will be led to the relevant texts by following footnotes from modern scholarly works; for many, it will be obvious from the outset what you need. If, for example, you are interested in writing about ancient comedy, you should not need this book to tell you that the first thing you have to do is read the comedies. Even in those cases where the modern writers have led you to the ancients, it is worthwhile to see if there is any new evidence you can bring to bear: often there are passages in ancient authors that the moderns who deal with your topic have not noticed, and there is only so much that you can do by rearranging the same old information from the same old sources, "like stale tea-leaves."[6] Nowadays one would seek information by choosing words for an online search, or by looking up appropriate words in a concordance; the appropriate databases of Greek and Latin literature[7] can often give you a lead on items that others have missed.

YOUR FINAL BIBLIOGRAPHY

Modern scholarly publishing requires not only that you be familiar with the literature relevant to your subject, but that you indicate to your readers the literature that you have used. In an article whose sources are of a manageable number the footnotes themselves may suffice, but to a book or thesis it is customary to append a bibliography, and indeed a book without precise footnotes and a bibliography may be unusable to scholars, who will not be able to evaluate whether the information being presented is accurate.

What you want to include in your bibliography and how you want to present it will depend on what you are writing and for whom. The most common practice, at least for modern sources, is to include in the bibliography all those works that you have used: if an item appears in your footnotes it should appear in your bibliography—some forms of footnotes, indeed, require this—and if you have never cited the work, it should not. There need be no pretense that you have read every word of every item in the bibliography: everyone knows you haven't and, in fact, you shouldn't, although reviewers sometimes forget the fact.

---

[6] The phrase is that of Zimmern, "Was Greek Civilization Based on Slave Labor?," 1–2.
[7] See above, p. 28, and below, pp. 36–8, 51–2 and 111–12.

As a general rule, however, it is always good to keep your purpose in mind. If a major purpose of your article is to provide a review of earlier literature, you will probably want to include in your bibliography even items that you have not seen at all; the custom is to note the fact by writing *non vidi* after the entry.[8] For other purposes, on the contrary, a shorter bibliography may be appropriate, giving only those sources that will be of use to the reader. Sometimes, as noted at the beginning of the chapter,[9] a short bibliography may be more valuable than a long one; the problem with using this criterion is that you do not always know what uses your reader may want to make of your text. In general this approach is used chiefly in books of a more popular nature, whose readers, if the book interests them enough, may want to read further but are not likely to want to check every assertion. For making up course syllabi it is the only reasonable approach; the student gains nothing by a bibliography whose main purpose is to demonstrate the teacher's expertise.

Bibliographies are usually given in a single list, organized alphabetically by the author's last name, and this is generally the form that is easiest on the reader, since looking for an entry in such a bibliography is a reasonably straightforward matter. Where a book deals with subjects so widely divergent that people interested in one subject are not likely to be interested in another, separate bibliographies may be offered for each subject—such, for example, is the practice of the *Cambridge Ancient History* (*CAH*). Classical authors are generally excluded from a bibliography, on the presumption that they are familiar to everyone; the common abbreviations are those used in the OCD[3] or, for authors who do not appear there, in the unabridged Liddell and Scott (LSJ[9]) and its *Revised Supplement*, or the *Oxford Latin Dictionary* (OLD). As Latin has lost out to English as the world's *lingua franca*, English names and abbreviations for particular works (Caes. *Civil War*) have become more popular and more intelligible than Latin (Caes. *Bell. Civ.*), though holdouts remain: the dictionaries use Latin, and works whose title may have various English translations usually have only one Latin title, and some less common works have no English translation at all. A list at the beginning of the bibliography or of the book—your publishers will probably have their own opinion—can include whatever abbreviations may be useful to you that do not appear in the OCD[3] and such. Where a particular edition of an ancient work has been used, that should appear in

---

8   The same phrase is used when citing at second hand a book you have not seen: in this case one writes "cited in —, page XX: *non vidi*." It is, however, a dangerous practice: see above, pp. 20–1.

9   Above, p. 29.

the bibliography. Where it is of interest to know which ancient sources have been cited, an index locorum is appended, listing all the relevant places and where they are discussed. There are some works—grammar books are the most obvious but not the only example—for which the index locorum may be the most important factor in making the book usable.

There are various forms of footnotes and bibliographical entries, and they are described in style manuals. I have my own opinions on the matter, but I shall not insist on them: you are entitled to yours. The most important thing, and the one thing that will do most to help the reader, is to choose a format and use it consistently.

MAJOR RESOURCES

Encyclopedias

RE stands for Pauly, Wissowa and Kroll, Real-Encyclopädie (often abbreviated PW after the names of its principal editors). This stupendous compilation is the closest that the classics have ever come to the original concept of an encyclopedia, a work that would encompass everything known to the human race. RE is not quite that ambitious: it deals only with knowledge about classical antiquity (klassische Altertumswissenschaft), and only with realia, items that are more or less concrete: elegy and jurisprudence are "real" enough, but there is no article on love or justice. Even with these limitations, it occupies a reasonable-size set of shelves almost from ceiling to floor: sixty-four volumes, confusingly numbered as "half-volumes"[10] from 1 to 34, fifteen supplementary volumes, and an index volume that was finally published in 1997, a hundred and four years after Georg Wissowa brought out the first volume.[11] The price is appropriate to the

---

[10] No less confusingly, the numbering of volumes was started again from R, in 1914, so that after volume 24 came the first volume of the "second row" (Zweite Reihe): later editions offer a single numbering, in which this volume is numbered 25.

[11] The original plan was simply to update and expand August Friedrich von Pauly's fifty-year-old six-volume encyclopedia (Pauly, Walz and Teuffel, Pauly's Real-Encyclopädie der classischen Alterthumswissenschaft), and the first volume got as far as Apollodorus, which—if we compare it with the percentage of the Neue Pauly up to that author— would have meant finishing in about seventeen or eighteen volumes; but things got out of hand. That the work was ever finished at all was the result of the heroic efforts of Wilhelm Kroll, Karl Mittelhaus and Konrat Ziegler, who continued the work, not without considerable assistance, through three more generations.

size: if you do not have money to burn, you will use your university's copy. Numbering is by column, not by page, so that the first leaf of a half-volume will be numbered 1–2 on one side, 3–4 on the other. Many of the articles were not ready in time, and these are published in the supplementary volumes; there are also addenda and corrigenda (*Nachträge und Berichtigungen*) at the ends of (half-)volumes. For many decades, a person looking for Thucydides would look in vain; after 1970, one could discover by searching a number of volumes or by asking a more expert scholar that he was dealt with in supplements 12 and 14. The appearance of a *Register der Nachträge und Supplemente* in 1980 and an alphabetical and categorical *Gesamtregister* in 1997–2000[12] has made RE, if not exactly user-friendly, much more manageable.

The intention of the compilers was to include all that is known, so that in most cases every relevant citation known to the author of a given article will appear in that article—a great boon if you are looking for ancient sources on a person or item about whom little has been written. It goes without saying that a work that restricts itself to *realia* has its blind spots; that a work compiled by hundreds of authors is a work of very uneven quality, with some articles being landmarks of scholarship while others are little more than compilations of quotes; and that many items in a work begun more than a hundred years ago and finished a quarter-century ago are now severely out of date. Articles are generally based heavily on the transmitted literature; information derived from archaeology, papyrology, numismatics and epigraphy—to name a few—is underrepresented. Moreover, the encyclopedia dates from a time and a place dominated by what today is called *positivism*: the belief that historical (and other) questions have a right answer and all other answers are wrong, so that writing history is a matter of determining *wie es eigentlich gewesen*, "the way it really was."[13] Postmodern scholars take a much more pessimistic view of the ability to determine an objective truth, and some even doubt its existence. But when what you need is what RE has to offer, this is the place you will find it; and nobody is ever likely to produce something like this again.

---

[12] Erler et al., eds., *Paulys Real-Encyclopädie der klassischen Altertumswissenschaft, Gesamtregister I, alphabetischer Teil; Gesamtregister II: Systematisches Sach- und Suchregister* (issued on CD-ROM).

[13] The phrase is that of von Ranke, *Geschichten der romanischen und germanischen Völker*, p. VII. Ranke himself did not use these words as a programmatic statement, but merely as a formula of modesty declaring his own unworthiness for the higher mission of "judging the past and instructing the present for the use of future years." Nevertheless, the expression has become a slogan often quoted, and much maligned.

Daremberg and Saglio, *Dictionnaire des antiquités* is a more modest and thus more accessible effort, no less dated than the early volumes of RE but nevertheless a convenient source of the sorts of information for which a person reading another book turns to a dictionary or an encyclopedia. How did the Romans name fractions? Under *arithmetica* you can find a simple table. What is an *aplustrum*? Gallicize it to *aplustre* and you will have an answer. Those matters which require a detailed discussion receive it: sixteen pages, for example, on *balneum*.

When Daremberg–Saglio had aged, and RE was both unfinished and unwieldy, a group of British scholars entered a new English candidate[14] by producing the OCD[1], a one-volume item that gives a brief summary and a very brief bibliography of each item. This has been thoroughly revised twice, and the third edition is still often the most convenient place for an English speaker to turn for a quick background of the people, places or things about which others seem to be writing with such confidence.

A modest-sized and up-to-date[15] encyclopedia remained a desideratum for German scholars until Ziegler and Sontheimer, *Der Kleine Pauly* (DKP), a five-volume abridged version of RE, "for all those . . . who for spatial or financial reasons must forgo the 'Large Pauly.'"[16] Another group of scholars produced the one-volume Andresen et al., *Lexikon der alten Welt*. Both have now been superseded to a large extent by Cancik and Schneider, *Der Neue Pauly* (DNP), an entirely new[17] compilation by contemporary scholars. The number of volumes (twenty numbered from 1 to 16 including an index, and five supplements so far) might give the impression of a mini-monster, but in fact the print is large and the articles of manageable size; no effort is made to tell the reader all there is to know about the topic.[18] A feature that will not be found in other encyclopedias is a multi-volume encyclopedia of

---

[14] The most popular classical encyclopedias in English at the time were the aging but thorough works of Sir William Smith, *A Dictionary of Greek and Roman Antiquities*; *A Dictionary of Greek and Roman Biography and Mythology*; and *Dictionary of Greek and Roman Geography*.

[15] The previous single-volume German encyclopedia, *Friedrich Lübkers Reallexikon des Klassischen Altertums*, had last been revised in 1914.

[16] DKP, vol. I, p. V.

[17] That, at least, was the intention; in fact many articles, as was bound to be the case, are condensations or retellings of the old material.

[18] Problems still remain with editing a series put together by so many different authors, and a young historian by the name of Mischa Meier managed to sneak into the first volume an item on *apopudobalia*, "an ancient type of sport, perhaps an early proto-form of the modern game football," complete with (invented) ancient and modern sources. The spoof was generally taken with good humor, but was not included in the English translation.

classical scholarship in volumes 13–15. The whole is now being translated into English[19] as Cancik and Schneider, *Brill's New Pauly* (BNP), which for English speakers will supplement, and for many purposes supplant, OCD[3].

There are also encyclopedias of subfields: the *Reallexikon für Antike und Christentum*, *Lexikon der Mythologie*, the polyglot *Lexicon Iconographicum Mythologiae Classicae* (LIMC), the lavishly illustrated *Enciclopedia Virgiliana* and many others, a number of which can be found in Jenkins, and some of which will be mentioned in following chapters. Lastly, although few students will need me to reveal this to them, *Wikipedia* and other online resources nowadays will often serve your needs as fully as, and often better than, any printed general encyclopedia—but be aware that it is designed as a resource for the general public, not for advanced researches; and double-check the information you find there.

Not an encyclopedia but similar in intent is the *Handbuch der Altertumswissenschaft*, conceived as a grand compendium of knowledge about the ancient world, arranged not alphabetically but topically, with all the study of antiquity collected under ten general categories and an eleventh for the Byzantine world.[20] This century-old enterprise is still going on, but its volumes (nearly all of them in German) are conceived, and are generally referred to, as independent works.

Bibliographies

What follows is a brief overview; Jenkins gives more information, and is often the place to look for the place to look. Halton and O'Leary, *Classical Scholarship: An Annotated Bibliography*, originally intended as an updating of McGuire, *Introduction to Classical Scholarship*, can also be useful, but a good deal happened in the twenty years after its publication.

In 1875 Conrad Bursian published a *Jahresbericht über die Fortschritte der classischen Altherthumswissenschaft*, a bibliography of all the classical scholarship

---

[19]   The English version is designed as a precise translation of the German, so that even those articles whose authors wrote them in English are being translated back into English from the published German text.

[20]   The categories are: I: Introductory and Ancillary Disciplines; II Greek Grammar, Latin Grammar, Rhetoric; III Ancient Orient, Greek History, Roman History; IV Greek Political Science, Greek and Roman Military Affairs; V History of Philosophy, History of Mathematics and Natural Sciences, History of Religion; VI Archaeology (now a separate *Handbuch der Archäologie*); VII History of Greek Literature; VIII History of Roman Literature; IX History of Medieval Latin Literature; X Ancient Legal History; XI Byzantine Handbook.

published in 1873, containing bibliographical surveys divided by topic and an index where every publication could be found. *Bursians Jahresbericht*, as it was always known, remained the authoritative bibliography of classical scholarship, universally admired until World War I undermined the international cooperation that had characterized the field until then. In 1928 Jules Marouzeau of the Sorbonne founded *L'année philologique* (*APh*), indexing material from 1924 onward, with short summaries included in the index. When *Bursians Jahresbericht* petered out in World War II and its aftermath, *APh*—also long known as "Marouzeau" after its founder, though it is no longer called by this name today—was left as the greatest bibliographical resource in the classics. Generations of classicists compiled their bibliographies by scanning the relevant pages of each issue of *APh*, a task that became more difficult with each passing year. The efficacy of such a search depended greatly upon the extent to which one's own topic corresponded to one of the subheadings under which *APh* grouped its entries. In recent years the *APh* has been put online, so that most of it can now be searched electronically: this allows you to define your own categories for searching, and to search the entire catalogue at once rather than going through it year by year. The task of deciding how relevant an article may be is greatly assisted by the fact that *APh* includes very brief summaries. These are not true abstracts of the article, but they will tell you more than the title does about what the article is about.

Lustrum was founded in 1957 to revive the topical bibliographies that *Bursians Jahresbericht* had provided but *APh* did not; of its two first editors, one of them, Andreas Thierfelder, had been the last editor of *Bursians Jahresbericht*. It publishes long bibliographical articles with titles like Schlam and Finkelpearl, "A Review of Scholarship on Apuleius' 'Metamorphoses' 1970–1998" or Touloumakos, "Aristoteles' 'Politik' 1925–1985"—this last an article that took twelve years and seven hundred pages. Obviously even a short bibliographical essay will take you much more effort and time than a quick online search of titles, but, for a research project of any great size, the effort will be well spent. A good bibliographical survey, should you be fortunate[21] enough to find one, can give you a better idea of what is going on in the field than any mere search of titles, since the

---

[21] You may consider yourself unfortunate, since you ignore an article like this at your own peril, and indeed you would hardly read a five-hundred-page bibliographical article on Aristotle's *Politics* in order to write a term paper or to justify a statement in a footnote. For larger projects, however, even if you are trying to keep your bibliography short, a good survey will help you find the items most appropriate to you and ignore the rest.

survey deals with (and reveals to you, at least in outline) what the articles actually say and the context in which they appear.

Greece and Rome: New Surveys in the Classics are similarly bibliographic essays, issued as separate volumes to subscribers to the journal *Greece & Rome*. These tend to have a wider scope than the essays in *Lustrum*—titles like Hardie, *Virgil* or North, *Roman Religion*—and are shorter and less detailed than the essays in *Lustrum*. This is not necessarily a disadvantage: the less valuable they are to you in fields about which you are expert, the more valuable they will be in those with which you are unfamiliar. *Classical World* published a series of bibliographical articles that were collected in 1978 in the *Classical World Bibliographies*;[22] though no longer current, these can still be useful.

The wide-ranging review *Gnomon* gave birth to the *Gnomon Bibliographische Datenbank* (GBD), once a searchable CD-ROM but now available at *Gnomon Online* for free download. It covers less ground than *APh*, but has some items that are not available there, notably a large collection of German and British doctoral dissertations, and a structured search-engine that allows searches in categories organized differently from those of *APh*.

TOCS-IN is a website where the tables of contents of classical and archaeological journals are listed and can be searched. Since the information here is entered in a more primitive way than for *APh* or the GBD— the contributing editors simply enter author, title, journal, volume and page for each item, without paying any attention to content—items are available on TOCS-IN long before they appear in the other sources, and this is the resource for finding the most recent articles. The online *Bibliotheca Classica Selecta* will help you locate as much of any journal as is available online.

When faced with an unfamiliar abbreviation it will usually suffice to look in the list of authors of LSJ[9] or OLD, the list of journals in *APh*, or the list of abbreviations at the front of the OCD[3]; but for a complete list there is now Wellington, *Dictionary of Bibliographic Abbreviations*, which will help you find бълг език as easily—well, almost as easily—as you could find RhM.

---

[22] Donlan, *The Classical World Bibliography of Greek and Roman History*; id., *The Classical World Bibliography of Greek Drama and Poetry*; id., *The Classical World Bibliography of Philosophy, Religion, and Rhetoric*; id., *The Classical World Bibliography of Roman Drama and Poetry and Ancient Fiction*; id., *The Classical World Bibliography of Vergil*.

4

WHAT ARE YOUR SOURCES?

PRIMARY AND SECONDARY SOURCES

For knowledge that all adults have, one book may be as good a source of information as another. If you do not know where Rome is located, you may look it up in any atlas or encyclopedia and feel reasonably confident that you have the answer without having to follow up references to see how the compilers found out.[1] For knowledge that is less certain—and in dealing with the ancient world, precious little is really certain—one cannot necessarily rely on just any book's information. Even such straightforward questions as when, or even whether, a particular person lived may turn out to be debatable. Whenever it makes a difference whether what we think is true or false, we have to find out what the sources are on which we base our knowledge.

The most important distinction to make is that between *primary* and *secondary* sources. A primary source has direct knowledge of the event or thing under discussion; a secondary source only knows what others have said or written. By this definition, all books written about the ancient world by modern scholars are secondary sources. Technically speaking, for that matter, most ancient books, particularly books of history or

---

[1] A certain amount of care is always in order; you might, for example, stumble upon one of the nine cities in the United States named Rome.

biography, are secondary sources: few authors wrote, as Caesar did, of affairs in which they participated personally.

Since, however, vast amounts of ancient literature have been lost, we usually treat as primary any source beyond which we cannot go, because its own sources are inaccessible to us. By this definition it often happens that a source that was once secondary is now primary. Livy's history of Rome was entirely derivative; Livy himself was a stay-at-home with no involvement in public affairs, and the information on which he based his own work was culled from books. Now that most of the books on which he based himself have been lost, his work for us assumes the status of a primary source: we usually cannot pick up an earlier book and check what was in front of Livy when he wrote. Herodotus, too, wrote of things in which he had taken no personal part, but, since his sources seem to have been mostly oral, his work was effectively primary as soon as it was first read in public: most of his own sources were not available to others.

What source is primary and what secondary also depends upon the problem with which we are dealing. For Roman history, Livy's books may be considered a secondary source, at least for those matters where his own sources are available to us; if what interests us is his style or his approach to history, then his books are the primary source. If we are interested in the history of the text of Livy's works, then a modern edition (which we could treat as a more or less primary source for his style) becomes an entirely secondary source, and the primary sources are the manuscripts, papyri and earlier editions that were before the editor.

SOURCE CRITICISM

There are people who find it tantalizing to try to reconstruct what Livy's sources, or Herodotus', may have been. Even for those of us who can control our curiosity, the question is often an important one: if we know that the author we are reading is repeating a story found in an unreliable source, the reliability of our own author is undermined. In some cases the analysis is relatively straightforward: where Livy is following Polybius, for example, we have the actual source in front of us, and in other cases a historian may tell us where a particular bit of information was found.[2] Sometimes—most famously in the case of the synoptic gospels—verbal

---

[2]   Hardly any ancient author regularly cited his sources as modern scholars do; the more common practice was to mention the name of a source only to disagree.

echoes make it clear that different books are basing themselves on the same source. An entire subfield of classics, known as "source criticism" or "higher criticism," dedicates itself to trying to identify the sources of a given author. The nineteenth century, particularly in Germany, put great store by source criticism; in particular, it was believed that, since ancient books, being written on scrolls, were not convenient for browsing, authors tended to follow one source or another for extended passages, rather than having a number of books open simultaneously. The extreme version of this theory, which considered it possible almost to see the earlier, lost author's words directly behind those of the later one, is no longer in favor; but there is still often a good deal that can be discovered about an author's lost sources. It is a job that requires careful reading of the transmitted text itself, of other texts on the same subject, and of whatever external information may be known about the author. The job is greatly helped by the compilations of fragments—isolated bits of other-wise lost works culled from quotations and from papyri—that scholars have painstakingly assembled. The total volume of ancient literature was so much greater than what has been preserved that an examination of fragmentary authors often shows us a different and more variegated picture than we can get from those whose works have survived.

THE RELIABILITY OF SOURCES

In almost every case, we must eventually base ourselves on the primary sources: the secondary source, by definition, can know nothing more than what was in the primary sources. The secondary author cannot—unless some other primary source is available—add to the story, and, if we find unsubstantiated additions, we will generally have to treat them as fantasy. But this does not mean that we can treat a primary source as if it were Holy Writ. Most obviously, the sources often contradict each other, or even themselves. The various dates given for the foundation of Rome caused confusion to the Romans, and two contradictory stories, one describing Aeneas as the founder and one speaking of Romulus and Remus, had to be harmonized to produce the clearly flowing story that Livy gives. Once we have worked out the contradictions among the literary sources, there may still be problems with other sources of information: the archaeological excavations around Rome support neither the story of Aeneas nor that of Romulus, and our own beliefs, whether religious or not, are such that nobody today believes that Hesiod's deities were ever born at all. Lastly there is the question of historical probability: Livy had his doubts about the idea that Romulus and Remus were raised by a wolf, and parallel modern cases, striking though they may be, do not suggest that children so raised could ever have been normal members of human society.[3] Classicists before the last two centuries tended to be over-trusting of ancient sources, and many stories found in ancient authors were retold many times before they were ever questioned. Nowadays, when one's academic career is made by questioning sources, virtually every statement is held up to scrutiny at some point; but there is still a temptation, born of laziness, to accept at face value whatever information is not central to our topic.

Not only inherent probability and internal consistency have to be taken into account; ancient authors had their own biases as we do. When Thucydides tells us[4] that the fall of Amphipolis—a military lapse for which the Athenians exiled him—came about by no fault of his own, we need not presume that he is lying, but we must remember that he has a clear interest in telling us the story in that particular way. Here the usual argument for preferring the older source must be turned on its head: the closer the source is to the event, the stronger the motivation to offer a distorted account. It was because of his distance from the events that Tacitus could claim to tell us the history of the early principate *sine ira et studio, quorum causas procul habeo*.[5] The fact that he produced a work notorious for its excesses of spite and hero-worship can only warn us that distance from the events, despite his claim, is no guarantee of evenhandedness: since we tend to see figures from the past in the light of the present, our present-day prejudices are still likely to cloud our vision of figures from whom we no longer have anything to hope or to fear.

WRITING FROM A SINGLE SOURCE

Perhaps the most common form of classical scholarship is the study of one particular ancient work. In a sense, works like this have one source only:

---

[3]   The most famous case was the case of Kamala and Amala, the wolf-children found in 1920 by the Reverend Joseph Singh and described in Singh and Zingg, *Wolf-Children and Feral Man*; Singh's diary is available on the web at http://feralchildren.com (access date 3 June 2010), where documentation can be found for many other cases, some better attested and some less so.

[4]   Thuc. 4.104–6.

[5]   Tac. *Ann.* 1.1; to speak honestly of the Flavians, to whom he was indebted, required *incorrupta fides* (id. *Hist.* 1.1.3). See Luce, "Ancient Views on the Causes of Bias."

any interpretation of the *Oedipus* must in the end show us something that is, in some respect or other, contained in the text. Some critical schools[6] have gone so far as to claim that, in dealing with a literary work, nothing but the text itself should be considered: what is important, according to these critics, is what the text says, not what its author meant it to say (perhaps the author did not succeed in saying it, and in any event how can we know?), nor what the reader feels it to say (unless we can demonstrate from the text that the interpretation is really there).

In point of fact, of course, no text stands alone. For one thing, as we shall see,[7] establishing the text itself is rarely a trivial matter: texts are transmitted to us with misspellings, mistakes, variations and infelicities that seem to cry out for correction. The meanings of the words in the text, not to mention its metaphors and symbols, can hardly be understood without reference to other texts. The text may include references to events and things outside of itself, and, if those references are significantly at variance with reality, we will want to know that, if only to establish whether the text is to be taken seriously or ironically. There is much more to be discussed in the matter of textual interpretation,[8] but at this point we must realize that, however focused our study, we can never write about one ancient text without looking at many others.

LITERARY AND DOCUMENTARY SOURCES

Up to now we have been discussing literary sources: works that were produced for the general public to read or to hear, to copy and to transmit to posterity. Many sources of information were not produced that way. Personal and business letters, receipts, financial accounts, religious dedications—all of these may shed light on our subject, often in ways their creators never intended. Physical items with no text at all may be sources, often sources that will tell us more than any description.

Nevertheless, we may not forget that even mute stones may have their prejudices. If we find a particular kind of stone used for building, it does not necessarily follow that this stone was commonly used for the purpose. If we find a dedication to a particular group of deities, it does not necessarily follow that there were many people who would have considered this group of deities to have anything to do with each other. The literary

---

[6] See below, pp. 122–4.
[7] Below, Chapters 9 and 20.
[8] Below, Chapter 10.

papyrus that we find with a reading different from all our manuscripts may simply be a scrap of a corrupt text. Even with mute sources, we can never suspend our critical sense.

WHAT IS CREDIBLE?

Much that is credible to one person is not credible to another; yet more, much that seems credible at first glance will not stand up to investigation, and many very surprising assertions turn out to be correct.[9] Asking a number of questions about a statement can help us define what we do and what we do not believe.

Is it reasonable? I do not have any personal knowledge of whether the Persian army in 480 was as large as Herodotus says it was, but the numbers seem extremely high, the more so when we try to calculate how many could pass a given road at once and how long it would take for an army of that size to assemble, to move and to encamp. His numbers for the Spartans at Thermopylae, on the other hand, though they have no more independent confirmation than do the Persian numbers, are not inherently implausible. As for Hesiod's story that woman was invented by the gods as a vengeance for Prometheus' theft of fire, that is a story whose factual likelihood I dismiss out of hand, though I would take it quite seriously—though not without examination—as evidence for the Greeks' beliefs about gender and about religion.

Is this source otherwise accurate? No source but the shortest can be right all the time, but some have better records than others, and we will obviously do better following a more reliable guide than a less reliable one. Even the best of guides will fail sometimes, and few ancient authors are so thoroughly reliable that we can consider them to approach infallibility. We will have to keep our eyes open at every stage to see whether this may be one of the cases when a less reliable source has preserved a more reliable story.

How does this source know this information? M. I. Finley famously asked whether Thucydides had had agents on the paths to Decelea counting the "more than twenty thousand" slaves who he said had escaped to that deme after the Spartans fortified it in the Peloponnesian War.[10] Ancient texts are full of information and extremely reticent about how they came

---

[9]   In the words that we find at the end of a number of Euripides' plays: πολλὰ δ'ἀέλπτως κραίνουσι θεοί, καὶ τὰ δοκθηέντ' οὐκ ἐτελέσθη (Eur. *Alc.* 1160–1, *Andr.* 1285–6, *Bac.* 1389–90, *Hel.* 1689–90, *Med.* 1416–17).

[10] Finley, *Ancient Economy*, 24, on Thuc. 7.27.5.

about that information. It is always worth asking how the author could have known what is being asserted. For that matter, it is worth asking it of modern-day public figures and academics.

What is the author's bias? Both Thucydides and Xenophon were Athenians who had been exiled from their homeland; Horace ate at the table of Augustus' chief financier; Julius Caesar wrote his early commentaries for publication in a time when his own position in the Roman state was not only contested but in serious danger. We may not be able to state in each case how the author's situation has affected the presentation of the material, but, if we do not keep it constantly in mind, we will fall victims to the propaganda of one side or the other in an ancient controversy where we would rather, if we could, find objective information.

What is my bias? Germans tend to favor Arminius against the Romans; Britons find Boadicea praiseworthy; Vercingetorix appeals to the French enough to have turned the comic-strip character Asterix into something of a culture hero. It is easy to recognize other people's prejudices, much harder to recognize our own: our natural tendency is to think that our own claim is simple fact—that, after all, is why we believe it. Some people, in trying to avoid their national prejudices, go to the opposite extreme, like W. S. Gilbert's

> . . . idiot who praises in enthusiastic tone
> All centuries but this, and every country but his own.[11]

We are not objective observers and we cannot entirely escape our prejudices, but we must do all we can to overcome them, because otherwise we shall be able to learn from the ancients only what we already thought without them—which is to say, we shall learn nothing at all.

WHAT FORM CAN TELL US

In reading a source, it is important to know the conventions of the form in which the author is writing. Comedy has to be funny; it does not follow that the subjects it treats were matters about which everyone felt light-hearted. Old comedy has to make fun of public figures; not everybody at whose expense Aristophanes jokes was an idiot. Lawyers have to try to win their cases; it does not follow that the opposing litigants were as vicious as the speeches we have make them out to be.

---

[11] W. S. Gilbert, *The Mikado*, Act I.

It was a regular feature of history books in the ancient world to quote speeches made at decisive moments; although Thucydides apologizes for unavoidable inaccuracies[12] and would say only that the speakers said "something like this" (τοιάδε . . . τοιαῦτα),[13] later historians felt no need for apology. When Josephus reports the speech that Moses made to the Israelites before the splitting of the Red Sea,[14] we need not suspect that he had some independent source for this otherwise unknown speech; it was simply a requirement of the form.

The meters of poetry also put certain constraints on authors. If a leader of Greeks or Trojans had a name that included a cretic (that is, three syllables of which the first and third are long, the middle one short) we will never know, for the dactylic hexameter in which Homer's epics were written did not allow any room for cretics. Any such person's name would have been distorted, altered or suppressed.

Sometimes the requirements of convention are so demanding that they seem to change the picture entirely. Herodotus never saw the Persian Wars about which he wrote, and his books about them were published decades after they took place. Aeschylus, on the other hand, fought at Marathon, and his *Persians* was produced only eight years after Salamis, in front of an audience that included the veterans of the battle. According to what we have said about primary and secondary sources, Aeschylus' version should be much more reliable, and in certain respects so it is; but in other respects the conventions of tragedy make it hardly usable as a historical source. Aeschylus is not likely to have asked any Persian before ascribing opinions to Darius, Atossa and Xerxes; the tragic form did not require that particular kind of accuracy. He had a message for the Athenians, and his play is designed to put across that message.

Within the conventions, we have to have our eyes and ears open for hints. When Plato's Socrates compliments somebody, he is often laying a philosophical trap. When Tacitus tells us that "some people suspected" poisoning in a particular figure's death, it is probably Tacitus himself who is trying to insinuate a suspicion into the reader's mind. When Homer's Agamemnon speaks with crudity about the jobs that Chryseis will perform "in our house, in Argos, far from her homeland,"[15] the crudity is supposed to show us something about Agamemnon's character. Hints like

---

[12] Thuc. 1.22.
[13] Ibid. 1.31.4, 1.36.4 and *passim*.
[14] Jos. *AJ* 2.15.5.
[15] Hom. Il. 1.29–31.

these abound in ancient literature, and we must always be aware of them. We must also be aware that they may be entirely false.

COMMENTARIES

Wherever we deal with classical sources, a good commentary is a great blessing. Depending on the sort of commentary it is, it may help you understand the Greek or Latin, explain the historical, mythological or literary background, offer parallel passages that can help illuminate this one, and alert you to issues in the text that have been the subject of scholarly discussion. These are very useful things, and only a foolhardy classicist will forgo the use of a commentary if one is available.

Commentaries, however, are not interchangeable, nor does a new commentary necessarily supersede an old one. Different commentaries have different goals in mind, and which commentary (or commentaries; you will not necessarily find all you need in a single commentary) is best for you depends very much on what you need to know.

School Commentaries

These are written chiefly to help the student understand the text. They vary widely in level: a commentary written for elementary school students who have learned a year or two of Latin will be written differently from one written for college students, even if the college students in question have themselves only recently begun to learn the language; for one thing, the elementary-school commentary is more likely to have a vocabulary at the back. School commentaries will pay more attention to points of grammar and to rare words than other commentaries would, and their explanations of historical or literary points are likely to be brief. Nowadays commentaries written for students may have a facing translation, a feature that was once considered cheating in the schoolroom but is now looked upon with more indulgence.[16]

---

[16] The claim has been advanced that literal translations are actually a more efficient way of teaching the ancient languages than the more traditional methods. The claim is not a new one; it was vigorously defended by John Clarke nearly three centuries ago in the preface to his edition of Justin's *History*. I am not aware of modern teachers who have actually had the temerity to use this method, which would seem worth consideration if the obvious abuses (students who skip the Latin and read the translation) can be controlled.

Scholarly Commentaries

Commentaries that are written for the use of scholars will not generally discuss points of grammar and vocabulary except insofar as the proper understanding of the text is a matter of real or potential disagreement. They will tell you more about the history of the text, about its background, and about what other scholars have had to say about it than the school commentaries will. They are generally longer, heavier and more expensive than school commentaries, and more likely to cite foreign scholars in their own language.

Specialized Commentaries

Some commentaries are written from a particular point of view, or with attention to a particular topic. Such works as HCT deal chiefly with historical issues, and may disappoint a person looking for a deeper understanding of Thucydides' style. De Jong, *A Narratological Commentary on the Odyssey* offers a literary discussion of the Odyssey, but does so from a particular point of view: it is an eye-opener on many issues that other commentaries miss, but it will not explain to you that Homer's subjunctives may have a short thematic vowel. Not every specialized commentary advertises its specialization in its title: How and Wells, *A Commentary on Herodotus* is no less a historical commentary than HCT, but the title does not admit the fact.

Not every commentary can be easily categorized. Some attempt to serve a number of different purposes; this is not necessarily bad, but it can be extremely difficult to do well. Other commentaries may have no apparent organizing principle at all. In general, the author of a commentary should have given careful thought to two questions: for whom am I writing this, and what does that person need to know? A commentary written without attention to these two questions will be of limited value at best. It is generally worth looking at the introduction before deciding whether a particular commentary is appropriate for what you want to get from it.

Ancient Commentaries

The first commentaries were written in the Hellenistic period, and commentaries continued to be written throughout the Middle Ages and down to our own day. Ancient commentaries, like the modern ones, were of various sorts and of various interests. Few ancient commentaries are preserved in full, and none at all from the earliest periods, though papyri have produced sufficient fragments to indicate something of what their form was. For the most part the work of ancient commentators is preserved in *scholia*, marginal comments in manuscripts of the work in question. These comments, usually brought without attribution, may be trivial, foolish, pedantic, polemical or illuminating. They may be based on information or quote sources not otherwise available to us. They may originate from anywhere from the Hellenistic period to the Middle Ages. Because they are so varied in nature and in provenance, and because their form and vocabulary tend to be technical and unfamiliar, few scholars take the trouble to delve into them,[17] and they have been published only rarely; the *scholia* on many authors have not been re-edited for over a hundred years, though the old editions are occasionally reprinted. Some individual *scholia* have achieved particular notice for one reason or another, and are cited repeatedly in modern discussions. *Scholia* are often signaled in footnotes with an upper-case sigma: Σ *Ar. Nub.* 905 means "a *scholion* on Aristophanes' *Clouds*, line 905."[18]

Characteristics of Commentaries

A beginning student tends to take a commentary as the sum total of everything that is known about the text: we can check the commentary and then feel secure that we are not missing any important information. Even scholars will often cite a commentary as a shorthand way of citing all previous literature. As mentioned above, only a certain kind of commentary tries to achieve this level of completeness, and even those that try do not necessarily succeed.

Certain prejudices are inherent in the nature of a commentary. The most significant is the commentary's tendency to concentrate on individual words and phrases. This is not accidental: ancient grammatical and educational theory saw learning as a process that began with understanding sounds, then letters, syllables, words, phrases, and so on in an ever-

---

[17] It is to be hoped, however, that this situation will change considerably now that Dickey, *Ancient Greek Scholarship* has made Greek scholarship, at least, considerably more accessible to the modern classicist, and Nünlist, *The Ancient Critic at Work* has elucidated the terms and concepts with which the ancient critics worked.

[18] Those who use this esoteric form of reference tend also to use the Latin (i.e., more esoteric) title for the work, though I know of no law requiring it.

widening area of comprehension.[19] There was no sense that one could accurately describe the forest without taking account of every tree. The result of looking at a book phrase by phrase, however, can too often be a failure to grasp the topic as a whole. Reading an entire commentary on Aeschylus' *Libation Bearers* does not necessarily prepare you to answer some very basic questions: who is the hero of this drama, Orestes or Electra? What does it add to the *Oresteia* that we do not get from the *Agamemnon* and the *Eumenides*? To counteract this tendency of the line-by-line commentaries, most modern commentaries offer an introduction[20] to deal with the larger questions raised by the work. Students, eager to get on with their assignment, often tend to ignore these introductions, but doing so may cause them to miss the editor's most important observations.

A further tendency of commentaries that must be taken into account is their tendency to favor the author on whom they are commenting. A scholar who feels no sympathy with a particular author will usually not be interested in devoting years to studying that author's works. There is a tendency to presume that whatever the author said was the right thing to say, and however the author phrased the text was the right way to phrase it: where Horace might take it amiss that good Homer may nod,[21] the commentator more often takes Alexander Pope's attitude: "nor is it Homer nods, but we that dream."[22] This attitude is not without its justification: a prudent scholar will indeed be well advised to presume that Homer's aesthetic judgment was better than the scholar's own, and few will want to copy the scholar who advised the reader that "any mistakes should be attributed to the original author, not to me." But no text is perfect, and sometimes a frank discussion of an author's shortcomings can be extremely illuminating. This is not to suggest that the proper attitude for a commentary to take is a hostile one,[23] but, when dealing with an author,

[19]   I owe this observation, as well as the general observation on the atomizing tendency of commentaries, to an excellent survey lecture offered by Ineke Sluiter at the Twentieth Triennial Conference of the Greek and Roman Societies at Cambridge in July 2005, on the basis of material that she is planning to publish as a monograph; I quote it with her permission. The lecture had so many other perceptive and worthwhile observations that I am sure that, when the monograph is published, nobody will consider that my own observations here have preempted Dr. Sluiter's study.

[20]   This is the case for commentaries but not for every edition of a classical work: the introductions to the Oxford Classical Texts and the Bibliotheca Teubneriana, for example, deal only with textual matters.

[21]   Hor. *Ars* 359.

[22]   Pope, *An Essay on Criticism*, 180.

[23]   Though occasionally such an attitude, as that of Wyse, *The Speeches of Isaeus*, can be very productive.

even a favorite author, both commentator and reader should be careful not to suspend their critical facilities entirely.

A last point to remember about commentaries is that each commentary is to a certain extent a compendium of its predecessors. Information is recycled, and errors and misunderstandings that creep in may be repeated for generations until somebody checks into the original source of the comment. For the same reason, the issues with which commentaries on a given work deal tend to remain the same. A commentary can be very useful in letting you know what people have thought about this and that aspect of the text. It should not command your implicit belief any more than any other secondary source; and you should not let it get in the way of your ability to take your own fresh look at the material.

CONCORDANCES

For many research projects in the classics you will want to know what ancient authors had to say about your topic; but since you probably do not know the entirety of ancient literature by heart, your own memory, and even that of your teachers and friends, may not suffice. If you know which authors are relevant to you and you can find an online text, the online search that we suggested above[24] for bibliographies can be helpful here, too; but a concordance may be even more helpful.

Before there were online searches there were concordances: volumes listing, in alphabetical order, every occurrence of a word in a given author. Compiling a concordance was a laborious matter: each word was written on a slip of paper, then the slips were sorted into alphabetical order and the results printed, bound and sold. Concordances were useful things: if you wanted to know, for example, what Demosthenes meant by ἀρετή, a glance at Preuss, *Index Demosthenicus* would direct you to all the places where he used the word, which would help you work out what his attitude was toward that concept. The online search has made the straightforward concordance obsolete: there is no need for an alphabetical listing when the text can be searched for any term in a matter of seconds. Concordances that merely list the words are no longer published, but for all that many of the old ones can still be useful.

For one thing, in a strongly inflected language like Greek or Latin, each word has many forms. There are search-engines that will come up with *tulerunt* when asked for occurrences of *fero*, but most will not, so that the

[24] P. 31.

electronic searcher has to try to remember all the possible forms of the word in question; a hand-made concordance will naturally put *tulerunt*, and all other forms of the verb, under the entry *fero*.[25]

Another advantage to a well-compiled concordance is that it distinguishes different meanings of the same word. If you want to find what Herodotus has to say about poetry, you might want to look up the verb ποιέω. An online search, if you remember all the forms, will turn up 1,215 occurrences. A peek into Powell, *A Lexicon to Herodotus* will reveal to you that only sixteen of them refer to poetry, and will tell you which they are. You will also find a great number of idiomatic uses whose interest the compiler will have noticed, but the computer, at least as computers are now built, never will. You may also find some variant readings that were not included in the TLG's text.[26]

When all of that is said, it is still true that there is always the possibility that an important reference that is very relevant to your subject does not use the particular word that you are seeking. If you were looking for ancient authors who deal with Augustus Caesar, Wacht, *Concordantia Vergiliana* would correctly inform you that the name Augustus appears only twice in the Aeneid, never at all in the Eclogues or the Georgics. You might conclude that Vergil was not particularly concerned with Augustus. Not many scholars would agree with you.

FRAGMENTS

In the Middle Ages, vast numbers of classical texts were lost. Out of more than seventy Aeschylean tragedies whose names we know,[27] only seven

---

[25] Progress has been made towards a system that will overcome the opacity of Greek and Latin morphology: the *Perseus* project has developed a program called *Morpheus* to identify Greek forms, and the Catholic University of Louvain has done its own work in this direction, specifically to make online searches better able to fulfill the role of a true concordance: Kevers and Kindt, "Vers un concordanceur-lemmatiseur."

[26] The problem of how to deal with variant readings was raised by Theodore F. Brunner, the founding director of the TLG, towards the end of his career, and it is to be hoped that the future will see good solutions. As long as copyright restrictions prohibit online sources from using the most up-to-date texts, there will be variants that they do not provide; but those variants are not available in the old concordances either, and new printed concordances, as of this writing, are not being produced.

[27] Seventy-three are named in a catalogue of Aeschylus' dramas copied in a number of manuscripts and easily available at the back of Denys Page's OCT edition; other names are known to us as well, and the Suda s.v. Αἰσχύλος claims that he wrote ninety.

remain; out of the 147 books of Livy's history, only thirty-five are in our possession. Of Sappho's nine books of poetry, which earned her the title of "the tenth Muse," not a single copy remains. All the early historians of Rome, all the tragedians except for Aeschylus, Sophocles and Euripides, all the philosophers before Socrates, and all the Republican orators except for Cicero were long known to moderns only insofar as their works had been cited by other authors whose works survived. In the last hundred years, papyri have increased our knowledge materially but tantalizingly, offering us thousands more scraps—literally—of ancient authors, and even, occasionally, complete or nearly complete works. Over the centuries, a small number of industrious classicists have dedicated their lives to finding and collecting all of these quotations: these are the "fragments" that tell us most of what we know about the lost works of antiquity.

Collections of fragments are generally divided into *fragmenta*, actual citations or paraphrases of a given work or an author ("ἀνδράκας means 'per man,' 'separately': Cratinus in the *Cowherds*"[28]), and *testimonia*, statements about the work or about its author ("The comic poet Cratinus lived ninety-four years, and at the end of his life produced the *Pytine* and won the prize, then died shortly thereafter"[29]). They can be very extensive: of Menander's comedies the nineteenth century possessed only an alphabetical collection of individual quotable lines (many of them not by Menander) and the knowledge that some comedies of his formed the basis for certain comedies of Plautus and Terence, although nobody knew how close these were to the original. Starting in 1897, some fortunate papyrus finds have given us a number of almost complete comedies. For other authors we may have summaries: for the lost books of Livy we have summaries that are called *periochae*, and a few later authors, such as Athenaeus at the end of the second century or Photius in the ninth, quoted at least some works extensively enough to give us an idea of what they were like. More deplorable is the situation of authors like Sappho, whose few surviving poems have now been joined by dozens of papyrus fragments, none of them more than a few lines long, and most of them containing only bits of lines whose beginnings and/or ends are lost.

Although it might seem that little coherent use can be made of these scraps, the fact is that the collections of fragments have gone a long way towards showing us what the lost works were like. The great collection of Diels and Kranz, *Die Fragmente der Vorsokratiker*, has been, since Diels' first edition in 1903, the basis of everything we know about presocratic

---

[28] Photius α 1748 = PCG Cratinus F 21.
[29] [Lucian] *Macr.* 25 = PCG Cratinus T 3.

philosophy, and by now we know a good deal. The *Annales* of Ennius,[30] the *Andromeda* of Euripides,[31] and the laws of Solon[32] are now well enough known for each to have merited an individual publication. Greek New Comedy was known only from fragments until the end of the nineteenth century; that is still the case with Middle Comedy.

There are pitfalls in the use of fragments. The most common danger is not checking the context. Each of the fragments in a collection has been taken from somewhere, many of them from other literary works that cite them. Checking the source may reveal to us that the fragment is being quoted for a particular purpose; that it may be being paraphrased rather than quoted; and sometimes even that its attribution to the author is uncertain. Looking at the context will also reveal to us when the selection of fragments available to us is less than representative. Athenaeus' *Deipnosophists* is one of our most important sources for fragments of Greek comedy; the great proportion of these fragments that deal with food give us an exaggerated picture, since food was Athenaeus' topic. Many fragments consist of a single word preserved by a grammarian or in a dictionary; these words are preserved precisely because they are bizarre, and can show us what was characteristic only by way of negation. Lastly, the very fact of dealing with fragmentary texts may lull us into a scholarship that pays attention only to the details we can tease out of the texts, or else—equally perniciously—into vast theories too big for the small and fragmentary foundations on which we are building.

HISTORICAL SOURCES

For literary studies of Sophocles or Vergil our chief interest is the text before us, and its historical context is a matter that interests us mainly for the light it throws on the text. When we study history, on the contrary, the texts we use are generally[33] of interest to us more as a source of information about what happened than for any virtue of the texts themselves.

---

[30] Skutsch, ed., *The Annals of Q. Ennius*.

[31] Bubel, ed., *Euripides: Andromeda*, more readily available for English speakers in Collard, Cropp and Lee, eds., *Euripides: Selected Fragmentary Plays*.

[32] Ruschenbusch, ed., *Solonos Nomoi*.

[33] Though not, of course, always: the study of historiography, how historians approached their subject, is a field in itself not necessarily less interesting than the study of what happened. See below, Chapter 13.

This fact, combined with a natural desire to seek for what we need in the most easily available place, leads to a lamentable tendency for some modern works of history to be little more than paraphrases of the ancient historians and biographers. The ancient historians undoubtedly had their virtues, and the best of them—and in most cases, though not all, it is the best of them who survive—were at least as good at what they were doing as any of their modern counterparts. But all the warnings given above about uncritical reliance on sources apply here, and there is a good deal of other information besides them. Literary works may occasionally make mention of historical events; few are as direct as Aeschylus' *Persians* or the *Octavia* attributed to Seneca, but even the very apolitical plays of Menander occasionally preserve a mention that reveals something of the time when they were written. More to the point, the literary works of the period often give us a much better feeling for how people thought at the time, a knowledge that may be very useful in understanding how they acted. The observations of Archilochus, Catullus and Horace about their military service show us ancient armies from a point of view that no historian quite reproduces—surely not Livy who, unlike these lyric poets, never served in an army.

Far beyond the literary sources are the things that can be learned from archaeology and its daughter disciplines, epigraphy, papyrology and numismatics. For some periods of ancient history, these sources become as important as the literary ones or more so; for all periods they have important contributions to make, most often complementing what the historians transmit, sometimes contradicting it, sometimes simply showing us information of an entirely different nature. This information may be much harder for a historian trained in the close analysis of texts to deal with. One of my major motivations in writing this book was the hope that it will make you more willing and more able to deal with all of the different sorts of information that we now have at hand.

No nation, not even the Roman Empire at the height of its power, lives alone. Studying the history of Athens inevitably involves us in the history of Sparta, Aegina and Persia, and the last, at least, is quite a different study from that of Athens. The fifth book of Tacitus' *Histories*, most of which is lost, begins with scraps of anti-Jewish fairy tales that masquerade as history; a comparison with the very voluminous contemporary Jewish literature that is preserved in Hebrew, Aramaic, Greek and more exotic languages shows us just how inaccurate an intelligent author could be when writing about a foreign culture. For few of the nations outside of the Greco-Roman sphere do we have the kind of documentation that we have for the Jews, but it will always be worthwhile for a historian of the period to pay attention as well as possible to what we do have.

BACKGROUND AND SURROUNDING INFORMATION

Even the histories of entirely unrelated nations may be of interest. We cannot help comparing the world of the ancients to our own, but that is not necessarily the most appropriate comparison. The way that the Chinese regulated their markets, the way that Africans and Europeans traded with each other without a common language, and the teeming capital of the Aztecs may all have interesting light to shed upon the ancient world despite the fact that they had no contact with the Greeks or the Romans. Visiting a historical site, or for that matter visiting a museum, will almost always show you something you would not have thought of inquiring about: my own thesis topic, which had nothing to do with Greek ceramics, had its origin in an afternoon at a museum whose display of Greek pottery suggested to me a question I had not previously considered. Your own experience, as mentioned above,[34] may be useful. For all that, however, you must decide—preferably at the earliest stages of a project—where to put the limits. Everything you learn will raise new questions, and if you follow them all up you will never publish your conclusions, if indeed you ever reach any at all.

[34] Page 19, n. 5.

5

BOOK REVIEWS

READING BOOK REVIEWS

In classics, as in the humanities in general,[1] the most influential research is published in the form of books: for a really thoroughgoing investigation or reevaluation, a journal article rarely suffices. It is impossible to read all the classical books that are published in a given year; nor, were it possible, would it be advisable. Some have little value for anybody;[2] even of those that are very important, most deal with subjects with which you are not currently involved. Book reviews serve at least three vital functions: they help their readers choose which books they should borrow or buy; they offer those who will never read the book a general idea of what it contains, information that may be useful for future research or teaching or simply as background knowledge; and they locate the book in the context of current research, indicating what is new about it, what is controversial and what other things might be worth reading.

---

[1] This is not the situation in the natural sciences, where most important advances are published as journal articles, and books serve chiefly for surveys of the state of research, including the work of many scholars besides the author.

[2] It is to be hoped that the process of peer review that often holds up a book's publication for months or years saves scholarly presses from publishing books that are entirely worthless, but there can be no doubt that in this field, as in all others, quality can vary very widely.

No review can be a substitute for the book itself; the review cannot go deeply into the details of the author's argument or the evidence with which the book's thesis is defended. Nevertheless, it is reasonable to expect of a book review that it will offer a fair summary of the book's central thesis, an evaluation (it should tell you whether or not the reviewer thinks the author has proved the case), and some idea of how it fits into, or how it affects, other scholarship. If the book contains serious errors, the reviewer should warn you of the fact.

The reviewer's attitude is not necessarily authoritative. Reviewers are normally people who have published in the same field as the author, and they may be more critical than they should be because the author disagrees with this or that thesis of theirs; alternatively, they may be more generous than they should be because of their own professional relationship with the author, who may in turn review the reviewer's next book, or even be asked for an opinion about the reviewer's upcoming promotion. Too often it is the reviewer who has not grasped the author's point—a problem in all fields but a particular problem in classics, where the information on which we base our claims generally consists of texts that are themselves already well known, so that the frequent references to familiar passages may obscure the originality of what is being said about them. Often a particular assertion may so intrigue (or so enrage) the reviewer that it seems to be a central premise of the book, and the reviewer does not catch what the real argument was.

For these reasons and dozens more, one can never rely on a review in place of the book. Even a seemingly straightforward quotation should be looked up before it is used: you will often be surprised to see that in its original context it does not say what it seemed to be saying in the review.

WRITING BOOK REVIEWS

Book reviews generally follow a more or less fixed pattern, in accordance with the functions they are expected to serve.

Preliminary Material

At the top of the review there is normally a summary of bibliographical information:

> SCHAPS, DAVID M. *Handbook for Classical Research.* Pp. xxii + 466, 34 figs. London/New York: Routledge, 2010. Paper, £22.99. ISBN: 978–0–415–42523–0.

The information included is standard: in this case author, title, number of pages (introductory matter numbered with Roman numerals is counted separately), whether it has maps ("maps"), figures ("figs."), illustrations ("ills.") or plates ("pls."), place of publication, publisher, year of publication, binding (cloth or paper), price, and ISBN (International Standard Book Number), a unique number assigned since 1970[3] to each edition of every book and normally printed on the back cover and copyright page. Different journals have different rules for precisely what information is printed at the top of a review and what its format is (the example above is in the format of CR), but the differences are not great. The information itself can be the most important part of the review: you can see at a glance if a book is priced beyond your means, or if it is too long for you to finish or too short to give you the details you need, or if the author or publisher is one to whom you would pay special attention.

Summary

The first thing the body of the review should tell the reader is what the book is about—sometimes a surprisingly difficult job. Every book has a title, but not every title is informative: Loomis, *Wages, Welfare Costs and Inflation in Classical Athens* is a title that gives a fair idea of the book's contents, but Loraux, *The Experiences of Tiresias* is less forthcoming about what the book's intentions are, and even the subtitle—"The Feminine and the Greek Man"—does not make the book's subject (the way in which feminine attributes are appropriated as part of the description of male heroes) entirely clear. Finley, *Ancient Economy* seems straightforward enough, and the author begins his preface with the words "The title of this volume is precise,"[4] but only a person who reads it carefully and knows such other books as Rostovtzeff, *The Social and Economic History of the Hellenistic World* will realize that the author has a thesis to maintain and is doing so combatively. Before you sit down to write your review, give some thought to what exactly the book is trying to do and how it is going about it. Once these two matters are clear to you, try to put them across to the reader.

The summary should also be written with the reader's needs in mind. The reader is generally interested in two questions: Do I want to read this

---

[3]   It was in 1970 that the International Organization for Standardization (ISO) adopted the ISBN system; this did not mean that every book published in every country immediately adopted the system.

[4]   Finley, *Ancient Economy*, 9.

book? Do I *have* to read this book? Although it is not a value judgment, your summary will be a major factor in my decision as to how relevant the book is to whatever I am interested in. Even if my answer to both questions is negative—no, I don't want to read this book, and I don't have to, either—it is the summary that is most likely to stay in my mind to remind me of this book when, in some unforeseen future time, it will be helpful to me.

Discussion

The opinions you express about the book may, and usually should, go beyond a general positive or negative evaluation. Real scholarly debate is not only permissible but desirable: if the claims of the book seem wrong, exaggerated or misconceived, it is the reviewer's job to say so, and to demonstrate why that is the case. Very often it is only the reviewers who will maintain an open debate in the face of a book that seems persuasive on its surface: it may take a generation before students who have grown up with the book realize that it is misleading them. Nevertheless, a certain caution is in order before jumping into the fray: the author has generally researched the book's particular topic more thoroughly than the reviewer, and, before taking issue with a book you review, you will have to challenge your own ideas and make sure that they are still tenable in view of the book's arguments.

Discussion should not only be free and frank, it should be pertinent. Picking at a few side issues may be a good way of demonstrating your own expertise, but it does not help the reader evaluate the book, and it does not do much for your professional reputation, either. There is a place in the review for discussing minor issues, but the main discussion section is not that place.

Judgment

Every reviewer should state a clear judgment about the book: does this book add to our knowledge or simply to our confusion? Your judgment may be nuanced: a book doesn't have to be either wonderful or worthless, and you may give a generally positive judgment while making allowances for problems, or a negative one that admits the book's strengths. Nevertheless, since the reader is interested in deciding whether or not to read (or to buy) the book, the reviewer's overall judgment is important, and not a responsibility that the reviewer can properly avoid. The natural order of giving your judgment would be to give the general judgment first, followed by the reservations: "This is an excellent book, though it does have its problem . . . ." Since, however, this order usually leaves readers with the reservations uppermost in their mind, many reviewers make a point of repeating their overall judgment at the end: "All these minor comments, however, do not diminish the merits of this fine book . . . ." Of course, one can do the same for a negative judgment ("But these few virtues cannot redeem this slapdash piece of work . . ."), but the charitable reviewer usually thinks it enough, if a negative judgment is required, to make that judgment once without rubbing it in.

It is easier to say on what basis you should not make your judgment than on what basis you should. Other people's judgments are not a good basis: if you are just going to say what others have said already, there is no real value to your review at all. There is nothing wrong with admiring a book that others have scorned, or with disliking a book that others have praised. Your own feelings about the author are also immaterial: if you think that you are incapable of saying anything bad (or anything good)— and most people have colleagues about whom they feel that way—you should not ask to review this book. The author's previous work is no guarantee: many authors write some excellent work along with some that is middling or downright embarrassing, and there is no reason to presume that this work is on the same standard, for better or for worse, as the others.

Hardest to avoid is judging the book according to its author's opinion of a matter on which you have your own ideas. For one thing, disagreement among scholars is healthy and constructive, and the fact that a scholar disagrees with you—even if you are right and the other is wrong, which is certainly the case—need not be taken as evidence of poor scholarship. Judge the book on its general merits, even if you disagree with its general thesis. A book may advance scholarship even if its central thesis is incorrect: the physics of Aristotle and Newton made enormous contributions to their subject even though the eventual judgment of scientists was that they were wrong in fundamental aspects. This fact does not require you to bend over backwards to speak with respect about nonsense: if a book is mistaken in its general thesis, it is not likely to be a great book. But if the thesis itself is debatable, the book may advance debate even though it comes down on a different side of the argument than you do. All this is said with regard to the book's major ideas; it should go without saying that you should never condemn a book because it disagrees with your own ideas in secondary matters. Had you expected to agree with everything the author said? Are there no books of value with opinions other than your own? And if that is the case—why do you read books?

Your judgment of the book should take account of its form as well as its content. Is it organized comprehensibly? If it is a commentary, are the comments presented in a way that makes them accessible and understandable? If illustrations are an important part of the book, are they clear, clearly identified and relevant? Will users of the book have to flip pages interminably to look up matters that should have been dealt with in one place? Is there an index, and is it helpfully organized? Some books of middling scholarship become classics because of their excellent presentation, and some brilliant books are utterly unusable because they are too difficult of access. You should note whether the achievement or the failure belongs to the author (poor organization, lack of proper documentation) or the publisher (unclear photographs, misspellings and typographical errors so frequent that they obstruct understanding); in either case, your honest criticism may help them improve their performance in the future.

Matters of Detail

Many reviewers use the end of a review for discussing matters of detail about which they have particular comments. This is perfectly legitimate and may be helpful both to reader and to author; in fact, the reviewer is more likely to have useful comments about points of detail than to be able to challenge effectively in a page or so a thesis that the author has developed in an entire book. For some types of book—a critical text, an atlas, a technical translation—the details may even be the most important part of the scholarship. Discussion of details, however, should not be there just for the sake of one-upmanship. Some reviewers make a point of noting every misprint in the book: for most books this serves no purpose except to show that the reviewer has actually read the book, and it is no compliment to the reviewer if we need such proof.

Another favorite form of one-upmanship is to mention a book or an article that the author did not mention: "I missed a reference to . . . ." Sometimes, indeed, an item of scholarship is so fundamental that an author who does not deal with it may be seriously compromised. This is not usually the case. The author is under no obligation to mention every single book or article that has ever been published, or even that has recently been published, on the subject under discussion; nor is it really honest to pretend that the reviewer (unlike the author) does know every-thing that has ever been written on the subject. If you are surprised that the author did not mention a particular article, ask two questions before you mention the fact. First, was the article available to the reviewer while the book was being written? Second, how much of a difference would it have made to the book if it had taken account of the article? If the answer is—and it usually is—"not much," then the author was probably right not to mention it, and you will be wrong if you do.

WHO WRITES REVIEWS?

Policy differs from journal to journal. Some journals only publish reviews by people they have invited to write the review; others welcome volunteers; some journals will accept unsolicited reviews and publish them if they think they merit publication. If you are interested in reviewing a book, it is probably worthwhile to get in touch with the editors of a journal to see if they are interested in having the book reviewed. It will usually be possible to find a journal that will accept the proposition warmly, and many will have a reviewer's copy sent to you for free. Of course, the editors will always reserve the right, once they receive it, to decide whether your review is appropriate before agreeing to publish it.

MAJOR RESOURCES

Journals Specializing in Book Reviews

Most classical journals publish book reviews, often taking up as much as a quarter of each issue. Certain journals are published entirely as collections of reviews, with other material rarely if ever included.

In English, the *Classical Review* (CR) is now (since 1975) devoted entirely to reviews; the *Journal of Hellenic Studies* (JHS) and the *Journal of Roman Studies* (JRS) between them cover most books appearing in English, and many appearing in other languages, though JHS covers considerably less than CR and takes much longer to get its reviews published. Also worth mentioning is *Phoenix*, though it does not compete for comprehensiveness with JHS and JRS, much less CR, and the *Journal of Roman Archaeology* for those publications that fall within its field. TLS is worth a particular mention, offering regular coverage of classical books written by first-rank scholars for a general but highly sophisticated audience.

A special mention should be made of the *Bryn Mawr Classical Review* (BMCR), an electronic journal that no longer publishes a paper edition at all. By virtue of uploading each review almost as soon as it is received, this journal is very often "first on the street" with reviews of new literature, and it casts an extremely wide net, often reviewing more than fifty books in a month. Because of the deplorable tendency of some reviewers to judge a book by what others have said about it, BMCR reviews can be very influential. The South African journal *Scholia* also publishes reviews on its website, *Scholia Reviews*, but does not attempt to cover everything: *Scholia* publishes in a year fewer reviews than BMCR publishes in a busy month.

Greece and Rome is not a journal devoted to reviews, but the Subject Reviews (formerly called Brief Reviews) offered at the end of each volume give a sentence or two to each book mentioned. These are a very convenient way of keeping an eye out for what may be worth looking into, and the opinions, if brief, are often judicious.

In German, Gnomon[5] and the Austrian *Anzeiger für die Altertumswissenschaft*— numbered, like RE, by column rather than by page—are devoted entirely to reviews; for books concerning history, *Klio*, the voice of East German scholarship during the years when Germany was divided, includes a large review section, as does the Swiss *Museum Helveticum*.

In French *L'antiquité classique*, *Les études classiques*, and the *Revue de philologie* all contain considerable review sections; for Latin items there are also *Latomus* and the *Revue des études latines*.

There is no Italian journal dedicated to book reviews; *Athenaeum* publishes a good number, and can be very useful for knowing what is going on in the world of Italian research.

Regularly consulting one of these will give you a good general idea of what books have been published recently in the field, but these journals are by no means the only places where books are reviewed, nor are their reviews in any sense "authoritative": a book that is panned in one may be praised in another. Many other journals include book reviews, and on occasion a review in any journal may raise matters of such importance that the review becomes an essential counterpoint to the book. For finding reviews of a given book the most valuable tool is *APh*, which gives a list of all reviews, including the name of the reviewer and the place the review appeared, under the rubric of the book itself; as a result of this policy, a book continues to appear year after year in the printed volume of *APh*

[5] See above, p. 38. In addition to reviews *Gnomon* regularly publishes a bibliographical index of recent work and obituaries of noteworthy classicists, along with a brief mention of the demise of the less noteworthy.

as long as new reviews of it are being published. *APh*, however, takes some time to appear, and simply entering the name of the book in an online search will often find a worthwhile review well before *APh* has recorded it.

PART II

LANGUAGE

6

LEXICOGRAPHY

USING DICTIONARIES

There is probably no area of classical studies where the student is as apt to relapse into the presumption that the grown-ups know everything as in the area of lexicography. We find an unfamiliar word, look it up in a dictionary, find the translation that seems most appropriate, and feel confident that we know what the meaning of the word is. Amazingly, we will accept from a dictionary even a word that means nothing to us. When Theophrastus[1] writes of the γλῖνος we can see that he means some kind of tree, and we go scurrying to our dictionary to find out more; when LSJ[9] informs us that a γλῖνος is a *Cretan maple, Acer creticum*, whether or not we have ever seen or heard of a Cretan maple, we feel that we have found out what there is to know, and return happily to reading Theophrastus.

The truth of the matter is that any dictionary's definitions are necessarily so brief that they often give us only a small amount of the information we need: a picture of the Cretan maple, for example, would have been helpful, but LSJ[9] does not come with pictures.[2] More insidiously, the

---

[1] HP 3.3.1.

[2] Some dictionaries, such as Gaffiot, *Dictionnaire illustré* and Autenrieth, *Homeric Dictionary*, do include pictures, though no real classical dictionary of which I know has gone as far as the outstanding Corbeil, *The Facts on File Visual Dictionary*, which dispenses with alphabetical order entirely in favor of a series of pictures meticulously labeled—in

definition may be much less certain than the dictionary admits: who, precisely, identified the γλῖνος with the Cretan maple, and on what grounds? Are there other possibilities? Worst of all, no word in any language is ever precisely equivalent to a word in another language.[3] Sometimes this may merely be a matter of sound and association—the name *Cretan maple* makes assertions about the tree's geographical location and its relationship to other trees, while the name γλῖνος does not—but more often it is a matter of a truly different referent. Did Theophrastus by γλῖνος mean only those trees that we would call Cretan maples? Did he perhaps include others, or exclude some that we would consider variants of the same type? And if this is the kind of problem that arises with a botanical term with a presumably specific referent, how in the world are we to translate such expressions as ὕβρις and ἀρετή?

Lexicography, in short, is no more exact a science than any other area of the classics, and the task of scholarship is no more finished or authoritative here than anywhere else; anyone with doubts can consult Boned Colera et al., *RBLG*, the third supplement to the still-evolving *Diccionario Griego–Español*, devoted entirely to a bibliography of its sources, including—after seventy-five large pages of indices and concordances and another sixty pages of lexicographical sources—some fifty thousand Greek words on which those sources and others have been consulted; another fifteen thousand have already been added in an online supplement (*RBLG Supl.*). When you want to know the meaning of a word, there is no reason to presume that what you find in LSJ[9] or OLD is all you can get. For day-to-day purposes, it will usually suffice: many readers of Theophrastus don't really have to know anything more about the γλῖνος than what Theophrastus himself has to say, and will be satisfied to be reassured by LSJ[9] that it is some kind of tree, without caring much what kind it is. But if it is important to you, there may be a good deal more to know; and *RBLG* may be a good place to start.

Not every lexicographical work is a dictionary. If you come across the expression ὦ δαιμόνιε LSJ[9] will tell you that it means "*good sir or lady*," that it is used to chiefs or commoners, especially strangers, used by husbands and wives, and frequently in comedy in an ironic sense. But what does it *mean*? Why does one sometimes say ὦ δαιμόνιε, sometimes ὦ βέλτιστε, and sometimes use the vocative of the person's name? You can find a short summary of the controversy surrounding this expression

the many bilingual editions since published, labeled bilingually—with the proper terms for all the items shown.
[3]   See below, p. 381.

in Dickey, *Greek Forms of Address*, 141–2; and the answers suggested there will tell you a lot more about your text than LSJ[9] did. Her companion volume, *Latin Forms of Address*, will do the same for questions like who would have called the poet *Catulle*, who (and when) *Gai Valeri*, and who *mi anime*.

COMPILING DICTIONARIES

Compiling a dictionary generally has two stages before the actual writing of an entry: *slipping*, in which the compiler reads through the works on which the dictionary will be based and records every usage that seems to be worth including; then an analysis, in which the information in the "slips" is condensed into a reasonable definition or set of definitions, and the citations to be used are put into an order that will illustrate the word's meanings. Many dictionaries are derivative from others, as abridgements of larger works, expansions of smaller ones, or translations of foreign ones: Liddell and Scott began as a translation of Passow, *Handwörterbuch der griechischen Sprache*, itself a reworking of Johann Gottlob Schneider, *Griechisch–Deutsches Wörterbuch*; Lewis and Short began from Freund, *Wörterbuch der lateinischen Sprache*. It was probably the tedious work of slipping that led Samuel Johnson to offer as the definition of a lexicographer "a harmless drudge"; it is precisely this job that has been made infinitely easier by the availability of electronic texts that can be sorted in short order and can easily collect together all uses of a given word.

Even when the compiler has collected the various uses they cannot simply be listed. As Henri Estienne complained about the lexica available in the sixteenth century,

> Even if a single Greek word could be translated by so many Latin ones . . . still, what would this be but to overwhelm the reader with an unclear and confused assortment of meanings? . . . Here is the word βαίνω, which struck my eye first when I opened the dictionary, with twenty-two interpretations listed under it in uninterrupted succession, namely: I hurry, I walk calmly, I go, I make to go, I approach, I come forth, I enter, I aim, I stroll, I enter upon, I set foot upon, I walk, I approach, I bring in, I go in, I follow upon, I march along, I go up, I make to go up, I go down, I love, I flatter. Most of these interpretations are either wrong or certainly inappropriate; but even if all of them were right, shouldn't they rather have been placed individually, that is, each one with appropriate examples?[4]

---

[4]   Stephanus, "Excerpta ex Epistola," xxix–xxx.

But the choice of how to arrange them is no simple matter:

> Only those who have made the experiment know the bewilderment with which editor or sub-editor, after he has apportioned the quotations for such a word as *above* . . . among 20, 30 or 40 groups, and furnished each of these with a provisional definition, spreads them out on a table or on the floor where he can obtain a general survey of the whole, and spends hour after hour in shifting them about like the pieces on a chess-board, striving to find in the fragmentary evidence of an incomplete historical record, such a sequence of meanings as may form a logical chain of development.[5]

The choice of which uses are significant and illustrative, and how they should be understood and organized, continues and will continue to require the judgment of the human compiler.

Dictionaries have been being produced since the Hellenistic age, and some ancient and medieval dictionaries have survived in fragments or even in their entirety.[6] These were generally collections of terms used by particular authors, or in particular subjects, or simply lists of rare expressions, and they were often intended to distinguish "correct" classical usage from "corrupt" later usage. These dictionaries, whose compilers had access to many works that are now lost, often preserve interesting linguistic, literary or historical information, though it requires a good deal of sifting to find the wheat among the chaff.

The idea that a dictionary should be an arbiter of proper usage had a long life; the dictionaries of Samuel Johnson and Noah Webster were both designed to maintain their language (the English and the "American," respectively) at the properly elevated level that their compilers considered appropriate. In the last half of the nineteenth century, however, a number of new principles came to be accepted in lexicography.[7]

---

[5]   Murray, *Caught in the Web of Words*, 203, quoting the presidential address of James Murray (editor of the OED) from the Philological Society Transactions (1882–84), pp. 509–10.

[6]   An important step towards making ancient and Byzantine lexicography has been the *Suda On Line*, where the Stoa Consortium is making a major lexicographical source available, with translation and commentary.

[7]   There is much more that could be said on the questions of principle involved in lexicography. Since there has never been a science of lexicography divorced from its practice, the most significant discussions of lexicography come from the lexicographers themselves. A few examples are Stephanus' "Excerpta" and the preface to his *Thesaurus*; the *Praemonenda* to the *Thesaurus Linguae Latinae*, published in seven languages as

One of these was that *a dictionary should list all the words of a language*. Gove, *Webster's Third New International Dictionary* caused something of a scandal as recently as 1968 by including such words as *ain't*, *irregardless* and *normalcy*. Even the principle of total inclusion, however, leaves a question about technical terms, invented words, jargon, and a large grey area of what does and what does not belong to the language. Is *supercalifragilistic-expialidocious* to be considered an English word simply because Mary Poppins uses it? What about *faux pas*? For classical languages the problems with this principle have not been the same as they are in a modern language: it is not our business to tell the ancient authors how they should write, but to help others understand what they have written, so any word that they use must be included—and the rarer and odder the word, the greater the need for it to be explained.[8] Problems arise rather in determining what exactly has been written by the ancient authors; our texts are never definitive, and sometimes a word may not appear in the dictionary, or a non-word may appear, because the compiler used a poor text.[9] Even when the compiler used an excellent text, the text in the hands of the reader may be different, and the word in this text may not be in the dictionary. And what about obscenities?[10] If Aristophanes was crude, does that oblige the lexicographer to be the same? LSJ[9] solves the problem by translating these expressions into Latin, but a less inhibited age filled the gap.[11]

---

a separate fascicle of the TLL in 1990; the introduction to Chadwick, *Lexicographica Graeca*; and various essays that have come out of the office of the DGE, among them Adrados and Somolinos, *La lexicografía griega*.

[8] LSJ[9], for one, applies this principle so scrupulously that it has an entry for the made-up tongue-twister λοπαδοτεμαχοσελαχογαλεοκρανιολειψανοδριμυποτριμ-ματοσιλφιοκαραβομελιτοκατακεχυμενοκιχλεπικοσσυφοφαττοπεριστερα-λεκτρυονοπτοκεφαλλιοκιγκλοπελειολαγωοσιραιοβαφητραγανοπτερύγων, a word that Aristophanes used at *Eccl.* 1169–75 and that is hardly likely to be used again except by people quoting him. But even LSJ[9] drew the line at Pseudartabas' mangled pseudo-Greek at Ar. *Ach.* 100, and the transliterated Punic in Plaut. *Poen.* 930–49 and the following scene is included neither by Lewis and Short nor by the OLD.

[9] "But I say that many more [such errors] can be added taken from those dictionaries, like Ἐπαπήνη, 'chariot': with an error that has arisen out of this verse of Homer, in Iliad 24: Σὺν δ' ἕταροι ἤειραν ἐϋξέστην ἐπ' ἀπήνῃ." Stephanus, "Excerpta ex Epistola," xxx.

[10] The OED omitted them entirely, against the opinions of its editor (see Murray, *Caught in the Web of Words*, 165); so did Gove, *Webster's Third New International Dictionary*. More recent dictionaries, in keeping with the spirit of the age, routinely include them.

[11] Henderson, *The Maculate Muse*; for Latin there is Adams, *The Latin Sexual Vocabulary*.

Another, related principle is that *the word means what the speakers of the language take it to mean*. It is not immediately obvious why the name of the Maccabees, the Jews who rebelled against the Seleucid Empire in the second century BCE, should have acquired the meaning that it has in the English term *macabre*,[12] nor why a person who asks "What's going on here?" is asking the same question as one who asks "What's coming off here?" But if those usages are the ones employed by speakers of the language, those are the ones that the lexicographer must give in the definition. For classical languages, this means not allowing ourselves to be misled by etymologies: often a word's actual meaning is far removed from its etymology, or even entirely opposed to it.

More important for classical lexicographers was the principle that *citations should be presented in chronological order*.[13] Once we have accepted that language change is natural and acceptable, chronological order becomes important so that we can establish when a word is first used, when it first acquires a particular meaning, and when it ceases to be used. Vergil may be a better poet than Ennius, but the citation from Ennius should come first if we want to know how the Latin language changed from the second to the first century BCE. Of course, the lexicographer has not necessarily found the first use of the word, nor the last, and surprises are regularly in store. Many words that cease to appear in Latin after Plautus have derivatives in modern Romance languages: insufficiently elevated for educated prose, they apparently survived in the spoken language for centuries after their last appearance in a written text.

The last principle of a modern dictionary is that *the meanings of a word should be ordered in such a way as to demonstrate its development*. In dealing with the word χαίρω, "I rejoice," one cannot explain why the third-person imperative χαιρέτω means "forget about it" without first showing the use of the second-person imperative to mean "good-bye." It is in this area that OLD is at its best, making the development of each word easily followed and easily understood; OLD also has the virtue of recognizing metaphors as such and calling them by their right name, rather than offering every metaphorical use as an independent meaning of the word.

---

[12] This etymology is not uncontested: see OED[2] s.v. *Macabre*.

[13] This principle was enunciated by Franz Passow in 1812 and adopted by Liddell and Scott in their first lexicon. This principle, however, may be violated when the limited linguistic base may make other distinctions more essential: it may be reasonable, for example, to see the distinction between medical texts and tragedians as a more essential one for a given word than the distinction between the fifth century and the first.

LSJ[9], which groups a word's meaning by logic more than by history, often leaves the user with no clear picture of how the various meanings are related to each other.

MAJOR RESOURCES

Dictionaries: Greek

Ancient Greek lexicography is dominated by Liddell, Scott and Jones (LSJ[9]), brought up to date by Glare, *Revised Supplement* (which can be bought separately if you have an earlier copy of LSJ[9]), and for serious scholarship this must always be consulted. Both LSJ[9] and the *Intermediate Lexicon* can be consulted online at the *Perseus* website,[14] and a CD-ROM edition of LSJ[9] is available. The total list of all appearances of a word can always be found through an online search of TLG, but, besides the fact that no definitions are offered, the number of citations that TLG can give will be manageable only for the least common words. In fact TLG and LSJ[9] do not precisely overlap: they are built on different editions of the authors, and cover different areas. The greatest difference is that the Greek of Christian authors, and indeed late authors in general, is almost entirely absent from LSJ[9]. LSJ[9] is also weak on technical vocabularies, a fact of which you should be aware if using it for specialized texts. As a scholarly tool the *Diccionario Griego–Español* (DGE) will apparently surpass LSJ[9], though English speakers will have to brush up their Spanish to use it, and it will not be completed for decades. In the meantime, on the website of the project and in the supplements produced—particularly the third supplement, the *Repertorio Bibliográfico de la Lexicografía Griega* (RBLG)—one can find a great deal of bibliographical material, opening up to us all more information about a given word than any dictionary, including the completed DGE, could ever do.

Lighter, easier, and quite adequate for a straightforward reading of the most commonly read authors is Liddell and Scott, *Intermediate Lexicon*; yet simpler is Liddell and Scott, *Abridged Lexicon*, originally designed for grammar school use and today worth the investment only for those who do not expect to go much past the stage where their textbooks provide them with the necessary vocabulary. Both of these are now seriously out of date. Other "college dictionaries" are available and are usable, though

---

[14] This edition, however, does not include the *Revised Supplement*.

you should always make sure you are getting a dictionary of ancient and not modern Greek, a distinction that is not always made clear on the cover or the title page. There are pocket dictionaries available, but these cannot be counted upon to have every word even in beginners' texts like Xenophon's *Anabasis*. A Greek Lexicon Project is now underway at Cambridge to produce a new intermediate lexicon, searchable online, which will finally, and apparently conclusively, replace the old standby. As a rule, one should not use a larger dictionary when a smaller one will suffice, since the additional material in the larger dictionary, which you do not need, will increase significantly the time it takes to look up a word.

To use any dictionary it is necessary to know the root form of the word one is seeking, often a non-trivial matter in Greek, where the forms of a single verb may number in the hundreds. There are a number of lists of verb forms for sale, such as Bodoh, *Index of Greek Verb Forms* or the older but more compact Marinone and Guala, *All the Greek Verbs*, though teachers sometimes try to hide the existence of these convenient aids from fear that they will prevent the students' ever learning the forms. If the text you are reading is part of the *Perseus* online database, a click on the form will provide help; the freeware program *Kalos* also offers help with morphology.

One set of Greek words that are not directly translatable into any modern language is the set of particles—δή, περ, που and the like—that have the great advantage (for us) of putting into the written text many shades of meaning that are transmitted in other languages by inflection of voice or by gesture. The monumental Denniston, *The Greek Particles* will reveal to you the particular meaning of a particle much more precisely than any general dictionary can, and in doing so will illuminate many a problematical text.[15]

For patristic Greek from Clement of Rome to Theodore of Studium, Sophocles, *Greek Lexicon* has been replaced by Lampe, *A Patristic Greek Lexicon*, though the latter does not cover late pagan authors or even Christian ones outside of its chronological boundaries. Both of these works take a knowledge of classical Greek for granted, so that they can be used only in conjunction with LSJ[9] or another dictionary of classical Greek. For a total picture of the Greek language from its beginnings until today, Dimitrakos, *Mega Lexikon* is a tremendous achievement, but, since it is made for Greek

---

[15] Even Denniston, for all its awe-inspiring comprehensiveness, is no longer the last word; as one can see from the articles in Rijksbaron, ed., *New Approaches to Greek Particles*, there is always something new to be said.

speakers and its definitions are in modern Greek, those who do not yet know the modern language will not be able to make much use of it.

Mycenaean Greek was still unknown when LSJ⁹ was compiled, and, although Glare, *Revised Supplement* gives the Mycenaean forms of classical words where they are attested, it is not a dictionary of all the words used in the Linear B texts. Davies, *Mycenaeae Graecitatis Lexicon* was an early and excellent effort at such a lexicon, but much has been achieved since then, and Aura Jorro, *DMic*, issued as a supplement to *DGE*, is more complete and more authoritative, and will be used by anyone who can read Spanish, even with difficulty.

The best, and almost the only, English–Greek dictionary is Woodhouse, *English–Greek Dictionary*, now available online: this has been useful not only to students of Greek composition but also to anybody who wants to look up a concept and cannot immediately think of the relevant Greek term. For the latter purpose, however, the *Perseus* website has an English–Greek feature that can give much more comprehensive results.

Etymology is not a matter to which LSJ⁹ gives much attention; the standard work is Chantraine, *Dictionnaire étymologique de la langue grecque*, and most classical libraries also carry Frisk, *Griechisches etymologisches Wörterbuch*. A new entry, Beekes, *Etymological Dictionary of Greek*, appeared too late for me to know whether or not it supersedes its predecessors. The beginner may wonder what the purpose of a dictionary arranged in backwards order might be, but it can be a very welcome tool for the epigrapher, papyrologist or palaeographer trying to figure out the beginning of a word of which only the last letters are preserved. Krestchmer and Locker, *Rückläufiges Wörterbuch* is a simple word-list; Buck and Petersen, *Reverse Index* is arranged morphologically by suffixes, a more useful arrangement for the historical linguist. For Greek names of which only the end is preserved, Dornseiff and Hansen, *Rückläufiges Wörterbuch der griechischen Eigennamen* can be helpful.

The great *Thesaurus Graecae Linguae* (TGL) of Henri Estienne, the younger Henricus Stephanus, has no parallel. Its arrangement of all the words derived from a single root under a single heading, so that, for example, ἀντίθεοις, θήκη and προστίθημι all appear together, made it from the first a clumsy tool[16] for the purpose of finding an unknown word, but the compiler's erudition and comprehensiveness have never been matched, so

---

[16] It would have been entirely unusable had Stephanus not appended to it an alphabetically arranged index, wherein one can find each word easily and trace it to the appropriate heading.

that a person who wishes to get an understanding of the range of meanings and uses of a Greek word has no better place to start than Stephanus—with the understanding, of course, that much has been discovered in the four hundred years since it was published. Stephanus' continued usefulness caused two groups of scholars to reprint and update his work, a British group under E. H. Barker,[17] whose nine-volume work, maintaining though somewhat modifying Stephanus' organization by roots, was published by A. J. Valpy between 1816 and 1828, and a group whose chief members were the formidable brothers Dindorf, whose work, rearranged in alphabetical order, was published by Ambroise Firmin-Didot from 1831 to 1865. These editions, both of which included voluminous additions in square brackets, are the editions which will usually be found in modern research libraries,[18] though the gain in scope and modernity is significantly offset by a less uniform and hence less comprehensible organization. Stephanus' first edition (of 1572) is now available online at *Gallica*, the rich and very useful website of the Bibliothèque Nationale de France.

The Stephanus of later Greek and Latin was Charles du Fresne, sieur du Cange, whose *Glossarium ad scriptores mediae et infimae Graecitatis* is still available in many research libraries.

Dictionaries: Latin

In Latin the field was ruled for many years by Lewis and Short, *A Latin Dictionary*, but this warhorse has been superseded by the more scientifically arranged and more understandable *Oxford Latin Dictionary* (OLD), a dictionary that one can browse for pleasure. Lewis and Short, however, is not yet dead. For one thing, the authors covered by the OLD go only as far as the second century CE,[19] while Lewis and Short go as late as Boethius and Cassiodorus in the sixth; for another, Lewis and Short can be consulted online at the *Perseus* site, which OLD, for copyright reasons, cannot. Even better, Clint Hagen's new *Glossa* website provides an easy, intuitive interface that makes L&S downright pleasant. Souter, *A Glossary of*

---

[17] The early proofs of the work were subject to such damning criticism that Barker's name does not appear at all on the published edition.

[18] Usually only one of them will be found, since librarians are not always aware that they are two very different works.

[19] In special instances the texts may "run over into the third century," and patristic writers of the late second century are not covered (OLD, vi).

Later Latin covers with definitions but no illustrative passages the period ignored by the OLD. In Latin as in Greek, the erudition of Stephanus—in this case not Henri Estienne but his father Robert—is legendary, and his *Dictionarium seu Latinae Linguae Thesaurus* is still valuable, and available at *Gallica*. But the ultimate research tool in Latin lexicography is TLL, which as of this writing, more than a hundred years after it was begun, has reached the end of the letter *p*; in this dictionary each entry is a research project, and postdoctoral fellows spend a year on writing a few entries. It includes not only definitions but etymologies, both ancient and modern; every attested spelling and every attested contraction of the word—a bonanza for epigraphers; and where, when and by which authors the word is used, and in what senses, including those cases where a particular author uses it only in certain ways. Both its size and the fact that it is written entirely in Latin make it forbidding to the beginner, but nobody who really has to know what there is to know about a particular word can afford to ignore it.

There are a number of smaller "college" Latin dictionaries, any of them sufficient for classroom purposes; Latin also boasts some pocket dictionaries, which like their Greek cousins can often be helpful but rarely sufficient. *Glossa* may make these dictionaries considerably less essential than they have hitherto been.

In Latin as in Greek, morphology must be understood before the dictionary can be used, and the online texts in *Perseus* allow the user to click on a form and see its morphology. Latin also boasts William Whitaker's *Words*, an online or downloadable dictionary program that allows you to type in the form before you and get both a morphological description and a brief dictionary definition.

For medieval and modern Latin the often-revised Forcellini et al., *Lexicon Totius Latinitatis*, a work whose first edition appeared in 1771, remains an important tool, as does the even older du Cange, *Glossarium ad scriptores mediae et infimae Latinitatis*; both of them, it must be mentioned, explain Latin in Latin, and du Cange deals only with medieval Latin: words that continue to have the same meaning they had in classical times are not treated. Niermeyer and Burgers, *Mediae Latinitatis Lexicon Minus* is much smaller— sometimes a disadvantage, more often a convenience—and it defines its words in French and English. Two projects for a new comprehensive dictionary of medieval Latin are underway, the *Mittellateinisches Wörterbuch* (with definitions in Latin) and the *Novum Glossarium Mediae Latinitatis* (with definitions in French). Both are useful for the letters already published, but neither, as of this writing, is complete. Since medieval Latin usually bears a heavy imprint of the vernacular, invaluable help can be gotten from dictionaries of medieval Latin of a particular area such as Latham's *Dictionary* for Britain, Fuchs' *Lexicon* for the Netherlands, and Bartal's *Glossarium* for Hungary.

No English–Latin dictionary compares with Smith and Hall, *English–Latin Dictionary*, which can be consulted online; like Woodhouse in Greek, this is a compilation that is likely to be reprinted but not, in the near future, repeated. Smaller compilations still appear, notably the English–Latin sections of James Morwood's *Pocket Oxford Latin Dictionary* (itself a reworking of a Woodhouse dictionary), D. P. Simpson's *Cassell's Latin Dictionary* and John C. Trauptman's *Bantam New College Latin and English Dictionary*.

The etymological dictionaries of Latin were Ernout and Meillet, *Dictionnaire étymologique* and Walde and Hofmann, *Lateinisches Etymologisches Wörterbuch*; but just as I was finishing this manuscript the impressive new dictionary of de Vaan, *Etymological Dictionary of Latin*, came into my hands, and it will supersede its predecessors.

Anybody who has read some literature knows or senses that there are certain terms inappropriate to an elevated context, but the modern reader of Greek or Latin, to whom all terms are equally foreign, is not likely to have this sense. Quicherat and Chatelain, *Thesaurus Poeticus Linguae Latinae* and Axelson, *Unpoetische Wörter* can make you one of the elite few who know which of the two words for "suddenly" (*subito* and *repente*) is more appropriate for poetry.

There are many specialized dictionaries: of specific authors (Powell, *A Lexicon to Herodotus*; Lodge, *Lexicon Plautinum*), of specific areas of research— the exemplary *Lexikon des frühgriechischen Epos* (LfgrE) sets a new standard for these—and of specific classes of items or terms (Thompson, *A Glossary of Greek Fishes*; Arnott, *Birds in the Ancient World from A to Z*). These will generally delve deeper into matters that the larger lexica gloss over; a few of them will be mentioned in the appropriate sections of this handbook. Almost all of the Greek ones can be found in *RBLG*.

7

GRAMMAR

USING GRAMMAR BOOKS

The world is full, and used to be much fuller, of people who think that the human race suffers from a surfeit of Latin grammar, people to whom there can be nothing more perverse than the pursuit of yet more knowledge about the subject. For more than two millennia, indeed, teaching of the classical languages has involved such a large dose of grammar that many—probably most—students never really come to appreciate what is being said in the text, let alone how it is being said, because their attention is taken up with subjunctives, ablative absolutes, concessive clauses and verbs of *fear* and *caution*. Many teachers of Latin and of other languages nowadays prefer methods that offer the student more text and less grammar, putting up with a certain amount of inexactitude in order to get closer to the wide experience of reading that alone can produce familiarity with the language. By now many people taught with these methods have graduated into the world of teaching (as, indeed, it was to be hoped that they would), and their grasp of grammar is not as firm as their teachers' was. Still worse, the pressure to publish in modern universities leaves the professional classicist much less time to read, so that few classicists feel as comfortable with the ancient languages as their teachers (much less their teachers' teachers) did; and even when we read, we often do so under time pressure that encourages us to gloss over grammatical difficulties rather than investigating them.

A further problem is that, although students usually have no trouble using a dictionary, they often avoid dealing with a grammar book as much as possible. If lexicology is the area of classics where childlike trust is most to be found, grammar is the area where fatigue and incuriosity are most likely to prevent questions from being asked at all. Students have generally learned to use a dictionary before reaching the university, and its organization is clear and offers few problems: the extra difficulties posed by the Greek augment and the uncertainties of Latin spelling are occasionally frustrating but not frightening. Grammar books, on the other hand, are a genre that the modern student has not encountered before, and people often continue to look up grammatical points in their first-year primer, through which they thumb desperately, with a vague memory of where the item they are seeking stood on the page.

In fact the organization of grammars shows a large degree of standardization. Phonology—how the language sounded, insofar as we know—and conventions of writing come first. Next comes morphology, the study of the forms: here will be found tables of declensions and conjugations, generally more comprehensive and more conveniently ordered than the lists in a beginners' book. Syntax, the last and largest section, will usually begin with the uses of the various forms, in particular the various cases of the noun and the voices, aspects, moods and tenses of the verb, and then describe the different forms of sentences and clauses (direct and indirect questions, conditional clauses, relative clauses, and such). Grammar books are not made to be read from cover to cover, but it does not take long to become familiar with their organization and to be able to find what you are seeking in short order. Most grammar books come with indices at the back, and in fact the index is one of the most important parts of the book. Often there will be a number of indices, one of words discussed, another of grammatical subjects, and often an index of passages quoted, a great convenience if the passage that is giving you trouble happens to be there.

WHERE GRAMMAR CAME FROM

That language has to be spoken according to a set of rules that can be set down in a book is not a self-evident fact. It was controversial even in ancient times. Some people defended the principle of *anomaly*, that language was a natural growth of human intellect, with forms that did not necessarily follow general rules; the stoic philosophers supported this position. Others held to a position called *analogy*, that language was ideally characterized by regular forms that repeated themselves throughout the language; Julius Caesar wrote a tract defending this principle, and followed it so rigidly that even in matters of vocabulary he considered certain forms proper and others improper: a river in Caesar is always a *flumen*, never a *fluvium*. His strict adherence to grammatical rules was the basis of the much-admired "purity" of his Latin; and it is what makes his works so convenient for beginners.

On the basis of the principle of analogy it should be possible to identify the regular forms and the rules that characterize them; and early grammatical research consisted of precisely this, finding how different forms were used identifying the rules that governed what was, and what was not, a grammatical sentence. The ideal method of proof is the *minimal pair*, two expressions that differ only in a single respect, and so can illuminate what the effect of that particular difference is. On the basis of research like this, the grammar books that we use today were painstakingly built up over centuries.

GRAMMATICAL RESEARCH

There always remains more to do. There are details to be worked out: the reasons behind Greek and Latin word order in many texts remain opaque, the local and chronological variations are unclear, and the precise meaning of thousands of texts remains uncertain. More of a problem is the lack of a good theoretical understanding of what is really behind the grammatical structure of the classical languages. If prolixity is the sign of a person who has not grasped the essential point, there are grounds for uneasiness when Kühner and Stegmann, *Ausführliche Grammatik der lateinischen Sprache* take more than sixty pages to explain the genitive. The major dictionaries that are now in use were built by large-scale slipping and fresh analysis of the data; the major comprehensive grammars, all of them old, are essentially reworkings of their predecessors. Classical grammar is ripe for a new approach.

One approach to grammatical research is to proceed the way lexicography does, by slipping and analysis: compiling a list of all the occurrences of a given construction or usage and then analyzing them. Computers are of less help here than in lexicography: it is easier to program a computer to find all forms of the verb *fero* than to program it to identify ablative absolutes, and, since it is more likely to produce erroneous results, the results of a computer-based search, even where one is practical, have to be double-checked by reading the text. For this reason, grammatical research that is done by slipping will generally be restricted to a single author, or at least to a manageable number of authors. Much good work continues to be done by this inductive method, deriving a general theory from analysis of individual examples.

A second approach, recognizing that language is by no means as rigid or universal as grammarians have tended to portray it, deals with peculiarities of certain authors, dialects or contexts. Threatte, *The Grammar of Attic Inscriptions*, an enormous undertaking, illuminates many respects in which the grammar of the inscriptions seems to differ from that of received texts; but in fact similar studies, on a smaller scale, may be made of individual authors, none of whom uses the language in quite the same way as any other.

The comparative approach is also fruitful: comparative grammars of Greek and Latin have long been available, and even beginning students learn that Vergil uses a "Greek accusative" or that Greek may use the subject of the sentence in the nominative as the subject of indirect discourse but Latin does not. The reasons for the differences are often illuminating. Less well investigated are comparisons with other languages, particularly other languages with which the Greeks and Romans came into close contact. Everybody knows that words are borrowed from one language to another; to many people it is less clear that grammatical structures are borrowed, but in fact grammatical borrowing is quite as certain, and almost as widespread, as lexical borrowing. Even where no borrowing has occurred, comparison of two languages can illuminate what possibilities exist other than those that the language in question uses.

Yet another approach attempts to apply to the text a new conceptual framework. The grammatical categories in which we think about the classical languages today are still essentially the same as the categories established by the Greek and Roman grammarians. Up to the middle of the twentieth century, they were generally accepted, and even applied unthinkingly to languages for which their applicability was dubious. But the last fifty years have seen a revolution in linguistic thinking, which we shall mention in the next chapter; and this revolution has begun to produce interesting new work as scholars probe its applicability to the classical languages.

Much recent work is based upon seeing grammatical constructions within their larger context. A Latin speaker might say *alea iacta est, iacta est alea, iacta alea est* or, for that matter, *aleam ieci, aleam iactam esse dico* or simply *iacta!* Each of these grammatically correct utterances says that a die, or the die, has been cast; in what circumstances would each be appropriate? A person who says *i domum* expects the same reaction as one who says *te mitto*.

Under what circumstances would I use each of these expressions to try to get the person to go away?

Beside the more general works, articles are constantly being produced on the basis of single problematical texts for which a scholar, by finding a few parallel cases, can offer a way out of a difficulty. These articles, though numerous, generally have a small readership; their main hope of reaching the knowledge of classicists in general is through the incorporation of their insights into commentaries on the texts for which they were first conceived.

Lastly, as modern scholarship gets less and less tied to the written text, scholars have become more aware that not all communication is verbal. A few recent works have begun to delve into the matter of gesture and body language, getting us a bit closer to what the ancients themselves could understand when they not only read a text but heard it and saw it performed.

MAJOR RESOURCES

Grammars

Grammar formed the basis of elementary education from Greco-Roman to modern times, and many works of the ancient grammarians are preserved, conveniently collected in the multivolume sets of Schneider and Uhlig, *Grammatici Graeci*, Keil, *Grammatici Latini* (the use of Keil has been made considerably more practical by Lomanto and Marinone, *Index Grammaticus*) and Funaioli, *Grammaticae Romanae Fragmenta*; to these collections must now be added Lallot, *Apollonius Dyscole, De la construction*. The German publishing house de Gruyter has been publishing in the series *Sammlung griechischer und lateinischer Grammatiker* a number of new editions of grammarians, some complete and some fragmentary.[1] A person interested in reading these works will get invaluable help from Dickey, *Ancient Greek Scholarship* and from Schad, *A Lexicon of Latin Grammatical Terminology*.

The ancient grammarians are of interest for the history of grammar, but nobody today goes to them for help with a difficult expression or sentence. At the beginners' level there are dozens of primers, with new ones appearing regularly: although the number of students learning

---

[1] Linke and Haas, eds., *Die Fragmente des Grammatikers Dionysios Thrax, Tyrannion und Diokles*; Montanari, ed., *I frammenti dei grammatici Agathokles, Hellanikos Ptolemaios Epithetes*; Theodoridis, ed., *Die Fragmente des Grammatikers Philoxenos*.

classical languages today is tiny by comparison with those who learned them two or three generations ago, this very fact, by causing dissatisfaction with the books available, has only encouraged the production of new ones. College grammars, with the features of the language on "rational" rather than pedagogical principles, are much fewer, but they are available, both in book form and on the internet, where a search on the words "Latin grammar" or "ancient Greek grammar" will direct you easily to what you need. Like the college dictionaries, these are adequate for most purposes, but cannot be counted on to deal with every problem you will come across. Nevertheless, you will get to know the languages much better by using them than you will by relying on your old textbook knowledge and guessing the rest.

For comprehensive grammars, nobody competes with the Germans. The standards for Greek are the revered Kühner and Gerth, *Ausführliche Grammatik der griechischen Sprache* and Schwyzer and Debrunner, *Griechische Grammatik*, for Latin Kühner and Stegmann, *Ausführliche Grammatik der lateinischen Sprache*. That said, it must be admitted that these standards are severely out of date; the new understandings of recent decades are not yet reflected in any comprehensive grammar. The "new Menge" (Menge, Burkard and Schauer, *Lehrbuch der lateinischen Syntax und Semantik*) is designed for use by students and is indeed in many respects much more user-friendly than the comprehensive grammars, but it restricts itself (unlike the 1873 classic on which it is based) almost entirely to Ciceronian Latin.

An older but very much admired Greek grammar was Krüger, *Griechische Sprachlehre*, which has now been substantially augmented and updated by Cooper, *Greek Syntax*. Cooper's discursive style makes his work much more readable than its original (or any other), but it must be used with caution, both because of numerous typographical errors and because of difficulties of formulation that may cause the text to be misleading; the absence of notes or an adequate index compounds the problem. Those of the German-challenged who want a more traditional grammar will still have to make do with Smyth, *Greek Grammar*, which is usually adequate: Smyth's doctorate was from Göttingen, and his book is heavily based on Kühner and Gerth, which he considered "the only modern complete Greek Grammar."[2] There are two American grammatical classics: Goodwin, *Syntax of the Moods and Tenses of the Greek Verb* and Gildersleeve, *Syntax of Classical Greek*. For a general description of the verb Rijksbaron, *The Syntax and Semantics of the Verb* represents more than a century's advance on Goodwin; for the details, the old book remains unsurpassed.

[2]   Smyth, *Greek Grammar*, 5.

Some subsets of Greek have an independent grammar of their own. For Mycenaean Greek there is now Bartoněk, *Handbuch des mykenischen Griechisch*, and, for the papyri, Mayser, *Grammatik der griechischen Papyri aus der Ptolemaërzeit* and Gignac, *Grammar of the Greek Papyri*. Threatte, *The Grammar of Attic Inscriptions* is a remarkable compendium of grammatical information based on the only written texts from the classical period that are still extant as written and not in later copies. So far only the first two sections, on phonology and morphology, have appeared; on the basis of their outstanding contribution, the section on syntax is eagerly awaited. Langslow, *Medical Latin in the Roman Empire* makes a promising beginning on the much neglected subject of technical language and the way it works.

Greek accentuation is often treated telegraphically if at all. Chandler, *A Practical Introduction to Greek Accentuation* will tell you all the details; short and practical summaries are Lejeune, *Précis d'accentuation grecque* and Probert, *A New Short Guide to the Accentuation of Ancient Greek*, the latter with exercises.

There is no comprehensive English grammar for Latin; the hundred-year-old stalwarts, *Gildersleeve's Latin Grammar*, *Allen and Greenough's New Latin Grammar*, and Bennett's *New Latin Grammar*, all available on the web, are still the best we have, though they have nothing like Teutonic thoroughness. A new grammar in French, Serbat, *Grammaire fondamentale*, is still a long way from completion.

The word order of Greek and Latin has long been a rather marginalized area of grammatical studies. After the interesting but still traditional work of Dover, *Greek Word Order*, two more recent path-breaking books, Dik, *Word Order in Ancient Greek* and Devine and Stephens, *Latin Word Order*, have put the matter on a new and firmer foundation that should add a significant new dimension to our appreciation of the nuances of the language of the ancients.

The fact that Latin continued to be written well into the modern period—it is, in fact, still written today, though for an ever-shrinking group of readers—produced a number of books designed to warn the writer against the easy transposition into Latin of words ("false friends") or usages ("calques") from one's native language. The greatest of these works is Krebs, *Antibarbarus der lateinischen Sprache*, and, even for those who do not write Latin, browsing through this book can correct many a misapprehension about what the Latin means.

On gesture and body language see Boegehold, *When a Gesture Was Expected*, and Cairns, *Body Language*.

8

LANGUAGE AND LINGUISTICS

HISTORICAL LINGUISTICS

The study of the classical languages was changed forever in 1786 when
Sir William Jones[1] demonstrated their connection with Sanskrit and scholars
of the early nineteenth century began to discover a historical development
whose elaboration underlay and in large measure explained many aspects of
the languages that had hitherto been only imperfectly understood. Grimm's
Law, describing the sound shift that had taken place between the other Indo-
European languages and the Germanic branch, first demonstrated the
possibility of describing these developments by a series of rigorously
applied principles rather than mere impressions of similarities; Ferdinand
de Saussure's description of *apophony*, the alternation of vowels within the
Indo-European root, showed that vowels, too, as much as they seemed to
vary from language to language, had a distinct and ascertainable role in the
development of word forms. By the mid-twentieth century the general
outline of the Indo-European family and the position of the classical
languages within it were well established, and the work that remained to be
done was chiefly a matter of working out details. It was possible to publish
not only a list of Indo-European roots[2] and etymological dictionaries of

---

[1] Jones was not the first to notice the similarity, but it seems to have been his discovery
that sparked the interest of philologists.

[2] Watkins, *The American Heritage Dictionary of Indo-European Roots*; the first edition appeared in
1969, appended (as the new edition is) to *The American Heritage Dictionary of the English Language*.

Greek and Latin[3] but a general picture of the morphology and even the syntax of the long-vanished ancestor of hundreds of modern languages.[4] The comparative method, by which these results were obtained, was a well-established methodology whose usefulness had extended into the entire field of descriptive linguistics, enabling us to reconstruct, within limits, the conceptual world of vanished societies in a way that study of their material remains could never really achieve.

The comparative method, helped somewhat by the writings of the ancient grammarians, had also made possible a good deal of reconstruction of the ancient languages themselves. The sound of ancient Greek and Latin was known well enough to put an end, finally, to the British practice of using English pronunciation for the ancient languages (a custom by which βουλή, for example, rhymed with "foully"). The development of epigraphy and the availability of large corpora permitted the history of sound-change to be mapped out both chronologically and geographically on the basis of changes in characteristic spelling errors. The history of Italic dialects—a subject based almost entirely on epigraphy—gave a much clearer picture of the prehistory of Latin than the Romans had had; the history of Greek dialects, likewise epigraphically based, could be traced clearly enough that moderns could see clearly the differences between Doric Greek as the Spartans spoke it and Doric Greek as the Athenians imitated it in their tragic odes. The accuracy of these reconstructions was dramatically demonstrated when the decipherment of Linear B showed the language of the Mycenaeans to have been dialectically closer to Arcado-Cypriot than to any other later dialect—just as historical linguistics had said that it must have been.

For all of its successes, historical linguistics had by no means played itself out. In addition to the work of fleshing out the details—work that has an endearing or exasperating way of producing surprises that bring into question the presumptions on which an apparently successful enterprise has hitherto been based—the new insights into the ancient languages raised questions about the entire mechanism of linguistic development. Why did the Romans one day start saying *bellum* where they had previously said *duellum*? We never say *bell* when we mean *dwell*; why did they? The comparative method has since had a good deal to say about this, too, demonstrating which kinds of developments occur commonly and which are rare, and what kinds of environments are conducive to

---

[3] Cf. above, pp. 77, 80.
[4] Meillet, *Introduction à l'étude comparative des langues indo-européennes.*

linguistic change. As field linguists raised the number of known languages into the thousands, these questions no longer needed to be treated by methods based on the fertile but restricted imaginations of classical linguists; more significantly, a theoretical basis was developed that could serve to explain phonological change rather than just chronicling it.

Nor does historical linguistics necessarily go backward. The history of vulgar Latin and its development into the modern Romance family, and of Greek into *koine* and thence into modern Greek, provided more grounds for study. Had nothing else happened in linguistics, there would have been plenty of work left for those interested in reconstructing and understanding the way the classical languages developed, the way they functioned and the way they passed into modern languages to which the ancient ones are neither intelligible nor entirely foreign. There still is.

THE LINGUISTIC REVOLUTION OF THE MID-TWENTIETH CENTURY

The book that changed the face of linguistics in 1957 was Chomsky, *Syntactic Structures*. The observation behind the book was a simple and incontrovertible one. Linguists had generally taken it for granted that describing a language was essentially a matter of describing its components: the sounds, words and utterances by which the users of the language communicate. Chomsky observed that, although a language has a finite set of sounds and a finite set of words, there is no limit to the number of sentences that can be generated.[5] This was well known, and it was just as well known that not every combination of words constitutes a sentence; on the contrary, speakers of a language recognize immediately certain combinations of words as being acceptable ("grammatical," in our terms) and others as being unacceptable or nonsensical. What this must mean, Chomsky reasoned, is that speakers of a language have an understood set of rules by which the grammatical sentences of the language can

---

[5]   If anyone doubts this assertion, it can be proven easily. If there is a finite number (call it N) of grammatical sentences, one or more of them have the most words of any of them—call this sentence x. But since the sentence "My mother says x" is also a grammatical sentence, there is a sentence yet longer than the longest sentence in our finite number, so our original presumption, that there were only N sentences, was false. This procedure can be repeated for any number N; so there is no such number, however large, that includes all possible sentences.

be generated; and a proper description of the language must identify and include these rules.

So far, so good; but the implications of this observation are vast. Speakers of a language may be consciously aware of what sounds and what words belong to the language, but only the most scholarly of them, if any, are aware of the grammatical rules. Conscious descriptions of grammar are a phenomenon that develops only when the language already exists; if every language includes a set of grammatical rules, they are rules that the speakers use without having formulated them consciously. This, in turn, means that the ability to form language-producing rules is an innate part of the human brain—an observation, indeed, that agrees with the fact that animals, no matter how much they are exposed to human speech, do not form original grammatical sentences.

This observation leads to another: if the ability to form these rules is built into the human brain, the kind of rules that are formed will presumably be the same in any language. The particular rules, of course, will vary from language to language, but underlying them will be a basic structure, imposed by the structure of the brain, that determines how language works. Linguistics, in this sense, ceases to be a matter merely of describing languages, and becomes a window into the way the brain structures and communicates human experience. To speak of it otherwise, as Chomsky memorably put it, "is as if natural science were to be designated 'the science of meter readings.'"[6]

Chomsky's observations have not gone unchallenged. That animals cannot learn human language does not necessarily imply that humans have a particular "language mechanism"; the ability to form grammars may be a result of more general abilities that humans have. Nor does the universality of language necessarily imply that it is innate: the similarities of languages may be imposed by other constraints.[7] As of this writing, the underlying questions continue to be a subject for lively disagreement.

But Chomsky or no Chomsky, the approach to linguistic questions has changed enormously in the past half-century. For one thing, the question of whether language determines the form of social communication or is determined by it has been a major point of controversy; for another, it has

---

[6] Chomsky, *Language and Mind*, 57; the lectures were first published in 1968.

[7] As Malcolm Heath put it in a comment on this chapter, "it is not the structure of the human brain that made Egyptians and meso-Americans converge on building pyramids with the pointy bit facing up." For a good summary of the issues involved and the research brought to bear on the innateness controversy, see Fiona Cowie, "Innateness and Language," in Zalta, *Stanford Encyclopedia of Philosophy*.

become increasingly clear that the internal rules of a language are in fact in constant flux, and are constantly being violated, and thus reformulated, by speakers of the language.[8] It is moreover obvious, as Saussure observed a century ago, that words are not the only medium by which human beings communicate;[9] and it does not take much thought to realize, as quarreling couples do every day, that words themselves may transmit more information than their simple meaning encodes. The purview of linguistics has become much wider than it once was, spawning a host of new approaches, of which we can mention only a few.

Semiotics

Saussure's observation that communication takes place by various means led him to suggest that linguistics itself was merely a subfield of a larger science that he called *sémiologie*, the study of all the methods by which people communicate. He recognized that this science did not yet exist, but in the century since his comment the study of semiotics has come into its own, concentrating on the meaning of different signifiers within the society that uses them. Not much work has been done on the semiotics of the ancient world, but there is undoubtedly a good deal to do, since many "signifiers" were particular to the Greeks and the Romans: the gymnasium, the phallus, the triumph, the taking of the auspices—the list goes on and on. What exactly was it that made somebody mutilate the faces of most of the herms of Athens on the eve of the Sicilian expedition in 415 BCE? And why did the Athenians believe that it was connected with a plot against the democracy? The difficulty of those still-disputed questions shows how much we still have to learn about signifier and signified in the ancient world.

---

[8]   Saussure, *Course in General Linguistics*, 71–8 observed correctly that although a speaker of the language cannot change it arbitrarily—to try to do so would cause misunderstanding at best, derision at worst—the language nevertheless changes, and its speakers, paradoxically, are as powerless to prevent the change as they are to initiate it. Conscious change of language does take place, but it is usually for social or political reasons rather than linguistic ones (as Roy Harris points out in Saussure, 73, n. 1). In a scholarly book like this one, of course, rules of grammar can never be violated. To do so would be, well, you know.

[9]   Saussure, *Course in General Linguistics*, 15–17.

Psycholinguistics

Psycholinguistics is the subfield of linguistics that has, at least so far, found the least application to the classical languages. The basic question with which it is concerned—what psychological phenomena are involved in language production and processing—is one that, since it deals with subconscious mechanisms, is accessible to us only with difficulty even when we are dealing with living languages; it is hard to see how we could defend any theses we might wish to propound on this subject by reference to the ancient languages. I am not aware of any work in psycholinguistics that has made particular use of the classical languages.

Sociolinguistics

Sociolinguistics, which deals with the study of language in its social context, has begun to have some effect on the study of the classical languages. Facts that were once considered interesting only with reference to the particular matter at hand—a bilingual inscription, for example, or the use or avoidance of certain words by a given author—are now seen as facts that have something to tell us about the society at large. Why did the Romans use Greek throughout the eastern half of the Empire, but Latin in the army? For that matter, how general was the use of Latin in the army? How many people were bilingual or trilingual, and what was their social status? To what extent can we recover the differences of language between different social strata and different geographical areas, and what do these differences tell us? Some important studies have begun to explore these areas, but there is a good deal more to be done.

Generative Grammar

If the production of sentences involves the observation of certain underlying rules, it would seem that a grammar should not merely catalogue usage, but expose the rules themselves in their proper logical order. To take a well-known sentence:[10]

---

[10] This is not the only possible way of analyzing this sentence; I seriously doubt that it is the most accurate. But it is the simplest, and so serves best the purpose of showing how a sentence can be generated out of an ordered set of rules.

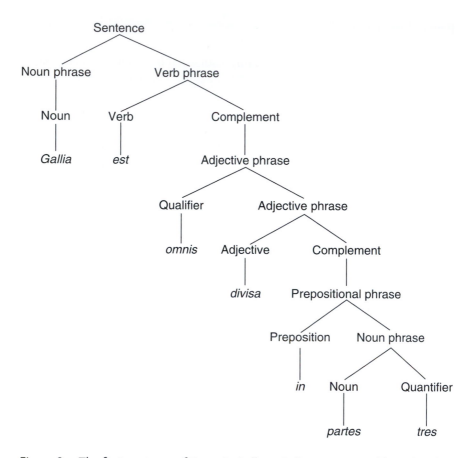

Figure 8.1 The first sentence of Caesar's *Bellum Gallicum* generated by ordered
grammatical rules

Here taking the rules for sentence-generation in order—first, a
sentence may consist of a noun phrase and a verb phrase (this is not the
only kind of sentence possible in Latin, where a nominal sentence, such as
facilis descensus Averno, has no verb phrase); then, a verb phrase may consist of
a verb with a complement (in this case, the verb is a copula and the complement is an adjective phrase—it could also have been a noun phrase);
then, an adjective phrase may consist of an adjective plus a complement,
etc.—should, when combined with a dictionary that defines words that
can be subjects, words that can be copulas, etc., produce all grammatical
sentences in the language, and only those sentences.

This example restricts itself to rules governing phrase structure; there
are other types of rules (morphological rules and transpositions, to give

two examples), but the essential point is that these are rules for *producing* sentences, not merely for *describing* them. They are derived, undoubtedly, from observing the language; but what we are finding, we hope, is the system[11] of rules that generate all grammatical sentences—a generative grammar.

When *Syntactic Structures* first appeared, there were almost immediate efforts to write such grammars; but it soon transpired that the nature of these rules was much less clear than it had seemed, and nobody has yet written a successful and comprehensive generative grammar of ancient Greek or Latin, nor of any other language. The effort to unravel the underlying rules involves a rethinking of almost every aspect of the language; and this requires a fresh look at the material itself. As this rethinking has progressed, it has become clear that generative rules, at least as originally formulated, do not seem to account for all the phenomena of language. The functional grammar developed by Simon Dik, conceiving language as a means of communication rather than a set of grammatical sentences, has had noteworthy success in explaining features of the classical languages for which neither traditional nor generative grammar gave a satisfying explanation. In general, many aspects of language seem to be driven by meaning or function rather than by grammar; and much of what happens in language seems to be defined in these terms better than it was described in the grammars on which we grew up.

Cognitive Linguistics

Linguistics has traditionally treated language as a system whose rules, however defined, are essentially arbitrary: nothing in the fruit itself makes *apple* a more appropriate term for it than *malum*. While this presumption is generally unexceptionable when applied to particular words,[12] certain features of language do not seem to be arbitrary at all. The presumption, for example, that when Caesar said *veni, vidi, vici* he was describing his actions in the order in which they took place is not an arbitrary one; and

---

[11] And the hierarchy; it is basic to generative grammar that rules must be applied in the proper order.

[12] Even here it may not be universal; it can be argued that the ancient Egyptian MIW was a name more naturally appropriate to the domestic cat than either the Greek αἴλουρος or the Latin *feles*.

many such presumptions may be made about statements, allowing speakers to transmit, and hearers to understand, information that is not said explicitly. In a short, persuasive and influential book, George Lakoff and Mark Johnson claim that metaphor is not merely a literary device, but a mode of thought by which people make sense of the world.[13] By this understanding no word has a unique meaning, because the meaning of any word can be—and inevitably is—extended by metaphor; moreover, the metaphors have a logical order, because the order in which we come to understand them is universal. A child understands spatial relationships before learning to speak, and understands logical relationships only later. When Cicero urged his wife to write him *de omnibus rebus*, "about everything,"[14] he was using a metaphorical sense of *de*; when he wrote to her *de Venusino*, "from the area of Venusia,"[15] he was using a spatial meaning that—although in his day it was hardly ever used, having been supplanted by *ab* and *ex*—was more basic. Moreover, different languages may use different metaphors: an English speaker speaks "about" or "on" a subject, whereas an ancient Greek speaker spoke "about" (περί) or "over" (ὑπέρ[16]) a subject, a Roman "from" (*de*) a subject. Understanding a language, by this approach, involves understanding the cognitive mechanisms by which people make sense of their environment, and by which they encode that understanding in language: the structure of a language is not imposed independently on the world, but arises out of our perception of the world.

Pragmatics

Pragmatics deals with the principles of language in use, and how it functions. The moment we speak of the function of language, we are insisting on taking it in context: identical utterances may have different meanings in different contexts, and different contexts may require different utterances

---

[13] Lakoff and Johnson, *Metaphors We Live By*. In Lakoff and Turner, *More than Cool Reason*, the authors discuss the phenomenon of literary metaphor and its relationship to the underlying mental process.

[14] Cic. *Fam.* 14.21.

[15] Ibid., 14.20.

[16] For this use see LSJ[9] s.v. ὑπέρ A III. The more usual meaning of ὑπέρ with reference to a subject of discourse is "in defense of" or "in behalf of" (ibid. A II), which is based on a different metaphor, whereby the subject protects someone by—as the English metaphor puts it—"covering" that person.

to produce the same result. Many utterances are acts in themselves ("speech-acts"): when Hippolytus swore not to reveal what the nurse would tell him, he was performing an act that changed drastically the status of his later determination to reveal Phaedra's guilty secret, and when a Roman legion shouted *Imperator!* to its commander, the shout might determine the fate of the Empire. But many utterances that may seem more innocuous are made not simply as observations on what is happening, but as ways of making things happen. When Plautus' Menaechmus says to Peniculus the parasite "Say that I am a real dandy!" and gets the answer "Where are we going to eat?" Peniculus is using the opening— Menaechmus wants admiration from him—to try to force Menaechmus to give him what he wants, an invitation to dinner.[17] Without this opening, he would simply have had to wait quietly, like Martial's Vacerra, who spent all day in public restrooms in the hope of getting an invitation ("Vacerra has to go to the dining room, not the bathroom" is Martial's way of putting it[18]): to request an invitation directly would likely have failed. It follows that various utterances, all of them grammatically correct, may be more or less acceptable in a given social situation. Many examples have to do with matters like politeness and ability to communicate; in ancient languages the interest of pragmatics is often in explaining to us why something is said in a particular way: why the words appear in this order, why the potential optative is used when the indicative would have been possible, why the author uses *subito* instead of *repente*. The use of pragmatics as an approach to the understanding of ancient texts has opened up a window to understanding many aspects of our texts that seemed arbitrary or meaningless when looked at from a purely syntactical point of view.

Applied Linguistics

Applied linguistics may appear to be of little use to languages whose users are all dead, and indeed so it would be were that really the case. Users of the classical languages, however, are not yet dead. I do not know whether I shall still be alive when you read these words, but you are, and you, too, are a user of the classical languages. Applied linguistics has made a good deal of progress in areas some of which are of urgent importance to

---

[17] Plaut. Men. 147.
[18] *Cenaturit Vacerra, non cacaturit*: Mart. 11.77.3.

classicists, particularly the question of methodology in teaching a foreign language. So far relatively little of the work of the applied linguists has rubbed off on the classicists, but it is to be hoped that a generation willing to read more broadly outside of its own field will bring the insights of the applied linguists to the teachers of Greek and Latin. When that happens, the classicists may have a good deal to tell the applied linguists about the particulars of what is and what is not appropriate to the teaching of languages whose teachers have never heard them spoken by natives, and whose learners will probably never speak them at all.

MAJOR RESOURCES

Indo-European Linguistics

Everything there was to know about Indo-European linguistics was compiled in Brugmann and Delbrück, *Grundriss* and condensed into Brugmann, *Kurze vergleichende Grammatik*. That was more than a hundred years ago, and, although nothing has ever taken the place of Brugmann and Delbrück, a huge amount of progress, including the discovery of entirely new Indo-European languages, has taken place since then. A previous generation was raised on Meillet, *Introduction à l'étude comparative des langues indo-européennes*, but today there are a number of up-to-date accounts, among them Beekes, *Comparative Indo-European Linguistics*, Szemerényi, *Introduction to Indo-European Linguistics* and Fortson, *Indo-European Language and Culture*.

Historical Accounts and Comparative Grammars of the Classical Languages

The old standbys Meillet and Vendryes, *Traité de grammaire comparée des langues classiques* and Buck, *Comparative Grammar of Greek and Latin* have now been replaced by Sihler, *New Comparative Grammar of Greek and Latin*, a greatly expanded updating of Buck.

The standard English-language histories of the classical languages in their time were Palmer, *The Latin Language* and Palmer, *The Greek Language*, though the latter did not have the thoroughness of Meillet, *Aperçu d'une histoire de la langue grecque*. More recent but lacking Palmer's readability are Adrados, *A History of the Greek Language* and the monumental if uneven Christidis, *A History of Ancient Greek*; for Latin Baldi, *Foundations of Latin* is both more up to date and more thoroughgoing than Palmer but does not deal with syntax. A breezy and fascinating description of the later development of Greek is Browning, *Medieval and Modern Greek*; fuller and no less rewarding is Horrocks, *Greek: A History*.

Such information as we can reconstruct about how the classical languages sounded is summarized by Allen in *Vox Latina* and *Vox Graeca*; a more systematic and theoretically informed presentation of the information for Greek can be found in Sommerstein, *The Sound Pattern of Ancient Greek*, which was begun under Allen's direction.

For the many Greek dialects, the most thorough treatment is still Bechtel, *Die griechischen Dialekte*; more accessible to English speakers is Buck, *The Greek Dialects*. Almost any non-Attic text from the archaic or classical period will require some use of one or the other of these books. The enormous collection of inscriptions on which Bechtel based his work was published separately as Bechtel and Collitz, *GDI*, and is for many purposes even more informative than his own descriptive volume.

Developments in Modern Linguistics

Classicists and the classical languages have not been major players in the lively linguistic controversies of the past fifty years, nor is there any longer a single school of thought that can be said to represent modern linguistics, for which I could give a major work as a source of background. Malmkjær, *The Linguistics Encyclopedia*, however, will give the beginner a decent background to the professional vocabulary, where such terms as *generative grammar*, *pragmatics*, *semiotics* and *speech-act theory* are often unfamiliar to classicists trained in an older tradition.

A number of works have applied the new approaches to the classical languages. The groundwork for a generative approach to Latin grammar has been laid in Oniga, *Il Latino: Breve introduzione linguistica*; cognitive grammar forms the basis for Luraghi, *On the Meaning of Prepositions and Cases*; the functional grammar developed in Simon Dik, *Theory of Functional Grammar* is the basis for Pinkster, *Latin Syntax and Semantics* and Helma Dik, *Word Order in Ancient Greek*. These are just a sampling of recent work; but reading any one of them will expose you to a way of looking at the classical languages that is probably very different from the one by which you were taught Latin, Greek or even English. Many people, including a good number who found the traditional descriptions hugely yawn-inducing, find the new approaches exciting.

For historical linguistics good introductions can be had from Campbell, *Historical Linguistics: An Introduction* or Trask and Millar, *Trask's Historical Linguistics*.

9

USING CLASSICAL TEXTS

WHAT DID THE AUTHOR WRITE?

Among the illusions with which we approach the ancient world is the illusion that we know, at least in those works that are still extant, what the ancient authors wrote. This is never the case. There is not a single work of ancient literature for which we have the author's autograph. Even the items inscribed on stone, which though rarely of literary value were at least recorded almost immediately upon composition, were inscribed by a mason, not by the author, and stonemasons make mistakes.[1] The earliest manuscripts we have were generally written hundreds of years—often more than a thousand years—after the work of which they claim to be copies. There are always discrepancies among different manuscripts,[2] usually minor but often significant or even quite substantial. A copy of Caesar that puts before us, as this or any other modern book does, a single text that can be read from start to finish without significant uncertainties is seriously misrepresenting what we know about Caesar.

---

[1] So, for that matter, do authors, so that even an author's manuscript may contain slips of the pen; but that is a problem for scholars of more modern texts, who may have an author's manuscript.

[2] Except for those unfortunate works of which only a single manuscript has survived; and our experience with manuscripts in general assures us that having only a single manuscript gives us more, not fewer, doubts about what the author really wrote.

All of us first learned to read Greek and Latin from such texts; a teacher of beginners is, and should be, quite satisfied if the student can understand any text at all. At some point, however, the student buys a real classical text for the first time and discovers that it is full of apparently incomprehensible things other than the text. The introduction, which should have given the student background for understanding the text, is in Latin. At the bottom of the page, where the student hoped to find help with difficult passages, is a mass of comments, apparently on various words in the text. These comments, which the teacher or older students call the *apparatus criticus*, are rarely more than single words, sometimes misspelled, with various letters, often from more than one alphabet, attached to them, an occasional proper name in italics, and often a brief word or two of Latin, which may not be written out fully. This is not what the student was looking for, and it does not generally seem to clear up the difficulty, whatever it was. The student, if not otherwise instructed, politely ignores these intrusions and reads the text in the middle of the page, perhaps with a slight pang of inadequacy.

The student wants to be told what the text means, and the *apparatus criticus* will not do that. For most problems, the first place to run will be a dictionary or a grammar book, but for the deeper problems this just will not work. In most printed texts the Aeneid begins with the words *Arma virumque cano*; in a few it begins *Ille ego*, and reaches arms and the man only in line 5. This is a significant difference, but which did Vergil write? No dictionary or grammar can tell us, for the extra lines are perfectly good Latin. It is to the *apparatus criticus* that we must go to see where the lines come from, and why there is doubt as to their authenticity. The *apparatus criticus* is a telegraphically terse compendium of the difficulties that scholars have had in establishing what it is that the author really wrote.[3] Through careful attention to it we will find ourselves required to delve deeper into the text, the language, the author and the context than we ever dreamed of doing. We may not reach our goal of knowing for certain what the author wrote, but we will begin to see the text as it really is today, through the uncertainties, the disagreements, the brilliance and the stupidity of those who have tried to understand it in the millennia since it was written, and particularly in the last few centuries.

[3]   That it continues to be written in Latin reflects the fact that editors have succeeded in reducing its usual vocabulary to a few dozen easily abbreviated words, a feat hard to reproduce from scratch in another language. Dickey, *Ancient Greek Scholarship*, 135–8 gives a convenient list of the most common terms used, and West, *Textual Criticism and Editorial Technique*, 86–94 useful observations on how an apparatus is (or should be) put together.

READING A CRITICAL EDITION

Figure 9.1 is a page from I. Bywater's OCT edition of Aristotle's *Nicomachean Ethics*. First for some orientation as to where we are: the page number on the top (35) is the page of this edition, and the top header (II.7) tells us that we are in Chapter 7 of Book II. Almost every classical text of any importance has its conventions as to numbering; for Aristotle the medieval numbering by books and chapters is sometimes used,[4] but the standard way of referring to a passage is by page number of Bekker's edition.[5] Here the inner margin (left on this page; on even-numbered pages it would be the right) gives the section number within the chapter, the outer margin (right on this page) the Bekker number (1108a[6] begins in the middle of the page). This particular edition, by an optional but not uncommon[7] printer's *tour de force*, manages to maintain the same lines (though not the same pages) as Bekker's edition, so that the line numbers in the outer margin give us the line number on Bekker's page. We have, then, the end of 1107b and the beginning of 1108a on the page before us.

But what is meant by those notes in the *apparatus criticus*? The truth is that they are so standardized that after a very brief period they become self-evident; but in case you have not yet done your apprenticeship, we will walk through them item by item.

Before beginning, however, we must know the symbols, for an essential way to keep the apparatus manageable is to use symbols for those terms that occur throughout, usually the manuscripts or other sources from which the text has been compiled. For this there is usually a page of "Sigla"—particular abbreviations used in this edition—prefaced to the work, and indeed we find there that K^b is cod. Laurentianus LXXXI.11, L^b is cod. Parisiensis 1854, M^b is cod. Marcianus 213, and Γ is "antiqua traductio (ed. Paris. a. 1497)"—that is, an old translation, edited in Paris in 1497, which the editor treats as an independent source because it allows us to draw conclusions about the Greek that was in the manuscript from which the translator worked. "Vulg." means here, as it usually does, "most manuscripts."

---

4 Even of this there are two versions: this particular passage, as it happens, is 2.7 in both numberings.

5 Bekker, ed., *Aristotelis Opera*.

6 Bekker's edition had two columns per page, which subsequent editions refer to as "a" and "b."

7 That is, not uncommon for editions of Aristotle; such correspondence is extremely rare for other authors.

II. 7.   35

7 ἐλευθεριότητα, πῇ δὲ διαφέρουσιν, ὕστερον ῥηθήσεται. περὶ
δὲ τιμὴν καὶ ἀτιμίαν μεσότης μὲν μεγαλοψυχία, ὑπερβολὴ δὲ χαυνότης τις λεγομένη, ἔλλειψις δὲ μικροψυχία·
8 ὡς δ᾿ ἐλέγομεν ἔχειν πρὸς τὴν μεγαλοπρέπειαν τὴν ἐλευθεριότητα, ⟨τῷ⟩ περὶ μικρὰ διαφέρουσαν, οὕτως ἔχει τις καὶ 25
πρὸς τὴν μεγαλοψυχίαν, περὶ τιμὴν οὖσαν μεγάλην, αὐτὴ
περὶ μικρὰν οὖσα· ἔστι γὰρ ὡς δεῖ ὀρέγεσθαι τιμῆς καὶ
μᾶλλον ἢ δεῖ καὶ ἧττον, λέγεται δ᾿ ὁ μὲν ὑπερβάλλων
ταῖς ὀρέξεσι φιλότιμος, ὁ δ᾿ ἐλλείπων ἀφιλότιμος, ὁ δὲ
μέσος ἀνώνυμος. ἀνώνυμοι δὲ καὶ αἱ διαθέσεις, πλὴν ἡ 30
τοῦ φιλοτίμου φιλοτιμία. ὅθεν ἐπιδικάζονται οἱ ἄκροι τῆς
μέσης χώρας· καὶ ἡμεῖς δὲ ἔστι μὲν ὅτε τὸν μέσον φιλότιμον καλοῦμεν ἔστι δ᾿ ὅτε ἀφιλότιμον, καὶ ἔστι μὲν ὅτε
9 ἐπαινοῦμεν τὸν φιλότιμον ἔστι δ᾿ ὅτε τὸν ἀφιλότιμον. διὰ 1108ᵃ
τίνα δ᾿ αἰτίαν τοῦτο ποιοῦμεν, ἐν τοῖς ἑξῆς ῥηθήσεται· νῦν
δὲ περὶ τῶν λοιπῶν λέγωμεν κατὰ τὸν ὑφηγημένον τρό-
10 πον. ἔστι δὲ καὶ περὶ τὴν ὀργὴν ὑπερβολὴ καὶ ἔλλειψις καὶ
μεσότης, σχεδὸν δὲ ἀνωνύμων ὄντων αὐτῶν τὸν μέσον 5
πρᾶον λέγοντες τὴν μεσότητα πραότητα καλέσωμεν· τῶν
δ᾿ ἄκρων ὁ μὲν ὑπερβάλλων ὀργίλος ἔστω, ἡ δὲ κακία ὀρ-
γιλότης, ὁ δ᾿ ἐλλείπων ἀόργητός τις, ἡ δ᾿ ἔλλειψις ἀορ-
11 γησία. εἰσὶ δὲ καὶ ἄλλαι τρεῖς μεσότητες, ἔχουσαι μέν
τινα ὁμοιότητα πρὸς ἀλλήλας, διαφέρουσαι δ᾿ ἀλλήλων· 10
πᾶσαι μὲν γάρ εἰσι περὶ λόγων καὶ πράξεων κοινωνίαν,
διαφέρουσι δὲ ὅτι ἡ μέν ἐστι περὶ τἀληθὲς τὸ ἐν αὐτοῖς,
αἱ δὲ περὶ τὸ ἡδύ· τούτου δὲ τὸ μὲν ἐν παιδιᾷ τὸ δ᾿ ἐν

----

21. πῇ Kᵇ Γ : ᾧ vulg.   25. τῷ add. Ramsauer   26. τὴν om. Kᵇ
27. μικρὰ Kᵇ Lᵇ   33. ἔστι μὲν ὅτε scripsi : ἔστιν ὅτε Kᵇ Γ : ἔστιν
ὅτε μὲν Lᵇ Mᵇ   1108ᵃ 4. τὴν add. Kᵇ   6. καλέσωμεν Kᵇ : καλέ-
σομεν vulg.   7. ἐστὶν Kᵇ   8. δ᾿ ἔλλειψις] δὲ κακία Kᵇ   12.
ὅτι ἡ μέν] ἡ μὲν ὅτι Kᵇ

Figure 9.1 A page of I. Bywater's Oxford text of Aristotle's *Nicomachean Ethics*
with its *apparatus criticus*

More information about these different manuscripts is usually available in the preface, though in this particular edition Bywater has been very parsimonious; he presumes that anyone who is interested in reading the preface will know that "cod. Laurentianus" refers to a manuscript book that is, or was,[8] in the Biblioteca Medicea Laurenziana in Florence ("LXXXI.11" is the manuscript number, which you will need if you go to Florence to look it up), "Parisiensis" in the Bibliothèque de l'Institut de France in Paris, and "Marcianus" in the Marcian Library in Venice. In the preface you will discover that Bywater considers the Laurentian manuscript to be the best—that is, the freest of errors—but has used the others to correct some of its obvious errors (*vitia manifesta*); he also gives some indication of the principles on which he has chosen his readings. This is an important bit of information, since there has been not a little disagreement among editors as to the proper principles for producing a good text.

Now for the comments in the first line of the *apparatus*:

21. πῇ Kᵇ Γ: ᾧ vulg. In line 21—actually the first line on this page, but the editor is using the line numbers in the outer margin—the word πῇ appears in the Laurentian manuscript and seems to be behind the 1497 translation; most manuscripts give ᾧ. This is as much information as the *apparatus* will give you; it is now up to you to see what the difference is (πῇ δὲ διαφέρουσιν means "how they differ," while ᾧ δὲ διαφέρουσιν means "in what they differ"; how, or in what, would those meanings differ? Since Aristotle promises to tell us later [ὕστερον ῥηθήσεται], a glance at the later discussion may give us an indication of which is more appropriate). For most purposes the difference will be negligible; for others, it may be crucial.

---

[8] Manuscripts generally retain their names even when moved; if you are planning to consult a particular manuscript, make sure it is still in the library after which it is named before making air reservations. Kristeller and Krämer, *Latin Manuscript Books* is the first book you will want to consult, and if a photographic or diplomatic edition will suffice for your purposes it will be worth looking in Boyle, *Medieval Latin Palaeography* to see if such a thing is available. Today it is also possible, though still not common, that the manuscript is available online; other libraries that have not digitalized their collections may at least have an online inventory of their manuscripts. Even after consulting these resources, get in touch with the relevant library to make sure that they have the manuscript and will be willing to make it available to you.

25. τῷ add. Ramsauer. In line 25 the word τῷ (which is printed in the text in angular brackets) does not appear in any manuscript, but was added by Ramsauer. It is not the business of the *apparatus* to give you Ramsauer's reason—that would expand the *apparatus* unduly—and so, if you cannot figure out his reason and want to see what it was, you will have to find Ramsauer's edition. In Bywater's day it was not normal practice to offer a bibliography with the text; all editors were mentioned by name, and it was the reader's job, if the reader cared, to look up the edition. Newer editions will often have a bibliography in the prefatory material, which is a great help for this kind of note; but if none is available, an internet search of a major library catalogue will usually help you—and you may find that the edition is available on the net or at a nearby library.

What you will find in Ramsauer[9] is the following note:

περὶ μικρὰ διαφέρουσαν i.e. οὖσαν περὶ μικρὰ καὶ τούτῳ διαφέρουσαν (v. b 18) vel διαφέρουσαν τῷ περὶ μικρὰ εἶναι. Et puto equidem Aristotelem scripsisse τῷ περὶ μικρὰ εἶναι.

That is to say,

Differing about small things, that is, *being about small things and differing in this* (see line b18) or *differing in being about small things*. But I think that Aristotle wrote *in being* about small things.

Ramsauer here remembered (or checked) the words to which Aristotle is referring, which indeed are only seven lines above, and he finds that Aristotle did not say that magnificence and liberality differ about small things, but that they differ in that magnificence deals with large things and liberality with small things. He is thus forced to interpret Aristotle's words here in the same vein, which he does in the two paraphrases he offers; but finding it hard to force that meaning on the Greek, he suggests that the addition of two letters (τῷ) would make the Greek mean what it should, and he suspects that those two letters were omitted at some early stage by a copyist and so do not occur in any of our manuscripts. He leaves it to the reader to look at the text and see whether such an omission is plausible; in this case, he presumably thought that, after the previous

---

[9] Ramsauer, *Aristotelis Ethica Nicomachea*.

word, in a manuscript that had ΤΗΤΑΤΩΙΠΕΡΙ it was easy for the scribe to omit the last of three consecutive syllables beginning with tau.

26. τὴν om. Κ^b. Although the Laurentian MS, which Bywater considers the best, omits this word (the others, apparently, have it), Bywater has decided to print it. Looking at the text will give a reason: Aristotle says that what he said with respect to the relationship of liberality to magnificence (πρὸς τὴν μεγαλοπρέπειαν) can also be applied to magnanimity (πρὸς τὴν μεγαλοψυχίαν): the parallelism of the two phrases makes it virtually certain that Aristotle wrote τὴν in the second phrase as he had in the first—or omitted it in the first as he had in the second; and since all the manuscripts, apparently, have it in the first place, it probably appeared in both. It makes no difference to the philosophical argument, but might be of interest to a grammarian: in English we would never use a definite article with an abstract noun like this. Looking only at the main text, our grammarian might think that this passage was a good example of the phenomenon; attention to the *apparatus criticus* will encourage caution.

These three notes, I hope, will suffice to give an idea of what reading an *apparatus criticus* can offer. Bywater has given in a single line of text information that, expanded into normal prose, has taken me a few pages to explain; he has also shown us the questions that have arisen from careful reading of the text, and at least one of them—the τῷ in line 25— turns out to be of significance in construing the Greek. An *apparatus criticus* is not something that can be taken in at a glance. Hardly any entry in it will reveal its significance without some consideration; but anyone who is seriously interested in what the author had to say in a given place will not be able to ignore it. Chapter 20 of this book, which deals with how texts are edited, will give some further ideas on how to recognize likely readings and likely mistakes.

MAJOR RESOURCES

Classical Texts: Collections

Any student of classics discovers that classical texts are available in various editions. These editions are not interchangeable. The various editions have been edited with different purposes and different audiences in mind; editorial policy varies from series to series, and of course from editor to editor. The edition that is best for tracing the manuscript tradition is not necessarily—in fact, necessarily is not—the best for teaching the work to beginners. The editions also vary in quality: some editions are simply poorly done. It is often worth asking people who specialize in a given author which edition is likely to be best for your purposes.

Text Alone

Most students in English-speaking countries, when seeking the text of an author, will turn first to the Oxford Classical Text.[10] These texts, edited by leading scholars and generally reliable, were originally designed for the use of students: the idea was that, instead of purchasing, shall we say, a student's edition of Iliad 1, the student would purchase, for a reasonable price, an edition of the entire Iliad; after a few years, the student would have the beginnings of a good classical library. Although the age of the students for whom the text is designed has increased as classical education has declined in elementary and secondary schools, the essentially student-oriented policy has remained. This means that the texts included in this series are generally the canonical ones: one will find Homer and Vergil, Thucydides and Livy, Aeschylus and Plautus, but not—or at least not yet, though the series is more than a hundred years old—Valerius Flaccus or Dio Chrysostom. The same student-oriented approach has produced a number of very useful anthologies of authors or genres whose works survive in fragments: these anthologies, with names like *Lyrica Graeca Selecta* or *Menandri Reliquiae Selectae*, conveniently offer the major fragments available without hiding them among the myriad smaller ones. The *apparatus criticus* of an OCT will generally attempt to include all significant variants and conjectures, but (again because of the orientation to students) will make no effort to be exhaustive. The introduction, almost always in Latin,[11] gives a brief account of the manuscripts from which the text has been

---

[10] Although the texts are universally referred to as OCTs, the books themselves always give the name of the series in Latin, *Scriptorum Classicorum Bibliotheca Oxoniensis*.

[11] In 1990, for the first time in the history of the OCT, Hugh Lloyd-Jones and N. G. Wilson wrote the introduction to their new edition of Sophocles in English. "This is the end of civilisation as we have known it," wrote M. L. West in his CR review. Anyone who has wondered what the Latin introductions contain but has not had the patience or capability to read one of them can gain an impression from this edition. Some later Oxford editors, but not all, have followed the lead of Lloyd-Jones and Wilson.

compiled and their supposed connections; the reader who wants to know when the author lived or what sort of work the book contains must look elsewhere.

The Teubner[12] series (whose official name is *Bibliotheca Scriptorum Graecorum et Romanorum Teubneriana*) is today similar in format, with a Latin introduction discussing textual issues and an *apparatus criticus* at the bottom of the page; very old editions printed the *apparatus criticus* separately or (in the cheaper, student editions, which are no longer printed) omitted it entirely. The Teubner series, like the Oxford one, was begun with students in mind, offering a high-quality text at a low price; this series, however, is today much broader, covering many more authors and often offering a more complete apparatus. During the period of divided Germany after World War II, Teubner was split into two houses, the East German one in its traditional Leipzig home and the West German one in Stuttgart; in this period there were sometimes competing Teubner editions of the same work. In cases where both Teubner and Oxford texts exist, the choice will generally depend on the relative merits of the particular editions. The publishers now offer the Latin texts in digital format, easy to use but difficult to afford.

For Christian authors, the series *Corpus Christianorum*, begun by Elegius Dekkers under the aegis of Brepols publishers, is the first place to look; this project, already more than fifty years old, plans to produce reliable texts of all the church fathers, and even non-Christian and anti-Christian authors who dealt with Christianity, and its volumes—including many other projects that have been born out of it—already number more than a thousand. Better, they are computer-searchable at *Brepolis*, the collection of databases managed by Brepols, if your institution has a subscription or you can afford a private one. Before the *Corpus Christianorum* there was (and still is) the *Corpus Scriptorum Ecclesiasticorum Latinorum* (CSEL) of the Österreichische Akademie der Wissenschaften; failing that, Jacques-Paul Migne's monumental PCC, hundreds of volumes published long ago in only a few years,[13] offers poor texts of almost everything. Migne took whatever text was available, and even the best texts of his time would not be used now where a better one can be had. Most large university libraries will have a set; the *Patrologia* is also available on CD and on the web, though

---

[12] The B. G. Teubner publishing house, founded in 1811, continued to publish this series until 1999, when it sold the rights to K. G. Saur; the current publisher is Walter de Gruyter.

[13] Migne, PL was published in 221 volumes in the years 1844–45; Migne, PG in 165 volumes, with facing Latin translation, in 1857–58.

the CD is expensive and use of the website requires explicit permission of the owners, on terms specified there. Migne was revolutionary in making all of the church fathers easily available, and, although the texts are now woefully out of date, they are still occasionally the only ones available.

Texts with Translation

The Loeb Classical Library, founded by James Loeb[14] in 1911, covers a very wide area, and has played a key role both in making classical texts available to the broader public and in allowing people with less than perfect command of Greek and Latin to approach the texts in their original languages. Some read the Latin and peek at the English when stymied, some read the English and glance at the Latin when they want to know more precisely what the author wrote, but all are offered an opportunity to approach directly a work that would otherwise require more ability or more time than they have available. The Loebs are small (originally designed to be of a size "to fit in a gentleman's pocket," but pockets have become smaller since then) and their *apparatus criticus*, if any, is restricted to bare essentials, but the texts are not carelessly edited. The Loeb introduction to a work, unlike that of an Oxford or a Teubner text, does not restrict itself to textual matters, but offers a general background to the work at hand.

Loeb at first had some difficulty finding a publisher, but by the end of World War I it was obvious that he had had a good idea. In 1920 the Association Guillaume Budé began a series of bilingual texts with French translation.[15] The Budés, which like the Loebs cover the entire spectrum of ancient literature, often aim slightly higher: their *apparatus criticus* may be more ample, and they often contain a commentary, though this will usually be designed as an aid to understanding the text, not a broad-ranging discussion of everything connected with it. The differences between individual Budés and individual Loebs are much greater than the differences between the two series, and your choice, if not dictated *a priori* by language, will depend on the particular work you are looking at.

---

[14] Loeb, the scion of a family of German-Jewish bankers from New York, spent his last years in Germany; his funeral in May 1933 was one of the last public tributes to a Jew as the Nazi night descended.

[15] The official title is *Collection des universités de France, publiée sous le patronage de l'Association Guillaume Budé*.

More recently the Fondazione Lorenzo Valla has begun printing a set of bilingual texts (*Scrittori greci e latini*) with Italian translation. These editions often include a full *apparatus criticus* and an ample commentary; some of these (notably the *Odyssey*[16] and Herodotus[17]) have appeared in English under the aegis of publishers who considered them, not without reason, superior to anything available in our native tongue. There is also a bilingual series published in Spanish under the title *Alma Mater*.

Texts with Commentary

Many editions are published with an accompanying commentary. These may be "school editions" designed to aid the beginner, concentrating on matters of grammar and sometimes even including a vocabulary list or a translation; they may be more advanced commentaries discussing issues of substance, designed for people for whom understanding the text is not the goal but the beginning; and they may be wide-ranging works of scholarship for which the commentary is merely a form into which to put a scholarly discussion much broader than the bounds of the work being commented on. Since the problems of beginning readers do not change much from year to year, school editions may remain valuable for generations, and a number of nineteenth-century editions with commentary are still periodically reprinted. In the modern situation, when many if not most students began to study the classical languages in colleges and universities, a need has been felt for editions that would offer help that goes beyond mere construal.[18] The pioneers of this were the "Oxford Reds," a number of works (never officially a series) published by Oxford University Press from the 1930s until the 1980s, offering an introduction and a detailed commentary that were on quite a respectable scholarly level: some of these editions, indeed, became the scholarly standard for decades. The text used was usually that of the OCT, occasionally with minor deviations. In recent years the Cambridge University Press has taken up the banner, with the *Cambridge Classical Texts and Commentaries* (the "green and yellows"), geared to a somewhat more elementary level than the Oxford Reds but still quite respectable in their treatment of scholarly

---

[16] Heubeck et al., eds., *A Commentary on Homer's Odyssey*.

[17] Asheri, Lloyd and Corcella, *A Commentary on Herodotus I–IV*.

[18] The modern student, on the other hand, may need more help than a Victorian schoolboy in understanding the ancient text; modern university editions often take this into account.

issues, and the *Cambridge Greek and Latin Classics* (the "orange and blacks") directed at a more advanced and scholarly audience. The Aris and Phillips series includes a facing translation, making it usable both for those who can read the original languages and for those who cannot; the commentary, more restricted than the Oxford or Cambridge ones, is keyed to the translation.

Classical Texts in Translation

In the late nineteenth century Bohn's Classical Library offered all the major works in a rather literal English translation that was exceptionally useful for preparing for exams; many people today still "bone up" for exams, unaware (as the current spelling shows) of the expression's origin. Penguin Classics and Everyman's Library in England and the Modern Library in America performed a great and often unappreciated service in keeping classical literature a part of the general culture.[19] Of these only the Penguins continue to appear, but translations of major texts, although they do not today make a person's fame and fortune as Alexander Pope's translation of Homer did for him, may still be quite marketable if done well. Lesser texts, when not part of a general series, will of course fare less well. It is to be hoped that enterprising publishers will once again take up the gauntlet of introducing the public to works that, when properly edited and produced, have a much wider audience than is often supposed. Oxford University Press has begun producing quite a respectable line of texts in translation, perhaps still geared more to academics than to the general public.

Online Texts

Many worthy projects have made numerous classical texts available online. Outstanding (as of this moment) are *Perseus*, where you can click on a Greek word and get its entire morphological analysis, dictionary definition and other relevant information; and the *Thesaurus Linguae Graecae* (TLG), where you can search the entire corpus of Greek literature (or any subset

---

[19] Indeed, in the mid-twentieth century even children got a dose of the ancients in the long discontinued *Classics Illustrated* comic books, which according to recent reports may yet be revived.

thereof) for any Greek word you choose. (Neither *Perseus* nor the TLG has an *apparatus criticus*.) There are many online collections of texts, and in my experience you can more often than not find whatever classical work you are looking for online, either in the original language or in translation—generally a choice of translations. Entering the name of a Greek author into your search-engine in Greek characters makes it possible to find the author on sites maintained by and for Greek speakers, another rich source; if you cannot find a Latin text on a site like *The Latin Library* or *LacusCurtius*, entering the Latin form ("Ovidi Nasonis Amatoria" instead of "Ovid Art Love") may find it elsewhere. Online texts are quite convenient, but they are sometimes very out of date: the most recent editions are often protected by copyright and so cannot legally be uploaded, though many publishers have cooperated with the TLG, to the advantage of scholars.

PART III

THE TRADITIONAL FIELDS

PART III

TRADITIONAL EMCEE

10

READING AND UNDERSTANDING LITERATURE

CLASSICS IS ALMOST ENTIRELY LITERATURE

It might reasonably be held that literature is not a subfield of classics, but the field itself; surely many people who are considered classicists spend their entire careers dealing only with literary texts, and many university departments carry the name Classical Languages and Literature. Almost any Greek or Latin author whose works have survived is an independent subfield: about 40 percent of the publications listed in *L'Année philologique* are catalogued under the names of individual authors. More than that: most authors require expertise far beyond their texts. Studying Aeschylus or Terence requires that you learn what there is to know about Greek or Roman theatrical performance and conventions; studying Homer means familiarizing yourself with epic poetry as a genre, with oral poetry and with the remains of Mycenaean and Dark Age Greece; studying Augustine means getting to know the other early church fathers and the social milieu of late antiquity. This book's chapters on epigraphy or ancient music try to give a short introduction to those subjects for a person who has had little previous exposure; that kind of chapter on literature would probably be less helpful to readers of this book, who have had enough exposure to classical literature to interest them in spending a good deal of their time on earth researching that literature. I restrict myself, therefore, to a short overview of the various theoretical approaches that have been taken in recent years, approaches that have mostly originated outside of our field but are often useful to classicists.

WHAT BOOK WILL MOST HELP ME UNDERSTAND AN ANCIENT WORK OF LITERATURE?

Undoubtedly, the work itself: there is no substitute for your own experience of the book, nor can you ever think intelligently about a book you haven't read. Even rereading a book you have read will probably give you more new insights than reading somebody else's book about it. Every work of literary criticism would seem to suffer from the same dilemma: if what it says is already in the original work, what does it add? And if what it says is not there, then isn't it simply wrong?

If every book, or any book, had a single, obvious, correct meaning, then indeed there would be no point in writing another word about it; but no book is that simple. If you think there is such a book, try sitting down with a friend, reading the book line by line, and explaining to each other what it means. You will probably be surprised by the results. Since each reader sees different things in the book, reading what someone else has to say about it will probably open your eyes to aspects you hadn't noticed. It will probably also annoy you by saying things that you think are demonstrably untrue, but this, too, is likely to sharpen your own understanding as you try to clarify why you disagree.

It is important to realize that a book about Vergil is never going to give you *the* meaning of Vergil. What you yourself see in Vergil—even the first time—is not something that you should simply "correct" the way you would be likely to correct the meaning of a grammatical form that you had misread. There is such a thing as a wrong interpretation,[1] but much more often different readings of a work are just that: different readings, each of them with some basis in the work itself, each of them with a claim to legitimacy that cannot be determined by the academic rank of the reader or the number of other people persuaded by one reading or the other. Reading another opinion will probably change your own, and so it should; but it should not simply replace your own as if it were axiomatic that the printed (and perhaps even assigned) book is right and you are wrong.

A secondary book, however, can have more to add than just another reading. One thing that it may be able to offer is information about other texts that illuminate the text at hand. When you read the Aeneid and begin—if that is how your text begins[2]—*arma virumque cano*, you may not need anyone to point out to you that Vergil is stating his topic, and that his

---

[1] I refer any reader who thinks that no interpretation is ever completely wrong to Kovacs, "A Cautionary Tale."

[2] See above, p. 101.

topic will be arms (i.e., war) and a man (i.e., the nature of a particular hero). But if someone tells you that Homer began the Iliad with the words μῆνιν ἄειδε and the Odyssey with the words ἄνδρα μοι ἔννεπε, you will see something else that you would not have known without this information: Vergil is announcing that he will write both an Iliad and an Odyssey. This connection among texts, once treated in terms of an earlier author's influence on a later one, is now subsumed under the term *intertextuality*, a matter of which we shall have more to say presently.

References to other texts are not all that secondary literature has to offer; other background information may be no less informative. Perhaps you already knew that books in Vergil's time were written in scrolls, and had no title page. A book might point out to you that this is probably why Vergil, like most other ancient writers, put the topic of his work in its first words: these are the words that would confront a potential reader who opened the scroll to see what it contained. Information about the political situation at the time the Aeneid was written and before it may also be significant, though the significance of the information may be as much a subject for debate as the meaning of the book itself.

LITERARY HISTORY

Contemporary books do not usually require any explanation of their literary background. Authors have usually read quite a few books before writing any, and those books have undoubtedly affected how they think a book should be written; but they generally write for people of their own time and place,[3] in a form and language intelligible to the reading public.

This is not the case for classical literature. When I first spent fifty cents for a pocket edition of Homer's Iliad for a high school course, I encountered this in the second paragraph:

> What god, then, made the feud between them? Apollo, son of Leto and Zeus. The King had offended him: so he sent a dire pestilence on the camp and the people perished. Agamemnon had offended his priest Chrysês, when the priest came to the Achaian fleet, bringing a rich treasure to ransom his daughter. He held in his hand a golden staff,

---

[3] There are exceptions: the novels of James Joyce and the *Cantos* of Ezra Pound were not easily understandable by the reading public at the time they were written, nor are they today. For some, that fact increases their appeal.

twined about with the sacred wreaths of Apollo Shootafar, and made his petition to the Achaian people in general but chiefly to the two royal princes of Atreus' line.[4]

Leaving aside the problems of translation (this was not the first translated book I had ever read), and despite the translator's help (Homer doesn't really give Apollo's name at first), I was made acutely uncomfortable by the author's apparent presumption that I knew who Leto was; that I knew which side the Achaians fought for (I had thought, on the excellent authority of a Hollywood epic seen when I was eight, that the Trojan War was fought between Greeks and Trojans, but Greeks were nowhere in evidence here); who Chrysês was, and how I was supposed to pronounce the circumflex over the "e"; why Apollo seemed to have the family name Shootafar; and who the royal princes of Atreus' line were.[5] Most of these problems are usually solved for modern college students by courses in literary history, courses that start from Homer (where, of course, they must still deal with the same lack of background) and continue through the rest of ancient literature, helping to understand the literature of each period by a consideration of what went before.

Such courses, though rarely exciting—the necessity of rushing through vast expanses of literature generally prevents any deep appreciation of the subject matter—are often useful in providing a background against which literature can be read. A better understanding of the environment that produced a work, however, will include much other information as well. Discussions of Greek tragedy and comedy may be enriched by knowledge of the Dionysiac worship of which they formed a part; a comparison of Hellenistic epic with Homeric epic will have a lot to do with the differences between the cultural world of the Hellenistic age, where Greeks were a dominant class ruling over far-flung multiethnic empires, and that of the archaic age, where Greeks were a small but warlike nation in a sea of barbarians. The changes affected not only the poets but their audience; and here is where questions of influence turn into questions of intertextuality.

---

[4]   Rouse, Iliad: The Story of Achilles.

[5]   In fact there is no necessity to believe that Homer expected his audience to be familiar with Chrysês, a character internal to the Iliad; but assaulted by all the other unfamiliar names, I had no way of distinguishing him from the royal princes of Atreus' line.

INTERTEXTUALITY

In the words *arma virumque cano*, and in almost every verse of the Aeneid, Homer has undoubtedly influenced Vergil. The influence, of course, could not have gone in the other direction: Vergil undoubtedly read Homer very carefully, and Homer could know nothing of Vergil. With a little thought, we will realize that influence can pass even without the later author's reading the earlier one: most writers of modern comedies are influenced by the conventions of Greek New Comedy—where comedy flows from difficulties in uniting a pair of young lovers, and ends happily with their marriage—even if they have never read any New Comedy, and even though the Greek originals themselves were totally unknown until little more than a century ago, and remain most imperfectly attested even today.

But if Vergil could not influence what Homer wrote, he can and does influence the Homer that we read. When some readers see in Homer a vigorous poet close to the world of the warriors and adventurers of whom he sings, and others see in him a primitive singer still innocent of the sophistication and beauty that Vergil could attain, both are reading Homer with eyes that react differently because they have seen Vergil. Sometimes a particular work becomes so thoroughly accepted that it becomes, as it were, sanctified: either literally, in that the work is accepted as divinely written or inspired, or figuratively, in that the work becomes the standard for its genre. In either case the text has been transformed. Once the Christian world has accepted certain texts as "the gospel truth" none of us, Christians or not, can read those texts as if that had never happened. If the Aeneid had not become Rome's national epic, we might still have Ennius' *Annals*, and we would certainly read them differently than we would today after reading Vergil.

Sometimes, particularly when we are dealing with writers who are contemporary to each other, intertextuality is simply something that was in the air: Tibullus and Propertius, regardless of the question of whether and when they actually read each other's poems, were both moving in the same ambience, following the same conventions, and trying to do much the same thing. Ovid takes those same conventions and treats them in an almost parodic fashion, and he did not necessarily have to have Tibullus and Propertius in front of him to do it. Nor can we read Tibullus and Propertius with quite the same seriousness once we have read Ovid. Influence passes in only one direction, but texts interact in all directions, and that is what we mean when we speak of intertextuality.

It is not only literary developments that may affect the reading of a text. Democritus appears on modern Greek money and has a university named after him not because of the innate superiority of his cosmological theories to those of Heraclitus, but because modern physicists, whose understanding of the universe is by no means that of Democritus, take him as the father of the atomic theory. The essence of Democritus' theory was that every substance is made up of particles whose shape determines the properties of the substance and cannot be split (ἄ-τομοι), whereas modern "atoms" are mere building blocks of most substances, can be split, and are themselves composed of smaller particles that have entirely different properties. The physical demonstrations on which modern atomic theory is based were entirely unknown to Democritus. Nevertheless, it is very difficult today to look at the disagreement of Democritus and Heraclitus without considering, at least in some sense, that Democritus was right and Heraclitus was wrong. Political developments also have their effects. As far as I know neither Nietzsche nor Wagner ever killed a Jew, but today we cannot read Nietzsche's antinomianism or Wagner's anti-Semitism without an awareness of how the Nazis used those ideologies. Plato's *Republic* does not ask how far the state should interfere in its citizens' private lives, a non-issue in ancient Greece,[6] but, for those who saw the totalitarian regimes of the mid-twentieth century, that issue overshadows every other aspect of the ideal state he proposed.[7]

In all of the examples discussed, the text itself has not changed. Texts of authors may indeed change over time, through accident, negligence or downright forgery, and it can even happen that a later author's words may unwittingly be inserted in the text of an earlier one, but that question belongs not to the current chapter but to the previous one. What has changed is the way we read the text, but it is very hard, and usually impossible, for us to escape the effects of the change. Should we try? Should we try, as far as we are able, to experience the *Agamemnon* as Aeschylus' contemporaries did? Are we falsifying Aeschylus when we read him in light of later developments? Is that what Aeschylus meant? Do we care what Aeschylus meant? These questions are basic to the enterprise of literary appreciation and criticism, and they have been discussed at length. I cannot give a thorough account of the debate, but we must at least take note of the issues.

---

6 Thucydides' Pericles, indeed, brags that the Athenians do not pry into one's private life too much (Thuc. 2.37.2), but he does not suggest that they had no right to do so if they had wished.

7 The first statement of this was Popper, *The Open Society and Its Enemies*, whose first edition appeared, not coincidentally, in 1945; it has been an important theme in the discussion of Plato's political philosophy ever since.

THE AUTHOR, THE TEXT, AND THE READER: THEORETICAL ISSUES

Until the twentieth century, literary appreciation was essentially a non-academic activity carried out by the educated elite: that Homer and Shakespeare and Pushkin were great writers was a matter generally agreed upon in those segments of society who were considered the better people, and whose taste was accepted as being more refined than that of the commons. With the advent of "the century of the common man" that standard could no longer be maintained. When the aristocracies crumbled at the end of World War I, it could no longer be accepted that what the well-to-do liked was the best that culture had to offer—particularly as the triumph of the commercial class in the west and the bureaucratic class in the east led to a dominance of Babbits on the one hand and *apparatchiks* on the other, people notoriously ignorant of literature, music and art. Even worse, precisely those artists who rebelled against the established standards— Pound, Eliot and Joyce in literature, Stravinsky and Schoenberg in music, Picasso, the Dadaists and a host of others in graphic art—were not only unpopular with the multitude, but utterly incomprehensible to them. Good taste could no longer simply be defined as the taste of the upper class, nor was the more democratic criterion of popularity accepted. There came about, in the new departments of modern literature that had arisen towards the end of the nineteenth century,[8] a spirited discussion as to what precisely it is that an intelligent reader sees in a literary work; and how one work differs from, and may be considered better than, another; or whether, indeed, it is even reasonable to speak of one work as better than another.

A history of the literary debates of the twentieth century is beyond the scope of this book, but the aspiring researcher has to be warned that professors tend to have very deeply held opinions about the various schools of thought. A referee may recommend rejecting an article because it agrees or disagrees with a particular theory that the referee considers important, or simply because it does not take that theory into account. There is also the opposite danger, that you may lose yourself in theoretical issues so deeply that you will have little to say about the literary work itself, or else what you do have to say will be so deeply embedded in theoretical jargon as to be impenetrable to the uninitiated. Each of the theoretical schools that I will mention—and I will mention only some,

---

[8]   On the relatively late flourishing of departments of English literature see Parker, "Where Do English Departments Come From?"

and those briefly—has had something significant to say; each of them can also be, and each of them has been, overdone to the point of parody by enthusiasts. In this, as in much of research, it is important to be informed but essential to maintain common sense.

"Internally Generated" Schools of Literary Theory

Some theoretical viewpoints arose directly from the study of literature; others are rather the application to literature of theories that originated in other fields of study. Probably the first self-conscious literary theory was the school that in its day was called "the new criticism." The new criticism arose in reaction to the approach of literary history sketched above, according to which it would appear that no work of literature can be properly appreciated without knowing the author who created it and the audience for which it was created. The new criticism argued, on the contrary, that the author's intentions are irrelevant, and that the feeling a work arouses in a reader is an individual phenomenon that cannot define the work's nature. Ascribing importance to the author's intentions is called *the intentional fallacy;*[9] ascribing importance to the reader's emotions is *the affective fallacy*. According to the new critics, the way to understand a text is by reading it closely, paying attention to alternate meanings, hints and echoes whereby the text says more than it seems to on a superficial reading. It is not accidental that some of the major figures of the new criticism were lyric poets, specialists in the production of short texts designed to be read very carefully and to mean more than they say.

Wimsatt and Beardsley's use of the polemically loaded term "fallacy" did not bring about the immediate surrender of everybody who thought that a reader should indeed try to understand an author's intention. Many respectable theorists will still argue for intentionalism,[10] and there are those who would claim that, insofar as writing is a form of communication, its entire purpose is to convey the writer's intention to the reader.

Structuralism holds that every element of a situation has meaning only in relationship to all the other elements of the situation, so that meaning can only be analyzed in the context of the total structure in which it is embedded. For a simple example: Jews and Christians in the ancient world were often considered atheists, since they denied all the gods who were

---

[9]   The philosophical text arguing this point is Wimsatt and Beardsley, *The Verbal Icon.*
[10]   See, for example, Heath, *Interpreting Classical Texts.*

worshipped by everyone else; in the modern west the word "atheist" would never be held to include a believing Jew or Christian. The basic meaning of the word (one who denies the existence of a deity) has not changed; what has changed is the structure around it, the society's underlying concept of godhead. Similarly, a work of literature can best be analyzed by its underlying structure: by this analysis many apparently different works are seen to be essentially the same, or else to be variations on a different structure that appears elsewhere. This kind of analysis has been elaborated into the discipline of *narratology*, an approach that by distinguishing the way a story is told (the "narrative") from the events of the story itself makes the way in which the narrative is structured—and the way in which the narrative structures the reader's or listener's perception of the events—the basic subject of study.

Structuralism should perhaps be listed among the "externally generated" theories, since it was first advanced as a psychological theory, and its twentieth-century version started from the linguistic theories of Ferdinand de Saussure in his *Course in General Linguistics*, the original of which was published posthumously by his students in 1916. Its most celebrated application was in the anthropological work of Claude Lévi-Strauss.

New historicism holds, against the new criticism, that historical information must be taken into account in understanding a text; unlike the "old" historical approach against which new criticism reacted, it does not take a text's historical background as a known objective fact, but treats all historical information as part of the "discourse" of which the text itself forms a part. The Aeneid is not to be seen without reference to the history and sociology of Augustan Rome; but neither is that history and sociology to be seen without the Aeneid, which forms a part of it no less essential than the more "historical" sources from which it is known. The new historicism considers all historical narrative to be necessarily subjective, but this subjectivity can be identified as such and itself taken as a component of the larger cultural narrative of which all literature forms a part.

Postmodernism is a broad term for various philosophical and artistic movements that react to the "modern" philosophy and art of the period between the two world wars. In some areas postmodernism carries modernism to extremes, and in others it reacts against it by reintroducing classical elements, but there are some general points of similarity among the various strands of postmodernism. The job of describing it is made somewhat easier, but not much, by the fact that I can limit myself here to postmodern literary criticism.

One recurring strand denies that there is any identifiable structure that can be determined for a text.[11] Every text involves a play of different meanings, all of them possible and none of them inherently more correct than another. The idea that at the basis of a text is a unique correct understanding is a way in which wielders of authority attempt to control the text's meaning, both to establish their own authority as guardians of the truth ("hegemony") and to defend against other, inherently sub-versive understandings; the job of criticism is to *deconstruct* the text, revealing the hidden (or, more polemically, "suppressed" or "silenced") meanings that are no less legitimate than the "authoritative" under-standing. This argument contains an obvious contradiction, for in defin-ing the job of criticism it treats certain forms of criticism as legitimate and others as illegitimate—exactly the phenomenon against which it is ostensibly rebelling. Many postmodernists, however, embrace contradic-tion: that, too, is part of the human condition, something we cannot remove from ourselves or from our literature. There is often a certain amount of irony and even self-parody in postmodernism—and that, too, is acceptable in the critic, and often seen by postmodernists in literary works that earlier critics treated with a high seriousness.

Like the new critics, the postmodernists deny the right of the author or any reader to establish a definitive meaning for the texts; unlike them, they also deny the existence of any definitive meaning at all. This does not mean that texts are meaningless, but only that their inherent ambiguities can never be exorcized by authority or by analysis. A corollary of this approach is the idea that every analysis, being itself a text, is itself subject to its own ambiguities and uncertainties: the more we try to explain, the more we multiply possible meanings, for we can never escape the net of language in which we express ourselves.

"Externally Generated" Schools of Literary Theory

Many theories whose origins lie in fields outside of literary studies have been applied to literature, with results no less significant than those of the internally generated theories.

Marxism, which sees culture as a phenomenon ("ideology") produced by the dominant economic class as a rationalization for its continued dominance, invites the investigation of texts as justifications of economic

---

[11] Derrida, "Structure, Sign, and Play in the Discourse of the Human Sciences," a lecture originally given at Johns Hopkins University in 1966, has become the seminal text of this approach.

dominance, as reflections of it or as attempts to subvert the dominant ideology. During the Soviet hegemony in Russia and eastern Europe more or less all work published there was expected to be, at least outwardly, Marxist, and as such was ignored in the west even more thoroughly than the language barrier might otherwise have dictated.[12] Recent Marxist criticism has tended to take a more nuanced view of literature, admitting the possibility of a more complex relationship between works of art and the society in which they are produced.

Psychoanalysis, specifically the school of psychological thought initiated by Sigmund Freud (and also those of the later theorists Karl Jung and Jacques Lacan), in positing that underlying a person's own perceptions of self and surroundings is a significant subconscious element, which the conscious perception sometimes suppresses and sometimes encodes, invites the analysis of literary texts according to the same rules. Freud himself employed literary texts in this way, most famously in the case of the Oedipus myth. A school of psychoanalytic literary criticism has grown up on the boundary between clinical psychology and literary theory, with interpretations often no less alarming than Freud's analysis of his patients' subconscious wishes.

The *feminism* of the late twentieth century (as opposed to earlier feminism, which concentrated on questions of women's political and legal rights) developed an extensive cultural agenda, claiming that much or all of culture hitherto has been a vehicle for the maintenance of male dominance. This understanding, no less than Marxism and psychoanalysis, proposes a new framework that is claimed to apply to all literature, and therefore demands that every text be reread in view of the relationships between the sexes reflected or prescribed in the text, in particular with a view to questions of power and its exercise within the family and without. With time feminist analysis has also produced "gender studies," as it has become increasingly clear that differing views of what women are or should be correspond to differing views of what men are or should be. Feminist studies have been much more widespread in the classics than Marxist or psychoanalytical studies ever were, a fact that is undoubtedly connected with the fact—itself a result of political feminism—that women are much more common and much more prominent in modern classics departments than Marxists or psychoanalysts.

---

[12]   There was a certain amount of Marxist literary analysis in the west; in English classics the most notable example in the Soviet heyday was Thomson, *Aeschylus and Athens*. Later de Ste. Croix, *The Class Struggle* dealt only tangentially with literature but offered a much less ideologically rigid analysis.

THE PLACE OF THEORY AND IDEOLOGY IN THE STUDY OF LITERATURE

Many students of literature balk at the claims of all the schools; they hold that literary works must be approached with an open mind, and dealt with without theoretical preconceptions.[13] The devotees of literary theory argue in opposition that preconceptions are inevitable, and not discussing them simply means accepting uncritically the preconceptions that we have built up over our lives. It is indubitable that every theory mentioned has its weaknesses, and every one can be abused when over-applied. I have refrained from criticizing any of the theories mentioned, for a handbook for researchers is not the place for polemic; but for each of them, considerable and even wearisome discussion pro and con is easily available. The websites of many literature professors can be helpful in supplying basic orientation and bibliography.[14]

Beside the controversy over the importance of theory lies another controversy, no less bitter, over the proper place of ideology in literature. The controversy is ancient: Vergil felt obliged to apologize for not writing on the more patriotic topic of *reges et proelia*,[15] and times of civil strife tend to encourage the feeling that literature is evading its duty if it does not contribute to the general struggle. Engelbert Drerup, at the height of World War I, published a bitter attack on Demosthenes, dedicated it to his son who had fallen in the war, and identified his work on its title page as "auch ein Kriegsbuch";[16] Georges Clemenceau, who became prime minister of France in the following year, later published his own laudatory biography of the same Athenian orator.[17] In calmer times, both authors and critics tend to defend the autonomy of the muse and to view works of open social advocacy as a lesser form of literature. I could wish the readers of this book the pleasure of living in the calmer sort of time when social advocacy appears less essential—on the condition that such appearance is not merely a sign of the shortsightedness of the author.

---

[13] For an outspoken expression of this view, see the Classical Association Presidential Address of David West, *Cast Out Theory*; for more detailed critical views of the currently fashionable theories see Patai and Corral, eds., *Theory's Empire*.

[14] I myself made use in the preparation of this chapter of the excellent and succinct summaries of Dr. Kristi Siegel at her website *Introduction to Modern Literary Theory*.

[15] Verg. *Ecl.* 6.3.

[16] Drerup, *Aus einer alten Advokatenrepublik*.

[17] Clemenceau, *Demosthenes*.

MAJOR RESOURCES

Introductions to classical literature are many, and you have probably been exposed to one or more; for this, too, Jenkins can provide a beginning if necessary. An exhaustive list of Greek authors, each with a number and a computer-appropriate label, is Berkowitz and Squitier, *TLG Canon*; it has been enlarged and kept up to date at the *TLG Online Canon of Greek Authors and Works* website. More thoroughgoing, with information about manuscripts and editions, and even a short description of each work, is Landfester, *Dictionary of Greek and Latin Authors and Texts*. For more serious articles on major authors and groups of Greek and Roman authors ("Asiani [oratori]," "Annalisti," "Pitagorici") one can consult Della Corte, *Dizionario degli scrittori greci e latini*. Most introductions to classical literature are organized by author, and can themselves offer a starting-point.

One matter that many students will want to know more about is metrics; for this the handiest summary of the meters themselves is still Halporn, Ostwald and Rosenmeyer, *The Meters of Greek and Latin Poetry*; D. S. Raven's *Greek Metre* and *Latin Metre* give somewhat more discussion, and for Greek poetry M. L. West, *Greek Metre* characteristically gives a thoughtful, if innovative and hence somewhat idiosyncratic, historical account that offers more to the student who wonders why and how these particular meters came to be used.

Since each author requires a complete bibliography, attempting a bibliography even of the major resources would inflate this chapter beyond reasonable proportion. Fortunately, a good and reasonably up-to-date brief bibliography of the major authors is available in Jenkins, to whom I refer the reader. Jenkins is a guide only to the reference literature, but he lists specialized bibliographies for each author where they exist. APh lists current bibliography by author, where possible, and so provides an easy source for more up-to-date references. For individual works Nickel, *Lexikon der antiken Literatur* offers a brief description of content, sources for the work, historical background, the theme, reworkings, editions, translations and secondary literature—a good place to find basic information about an unfamiliar work.

Collections of Fragments

Since many classicists are less aware of where to find those authors who have reached us in fragmentary condition, I include, at the risk of seeming perverse, a list of some major collections of fragments.

Drama: Comedy. For generations, as Meineke, *Poetarum comicorum Graecorum fragmenta* got more and more out of date, the efforts to provide a new collection were of dubious value; and as useful as it was to have a full collection of comic fragments with a verse translation, J. M. Edmonds' *magnum opus, The Fragments of Attic Comedy,* was permanently stigmatized when it turned out that the "Cairo palimpsest" on which he claimed to have read various items of great interest was no palimpsest at all, and the plot summaries he printed from it were apparently his own invention.[18] Fortunately, Kassel and Austin, *Poetae Comici Graeci* (PCG, sometimes abbreviated KA or K-A) has now finally given an authoritative collection of fragments; and although this does not include a translation, Olson, *Broken Laughter* does include (in an appendix) a translation of the selections he has chosen, and Jeffrey Henderson has published the major fragments of Aristophanes in his Loeb edition. The fragments of Roman comedy (except for Plautus and Syrus' *Sententiae*) were collected by Ribbeck, *Comicorum Romanorum Fragmenta* (CRF). There has been no complete collection since, but Frassinetti, *Atellanae Fabulae,* Daviault, *Comoedia Togata,* Rychlewska, *Turpilii Comici Fragmenta* and Manuwald, *Fabulae praetextae* have improved matters considerably.

Drama: Tragedy. Nauck, *Tragicorum Graecorum fragmenta* (TGF), the standard for years, has now been superseded by Snell, Kannicht and Radt, *Tragicorum Graecorum fragmenta* (TrGF). A convenient selection of the major tragic fragments is Diggle, *Tragicorum Graecorum Fragmenta Selecta.* Text and commentary are offered by Carden, *The Papyrus Fragments of Sophocles;* text, English translation and commentary by Sommerstein, Fitzpatrick and Talboy, *Sophocles: Selected Fragmentary Plays* and Collard, Cropp and Lee, *Euripides: Selected Fragmentary Plays.* A number of tragedies of which we have only fragments have been published in individual editions with commentaries,[19] and at least one, Euripides' *Hypsipyle,* has been presented in the theater at Epidaurus. The new Loeb editions of Aeschylus, Sophocles and Euripides all include the major fragments, heralding a new day when the major fragments of Greek drama are available to the undergraduate and the casual reader no less than to the expert. For Roman tragedy as for comedy

---

[18] See Marzullo, "Il Cairense di Menandro agli infrarossi" and Martin, "Un faux Ménandre." Volumes II and III of Edmonds' collection were published posthumously, and it cannot be asserted definitely that he intended for his invented material to be included. He had, however, published some of it in his lifetime: Edmonds, ed., *Samia* and Edmonds, "The Cairensis of Menander by Infra-Red."

[19] Diggle, *Euripides: Phaethon;* Harder, *Euripides' Kresphontes and Archelaos;* Müller, *Euripides: Philoktet;* Preiser, *Euripides: Telephos.*

it was Ribbeck who collected the fragments, in *Tragicorum Romanorum Fragmenta* (TRF); this has since been renewed by Klotz, *Tragicorum Fragmenta*.

Drama: Satyr-plays. Fragments of satyr-plays can be found among the tragic fragments in TrGF; the relevant fragments are reprinted in Krumeich, Pechstein and Seidensticker, *Das griechische Satyrspiel*, and those of the minor dramatists in Cipolla, *Poeti minori del dramma satiresco*. For the larger fragments we have individual volumes: Maltese, *Ichneutae* and Werre-de Haas, *Aeschylus' Dictyulci: An Attempt at Reconstruction of a Satyric Drama.*

Poetry: Greek: Elegy and iambus, of which fragments are most of what we have, are now represented by West, *Iambi et Elegi Graeci*, with a selection available more cheaply in West, *Delectus ex Iambis et Elegis Graecis*; for translations, the Loeb Classical Library, for which Edmonds, *Elegy and Iambus with the Anacreontea* did yeoman service for two generations of classicists, has now partially replaced it with Gerber, *Greek Elegiac Poetry*.

The fragments of epic are published in Davies, *Epicorum Graecorum Fragmenta.*

For lyric the two great collections are Lobel and Page, *Poetarum Lesbiorum Fragmenta* and Page, *Poetae Melici Graeci*, with a selection available in Page, *Lyrica Graeca Selecta*; a new edition of three authors (Alcman, Stesichorus and Ibycus) is available in Davies, *Poetarum Melicorum Graecorum Fragmenta.* The Loeb translation of Edmonds, *Lyra Graeca* has now been replaced by Campbell, *Greek Lyric.*

Poetry: Roman. The standard collection is Morel, Büchner and Blänsdorf, *Fragmenta Poetarum Latinorum*; Courtney, *The Fragmentary Latin Poets* and Hollis, FRP present a good selection with generous English discussion.

11

ORATORY AND RHETORIC

SPEECHES AND SOCIETY

Speeches hold a very limited space in our society. Some speeches have bent or strengthened a nation's will at a critical moment; some have catapulted unknown people into public prominence; some have decided elections, sent people to jail or freed them from it. For all that, speeches today are just one of the forms of persuasion that are brought to bear upon people, and not necessarily the most pervasive or the most persuasive.

Both in democratic Athens and in republican Rome, political and judicial decisions were made by large bodies of men who deliberated and then voted on the basis of their deliberations. In this setting, it was very often a good speech that decided the issue, and public speaking was one of the most valuable of talents. From the fifth century BCE onwards, moreover, there were people who claimed to be able to teach this art, and they made it into the basis of education, an art admired for its own sake long after the councils and assemblies had lost their control of public events. In the democracy and the republic, the greatest of orators were often the leaders of the state; in later times the best of them enjoyed imperial patronage, municipal honors, and a following of young men who gave them star status.[1]

---

[1] "After performing, people would envy him as he went home with a crowd of Greeks from all over . . . . [the young] felt towards him as children do towards a sweet and

Once Demosthenes, Cicero and their like were considered the out-standing figures of the ancient world; today, although the study of rhetoric is less widespread among classicists, the power of persuasion in society has not diminished and, although the media through which persuasion is exercised have changed, the study of ancient rhetoric may still have much to teach moderns.

THE SCIENCE OF RHETORIC

The Sicilians Corax and Tisias in the mid-fifth century BCE are said to have been the first people to have produced rhetorical treatises,[2] and Gorgias of Leontini, a few decades thereafter, is said to have given lessons, for an exorbitant fee, in the art of persuasion. Although we do not have any educational writings by him, his *Encomium of Helen*, intentionally promoting an outrageous thesis, gives an idea of the virtuosity that he offered, and such "sophistical"[3] set pieces continue through the ages. Similar in thrust are the *Tetralogies* of Antiphon, arguing both sides of imaginary court cases to demonstrate both the power and the technique of rhetoric. Isocrates in the fourth century spent most of his career as a very influential teacher of rhetoric, and left in his speeches a good deal of his rhetorical ideas. Gorgias had promoted the study of rhetoric as the way to power, but seems to have limited himself essentially to stylistic and structural matters; Isocrates made the study of rhetoric the basis of a general education. Aristotle wrote a treatise on rhetoric which has survived, and his pupil Theophrastus wrote one that has not. Cicero, Tacitus, the anonymous author of the *Rhetorica ad Herennium* and others added their own ideas; the elder Seneca gave a charming series of excerpts from the rhetorical schools, and the classic statement of oratorical principles is that given by Quintilian.

gentle father who can keep up with them in a Greek dance. I have known some of them to shed tears when reminded of that man, and some of them would imitate his intonations, some his walk, and others his elegant style of clothing." Philostratus, *Vit. Soph.* 587, on Hadrian of Tyre. My thanks to Maurice, *The Teacher in Ancient Rome*, for bringing both the citation and the phenomenon to my attention. Cf. Borg, "Glamorous Intellectuals."

[2] We are not well informed about the nature of these treatises, which may have been simply model speeches for imitation: Usher, *Greek Oratory*, 2.

[3] Whether the term "sophist" was a term of approbation or opprobrium depended upon the tastes of the day; today it is out of fashion.

Throughout antiquity, rhetoric was a hotly debated subject. General-izations were made, and rules were articulated, elaborated, disputed and violated. Each orator or speechwriter had his own style. Cato and Marcus Brutus were known for their straightforward, unadorned style; the speeches of Hortensius, the greatest orator of Rome until Cicero outdid him in the trial of Verres, were much more florid, and these two styles, known as "Attic" and "Asiatic" respectively, were two poles along which connoisseurs of rhetoric would range the great speakers of Rome. What different kinds of oratory there were, what the proper ways for dealing with them were, and what sorts of strategies were appropriate to which situations were questions that exercised some of the best minds of antiquity. In the course of this debate a technical vocabulary grew up, much of which survives today.

Rhetoric, like every profession, had to be taught to beginners, and the elementary teaching of rhetoric was dominated, as school subjects tend to be, by textbooks. These rhetorical handbooks defined and used the terms by which the great students of oratory had described their art. An arrangement of a few of the basic structural terms will give you an idea of the way the subject was taught, though when you start reading the rhetoricians you will discover that the field was much broader and much more contested than this schematic presentation suggests.

The Three Kinds of Speech (Genera, γένη)[4]

- *Deliberative oratory* (deliberativum, συμβουλευτικόν) argues for or against a particular future course of action; under this heading come speeches before public assemblies.
- *Forensic oratory* (iudiciale, δικανικόν) accuses or defends past actions; this includes courtroom oratory.
- *Epideictic oratory* (demonstrativum, ἐπιδεικτικόν) does not necessarily persuade at all, but speaks in praise or in blame of a topic before an audience of whom no decision is demanded; patriotic speeches from Pericles to presidents fall in this category.

---

[4]   Ar. Rhet. 1.3 1358b 7–8, Rhet. Her. 1.2.

The Five Parts of Rhetoric (Partes/Opera/Elementa Artis, μόρια/ἔργα/στοιχεῖα ῥητορικῆς[5])

- Inventio (εὕρεσις) is the discovery of ideas.
- Dispositio (διάθεσις/τάξις/οἰκονομία) is their arrangement in an appropriate order.
- Elocutio (λέξις) is their expression in appropriate words.
- Memoria (μνήμη) is learning the speech by heart.
- Pronuntio or actio (ὑπόκρισις) is delivering it.

It will be obvious to any reader that the speeches we have of the ancient world give us examples only of the first three parts of rhetoric; it will be obvious to anyone who has ever heard a speech that the last two—or at least, since the advent of the TelePrompTer, the last one—can be critical to a speaker's success. Isocrates never gave his speeches before an assembly because he did not feel that he was up to it; Demosthenes, on the other hand, famously practiced his delivery until he was the greatest in Greece.

The Parts of a Speech (Partes Orationis, μέρη λόγου)[6]

- The exordium (προοίμιον) begins the speech; its goal is to win the sympathy of the judge or the audience.
- The narratio (διήγησις) states the facts of the case in such a way as to make the speaker's claims plausible.
- Probatio (πίστις) proves the speaker's case, and
- Refutatio (ἀνασκευή) disproves the opponent's claims; these two are sometimes united under the heading argumentatio.
- The peroratio (ἐπίλογος) refreshes the audience's memory and influences its emotions in such a way as to bring about the desired decision.

---

5 Whether these were properly considered "parts," "tasks" or "elements" was a disputed point among rhetoricians; see Quint. Inst. 3.3.11–15. The parts of oratory are given here as in Rhet. Her. 1.3 and Quint. Inst. 3.3.1.

6 The number of parts of a speech was also a subject of lively controversy; I give Lausberg's categories, but the ancient rhetoricians varied greatly in their enumeration, from Aristotle, who held (Rhet. 3.13 1414a 31–b 18) that only two parts were essential and four were enough, to those who numbered five, six, seven and even more "parts." The question was largely taxonomic; in practice all agreed that different situations would be treated in different ways.

The Status of a Question (Status, στάσις)

Quintilian 3.6.85 defines four relevant *status*, things that must be proven by an accuser:

- *Coniectura* (στοχασμός): Was the thing done?
- *Finitio* (ὅρος): What was done?
- *Qualitas* (ποιότης): Was what was done unjust?
- *Translatio* (μετάληψις): Does the law provide redress, and is the redress being sought in the proper legal form?

Tropes and Figures of Speech

These are so many as to be beyond counting in a general handbook; and these are the terms that have had the longest shelf-life, still bandied about in literature departments around the world. Some of them—metaphor, oxymoron, hyperbole—are everyday terms, while other terms—epanalepsis, paronomasia, paraleipsis—are used by professional rhetoricians and looked up in dictionaries by students.[7] All of them are still used—sometimes unconsciously—by modern speechmakers, advertisers and politicians, and a knowledge of them may offer a certain amount of protection against the manipulation to which our opinions are subjected day in and day out.

The terms mentioned here are the barest skeleton of what the handbooks had to offer. Every possible approach was defined, subdivided and labeled; every possible difficulty was given a name and an approach for dealing with it; famous speeches were analyzed from top to bottom as sources for new insights and as examples for imitation. Rules were given for the best alternation of long and short syllables to use before a pause.[8] The best of modern speechwriters are mere talented autodidacts by

---

[7] A very clear and convenient list is given in Rowe, "Style," 124–50; Lausberg, *Handbook of Literary Rhetoric*, §552–910 is more exhaustive. Various modern stylebooks give the terms most commonly used today; but the easiest place to find them is on the internet, where a number of easily located websites (such as *A Glossary of Rhetorical Terms with Examples*, authored by Ernest Ament but put online by others) give the terms, their definitions, and examples of their use.

[8] For a brief and clear description of these *clausulae* see Nisbet, "The Speeches," 47–9, an excellent description of how the rules of oratory were used, and sometimes broken, by a master.

comparison to those who had been trained for years in the schools of rhetoric.

For all that, the rules given in the handbooks were made to be broken:

> But let nobody demand from me that sort of rules that are handed down by most of the technical writers, as if I were to give some laws decreed by immutable necessity to students of public speaking .... Rhetoric would be an easy and trivial task, if it could be contained in a single short prescription; but most things change because of the case, the time, the opportunity, and necessity .... What if you should instruct a general, whenever he draws up his troops, to put the front in line, to advance the wings on either side, to put the cavalry in front of the wings? And that would perhaps be the most proper method, wherever it was possible; but the nature of the place—if a mountain happens to be there, if a river is in the way, if he is hampered by hills, woods, or some other difficulty; the kind of enemy and the nature of the current struggle make a difference; in one case the battle will be in line, in another in column, in one with auxiliary forces, in another with legions, and sometimes it will even be worthwhile to turn tail and pretend to flee .... For these rules were not passed by vote or by plebiscite, but expediency figured it out, whatever it is. I will not deny that it is usually expedient to write thus—if that were not so, I would not be writing this—but still, if expediency should argue for something else, we will leave the authority of the rest of the teachers and follow it.[9]

RHETORIC IN OTHER GENRES

The science of persuasion was a very seductive one. The ability to convince was useful, and the technique by which a person could be brought to believe the opposite of what had seemed true a few moments ago was quite impressive, and inexorably made its way into other forms of literature as well. Historians from Herodotus onward inserted speeches at critical points in their narrative; Thucydides, in a famously ambiguous passage, claimed to "keep as close as possible to the general meaning of what was really said"; later historians did not even pretend that their speeches were authentic. Among the tragedians, Euripides was notorious for his use of rhetoric, and the arguing of outrageous theses shows up

---

[9]   Quint. Inst. 2.13.1–7.

again when Jason argues that he is acting in Medea's best interests by dumping her for a more politically advantageous wife,[10] or when Macareus in the lost *Aeolus* argued that the brothers and sisters should be married to one another.[11] Nor was Euripides alone; less outrageous but no less sophistic is Antigone's argument, in Sophocles' play, about why the death of a brother is more grievous than that of children or a husband.[12] As for the instances of the more common rhetorical figures—I forgo any attempt to enumerate them, out of consideration for the reader's patience and the world's supply of paper.[13] Plato, who argued in the *Gorgias* and the *Phaedrus* against the entire rhetorical enterprise, was himself a subtle rhetorician. The influence of the rhetorical tradition can be seen in all branches of ancient literature, and, although it is much less direct today than it was in the not-so-distant days when teenagers were schooled by means of mock debates (in many places they still are), it has still not disappeared from western literature, nor is it likely to.

RHETORIC IN EDUCATION

The elementary education of Greeks and Romans was relatively broadly based: music, art and sport were important to the Greeks, and, as long as citizen armies remained, military training was the most important and most universally required education of all. But for those who pursued advanced studies there were essentially two competing types of schools, the rhetorical and the philosophical. The competition, which dated from the time of Plato and Isocrates, remained quite vital throughout antiquity. Hardly any other subject made the claim that both philosophy and rhetoric made, to be a complete education for a man of culture. The important place of rhetoric in education meant that it was both praised and attacked in terms far more extravagant than we should think of using today. What it means practically is that an understanding of rhetoric is likely to be useful to a researcher in many other fields as well: the poet, or general, or philosopher that you are studying was probably educated in

---

[10] Eur. *Med.* 522–75.

[11] This lost speech is briefly described in Book 9, Chapter 11 of the *Ars Rhetorica* attributed to Dionysius of Halicarnassus.

[12] Soph. *Ant.* 905–12. The argument appears in a more natural context in Herodotus 3.119.4–7, and is cited, not inappropriately, by Aristotle *Rhet.* 1417a 32–3, as an example of how to deal with an unbelievable claim.

[13] The figure I am using here is *praeteritio*, Lausberg §882–6.

the forms of rhetoric, and may be using on the public, not excluding you, the lessons learned in school.

The controversy between philosophy and rhetoric over the control of education was never authoritatively determined in antiquity; both philosophical and rhetorical schools flourished until late antiquity. In addition to the schools of philosophy and rhetoric, schools of medicine developed relatively early, and under the Roman Empire schools of law developed as well. All of these enjoyed the patronage of various Roman emperors, though the pagan philosophical schools were finally inter- dicted by Justinian in 529. In the long run both the philosophical and the rhetorical traditions were absorbed, not without modification, into the theological study that came to dominate medieval learning; and it may not be accidental[14] that when the universities of Europe appear in the eleventh and twelfth centuries their dominant faculties are theology, medicine and law.

ORATORY AS A SOURCE FOR LAW AND SOCIETY

Few of the writings that survive from the ancient world give us the actual words that were spoken in a moment of crisis. The speeches we find in the historians are usually their own invention; there was no Congressional Record to transmit the words that were spoken in the Athenian ecclesia, and, although from the time of Julius Caesar there were transcriptions of Senatorial debates at Rome (the *acta senatus*),[15] they were not available to everyone, and are not available to us. Except for what we find in papyri, the speeches of the orators are about as close as we come to an actual recording of words as they were delivered. Many of them were delivered in a court of law, and almost all were delivered in order to persuade; and this makes the remnants of ancient oratory capital sources for the law of Athens and of republican Rome, and for the beliefs and prejudices of the men who formed the judicial and deliberative bodies before whom the speeches were given. They were no doubt edited before publication, and we hardly ever hear the other side; but they were edited for a readership similar to the

---

[14] This, at any rate, was the claim of Irini Triki in a short talk given at a conference in 2002 and thereafter published. Whether the connection she sketched out there is historically tenable will require more detailed documentation.

[15] On the *acta senatus* see Talbert, *The Senate of Imperial Rome*, 308–23; it is not impossible that they were verbatim accounts, but neither can it be proven. On their use by historians, particularly Tacitus, see ibid., 323–34.

body before whom the speeches had been delivered, and they are a mine of information about precisely the sort of things that literature often ignored. Insurance fraud, torture of slaves, electoral bribery, purchasing a call girl and then trying to get rid of her, ugly inheritance fights within a family, the corruption of a provincial governor—these are the sort of things we find in oratory, spelled out in detail for which a historian would not spare the space, and in words that cannot be too far from the actual words spoken at the time. For this reason students of ancient law and students of ancient society must perforce become students of ancient rhetoric.

Even where the orators treat subjects that are common in literature, they do so with an immediacy that poets can only imitate. It is one thing to hear a tragic Orestes speaking of his mother's infidelity, or Homer's Helen playing down the matter; it is quite another to read Lysias 1, where a man defends himself from a charge of murdering the man he claims to have caught in bed with his wife. It is one thing to read the *Seven against Thebes* and its Aeschylean rhetoric about defending the country; it is quite another to read Demosthenes' impassioned and ultimately unsuccessful efforts to get his countrymen to oppose Philip of Macedon while that could still be done. And the greatest of all was Cicero:

> How long will you abuse our patience, Catiline? How long will this insanity of yours laugh at us? How far will your unbridled arrogance go? Doesn't it disturb you that the Palatine has an armed guard at night, that the city is being patrolled, that the people are afraid, that the good people have all gotten together, that the senate has to meet in this heavily fortified place, that all these faces look at you the way they do? Don't you realize that your plot has been exposed?[16]

I do not know how close these words are to the ones that were actually spoken on that fateful night; but even so, the urgency in them reverberates as no later creation could ever do.

MAJOR RESOURCES

The classical study of Attic oratory is Blass, *Die attische Beredsamkeit*: although a milestone of classical scholarship, it will not be the starting-point for a

---

[16] Cic. *Catil.* 1.1.

twenty-first-century scholar. George A. Kennedy wrote the major works in English in his generation, the very readable volumes entitled *The Art of Persuasion in Greece*, *The Art of Rhetoric in the Roman World* and *Greek Rhetoric under Christian Emperors*. His *New History of Classical Rhetoric* is an abbreviated but updated version of these three volumes. A shorter (and hence more useful for the casual student) introduction is Habinek, *Ancient Rhetoric and Oratory*.

Editors of ancient oratory regularly take for granted a wide technical vocabulary with which students are often unfamiliar. Ueding, *Historisches Wörterbuch der Rhetorik* is valuable, though not yet complete as of this writing. Lausberg, *Handbook of Literary Rhetoric*, though not restricted to classical literature, is the most thoroughgoing summary of what the ancient handbooks had to say, though it gives perhaps an overly schematic impression of the subject. Porter, *Handbook of Classical Rhetoric in the Hellenistic Period*—and the Hellenistic period, by Porter's definition, goes as far as 400 CE, so that not only Roman but Christian rhetoric is here as well—is also well organized and an easier read.

The ancient Greek textbooks on oratory were published in nine volumes by Walz, *Rhetores Graeci* and a selection of them by Spengel, *Rhetores Graeci*; for the Latin authors we have Halm, *Rhetores Latini Minores*. There is no more recent complete collection, though Teubner continued Spengel's work with editions by Hugo Rabe and others of many rhetorical theoreticians. Some have recently been translated into English: Malcolm Heath and Cecil Wooten have translated works of Hermogenes, and George Kennedy has translated a number of important texts. The recently begun Patillon, *Corpus rhetoricum* promises a selection, with French translation, that should make a number of important late antique texts more easily available and usable; and Donald Russell's Loeb Quintilian includes not only an exemplary translation but notes that go beyond the usual Loeb minimum and useful end matter, including a 26-page index of rhetorical and grammatical terms.

For the orators themselves there are, shockingly, relatively few comprehensive commentaries. Nobody has done for the speeches of Demosthenes or Cicero what Gomme did for Thucydides, Jebb for Sophocles, or Shackleton Bailey for Cicero's letters. The problem is partly the sheer size of the opus and the breadth of scholarship required to produce a commentary on the various speeches, each of which is firmly embedded in a context that must be understood in detail; there are commentaries on selected speeches, and even comprehensive commentaries on those orators of whose works less is preserved. Particular mention should be made of Wyse, *The Speeches of Isaeus*, whose extremely critical (some say hypercritical) attitude towards his author's claims is a rare and exemplary illustration of how much room there is for doubt about the assertions of an advocate; and the appearance of Whitehead, *Hypereides: The Forensic Speeches* and Todd, *A Commentary on Lysias, Speeches 1–11* suggests that the time is finally coming when Greek oratory, at least, will reclaim its central place in classical scholarship.

12

PHILOSOPHY

THE CONTINUITY OF PHILOSOPHICAL QUESTIONS

Studying science is not the same as studying the history of science, and one may be a competent scientist, and even an extraordinary one, without knowing or caring about the history of the field; conversely, it might be doubted whether a person who studies only the history of science can truly be called a scientist at all. The same can be said, with only slightly less justification, for the study of literature or the study of history itself. The study of philosophy, on the other hand, is hardly separable, if at all, from the study of the history of philosophy. The basic questions of philosophy, being questions basic to life itself, show a remarkable continuity from antiquity to our own day,[1] and not for nothing did Alfred North Whitehead describe the European philosophical tradition as "a series of footnotes to Plato":[2] much has changed since Plato, and in many areas progress has been made, but to a large extent the questions that philosophy deals with are still the questions that Plato raised and others that arose out of the effort to answer Plato's questions. This means, on the one hand, that students of ancient philosophy will find that other philosophers know much more about their field than, for example, professors of modern literature know about ancient literature; on the other hand, it

[1] Frede, "Die wundersame Wandelbarkeit," 12–13.
[2] Whitehead, *Process and Reality*, 63.

will mean that a familiarity with modern philosophy is likely to be much more important for the student of Plato than a familiarity with modern literature is for the student of Homer.

But the continuity of subject matter is more than just an academic requirement: it reflects on what we are doing when we study ancient philosophy. Some study it as a self-contained phenomenon, just as we study ancient history without any particular reference to the two thousand years that have passed since then; but others study ancient philosophy as a forerunner to later philosophy, or even as its essence. For this kind of scholar Descartes and Kant are quite as relevant to Plato as any of his interpreters, for the questions they raised reflect, whether they said so or not, on the attitudes of Plato himself, and require reevaluation of the ancient philosopher in light of the modern.

THE PHILOSOPHICAL APPROACH AND THE HISTORICAL APPROACH

Even when put in the context of the history of the field, there are two basic ways of approaching ancient philosophy. One approach sees the questions as essentially static: when Hobbes discusses the power of the ruler within the state, he is still addressing the same matters that Plato discussed in the *Republic* and the *Laws* and Aristotle in the *Politics*. Hobbes' analysis, no doubt, raises new challenges to what the earlier philosophers had said and casts them in a new light, but the discussion of the ideal state is an ongoing dialogue in which the voice of the older participants is never drowned out by that of the younger ones.

Those who take a more historical approach, on the other hand, see the development of the field as being a one-way progression in which the ancients, important as they are, represent only the embryonic stage of philosophical analysis. Their questions are not necessarily our questions at all: the questions themselves have developed over time, and we have to be careful not to read into the ancients issues that they never addressed and answers that they never gave. This approach does not necessarily make the ancients less interesting, but, where the strictly philosophical approach tends to put them in more immediate dialogue with us, the historical one sees them as the beginning of a road that has gone a long way and that we are still traveling. Those who take these two approaches sometimes appear to inhabit entirely different worlds,[3] but there are scholars who have gone

---

[3] "No useful discussion is possible between the writer who tries to insert the word 'philosopher' into a synchronic perspective, which is still made up of the culture in

a considerable way towards combining them;[4] and even a philosopher for whom the ancient world and its problems are hopelessly remote from our own may still find their methods fruitful where their answers are no longer tenable.[5]

DAUGHTER FIELDS

Although the questions raised by the ancient philosophers tend to be important and difficult, they are not necessarily insoluble. Some areas of investigation have developed particular methodologies and approaches so radically different from that of the philosophers that they are now entirely independent subjects, whose practitioners read the philosophers, if at all, for purely historical interest.[6] Chief among these fields are what we now call "the sciences": physics, zoology, botany, astronomy, meteorology and psychology were all once parts of philosophy. Political science and economics, too, are daughter fields: they were treated by Plato and Aristotle,[7] and, as recently as Thomas Hobbes and Adam Smith, those who wrote on these subjects were considered philosophers.[8] In another direction, metaphysics is still treated by philosophers, but many of its concerns have

which the philosopher lived and breathed, and his colleague who is ready to clarify obscure points purely and simply through rereading other 'philosophers'": Capizzi, *The Cosmic Republic*, 6. One who preferred the strictly philosophical approach might agree, but would phrase the matter differently: "No useful discussion is possible between the writer who tries to insert the word 'philosopher' into a philosophic perspective, which is still made up of the actual questions that the philosopher raised with all their details and implications, and his colleague who is ready to clarify obscure points purely and simply by reference to the time and place in which the philosopher first raised these matters."

4   See, for example, Glock, "Analytic Philosophy and History: A Mismatch?" and Sorabji, "Ideas Leap Barriers."

5   My thanks to Alexander Nehamas for making this point to me.

6   It has been observed that a field of study reaches maturity when it develops its own vocabulary: at this point only those who specialize in the field can participate in its discussions, and it becomes independent. This well-known observation has had the unfortunate effect of encouraging the development and use of jargon throughout academia, a usage that often obscures more than it enlightens.

7   Both Plato and Aristotle devoted major works to politics, but their discussions of economics were generally secondary and often restricted themselves to rather rudimentary observations: see Finley, "Aristotle."

8   Today they are generally referred to as economists or political scientists; but when they cross the bounds of the modern discipline, they may, like Leo Strauss or Isaiah Berlin, be referred to as philosophers even today.

long been appropriated by the western religions, whose philosophical sophistication is much greater than that of the paganism of Greece and Rome.

THE PRACTICAL IMPORTANCE OF PHILOSOPHICAL QUESTIONS

In a number of places Plato stresses the importance of philosophical investigation for every human being, going so far as the famous statement that the unexamined life is not worth living.[9] Few would make such claims for literature or art; probably nobody would make them for epigraphy or papyrology. Because of the importance of the issues involved, many people, not all of them scholars, look to philosophy for guidance in living their lives. At the very least in ethics, in politics and in logic, ancient philosophy still offers us an approach that seems likely to help us deal with our own lives, and this is the motivation of many people for entering the field in the first place. Others are attracted by the intrinsic interest of philosophical questions, regardless of any potential real-world benefits. Whatever the initial impulse, however, the practice of scholarship tends, in this field as in others, to focus one's approach on understanding for its own sake, and questions of epistemology and metaphysics are no less significant to the philosopher than questions of ethics and politics.

THE SPECIALIZED LANGUAGE OF PHILOSOPHY

Every subfield has its own specialized terms: an outsider to the study of literature may be puzzled by such terms as *ecphrasis*, *deconstruction* or *intentional fallacy* or misled by the use of the words *discourse* and *engender*, and the same is true for such terms of textual criticism as *autopsy* or *stemma*. In philosophy, the technical language extends to the major issues of the subject itself. Entire areas of philosophic investigation have names like *ontology* and *epistemology* that may be meaningless to outsiders. Even words that we use in everyday discourse are likely to have a different meaning in philosophy. A person who thinks that there exists a quality of elephantness that is independent of the elephants in the zoo and in the savannah may be called a realist, which is certainly not the title that the untutored would use.

---

[9]   Plat. *Ap.* 38a.

Sometimes the very antiquity of the texts consulted can result in misunderstanding: when John Locke or David Hume speak of an argument as *specious* they mean that it is attractive, which was what *specious* meant in seventeenth- and eighteenth-century English; there is no implication, as there would be today, that the argument is false or misleading. Outsiders reading philosophical works should be wary of the language. If what is being said doesn't seem to make sense, check the meanings of the words in a philosophical dictionary to make sure the author is using them in the way you think.

THE DECEPTIVE SIMPLICITY OF PHILOSOPHICAL QUESTIONS

Many of the subjects of ancient philosophy can be expressed in questions of stunning simplicity. Who are we? What are we? Where did we come from? What should we do? What is good? What is beautiful? What do we know? How do we know it? The answers to these questions may be subtle and abstruse, but it is not clear that they must be so. They are, in fact, questions so simply phrased that one needs no background at all to reflect on them. Socrates regularly approached them by taking examples from everyday life to illustrate them—an approach that others sometimes found infuriating.[10]

The simplicity of philosophical questions means that philosophers, like theoretical scientists, spend a good deal of time with their feet on the desk asking themselves theoretical questions. Who am I? Well, who is anybody? What am I looking for when I ask that question? Will my name suffice? My family? My job description? What is the difference between asking who I am and asking what I am? What sort of things cause me to say "That's not for me" or even "That's not me"? Once the initial question has been raised and one takes time to think about it, a host of other questions suggest themselves. Philosophers thrive on asking this kind of question and trying to find an approach that will help answer it. A person who begins to read philosophy should be ready to put the book down regularly—for some books, almost at every sentence—and ask "What exactly is being said here? What would offer (if the author doesn't) an example of it? Does it correspond to what I know? Does it correspond to the author's other assertions?" These questions are helpful in any field of research; in philosophy, they are the subject matter itself.

[10] See, for example, Plat. *Gorg.* 490c–491a.

THE SCHOOLS OF ANCIENT PHILOSOPHY

The major philosophers of Greece organized schools, and, although later philosophers might be influenced by more than one stream of thought, they generally belonged to one school or another much more explicitly than modern philosophers do. The short descriptions that follow should not in any way be taken to be even a thumbnail account of the various schools and their doctrines; for that there is no choice but to read a philosophical account, short or long according to your needs. The descriptions that I offer are meant only to distinguish the various schools sufficiently to help the outsider keep clear the names of the various groups and enough information to distinguish them from one another.

Those before Socrates who expressed opinions on what we now think of as philosophical questions are generally referred to as the Presocratics, a catchall term that includes people as various as Thales, who was the first Greek to predict correctly a solar eclipse; the mystic Pythagoras, famous today for his theorem about the square of the hypotenuse but equally famous in antiquity for the doctrine of the transmigration of souls; Heraclitus, for whom fire was the primordial element and everything was in a constant state of flux; Parmenides, of the Eleatic school, who wrote in hexameters and for whom, on the contrary, "the one" permeated the universe, and everything that ever had been still was and always would be, with change an illusion; Empedocles, who conceived the world as consisting of four elements, a compromise among Thales' primordial water, Anaximenes' air and Heraclitus' fire; Anaxagoras, who held that all matter was infinitely divisible, and contained some of each element; and Leucippus and Democritus, who held that it was all a matter of atoms moving in space. Besides these "natural" thinkers we also find Gorgias, the teacher of rhetoric who is said to have held that nothing exists and that, if it did, we could not know it and that, if we did know it, we could not speak about it; and Protagoras, who held that truth was a subjective matter, since man was the measure of all things. All of these would have been called sophoi; the term sophistai, which was also used and was once complimentary,[11] has come down to us through Plato as a pejorative term used of people who sell a pretense of knowledge for money.[12] Later generations and modern scholars often reserve that term for the teachers

---

[11]   Diog. Laert. 1.12.

[12]   This is an egregious but not exaggerated simplification of the conclusion reached in Plato's Sophist.

of rhetoric, and in the Roman Empire for the rhetoricians themselves, rather than the natural philosophers.

Socrates himself left no writings and founded no school,[13] but his effect on his contemporaries was profound, and almost all philosophy afterwards descended in some respect from his students. His students represented him as an inquisitive, brave and logical person who considered questions of right conduct the most important questions that a person could ask; his detractors portrayed him as a head-in-the-clouds purveyor of abstruse, misleading and subversive ideas on every topic imaginable. Numerous thinkers, Xenophon among them, were known as Socratics, but it was not the name of Socrates that would attach itself to a long-lived school of philosophy.

The student who defines the Socratic school for us is Plato, whose voluminous writings, in the form of dialogues in which Socrates is generally the main character, formed the basis on which later discussion took place. Plato did found a school in the grove of Academe, and his school, the Academy, lasted for some three hundred years until it dispersed in the Mithridatic wars.[14] It was revived in about 410 CE and continued until 529, when it was finally dissolved by Justinian.

The dialogue form used by Plato is by its nature ambiguous: Plato never says anything in his own name in the dialogues (in the *Phaedo*, his description of Socrates' death in which he discusses the immortality of the soul, he even adds the disclaimer, "Plato, I believe, was ill"[15]), and the reader must judge which opinion expressed, if any, is Plato's own. In some of the dialogues there can be little doubt; in others it is not clear, and in many it seems that no conclusion at all is reached. The number of topics discussed in the dialogues and the opinions expressed would fill an encyclopedia, though to my knowledge an *Encyclopedia Platonica* has still to be written; the most famous of all is the doctrine of the forms (or ideas, though Plato does not mean by the Greek word ἰδέα what we mean by an idea, for his ideas are independent of the human mind that conceives them), according to which the physical world that we perceive through

---

[13] The effort to identify Socrates' ideas, as opposed to those of his students (particularly Plato), occupied students of ancient philosophy for generations. In the twentieth century scholars appeared finally to have despaired of the effort, until Vlastos, *Socrates, Ironist and Moral Philosopher* and *Socratic Studies* opened the question all over again.

[14] John Glucker's discussion in *Antiochus and the Late Academy* has been generally accepted as disproving the effort of Zumpt, *Ueber den Bestand der philosophischen Schulen* to trace an unbroken list of scholiarchs from Plato until the time of Justinian.

[15] Pl. *Phaedo* 59b.

our senses is only a vague and inaccurate reflection of the real world, which consists of forms that we cannot perceive through our senses but can appreciate through philosophy. Other theories have attached themselves to his name, particularly the philosophical communism of the *Republic* and the exalted love of the *Symposium*, but in fact every one of his dialogues is a gushing spring of original thought to which later philosophers returned again and again.

Aristotle, Plato's most eminent student, taught in the Lyceum, though buildings were provided for the school only under the leadership of his student Theophrastus; the covered walk (περίπατος) of those buildings apparently gave the philosophers of the school the name peripatetics. Although Aristotle rejected the theory of the forms, he sought no less than Plato basic principles that governed the sensible world, and developed rules of logical argumentation on which, along with minute observation of nature and of polities, a shrewd common sense and a brilliant ability for generalization, he based a philosophy that ranged over biology, physics, metaphysics, ethics, rhetoric, politics and much more, not all of which has been preserved.

Diogenes, whose insistence on fulfilling his natural wants with no shame in the simplest and easiest way possible earned him the nickname of "the dog" (ὁ κύων), never founded a school, but those who imitated his thoughts and actions were known as *cynics*, and throughout antiquity they remained a significant group of oddballs, their claim to be considered philosophers not undisputed.

Epicurus' greatest contribution, if we are to judge from the *De rerum natura* of his Roman follower Lucretius, was the denial of the immortality of the soul, a denial based on a materialism that explained the entire universe in terms of the interplay of atoms. Epicurus claimed that precisely this denial freed a person from fear of death, since there was no reason to fear what would cause us no suffering when it arrived. Freed from death, the philosophically enlightened soul should pursue its own pleasure, which Epicurus conceived as *ataraxia*, a state of calm contemplation. His followers continued after his death to live in his house and garden, forming a semi-monastic group known as *Epicureans*; their philosophy was influential far beyond the limits of their own headquarters.

Zeno of Citium held that destructive emotions were the result of error, and that a proper understanding would purge a person of all such emotions; what a person should follow were the virtues of wisdom, courage, justice and prudence. Zeno taught in the "multicolored colonnade" (ποικίλη στόα) in Athens; his school was known as "the stoa," and his followers as *stoics*. The school continued in existence for centuries; its last great adherent was the emperor Marcus Aurelius, who died in 180 CE. Both Epicureans and stoics held theories about the physical universe that explained and reinforced their ethical beliefs.

The later heads of the Academy (in what is now called the New Academy) continued to revere Plato, but they developed his philosophy—apparently in reaction to stoicism—so far in the direction of Skepticism that they eventually brought about a counterrevolution. Antiochus of Ascalon, who died in 68 BCE, attempted to revive the actual opinions (*dogmata*) of Plato rather than just the uncertainties (*aporemata*); the philosophers who followed in this direction are referred to as *middle Platonists*. Along with the written dialogues, the middle Platonists relied on "unwritten doctrines," handed down as part of the tradition of the Academy, that appear to have had a strong Pythagorean element. From the time of Plotinus, the third-century CE Platonist who was one of the most influential philosophers of all time, begins a period that moderns call *Neoplatonism*. The Neoplatonists no less than their predecessors considered themselves to be followers of Plato, but their emphasis on a unifying metaphysics through which a person could actually become one with the transcendent god makes Neoplatonism much more like a religion than the earlier forms—and, as such, a serious competitor with Christianity. Although organized Christianity won the battle against organized Neoplatonism, the ideas of the Neoplatonists had considerable influence on the church fathers, particularly through the works of Augustine.

The Skepticism of the New Academy held that truth was unknowable; another branch of Skepticism called *Pyrrhonism* (after Pyrrho of Elis, who flourished in the late fourth and early third centuries BCE) was based rather on the suspension of judgment, without asserting that correct knowledge was unattainable.[16] The extreme nature of ancient Skepticism made it unpalatable to most philosophers, but the questions it raised were not then, and are not now, easily disposed of.

The voluminous works of Aristotle were elucidated with commentaries both in Greek and in Latin, and later in Arabic; the commentators themselves are some of the most important names in the philosophic tradition, including Alexander of Aphrodisias, John Philoponus, Simplicius and later Avicenna (Ibn Sina) and Averroes (Ibn Rushd). Not all of the commentators

---

16 This, at any rate, is the description of Sextus Empiricus, PH 1.1–3; the logical problems with both positions (if correct knowledge is unattainable, how can you know that? And if it is not, what requires you to suspend judgment?) make the actual distinction less clear to our eyes, which is perhaps an appropriate way for us to approach ancient Skepticism.

were themselves Aristotelians; the later Greek commentators on Aristotle were Platonists, and some have argued—indeed, many in antiquity argued—that the differences between Aristotelians and Platonists were much less than is usually claimed.[17] A more important point to be made is that commentaries became increasingly the form in which philosophic debate was carried on, so that the commentators themselves are philosophers in their own right, not simply expounders of the books on which they commented.

Although the major schools (the Pythagoreans, the Academy, the Lyceum, the "garden" of the Epicureans, and the stoa) often had an organizational existence and generally a real intellectual coherence, none of them existed in a vacuum, and there was a significant amount of interchange and influence among them. Among the Romans this mutual influence became more pronounced: in this as in their art and architecture the Romans treated the Greeks eclectically, taking what seemed appropriate without feeling required to adhere entirely to one school or another. The epic poet Lucretius was an Epicurean, and his poem De rerum natura is the main source we have for Epicurean philosophy; Cato the Younger was famous as a stoic, as was Seneca the Younger, whose writings, along with those of Cicero, formed the basis for western ethical philosophy for more than a millennium.

In the republican period and the principate the Epicureans and the Stoics were the most influential philosophical schools, but by the third century Neoplatonism and other movements had gained considerable importance. To the Christians Epicureanism was anathema, and, when Christian intellectuals came, as they eventually had to, to deal with the challenge of philosophy on an intellectual plane, it was the philosophy of Plato, which they fought so vigorously, that was nevertheless the most intellectually congenial to them. Aristotle, however, whose logical demonstrations were very hard to deny, was a force that first swept across the philosophical thinking of the Muslim philosophers and afterwards, from the twelfth century on, spread to Christendom; and since then Platonism and Aristotelianism have been the two most influential of the ancient philosophical schools.

---

[17] Notably Gerson, *Aristotle and Other Platonists*; see also Karamanolis, *Plato and Aristotle*, Sorabji, "The Transformation" and Tuominen, *The Ancient Commentators*.

THE MAJOR SUBJECTS

No one can list all the subjects of philosophy, for of course anything that can be thought can be discussed in a philosophical way,[18] and merely listing the subjects of the works of Plato and Aristotle would be a large task and not a very fruitful one, since not every matter they treated has developed into a significant branch of philosophy. It may, however, be helpful to a non-philosopher to mention some of the branches and what they deal with. I exclude the "daughter branches" such as physics, psychology and political science not because they are any less important in the study of ancient philosophy, but because they are well known today even outside of philosophical circles.

- *Logic*: How can anything be proven? How can we distinguish the true from the false? Can everything that is true be proven? Can anything? For Aristotle this is not really a branch of philosophy, but an essential tool without which philosophy cannot really be pursued.
- *Epistemology*: What do we know? How do we know it? What does it mean to know something?
- *Metaphysics*: What are the causes of things? What are the principles according to which the world exists? What is the substance, or what are the substances, of which the universe is composed? Perhaps the most significant part of metaphysics is
- *Ontology*: What exists? Are the things we see real, or is there another reality lurking behind them? Are the concepts in our minds real?
- *Aesthetics*: What is beauty? How do we perceive it, how do we recognize it, and how does it affect us?
- *Ethics*: What should a person do in life, and what should a person want to do? What is justice? What is happiness? What contributes to justice and to happiness? How can we establish which course of behavior is the better one? Better for whom?[19]
- *Philosophy of science, of history, of religion, etc.*: All of the "daughter fields," and many others that did not arise from philosophy, have evolved their own ways of determining the truth, but in doing so they necessarily make

---

[18] At least, that has been the traditional view and practice, though Wittgenstein, *Tractatus* argued famously that it was neither tenable nor meaningful.

[19] I speak of ethics as if it were a subject in itself, and to many philosophers it is; but it is worth noting that, to Aristotle, ethics is a part of politics, which includes ethics (governance of the self), economics (governance of the *oikos*) and politics (governance of the city).

many presumptions, many of them unstated or even unrealized. What are we trying to find when we pursue these different fields? What is religious truth, and how would we recognize it? What are we describing when we write about history, and what, if anything, can we learn from it? What has science proven about the world, and what unspoken presumptions does it make in doing so? A special position in the "philosophy of such-and-such" category belongs to the *philosophy of language*, because it is through language itself that philosophy is conducted, so that understanding what language means, and how it means it, underlies the entire philosophical enterprise. A good deal of English and American philosophy in the twentieth century centered around linguistic questions, but in fact problems of what words mean and how they mean them go back as far as the Presocratics.

MAJOR RESOURCES

For the vocabulary of ancient philosophy one can consult Peters, *Greek Philosophical Terms*; Urmson, *The Greek Philosophical Vocabulary* is a list of terms with a collection of illustrative passages from the philosophers. These, however, are to philosophy mere specialized lexica; for philosophy in general the most comprehensive work is Audi, *The Cambridge Dictionary of Philosophy*, whose entries give not only a definition but a concise introduction to whatever is being sought. Shorter but quite respectable is Blackburn, *The Oxford Dictionary of Philosophy*. Mautner, *A Dictionary of Philosophy* is organized differently, offering many more entries but restricting itself to brief but clear definitions of the term in question. Audi is the work of choice for an outsider trying to get a basic orientation; Mautner is appropriate for checking a term for which one does not need more than the straightforward meaning. An earlier effort, Runes, *Dictionary of Philosophy*, is available on the internet, but it is old and was never authoritative.

For longer discussions of general philosophy there is now the ten-volume Craig, *Routledge Encyclopedia of Philosophy*; Edwards, *The Encyclopedia of Philosophy* is respectable but belongs, both in its approach and in what it covers, to an earlier generation. For those who feel more comfortable with a single volume, there is Honderich, *The Oxford Companion to Philosophy*, which despite its modest name admits that its "brave, large aim . . . has been to bring philosophy together between two covers better than ever before."[20]

---

[20] Honderich, ed., *The Oxford Companion to Philosophy*, vii.

Very different, despite the similarity of name, is Bunnin and Tsui-James, *The Blackwell Companion to Philosophy*, a collection of twenty-one sections each offering a full discussion of one area of philosophy and another twenty-one sections each dealing with a period in the history of philosophy. Zalta, *Stanford Encyclopedia of Philosophy* is an internet project that has no print edition.

There is no comparable encyclopedia of ancient philosophy. Zeyl, *Encyclopedia of Classical Philosophy* is a collection of brief articles, mostly about individual philosophers. For a general and thorough background there are the Cambridge Histories: Rowe and Schofield, *The Cambridge History of Greek and Roman Political Thought* and the much older Armstrong, *The Cambridge History of Later Greek and Early Medieval Philosophy*; the broader field is covered no less thoroughly by Flashar, *Philosophie der Antike*. Shorter going are the Cambridge Companions: Long, *The Cambridge Companion to Early Greek Philosophy* and Sedley, *The Cambridge Companion to Greek and Roman Philosophy*. The series *Cambridge Companions to Philosophy* also offers "companions" to many individual philosophers, specialties and periods.

In addition to these general works there are dictionaries and encyclopedias of many of the subfields of philosophy; I omit their mention on the presumption that, once one is deeply enough involved in philosophical questions to be interested in such works as Kelly, *Encyclopedia of Aesthetics*, Becker and Becker, *Encyclopedia of Ethics*, or Embree et al., *Encyclopedia of Phenomenology*, one is no mere classicist, in need of this beginner's handbook, but a philosopher.

Brief summaries of new works in some of the main branches of ancient philosophy (Presocratics, Plato, Aristotle and Neoplatonism) are offered as a regular feature of the journal *Phronesis*; like the Subject Reviews of *Greece and Rome*,[21] these offer an easy way for a non-specialist to keep abreast of the field.

Philosophic Fragments and Commentaries

Diels and Kranz, *Die Fragmente der Vorsokratiker* (DK) has been since its publication the basis of all discussion of Presocratic philosophy. It includes a German translation; an English translation is Freeman, *Ancilla*, but the introduction of choice is Kirk and Raven, *The Presocratic Philosophers*, which combines a historical account with a generous selection of fragments with commentary. Fragments of the peripatetic philosophers are collected in

---

[21] Above, p. 38.

Wehrli, *Die Schule des Aristoteles*, with two *Supplementbände*; further new texts and updates of the old ones are appearing, with translation and discussion, in the Theophrastus project of William Fortenbaugh.[22] For Stoics, Epicureans and Skeptics the selection of Long and Sedley, *The Hellenistic Philosophers* is well organized and user-friendly; the older complete editions of fragments can be found in their bibliography.

Many of the numerous commentators on Aristotle were edited in the series *Commentaria in Aristotelem Graeca* and have been being made available in English by the Ancient Commentators on Aristotle project under the auspices of Richard Sorabji at King's College London, which has by now produced more than seventy volumes. Sorabji's user-friendly *Philosophy of the Commentators* makes a good selection of their ideas available by subject.

---

[22] Fortenbaugh et al., eds., *Theophrastus of Eresus*; Fortenbaugh and Schütrumpf, eds., *Demetrius of Phalerum*; id., eds., *Dicaearchus of Messana*; Fortenbaugh and White, eds., *Aristo of Ceos*; id., eds., *Lyco of Troas and Hieronymus of Rhodes*; Schütrumpf, ed., *Heraclides of Pontus*.

13

HISTORY

THE SPECIAL PLACE OF HISTORY IN CLASSICAL STUDIES

The most salient fact about the world of the ancient Greeks and Romans is that it no longer exists. However deeply our lives may be touched by the classical heritage, we can never speak to an ancient Greek or Roman, never visit them in their homes, never walk through their streets as they knew them. They are situated in the past, and our encounter with them is inescapably a historical one. It follows that, whatever particular aspect of their civilization we may choose to investigate, our investigation will always have to be historically informed. It is possible, though perhaps inadvisable, to discuss ancient history with only slight reference to ancient poetry, historical linguistics or ancient art; but it is hardly possible to discuss any of those subjects intelligently without at least a basic grounding in the history of the Greeks and the Romans.[1]

WHAT IS HISTORY?

Many books have been written on this question, and outsiders may find it peculiar that a discipline can thrive for centuries as its practitioners

---

[1] For this very reason, I take it for granted that the reader has taken at least a survey course or two in ancient history, and have not included basic textbooks in the list of major resources.

continue to ponder what exactly it may be. Like many other professionals, most historians engage in their profession without having worked out a consistent theoretical basis to explain what they are doing, and it is surely not the job of a handbook to develop and argue a theory of history. I think, however, that it will be useful to state some of the issues that determine what we think of as history.

It certainly is not the study of everything that happened in the past; there are now a few billion people in the world, and simply to establish what each of them had done in a given hour would be far beyond the abilities of all the world's historians working together—and of interest to nobody. The term *history*, when it was first used for our subject, seems to have meant simply "knowledge" or "results of research"; it is cognate with English *wisdom*, and its etymology does not even tell us that history has anything to do with the past. It was Herodotus who first called his work *historiē*, but there are those today who have reservations about calling Herodotus' work history at all; surely Book II reads more like what we should call geography or anthropology than history. We speak today of political history, of military history, of intellectual history, of social history, of economic history; and although none of these can be pursued in entire isolation from the others, you will know better where to look for information if you have defined for yourself what aspects of the past interest you.

Whichever form of history we are pursuing, however, we always do so on the presumption that at some level there is a sequence of cause and effect that we can perceive; otherwise history would be, as Elbert Hubbard described life, just one damned thing after another. A distinction popular among teachers of literature runs as follows: "'The king died and then the queen died' is history; 'The king died and then the queen died of grief' is a story." Both sides of this antithesis identify only the beginnings. "The king died and then the queen died of grief" may indeed be the point from which a storyteller begins, but it will take a good deal of elaboration to turn it into a story that will be worth telling or hearing; similarly "The king died and then the queen died" may state two historical facts, but it will not be history worth writing or reading until we have asked a number of questions, the first of which will surely be: was there any connection between these two deaths? The connection may be that one caused the other, as in the example above, or that they had the same cause (after the rebels had executed the king, they sought out the queen and killed her, too[2]) or the results may have been particularly catastrophic because of the

---

[2]   This is the story of the deaths of Yoram and his mother Jezebel, II Kings 9.

two deaths (the king died and then the queen died, leaving a two-year-old orphan on the throne[3]). History is never simply a list of dates and events to be memorized.

History, then, always involves a *selection* of the information and a *structuring* of the information; moreover, to at least some degree the principles by which the information is to be selected and structured are decided on by the historian, consciously or unconsciously, before the actual collection of information takes place: the very term "research" implies that we know more or less what we are looking for.[4] This being the case, it will take a good deal of open-mindedness to avoid the danger of seeing in history only what we want to see in it, filtering out or explaining away the things that do not fit our preconceptions. Not all historians avoid this pitfall; some, indeed, embrace it, and write explicitly polemical histories designed to advance a social, political or national cause that they consider more important than mere knowledge for knowledge's sake. The short-term fate of this kind of history will depend upon the success or failure of the cause it is designed to support; in the long run, however, when the passion of the present has abated, polemical history tends to be forgotten.

THE SUBJECTS OF HISTORY

Political History

The great historians of antiquity generally wrote about politics and war, and so have most of their successors. At certain periods, history consisted of nothing but the chronicles of kings and their campaigns, and, although history today takes a much wider view, the centrality of politics and wars was not unreasonable: these are the two things that are of interest to everybody, since hardly anybody can avoid being affected by them, and they are things that have a clear line of causation that offers a good "story-line": Julius Caesar's political ambitions had a good deal to do with his military accomplishments, and these in turn played a major part in

---

3   This was the story of the death of Zaitian, emperor of China, on the fourteenth of November, 1908, and the death of his aunt Cixi, the dowager empress, the following day, leaving Puyi, Zaitian's nephew, on the throne. Not surprisingly, Puyi was overthrown by a republican revolution when he reached the age of five.

4   In the words of Bachelard that Hayden White used as the epigraph for *Metahistory*, "One can only study what one has first dreamed about."

making him dictator of Rome, a fact that brought about his assassination, which in turn provided the opportunity for his eighteen-year-old grandnephew to become, in the fullness of time, Augustus Caesar—the story goes on and on, and we know and can follow the major characters and their deeds. Literary history or social history may have causal relations that are harder to determine, and that may constantly be being impinged upon by kings and by their wars. For this reason, political history continues to provide the background for all others: we say that Vergil wrote in the Augustan era and that Aristophanes' early plays appeared during the Peloponnesian War, but we do not often say that Augustus reigned at the time of Vergil or that the Peloponnesian War ended around the middle of Aristophanes' career.

Institutional History

Even a political historian is not likely today to treat universal history as simply "the History of Great Men,"[5] producing the kind of naive chronicle that entertained the Middle Ages. As early as the seventeenth century, when Hobbes translated Thucydides and wrote the *Leviathan*, English-speaking scholars have seen their national political institutions as man-made and changeable, the subject of legitimate dispute; the French revolution in the eighteenth century, German and Italian unification in the nineteenth, and the Russian revolution in the twentieth testify to the acceptance of this attitude throughout Europe, turning a good deal of interest to *institutional history*: in the first place political institutions (the Athenian democracy, the Roman republic, the Catholic church), but also legal ones (inheritance law and *patria potestas*), social ones (*proxenia* and *clientela*), and whatever other institutionalized forms human beings in the ancient world may have had through which their relationships with each other and with the community at large were maintained.

National or Ethnic History and Regional History

The national history of the Romans is generally treated as being more or less coextensive with their political history: those who study Roman

---

[5]   The phrase is that of Carlyle, *On Heroes, Hero-Worship, the Heroic in History*, 3. The capitals are Carlyle's.

history of the fourth century BCE study the city of Rome and its central Italian neighbors, whereas those who study Roman history of the fourth century CE study an area that stretches from Hadrian's wall to the Euphrates—and indeed, by that time, all free people in that area were Roman citizens. For Greece the situation is murkier. Throughout the classical period no political structure encompassed all those people who considered themselves Greek; in the Hellenistic and Roman periods most Greeks belonged to states that were Greek either in a qualified sense or not at all. Since Greeks did (and do) consider themselves a single nation despite political boundaries, it is quite reasonable to write a history of the Greeks; but this history should properly include things that happened in Marseilles, Cyrene and Bactria, while excluding, or at least relegating to the margins, the Minoans of Crete and the indigenous population of Egypt. A history of a nomadic or a migratory people will have to move from place to place, as modern histories of Americans begin in Europe. Alternatively, one can write the history of a region, including various peoples as they move in and out: by this measure, a modern history of America should—and some do—include the Mayas, the Incas and the Natchez, and treat Europe as something of a footnote.[6] In either case, a historian should be aware both of the ethnic situation and of the geographic one: it is easy to fall into the trap of taking Athens for Greece, or, for that matter, the city of Rome for the entire Roman people.

Defining the group or the region that we are studying is a necessary preliminary to research; but the groups or regions excluded do not thereby vanish from the historical record. A history of Mycenaean Greece will not be a history of the Hittites and the Egyptians, nor will a history of the Roman Empire be a history of the Germans and the Parthians; but neither can entirely ignore the people who were in contact with, and often vitally important to, the people at the center of our interest. Two hundred years ago relatively little was known about ancient peoples other than the Greeks, the Romans and the Jews; today the writings of the Egyptians, the Babylonians, the Hittites and the Persians are available to us, and the early history of the Celts, the Germans and the Scythians no longer need be written exclusively from Greek and Latin sources. Few classicists

---

[6]   Either approach can be carried to extremes. The French in Indochina were probably overdoing the sense of national continuity when they taught Vietnamese children to read French from a book entitled *Nos ancêtres les gaulois*; the Lithuanians were probably stretching the geographical claim when they insisted on keeping the Hebrew books of Lithuania's exterminated Jews on the grounds that they were Lithuania's national heritage.

can read Hittite or are well acquainted with German or Celtic archaeology; those few who are will always be an invaluable source of information and perspective to those who are not, and any of us can make the
effort of acquainting ourselves with scholars who study the peoples,
places and times that are outside of our purview but not irrelevant to it.

Military History

Much of history has been decided by wars and battles. It is hardly possible
to imagine what history would have been had Alexander the Great or
Julius Caesar—or, for that matter, Muhammad—been defeated and killed
in his first battle. But the events and people that fill political histories are
not the only, and often not even the decisive, factors that determine
success or failure in battle. Since the military success of the Greeks and the
Romans is not a negligible factor in their continuing interest for us, the
story of how they achieved that success continues to hold fascination, and
even important lessons, for the modern day. Since many of the basic
principles of warfare remain the same—the advantage of high ground,
tactics of encirclement, and the element of surprise, to mention just a
few—ancient battles continue to be taught in modern war colleges, when
so many other aspects of the ancient world have ceased to interest the
more practical-minded of our contemporaries.[7] The Roman army, which
ruled over millions of square miles of territory for more than half a
millennium, which subdued and guarded provinces and which made and
unmade emperors, is a particularly fruitful area of research, the more so
because it has left so broad an imprint in the archaeological and
epigraphical record. Military history is sometimes the province of former
military officers; those who have never seen battle run the danger of
glaring errors.

---

[7] "Ike . . . was . . . more than usually well-read in the triumphs, glories, and tragedies
of military history. As a boy he had combed through his mother's books for stories
of Hannibal, Caesar, Pericles, Themistocles, Miltiades, and Leonidas . . . imbibed,
despite his mother's pacifism, the heady, inspiring accounts of bloody battles, noble
sacrifice, and heroism—Hannibal crossing the Alps. . . . 'The battles of Marathon,
Zama, Salamis, and Cannae,' Ike would later write, 'became as familiar to me as the
games (and battles) I enjoyed with my brothers and friends in the school yard.'"
Korda, Ike, 128–9.

Intellectual History

Everyone has heard about the power of an idea whose time has come; but how does the time come for an idea? Why did thinkers continue to be fascinated by Socrates' ideas for almost a millennium after the Athenian democracy executed him? How did the knowledge of mathematics progress from Pythagoras to Archimedes, or the knowledge of medicine from the mythical Chiron to Galen—and why did it progress no further? Why was monotheism, so repugnant to the Romans of the first century CE, acceptable and even attractive to them three hundred years later? Ideas have a history no less than states, and much has been written on the history of philosophy, the history of rhetoric or, for that matter, the history of metallurgy or accounting. The less thoughtful investigations of this genre, as in every historical genre, tend merely to tell one thing after another, with the presumption that each new development is an improvement upon its predecessors, and each age wiser than its parents'; the more thoughtful ones interest themselves in questions of relationship of each intellectual development to its own age and those that preceded it.

Literary History

Literary history is a form of intellectual history. Literature undoubtedly exhibits development from one thing into another: if Homer had never written the Iliad and the Odyssey, Vergil would never have imagined writing the Aeneid. More strikingly, Dante, whose epic was so different from either, considered Vergil his teacher. But just as in other forms of history, the interesting questions are deeper and broader than simple matters of imitation and development: what did Vergil do with the Iliad and the Odyssey? How does Vergil's Aeneas differ from Homer's heroes? What changes in the way we read Homer after reading Vergil? The need for literary history, as for intellectual history in general, becomes clear to almost anyone who tries to describe a literary form for a modern audience: it is very hard to understand where we are now without describing the path by which we got here.

Social and Economic History

Most of the forms of history that we have so far described concern themselves with a very restricted class of people: kings, lawmakers, generals, philosophers, poets. The vast majority of human beings, of course, were none of these; and when ordinary people say that a person or an action will "go down in history," they admit that history is something in which they themselves do not figure. Not every historian has been willing to accept this restriction of the subject to a small cadre of exceptional individuals. Social history attempts to observe and analyze those aspects of society that affect larger groups of people: How do they interact? Do they all marry and, if so, whom? How do they educate their children? Sometimes we read a work of ancient literature and feel as if its author is just like us; then we see the Athenian men parading around with *phalloi* or a Roman father calling a family *consilium* to judge his son for treason and feel ourselves in very alien territory. Here, too, a historical approach can illuminate both how the ancients lived and how that life was or was not different from our own.

The question of how the people make their living ("microeconomics") and how the society as a whole provides itself with necessities and luxuries ("macroeconomics") is an aspect of social history that has developed over the last two and a half centuries into an independent discipline. Since the usual sorts of information on which economic calculations can be based are either totally lacking or extremely scarce for the ancient world, ancient economic history is a very different field from economic history as a whole; textbooks on economic history often begin with medieval or even early modern Europe, ignoring the ancient world entirely. But precisely for that reason, economic historians of the ancient world often find themselves with a unique ability to judge the extent to which the laws of modern economics, laws which have been deduced from observation of modern economies, are valuable tools for understanding an economy that never had any connection with the economy of modern Europe and America.

Many, however, put social and economic history much closer to the center of what all historians are studying. Marx and Engels famously maintained that "the history of all hitherto existing society is the history of class struggles,"[8] and Marxists to this day consider the concept of class struggle to be "much the most important and the most fruitful [tool] for actual use in understanding and explaining particular historical events."[9] Even those who are not Marxists often find that class—a concept of which

---

[8] *The Communist Manifesto*; I quote it from Marx and Engels, *Collected Works*, VI 484.
[9] de Ste. Croix, *The Class Struggle*, 3.

both Greeks and Romans were acutely aware[10]—was an important and often a driving factor behind the main developments of ancient history. Debate still rages between those who consider economic class to be the essential factor and those who prefer to see, as our sources tend to, "orders" or "statuses" of a more social and legal nature as the essential matters to which we should pay attention; but there is little doubt that beneath the political and military history there is also a social and economic story that, while it may not have determined everything the leaders did, had quite a bit to do with the possibilities among which they had to choose and the goals that they could realistically hope to achieve.

HISTORY AS FACTS OR HISTORY AS TEXT

A Roman or a Carthaginian who fought at Cannae may reasonably have felt that he was making history, even if he fought in grim silence; Livy, who described the battle two centuries later, may legitimately have thought that he was composing history, even though he produced nothing but words. Which is history, the events that happened or the story that is told of them? The commonsense answer is surely that history is both, the events and the story; but the connection is not a simple one. At one extreme is the opinion that the ultimate criterion for a work of history is its ability to reflect faithfully the things that happened; on this attitude, which is called *positivism* and has already been mentioned,[11] the real history was the events, and a historical narrative is a true and authentic one only to the extent that it represents those events clearly and honestly. Whether the narrative is well or ill written, whether the events described were of importance to many people, to few or to none at all, and what the author's moral judgment of the participants may be, may be questions of interest, but they do not affect the value of the narrative as history.

At the other extreme is an opinion that was widely held in the ancient world according to which history is a branch of literature, and its value is to be judged by the same criteria that apply to other works of literature. A

---

[10] For this claim I might cite ibid., 69–80, but in fact it suffices to remind the reader of the internal difficulties with which Solon dealt in Athens, or the continued struggles there between the *demos* and the "oligarchs," or the Struggle of the Orders in Rome, to make it clear that the idea of class solidarity and class struggle was by no means foreign to classical antiquity.

[11] Above, p. 34.

boring history, by this criterion, is worthless, appropriate for burning or worse,[12] and an unedifying one misses its major purpose.[13] This opinion is no longer taken seriously in the academic world; good style alone will not win you a degree, promotion or tenure. But it is still true that a single well-written book may be more influential than a dozen poorly written ones.[14]

Nobody today would claim that a history is ever entirely fact; narrative is never identical with the events it describes, and the study of narratology has elucidated very compellingly what kinds of transformations take place when events are turned into narrative.[15] But even granting that our main interest is in establishing what the facts were and constructing a reasonable and significant narrative out of them, there remains a tension between the need to make our narrative understandable to ourselves and our contemporaries and the need to make clear the differences of outlook, circumstance and all the other factors that make the past different from the present. Some historians pursue a consciously distancing approach, broadening our understanding precisely by making us realize how unlike us human beings have been; others prefer a familiarizing approach, seeing people of very different backgrounds and situations wrestling with the same basic problems that we ourselves face. Which approach we choose, or whether, like most historians, we fall somewhere in the middle, will chiefly depend upon the reasons that have attracted us to the study of history in the first place.

[12]   *at vos interea venite in ignem,*
       pleni ruris et inficetiarum
       annales Volusi, cacata carta (Cat. 36.18–20). Catullus, it must be admitted, was writing of a history in verse, of which it might be more reasonable to hold that its literary qualities were its most important feature.

[13]   *Hoc illud est praecipue in cognitione rerum salubre et frugiferum, omnis te exempli documenta in inlustri posita monumento intueri; inde tibi tuaeque rei publicae quod imitere capias, inde foedum inceptu foedum exitu quod vites* (Liv. Praef. 10).

[14]   One of the most remarkable examples was Irving, *A History of the Life and Voyages of Christopher Columbus*, which originated—apparently out of whole cloth—the story that until Columbus everyone believed the world to be flat. The story is a flagrant fabrication. The Greeks in the Hellenistic period not only knew that the world was round but had a very nearly correct measure of its circumference, and the Romans, as every student of elementary Latin knows, spoke of *orbis terrarum*; nor had this knowledge been lost in Columbus' time. But the story is still repeated by elementary school teachers, and believed by most people who have heard the name of Columbus.

[15]   Above, p. 123.

ANCILLARY DISCIPLINES

Certain disciplines are so basic to any historical narrative that we often take them for granted, though in fact they require years of investigation and their conclusions, often presented in tabular or lapidary form as if they were entirely unassailable, may turn out, to the person willing to spend the effort and study, to be less certain than has generally been presumed.

Antiquarianism

We are surrounded by monuments of the past. Every office contains records of past transactions; every cemetery contains descriptions of people who no longer walk the earth; every person who can speak or write can tell of things that others have forgotten. An enterprising historian will pay attention to these monuments when their information is useful: an economic historian may pore over records of ancient transactions to discover changes in economic behavior, and a social historian may want to hear from people who have lived in a certain situation or a certain period what it was like. Many people, however, find the past fascinating in its own right, and have researched these kinds of monuments with no grander purpose than to tell the story of their own locality or family or profession. Historians denote this kind of research with the pejorative term of "antiquarianism," but antiquaries in fact provide large amounts of data on which more sophisticated historians can build more valuable conclusions.

Chronology

Chronology is so basic to history that it is often mistaken for the entirety of the subject. In modern history, chronology is generally so well known that it can be presumed: people and events are regularly mentioned with dates attached to them, and we rely on these dates to place them in their historical context. It is rare, though not unexampled, for there to be any uncertainty about the date of an event or of a person's birth or death.

The situation in ancient history, as every student quickly learns, is nothing like that. Each political unit has its own calendar, with no standardization even about when the year begins until the Roman period. Years are named by kings or by magistrates and, again, there are different magistrates for each polity. The idea of a single series of years that could be continued indefinitely first appears with the Seleucid era in 311—even here, there were two different ways of counting, depending on when the new year was taken to fall—and it was not adopted by other states. Our sources do not always give dates; where they do, we may not know when the archon or consul named held office. Sometimes our dates depend upon impressionistic evidence, as the style of lettering on an inscription or of sculpture associated with it. With these difficulties, it is a great accomplishment, a tribute both to the careful scholarship of our pre-decessors and to the meticulousness of our most chronologically sophisti-cated sources, that we have a pretty clear and detailed chronology of the ancient world; but it is well to be aware how much uncertainty remains, and to try, within reason, to know not only the date of a person or an event but how certain we can be of that date.

Periodization

It is useful to divide history into periods. There can be no doubt that much in Rome was different from the time of Augustus Caesar onward, and it is reasonable to distinguish this period, whether we call it empire or principate, from the republican period that preceded it. Sometimes, as in this case, the dividing line is pretty clear—we may perhaps disagree whether we should put the end of the republic in 49, 44, 30 or 23 BCE, but there is no question that the political life of Rome at Augustus' death was thoroughly and irreversibly changed from what it had been at his birth. In other cases it is much less clear. When does the archaic age of Greece end and the classical age begin? I was taught that it happened with the fall of the tyranny at Athens, but I don't suppose that the Greeks of Gela thought that something earth-shaking had happened. When did the Roman Empire cease to exist in the west? I was taught that it was with the deposition of Romulus Augustulus in 476, but then another claimant, Nepos, was still recognized by the eastern empire, and the emperors of Constantinople later continued to see themselves as emperors of the west, and were so seen by many others until Charlemagne took their crown in 800. Roman law was considered valid in Europe well into the nineteenth century. Periodization is debatable, and indeed changes from time to time: there was a time when Greek history was thought to have ended in 338 BCE. Nor is periodization universal: the Iron Age began in Greece hundreds of years before it reached Egypt. Sometimes a new periodization is suggested: the Hellenistic era was the invention of Johannes Droysen in 1833, and what was once treated simply as "the imperial period" of Rome was later often divided into "principate" and "dominate." Historians usually work within the periodizations that they learned in school, but it is well to be aware of the uncertainties surrounding them.

Prosopography

We learn the names of the major players on the historical stage very early: we had probably known about Julius Caesar and Alexander the Great before we ever took a course in classics, and Pericles, Leonidas and Scipio Africanus are easily identifiable. The historical record, however, is full of other people, and the fact that we do not recognize a name we come across does not necessarily mean there is nothing to know about its bearer. When Herodotus chooses to end his narration of the Persian Wars with the crucifixion of Artauktes by the Athenians under the command of Xanthippus, it is not without interest to note that Xanthippus is the father of Pericles, and that Herodotus settled in Thurii, a colony founded on the initiative of the Athenians when Pericles was a dominant figure in Athenian politics. A reader who has seen the virtue and naivety of Ischomachus' young wife in Xenophon's *Oeconomicus*, 7–10 will be surprised to read the lurid description of the same woman in Andocides 1.124–9.[16] Often the knowledge of who precisely a given person was, with the family connections and other items that may be known about that person, may give us a quite interesting view on the person's actions; and occasionally scholars have made great historical discoveries by carefully following up the personal histories and connections of the players on the historical stage.[17]

For relatively small groups, a prosopography will list every person known; but most people who appear in historical, epigraphical or papyrological records appear there only once, and, when the population to be covered is very large, it is reasonable to concentrate on those who are known to have played a role of some significance. This is not to say that there is nothing to be gained from a list of the insignificant—even a telephone-book tells us something about the place for which it was

---

[16] Harvey, "The Wicked Wife of Ischomachos."

[17] Perhaps the most famous case is Syme, *The Roman Revolution*, who demonstrated that by the end of the Augustan era the republican nobility had virtually ceased to exist. Davies, *Wealth and the Power of Wealth in Classical Athens* used prosopographical information to discover a similar discontinuity in the history of Athens, where the great families of the fifth century disappear from view in the fourth.

produced—but a prosopographical project can be made more manageable by restricting its scope.[18] A different kind of project, an *Onomasticon* or *Namenbuch*, collects all the names without discussing the details of each individual.

Taxonomy

One last issue of which a historian must be aware is that of taxonomy. We cannot speak of history without using an entire vocabulary—"state," "empire," "class," "revolution"—whose words are rarely clearly defined. History is not geometry, and not every term we use can or must be defined; but when we begin to generalize, it is often important to know what we are talking about. Is it proper to speak of money, or of anything, as belonging to "the Athenian state"? Did the plebeians form a class? When we speak of the Roman Empire, are we including client kingdoms like Pergamon or Herod's Judaea? Probably few of us will ever have the merit of discovering universal historical laws; but it is unlikely that we can say anything broadly valid if we do not take the care at least to try to define our terms.

MAJOR RESOURCES

Comprehensive Histories

The grand, all-encompassing history of the ancient world was a project not of Germans but of Britons. The original *Cambridge Ancient History* (*CAH*[1]) tried to be a universal and reliable history for the "general reader." It surely was not that; hardly any reader, general or otherwise, has read through all of its twelve volumes—not even J. B. Bury, its first general editor, who died more than a decade before it was completed.[19] Its

---

[18] This principle is stated by Henri Irénée Marrou in Mandouze et al., *Prosopographie chrétienne du Bas-Empire*, I 7. There is room for debate about the matter, and I do not know of anyone who has undertaken an *Onomasticon* of all known Christians; but it cannot be doubted that only this restriction made that work and others like it possible.

[19] Two of the editors, F. E. Adcock and S.A. Cook, served for all twelve volumes; whether they read every word of it or not is a question that can presumably no longer be answered definitively in this world.

particular disposal, with each chapter written by a different scholar, reflected an attitude that the question of "what was known" about history allowed of an answer definite enough that the differing opinions of different authors would not seriously blemish the total product. It covered what was for its time a broad chronological and geographical scope, including Egypt, Sumeria, Assyria and Babylonia, but nothing further east (much less west) of the Roman Empire; and once the classical age of Greece was reached, it restricted itself to Greco-Roman history, ending at 324 CE. Its subject matter, typically for its time, was overwhelmingly political and military. CAH[2], begun almost forty years later, maintained the same geographical range, though adding a thirteenth and fourteenth volume to extend its coverage to 600 CE.[20] Political and military history still dominated, though independent attention was now paid to literary, artistic, social and even a bit of economic history. The approach of general histories of the last few decades has been more that of such books as Cartledge, *The Cambridge Illustrated History of Ancient Greece*, making social questions the central ones and treating political history as a framework of mostly structural interest.

> In practical terms, this means that narrative is reduced to one chapter, which focuses more on processes than on individual men and events; the other chapters are devoted to such topics as Rich and Poor; Women, Children and Men; Work and Leisure; and Performance. Here as in *CAH*, the chapter numbering is significant: there the non-narrative chapters are implied to be fewer than they are; here there are twelve numbered chapters, but the Historical Outline is an Intermezzo without a number.[21]

Settis, *I Greci* charts a middle course, dedicating one of its four volumes[22] to history but including generous volumes on the classical tradition (placed first!), the Greeks abroad, and Greek art, culture and society.[23]

---

[20] The first and second volumes of CAH[1] had already been revised before the project for a complete revision was undertaken, with the result that volumes I and II of the revised edition bear the notation "third edition."

[21] Rhodes, "The *Cambridge Ancient History*."

[22] Or three of its seven, since the historical volume comprises three separately bound parts and the volume on Greek culture and society comprises two.

[23] Its companion work, Schiavone, *Storia di Roma*, follows a chronological structure.

Much larger than the *CAH*, but a good deal more difficult to use, is Temporini and Haase, *Aufstieg und Niedergang der römischen Welt* (ANRW), a series of comprehensive handbooks of everything that was, is or ever will be known about the Roman world, its articles in every major European language. Begun as a project in honor of Professor Joseph Vogt's seventy-fifth birthday, it is passing its own thirty-fifth as I write these lines, already of gargantuan size but nowhere near completion, and now suspended: the last volume appeared in 1998, but the homepage still lists a number of volumes in preparation. Planned in three parts—from the foundation to the end of the republic, the principate, and late antiquity—it completed the first part in four volumes, has not completed the principate in more than sixty, and has not even begun late antiquity. Its organization is not such that makes it possible to "look up" a given subject, nor, at least for now, is there a general table of contents or index. Alas, however, it includes much work of genuine value, so it is not a resource lightly to be ignored. The *ANRW* homepage can help you find your way around, as can the searchable database of the *VRoma: ANRW*.

Chronology, Fasti, and Magistrate and Regnal Lists

Since the ancients generally identified years by regnal years of a ruler or by an eponymous magistrate, lists of the rulers are often essential for dating a document or an event. Clear, convenient, up to date and comprehensive is Eder and Renger, *Chronologies of the Ancient World*, which ranges geographically from China to Wessex and chronologically from the third millennium BCE until the ninth century CE. The standard lists, which deal more directly with the problems involved, are Develin, *Athenian Officials* (AO), Broughton, *The Magistrates of the Roman Republic* (MRR), Kienast, *Römische Kaisertabelle*, and Bagnall et al., *Consuls of the Later Roman Empire*. Details of the various calendars and their astronomical rationale can be found in Samuel, *Greek and Roman Chronology*. Shorter accounts are Bickerman, *Chronology of the Ancient World* and Hannah, *Greek and Roman Calendars*; Bickerman's book also includes various astronomical tables, fasti, archon and regnal lists, and even a year-by-year table of historical events, reprinted for the most part from other books but very handy for quick reference.

Prosopographies

The prosopography of ancient Athens that was used throughout the twentieth century was Kirchner, *Prosopographia Attica* (*PA*), supplemented by Sundwall, *Nachträge zur Prosopographia Attica*; an obscure Athenian would regularly be identified by the appropriate number in *PA*. Davies, *Athenian Propertied Families* (*APF*) and *AO* were much more usable guides to those people (liturgists and magistrates) who were important enough to be included in them. For the century now beginning, Traill, *Persons of Ancient Athens*, now complete except for the index, will supersede *PA*; its searchable website, *Website Attica*, is regularly updated. A much wider geographical area, though not, as of now, including Asia and Egypt, is covered by Fraser and Matthews, *A Lexicon of Greek Personal Names*. For the Roman republic there is still no comprehensive prosopography. For the empire the old *Prosopographia Imperii Romani* (PIR[1]) is being superseded by a newer version (PIR[2]), which as of this writing is almost but not quite complete;[24] this, too, has a searchable, updated website. PIR[2] goes only as far as the accession of Diocletian in 284; for late antiquity (up to 641) there are two parallel volumes, Jones, Martindale and Morris, *The Prosopography of the Later Roman Empire* (PLRE), an index not of all known people, but of the members of the imperial elite,[25] and Mandouze et al., *Prosopographie chrétienne du Bas-Empire*, listing those who performed ecclesiastical functions, however minor, and those, Christian or not, who influenced the history of Christianity in any way. These are the broadest-based prosopographical works; there are many more specialized ones, of which the most notable are mentioned in Jenkins.

Commentaries

I mention here only the major scholarly commentaries, but for each author there are many students' commentaries, which for many uses are the commentaries of choice, but for research cannot, and do not intend to, take the place of the scholarly commentaries.[26]

---

[24] The death-defying PIR[2] has survived Nazism, Communism and—its closest call of all—bureaucratic budgeters: see Fuendling's BMCR review of Part 8, Fasc. 1.

[25] For a precise definition of the criteria for inclusion see PLRE I vi.

[26] On students' commentaries and scholarly commentaries in general see above, pp. 47–8.

The standard commentary on Herodotus for over a century has been How and Wells, *A Commentary on Herodotus*; this has now been superseded by Asheri et al., *Erodoto: Le storie*. As of this writing, half of the new commentary is available in English: Asheri, Lloyd and Corcella, *A Commentary on Herodotus I–IV*. For the second book, Lloyd, *Herodotus: Book II* did the essential work of correlating Herodotus' description with modern Egyptology; his commentary in Asheri, Lloyd and Corcella, though more recent, is less exhaustive. Gomme, Andrewes and Dover, *A Historical Commentary on Thucydides* has not outlived its usefulness, but Hornblower, *A Commentary on Thucydides* will give you a much more modern approach and a good deal of new information, and does not limit itself to narrowly historical questions. Walbank, *A Historical Commentary on Polybius* did for Polybius what his predecessors did for Herodotus and Thucydides. Nobody has taken on all the surviving text of Livy, but Oxford University Press has been working on it for half a century. By now we have *A Commentary on Livy* for Books 1–5 (Ogilvie), 6–10 (Oakley) and 31–40 (Briscoe). Sallust's *Jugurtha* has a major German commentary by Erich Koestermann, and his *Catiline* another by Karl Vretska. Tacitus' *Annals* have received the beginnings of a treatment in the commentary begun by F. R. D. Goodyear, which has now been continued by A. J. Woodman and R. H. Martin up to the end of the third book.

The less celebrated historians—Diodorus Siculus, Valerius Maximus, Ammianus Marcellinus and others—have generally not received such thoroughgoing commentaries; nor have some of the more celebrated writers on historical subjects, such as Caesar and Plutarch. Some of these, probably, could use a major commentary, but surely not all of them. The great historical commentaries have usually treated authors who are the major historical source for their period. For authors like these, the study of the author and the study of the times described are inseparable: it is hardly imaginable to discuss the Hannibalic war without Livy, or to read the third decade of Livy without reference to the war. The works of Julius Caesar, on the other hand, for all their fascination, are only one out of many sources for his well-documented career, and studying the period by reading a commentary on Caesar would give a skewed picture of the history of his times. Other authors, like Plutarch, are simply so immense and so diffuse that they defeat the most ambitious would-be commentator: if it is necessary to know everything about the Peloponnesian War to produce a commentary on Thucydides, it is necessary to know everything about practically everything—or at least everything that happened before the second century CE—to produce a commentary on all of Plutarch. As for an author like Diodorus, for certain periods—those for which a more reliable source exists—a commentary on him would reproduce a good deal of what is already available in the commentaries on the major source. This is not to say that there are not great commentaries still to be produced; but for many authors, the lack of a major historical commentary need not be a matter of simple neglect.

Fragmentary Histories

Greek: Jacoby, *F Gr Hist*. In three parts: I is Genealogy and Mythography, II Chronological History, III History of States and Peoples. Part III, which was left unfinished, is now being published from Jacoby's notes by Charles Fornara; Parts IV (Biography, History of Literature, and Antiquarian Literature) and V (Geography), including an English translation, are being compiled by international teams of scholars.[27] All parts except the first are divided into volumes and fascicles. The commentaries on the second and third parts are bound separately from the text, a fact that is not always marked on the binding, so that if you are careless you could come home with a volume of Jacoby's commentary without the text on which he is commenting. Still worse, his footnotes are in yet another fascicle, so that you might get only the footnotes without even the commentary! The commentary on the first parts is in German, but that on the last parts, written after Jacoby came to Oxford in the wake of Nazi persecution, is in English, an ironic end for a project whose second volumes were greeted by Wilamowitz with praise for "a work of which we can be proud of the fact that only a German could have produced it."[28] A complete index to the first three parts has also been undertaken. But all of this is superseded, for those who can afford it or who have access to it, by the online version, where the ability to search by word makes the corpus much more functional.

No less awe-inspiring in its time, though it has been put into the shade by *F Gr Hist*, is Müller, *Fragmenta Historicorum Graecorum* (FHG). These volumes, which include a Latin translation (and a French one in the last volume, whose posthumous publication was delayed for sixty-nine years), retain

---

[27] On the undertaking and its difficulties see Schepens, "Jacoby's FGrHist." The new editors have been careful to distinguish their own efforts from Jacoby's by publishing them under the title "Die Fragmente der griechischen Historiker *Continued*," and by beginning a new numbering from 1000.

[28] In the *Deutsche Literarturzeitung* 22 (1926), 1047. My thanks to David Sohlberg for directing me to this review.

some value for those authors that F Gr Hist has not reached, and for finding fragments referred to by books older than F Gr Hist.

Roman: The fragments of the Roman historians, represented for more than a hundred years by the selection printed in Peter, Historicorum Romanorum Reliquiae and made more accessible in Chassignet, L'Annalistique romaine and Beck and Walter, Die frühen römischen Historiker, will now finally get a full collection in Cornell, Fragments of the Roman Historians.

On historical atlases, see below, pp. 313–14. For basic data about the various poleis of which the Greek world was composed, Hansen and Nielsen, An Inventory of Archaic and Classical Poleis, the greatest work of ancient historical taxonomy in the last generation, is indispensable.

PART IV

THE PHYSICAL REMAINS

14

ARCHAEOLOGY

WHAT ARCHAEOLOGY IS

Archaeology today is the study of the human past on the basis of its physical remains. Since most of the physical remains of the past have been covered by dust, sand, silt, water or later habitations, archaeology is generally based on excavation. Excavation, however, provides only the raw materials of archaeology. The real contribution of archaeology to the study of the past is not so much the artifacts themselves as the new information that comes from their careful study and analysis. An archaeologist may (or may not) spend a few weeks in the summer excavating a site, but most of an archaeologist's research time is spent collecting, analyzing and reflecting on what can be learned from data both new and old.

Its basis in excavation makes the scope of archaeology radically different from the scope of other subfields of the classics. For one thing, it includes peoples and periods whose history is meager or nonexistent: while history begins with the development of writing in the second millennium BCE, archaeology begins in the Stone Age, and recent work has begun to treat the society of Neandertals as being no less worthy of investigation than their physiology. Virtually all of our knowledge of the societies, nations and empires of the Americas before 1492 has come from archaeology, and many worlds in which people once lived, from nomadic bands to vast empires, have passed from human memory and are known to us only from excavation.

Because of this broader scope, the position of classical archaeology within the general field of archaeology is somewhat different from that of ancient history within the field of history. Ancient history, no doubt, forms only a small part of the larger field of history, as can be seen at any gathering of historians; but since for almost two thousand years European society—the society that has occupied historians more than any other—has developed in the wake and the shadow of ancient Greece and Rome, classical civilization has a privileged position at the fount of a good deal of history. There are, however, important civilizations that have little or no connection with the classical world, civilizations that in the postcolonial world we no longer consider exotic or unimportant; and in the world-wide, ten-thousand-year sweep of archaeology—a field where information gets more interesting, not less so, the further removed it is from the modern world—the societies of Greece and Rome do not stand at the basis of the discipline. That classical archaeology nevertheless long maintained an important position in the discipline was a result chiefly of the history of archaeology, which can be said in a sense to have begun at Pompeii and at Troy, and of the continued effort of the people who worked in the field and the governments who fostered their work; but newer trends in archaeology have tended to marginalize classical archaeology from its larger discipline in a way that is still only beginning to be addressed.[1]

Classical archaeology is distinguished by a particularly close relationship with art history; many books, and even academic departments, carry titles that speak of "art and archaeology" as if they were two aspects of the same field. This is a result of the great success of classical archaeology in the old days, when it was chiefly a matter of searching for buried treasure. Most classical art that we have has been recovered by archaeology; that may be equally true for pre-Columbian art of the Americas, but, since the

---

[1]   On both the achievements of classical archaeology and its uneasy relationship with archaeology in general see Renfrew, "The Great Tradition versus the Great Divide," Snodgrass, "The New Archaeology and the Classical Archaeologist" and Snodgrass, *An Archaeology of Greece*, 1–35 ("So far, from the point of view of the narrow interests of classical archaeology *sensu stricto*, the advent of the new movement in archaeology has been something of a disaster. To be criticized, even attacked, is one thing; to have the very existence of one's subject ignored is another." Ibid., 6–7). The development of classical archaeology in the generation since has indeed been characterized, as Renfrew urged, by adoption of the techniques of "new archaeology," with consequences that promise to be revolutionary: Morris, "Classical Archaeology." For a less sanguine view see Davis, "Classical Archaeology and Anthropological Archaeology in North America."

study of art history still tends to focus particularly on the history of European art, the discoveries of classical archaeology have a particular importance in the field.

Classical archaeology differs not only from other fields of archaeology; it differs from other subfields of the classics, in that archaeology typically defines the limits of its study geographically rather than historically, socially and chronologically. Whereas narrative histories tend to follow nations and societies from place to place and literary history follows intellectual and aesthetic developments from author to author, an archaeological excavation is tied to a single place. An excavator of Jerusalem finds artifacts of Arabs, Crusaders, Samaritans, Idumeans, Jews, Israelites and Canaanites; of Turks, Mongols, Romans, Assyrians, Egyptians and other groups who conquered the land but did not settle it widely; of Hurrians, Hittites, Jebusites, Amorites and other nations known more from archaeology than from history; and finally of innumerable prehistoric peoples whose identities we must reconstruct without any written record to help us. Sometimes these people are closely connected; sometimes the only connection is that one group occupied the site after exterminating the other or upon finding it abandoned. The history of a site has a very different shape from the history that follows, shall we say, the Greeks from their first invasion of the peninsula through the Mycenaean flourishing, the collapse of Dark Ages, the renaissance of the classical period, the wide expansion of the Hellenistic period, the conquest by Rome, rise of Byzantium, and the conversion to Christianity.

The difference that we are describing, which is essentially the difference between geography and history, applies to an excavation and its report; it does not necessarily apply thereafter. Once the report has been published, it will be used by other archaeologists with different interests. One will notice a peculiarity about the pottery that may reveal trade connections of which we had been unaware; a numismatist may find that a coin found in a Syrian mound can give us new information about the emperor at Rome; another archaeologist may ransack the literature for information on other communities in the area and discover whether this one flourished along with its neighbors or at their expense. There is a good deal to be learned by integrating archaeological information into the historical record; but because of the different focus of the archaeological information, it requires broad reading and careful selection to get a clear picture that can be applied to history. And since archaeology, unlike history, has an almost inexhaustible source of new information, the picture is always changing.

WHAT ARE WE LOOKING FOR WHEN WE EXCAVATE?

Excavations were once essentially treasure hunts, searching for items of value under the earth. The items might be intrinsically valuable, like the buried treasure of *Treasure Island*, or they might be valuable because they were works of art or even, like most ancient coins, simply because they were old. Treasure hunters knew where the most likely places were for finding things of value; the most celebrated were the pyramids of Egypt and the ruins of Pompeii, but almost any locality had its more modest candidates, and occasionally a modern excavator is disappointed to find that the treasure hunters have been there first. Treasure hunting remains a popular hobby, and some of the most exciting finds of the twentieth century (most notably the Dead Sea Scrolls) were originally found by anonymous treasure hunters. But today treasure hunting is frowned upon—in those lands where archaeology is important enough to be of interest to the government, it is generally illegal—and modern excavations are not undertaken in the hope of finding gold, silver or exquisite statuary.[2]

Nor—but this is a more recent development—are they usually undertaken in the hope of proving, disproving, illuminating or elaborating literary texts, as early excavators tried to use excavation as a test of Homer or the Bible. History itself in recent years has come to focus less on wars, politics and the activities of famous men in favor of an effort better to understand society, economics and the activities of ordinary people; and in that area archaeology has pride of place. Literary and historical texts will always tell us more about the elite than about the masses, both because the elite were much more likely to be literate and because the activities of a particular ruler, general or author were likely to be of interest to more people than those of a particular wife, farmer or artisan. The archaeologist's proverbial spade, on the other hand, is almost as likely[3] to strike the home or the bones of a tailor as of a prince—much

---

[2]   This does not necessarily mean that excavations are undertaken for altruistic purposes. Modern archaeologists hope to gain both money and honor by their activities; but they do not expect to find the money underground and use it to buy honor, but to achieve honor and professional advancement by the quality of their academic contributions to their field. Nor is the treasure-hunting tradition entirely dead, as can be seen from the lavishly funded and successful expedition to find the wreck of the *Titanic*.

[3]   I say "almost" because archaeological sites are not chosen randomly, and there is still a certain unavoidable bias towards the elite since (a) urban centers have more artifacts than the countryside; (b) places of historical interest are still more likely to

more likely, in fact, since there were many more tailors than princes. The archaeologist thus has access to a much broader canvas than the written sources provide, and the knowledge that can be gained is of much wider interest than simply providing background for the history transmitted by ancient authors. The interpretation of these finds still remains a matter in which history, anthropology and sociology will loom large; but as more and more of our knowledge of the life of ancient masses stems from archaeology, its place in teaching us about the past must become greater and greater.[4]

If modern excavators are no longer looking for buried treasure, what are they looking for? It can be stated as a general rule that behind every excavation is an unresolved question. Sometimes we are looking for particular objects: Are there any more papyri hidden in that cave? Can we find the remains of the temple that Pausanias mentions? Famous ancient sites are still being re-excavated, both because they have not been excavated in their entirety—it is a rare archaeological expedition that has enough time, money and manpower to clear away an entire ancient city—and because every excavation raises new questions, which often require new excavations to settle them. Most excavations, however, are neither looking for specific objects nor merely expanding a previous dig. Archaeological excavations are research projects, with stated questions to investigate and an explicit plan for how the excavation can settle them. An excavation today is a continuation of archaeological analysis by other means.

The Limits of Excavation

In every field of scholarship ethical questions arise, but the questions are more insistent in archaeology because it involves more invasive techniques of investigation. Not in every case is a scholar justified in allowing curiosity free rein. Some limits are well known; we frown upon the

---

be excavated than undocumented cities, however populous; and (c) the rich by definition have more physical objects than the poor, and what they have is made out of more durable material.

[4]   This will only happen, of course, when students of ancient history and sociology are familiar with the work of archaeologists, a state of affairs to which I hope this book will contribute. A recent book that gives a good idea of what can be achieved by integrating archaeological research into the historical record is Whitley, *The Archaeology of Ancient Greece*, the current beginners' text for archaeologists who wish to introduce their students into the new archaeology from the start.

practice of peeping into our neighbors' apartments, or investigating their financial or medical condition when it does not concern us directly. There are limits, too, to how far we may indulge our curiosity about the dead. Digging up their graves in the hope of finding buried treasure or using their corpses for profit has traditionally been considered uncivilized at best and criminal at worst; although some archaeologists consider that scientific inquiry should be allowed to set aside such scruples, not everybody is so dismissive about the matter. In some places ancient graves are legally protected; even where they are not, civility demands that they be left undisturbed when doing otherwise would offend the people who still feel themselves connected to them, despite the obvious archaeological advantages to be gained by their study. Often what seems to an archaeologist like saving a site—removing buried bones, for example, before they are covered over with asphalt for a parking lot—may seem to others like destroying it.

Although treasure hunting is no longer a major goal of archaeology, amazing discoveries sometimes happen—the terracotta army of the first Emperor of China[5] or the tomb of Philip of Macedon[6]—and sometimes artifacts discovered long since are found to have astounding significance, such as the signature of Cleopatra on a royal gift of land[7] or the discovery that the fish sauce prepared in Herod's kitchen was kosher.[8] Although most materials excavated today derive their value from their assimilation into a picture of ancient society that is being continuously refined, there remains a great and lucrative market for antiquities, and the temptation to exploit the market can be hard to resist. Excavators are licensed and supervised, and museum curators can be prosecuted if tempted by an authentic artifact whose seller may not really be its rightful owner. The fact that nationalistic politics has now entered the picture makes it all the more important to exercise caution.

A further temptation is the use of archaeology to prove or disprove religious or political claims. There is no doubt that archaeology can illuminate many details of religious narrative, but it is rare in the extreme that it can actually be related to a particular event as told in the narrative, and rarer yet—in fact, as far as I know, wholly unexampled—for archaeology to provide a proof that succeeds in either converting the unconverted or unconverting the converted. The effort to use archaeology for

[5]   Portal, ed., *The First Emperor.*
[6]   Andronicos, *Vergina: The Royal Tombs.*
[7]   Van Minnen, "An Official Act of Cleopatra."
[8]   Cotton, Lernau and Goren, "Fish Sauces."

these purposes will generally produce much heat but little light, and will only encourage us to misinterpret what we find.

It is important for an archaeologist, like every other scholar, to maintain a certain amount of interpretative modesty. Because archaeologists deal with facts more solid than any other person who researches the past, it is easy to lose sight of the multiplicity of possible interpretations. The excavations that Schliemann carried out at Hissarlik convinced him absolutely of the truth of the Homeric epics. Nobody can any longer doubt that there was an important settlement at this site; that the settlement was called Troy (by its inhabitants or by anybody else), and that it was destroyed by an army from Greece, is not written anywhere in the stones—much less that the army (if it existed) was commanded by a man named Agamemnon, or entered the town inside a wooden horse. The opposite tendency, to deny the reality of an inherited narrative because we have not found the remains we should have expected, may be equally suspect. Thucydides warned against it with a clear and convincing example,[9] and the absence of archaeological remains is indeed a serious factor to be considered in interpretation; but a careful scholar will keep an open mind as far as possible.

Perhaps the strongest temptation of them all, because it involves no conscious ethical dilemma, is the temptation to excavate more than one can publish. Excavations in the Mediterranean basin normally take place in the summertime, when the weather is warm and students and professors are free of other responsibilities. It is a lost opportunity to let a summer go by without exploiting it. But the proper publication of an excavation's finds generally takes years, and many a site has been excavated carefully only to have its finds and its records lost or destroyed when the original excavator died. An excavation that is never published is worse than no excavation at all: the information gathered is no longer at the site, and if not published it is lost forever.

ARCHAEOLOGICAL SURVEYS

When archaeology centered upon sites that were considered either "typical" or "productive," surveying was undertaken chiefly to help locate such sites or to document their distribution. In recent decades, however, systematic surveys have increasingly been used as a data-gathering

---

[9]   Thuc. 1.10.

method in their own right, no less important than excavation in their ability to produce information about the past.

The purpose of a survey is to get a picture of the density of archaeological remains over a given area. Aerial photographs are a great help in getting the lay of the land, and often reveal telltale traces of previous human settlement. In relatively exposed areas it may suffice to have the surveyors, traversing the land at fixed intervals, identify every item of interest that they find on the surface. For areas where the surface is overgrown or partially inaccessible, or where the items of interest are unlikely to protrude above the surface, various sampling methods have been developed to give insight into distribution patterns. Some of these methods are "invasive," involving the digging of sample holes along the landscape; others, such as ground-penetrating radar, magnetometry or resistivity (changes in the earth's magnetic field or in electrical resistance that may be due to past human activity) can give information about the area without disturbing it. Not every area lends itself to surveying; sometimes the picture provided is incomplete or even distorted. Still, the technique of archaeological surveying has increased, often dramatically, the number of known settlements, and has made statistical studies more practical and more reliable than they could be when sites were hand-picked. More importantly, it has opened up new areas of knowledge by giving us a clearer picture of patterns of human settlement and human activity over wide areas and not only in urban centers—a picture of capital importance for the ancient world, in which agriculture and herding provided the basis of human nutrition, as they still do, and employed most of the human population, as in Europe and America they no longer do.

ARTIFACTS AND HOW WE CAN LEARN FROM THEM

Once an excavation is undertaken, it cannot restrict itself to the items it was looking for and the questions it was asking: it must record everything it finds that might be of interest to some future investigator. Any artifact— that is, any item produced or modified by past human culture—must be recorded, described and catalogued. Stones by themselves are not artifacts; but if they have been cut, polished or even simply piled up by human beings they are. An animal's bones are not artifacts, but, if they are burnt or broken in a way that suggests that the animal was cooked and eaten, they are. There are things to be learned merely by observing the soil: the level and type of *anthrosols*—levels of soil that have been loosened by human habitation or cultivation—give us information about the history of an area. Many items that were once disposed of as rubbish are now saved and catalogued, and the characteristic tool of the modern archaeologist is the sieve no less than the spade. Small-denomination coins that were once discarded unnoticed are now collected and catalogued; stones that were once considered pebbles may now be recognized as weights; even petrified human feces, now dignified by the name *coprolites*, may be analyzed for the information they can provide about human diet. Finding and cataloguing artifacts is not the final purpose of archaeology, but it is the foundation upon which the entire structure rests.

THE TRADITIONAL CATEGORIES

The major items remain as they used to be. Architectural remains are essential. Where houses are built of brick or stone, as they generally were in ancient Greece, or of the concrete that was one of Rome's greatest gifts to technology, the foundation of almost every house remains unless it has been intentionally dug up; these foundations not only give us the general layout of the settlement, but also reveal a good deal about the way the community lived and functioned. Life centered around the labyrinthine Minoan palaces will have been very different from life centered around a large hall of the sort that archaeologists call a *megaron*; the presence of an outdoor arcade or a marketplace shows us another aspect. Many of the great buildings of antiquity are architectural wonders; for the history of the common people, the ordinary houses are of no less interest.

Ceramic ware, which is easily shattered but hardly ever destroyed, is also indispensable. Not that the differences in pottery themselves have much to tell us about everyday life: cups were for drinking, amphoras for storage, frying-pans for frying and, with small variations, the sorts of vessels used were more or less the same throughout the ancient world. But styles of shape and decoration varied from place to place and changed from age to age, so that it is the shape and style of pottery found in a given archaeological context that give the best indication of its date. As this has become clearer, the study and classification of pottery styles have been refined to the point where even prehistoric sites can often be well dated by the presence of a style of ceramic ware for which another site has provided a reliable date. Modern physics and chemistry now permit even more precise analysis, determining a pot's place of origin and its date on the basis of the chemical content and radioactivity of its clay;[10] and we are now often in a position to identify even an unsigned pot not only by its era but by the town, and workshop, though not yet the individual, who produced it.

Metal artifacts have no less intrinsic interests than the pottery, but being more liable to rust, to robbery and to reuse they are less ubiquitous than ceramics. Often they can tell us about less durable materials that were in use: nails are evidence for carpentry, safety pins (fibulae) for fabric. One particular category of metal artifact, coins, forms a branch of study in its own right, and will accordingly get its own discussion in this book.[11]

NEWER INTERESTS

Modern archaeology, however, casts a wider net than that defined by stone, ceramic and metal. The rings in tree-trunks are wider in rainy years than in dry ones; by carefully cataloguing wooden items, archaeologists have been able to establish year-by-year sequences over millennia. This technique of *dendrochronology* was pioneered by the astronomer A. E. Douglass of the University of Arizona but is now more widely used in archaeology than in astronomy. It is not as simple a matter as simply measuring rings—as in any science, many factors have to be considered in order to get a reliable result—but where available it allows us to give a precise calendar date for the cutting of a particular piece of wood. This does not necessarily date the artifact of which the wood is a part: old wood may have been used or reused, or new wood may have been used to repair an older artifact. But when all factors are taken into account, dendrochronology can give us a very firm anchor on which to base our reconstructions; and this makes wooden artifacts much more significant than they used to be.

Archaeobotany studies the vegetable remains of a culture. Remains of seeds at cooking sites or in coprolites can tell us what people ate, and other con-texts can show us the uses of plants for clothing, for decoration or for

---

[10] The many various methods now available for coaxing information out of old broken pots are clearly and—as of the time of its publication—exhaustively described in Rice, *Pottery Analysis*, which includes the processes and purposes of pottery production as well as the methods by which we can recover information from the pots and sherds. Pollard et al., *Analytical Chemistry in Archaeology* offers a useful introduction to the chemistry that lies behind the new methods of analysis.

[11] See below, Chapter 16.

magic. For the ancient world literary texts provide copious information, and some archaeobotanists see the first-century physician Dioscorides, whose treatise *De materia medica* listed more than six hundred medicinal herbs, as the father of their discipline; archaeology, however, can help in identifying many of the plants we would otherwise know only by name. More to the point, examination of variations over time and place can build a picture of the ecology of the ancient world—of how the ancients used the vegetable world, and how, in turn, their uses and settlements impinged upon that world and changed it. The study of ancient flora requires a thorough grounding in botany, and in particular in identifying specimens of seeds and pollen; like other new special fields of archaeological investigation, it has spawned a small but valuable group of professionals.

The relationship of humans to animals is also a changing one, and this, too, can be illuminated by archaeology, a subfield called either *archaeozoology* or *zooarchaeology*. How large were the horses of the Greeks and Romans, and how did this affect the significance of cavalry in wartime? Dogs were surely used in hunting—the Greek word for a hunter is *kynēgos*, "dog-leader"—and in herding; were dogs common in the cities? What kind of dogs? How much meat, how much fowl, how much fish did an ancient family consume? Literature can give us impressions about these matters, chiefly as perceived by the well-to-do; but archaeology, if we are careful to collect all the evidence and not to over-generalize from a few finds, can give us a much broader picture. Animal bones interest modern archaeologists more than they interested those of the nineteenth century.

Of particular interest in the Mediterranean world has been *marine archaeology*, the investigation of sites that are now under water. Most of these are shipwrecks, and their systematic excavation has revealed and will continue to reveal much about ancient commerce, ancient seafaring and ancient warfare. Yet more, not only things that once floated on the water may today be under it, and the techniques of marine archaeology have also proved useful in excavating harbors and even inundated cities.

Many more techniques could be listed: petrography, chemistry (particularly, but not only, isotope analysis) and a host of other sciences have all now been enlisted in the service of archaeology. *Archaeo-metallurgy* studies the use of metals by ancient societies, and must of course be based on a good acquaintance with what is known today about metallurgy. Sometimes a specialist in one of these subjects will actually participate in an excavation; more commonly, artifacts will be sent to a laboratory for analysis. Each of these specialties, if properly consulted, can help us tease more information out of the physical remains of the past.

READING ARCHAEOLOGICAL REPORTS

Some fortunate people will find that the archaeological information of interest to them has already been made available in user-friendly form. The student of Homer, for example, will find in the series *Archaeologia Homerica* a group of monographs conveniently organized by topic that makes available the archaeological information so essential to Homer. Most researchers who want archaeological information will not be this fortunate, and will have to do their own work to familiarize themselves with what has been discovered.

The first place to look will be *APh*, which covers those archaeological journals that deal extensively with the classical world. You will often find that archaeologists have done the work of assembling and analyzing the information bearing on a historical topic. For an outsider, preliminary reports, published in archaeological journals, are generally more accessible and informative than the final publication: in the preliminary report the excavators summarize the results of the campaign and evaluate its significance, and that is usually what you are looking for. But since the ultimate source of information, short of re-inspection where possible, is the excavation report, you will probably have to look at excavation reports as well, and they can be forbidding. The careful description of six hundred amphorae, of each layer of bricks in a building that was rebuilt four times, of every broken bit of statuary, can be a powerful soporific for a researcher from another field who was interested only in a particular problem on which this excavation could shed some light. Excavation reports, however, must be exhaustive if they are to be worth anything; and so the researcher who is not specializing in this particular excavation must treat them as reference books. First you identify the part of the report that deals with your subject; then you find, usually in the introductory or closing paragraphs, what conclusions relevant to you the excavator or the author drew from the excavation; then you start looking into those parts of the reported material on which the claims are based, for archaeologists cannot be trusted to be right all the time any more than other scholars can. If your own research brings into question the entire interpretation of the site, you will indeed have to deal with all the information recorded, just as the original author did; but if, as is much more common for those who are not professional archaeologists, the subject of your interest is only tangentially affected by archaeology, you will pick out the relevant information and use it accordingly. You will probably discover aspects of ancient reality that you had not known, perhaps not even imagined. And your conclusions will now be better grounded.

MAJOR RESOURCES

Encyclopedias and Dictionaries

Encyclopedias of archaeology differ greatly depending on the purpose for which they were made. Those designed to give the public a general idea of the great excavations and the famous discoveries tend to have many photographs and non-technical articles describing sites and people; to this group belong the aging Charles-Picard, *Larousse Encyclopedia of Archaeology*, Sherratt, *The Cambridge Encyclopedia of Archaeology* and Murray, *Encyclopedia of Archaeology*. Those designed to help students come to grips with the methods currently used have fewer illustrations if any and articles dealing with issues of theory and method; to this group belong Barker, *Companion Encyclopedia of Archaeology* and Ellis, *Archaeological Method and Theory*. A middle position is occupied by Whitehouse, *The Macmillan Dictionary of Archaeology*, Fagan, *The Oxford Companion to Archaeology*, Shaw and Jameson, *A Dictionary of Archaeology* and Orser, *Encyclopedia of Historical Archaeology*, which are designed for a more scholarly public but remain focused on excavations and discoveries no less than on methods and theories. For the land of Israel, the *New Encyclopedia of Archaeological Excavations in the Holy Land* gives a comprehensive and, with the publication of a recent supplementary volume, up-to-date account of the excavations of the numerous sites (some two hundred) excavated in this small and contested country. Goffer, *Elsevier's Dictionary of Archaeological Materials and Archaeometry* is a list of technical terms with brief definitions, but has the special virtue of giving its terms in German, Spanish, French, Italian and Portuguese as well as English, a feature that can be very useful when reading articles in those languages.

Excavation Reports

The most authoritative archaeological information is that available in the final publications of excavations. These are often enormous, multivolume items that may have taken decades to produce. It would be beyond my ability and beyond the scope of this volume to try to list them all, invidious and arbitrary to try to choose the most significant.

Stillwell, MacDonald and McAllister, *The Princeton Encyclopedia of Classical Sites* will give you a short description and can direct you to the right place, but it is by now a generation old; de Grummond, *An Encyclopedia of the History of Classical Archaeology* is newer and includes not only sites but capsule biographies of major archaeologists. Using it as a bibliography, however, may take some effort: the volumes of the American excavations in the Athenian agora, for example, will not be found at the end of the four-page article on Athens, though the excavations are mentioned in the article itself and the bibliographical reference will be found under "Agora, Athens." For Rome, a site that could keep a tourist busy for years, Steinby, *Lexicon Topographicum Urbis Romae* is extremely useful for those who read Italian.

Current Excavations: Journals

By law all the results of excavations carried out in Greece must be reported to the Greek Ministry of Culture before being published, and on this basis the official journal Ἀρχαιολογικὸν Δελτίον (*AD*) contains regular preliminary reports of excavations. Despite its importance and its timeliness, neither *AD* nor Ἀρχαιολογικὴ Ἐφημερίς (*AE*), the other major modern Greek archaeological journal, is widely available in university libraries outside of Greece, since many libraries have little or no coverage of modern Greek. Each of the major foreign schools has its "house organ" that regularly prints preliminary reports of its own excavations, as follows:

American Academy in Rome	*Memoirs of the American Academy in Rome*
American School of Classical Studies at Athens	*Hesperia*
British School at Athens	*Annual of the British School at Athens*
British School at Rome	*Papers of the British School at Rome*
Deutsches Archäologisches Institut	*Mitteilungen des Deutschen Archäologischen Instituts.* There are many different journals with this name, each belonging to a different department (*Abteilung*); the ones of most interest to classicists are the *Athenische Abteilung*, the *Abteilung Istanbul* and the *Römische Abteilung*, and the *AA* published by the institute.
École française d'Athènes	*Bulletin de correspondance hellénique*
École française de Rome	*Mélanges de l'École française de Rome—Antiquité*

Each of these schools maintains a website on which the basic information about its activities can be found. The researcher who wants to know what is happening in particular excavations can find some guidance by looking at the description of their archaeological activities; a graduate student interested in archaeology will probably be more interested in looking into information about their academic programs, which offer considerable resources beyond those available in one's home department.

A general review of all recently published classical excavations in Greek lands is given each year in almost telegraphic concision in the *Archaeological Reports* that are distributed together with the *Journal of Hellenic Studies* (JHS), and in the *Bulletin archéologique* that is published annually in the *Revue des études grecques* (REG). These very convenient summaries are produced through Herculean efforts; nobody yet performs the same service for the wider world of Roman archaeology, though there are some regular local summaries.

It is a disappointing excavation about which there is nothing more to say once the excavation report has been produced. Many journals publish articles about archaeology; the most prominent, in addition to the "school journals" mentioned above, are the *American Journal of Archaeology* (AJA), published by the American Institute of Archaeology, the *Journal of Roman Archaeology* (JRA), and Chiron, published by the Deutsches Archäologisches Institut; the *Bulletin of the American School of Oriental Research* (BASOR) also deals with items of Hellenistic and Roman archaeology. For each area of the Greco-Roman world, at least one journal, and often more, specializes in the ancient history of that area; important information is included in these journals, which for their own area may be as important as the major ones or more so. Popular journals, glossy and attractive, are common in this field as they are not in most fields of classics; perhaps the most notable are *Archaeology* and the *Biblical Archaeology Review* (BAR); the latter, despite its name or because of it, often deals with items of interest to students of the classical world.

15

MYCENAEAN STUDIES

THE DISCOVERY OF THE MYCENAEAN WORLD

The Buildings, the Treasures and the Romance

Not only the scholarly world but the entire European world of letters was astonished and excited by Heinrich Schliemann's discovery of a large and wealthy city on the mound of Hissarlik, which others before him had argued was the site of ancient Troy.[1] Yet more amazing was the wealthy citadel he found at Mycenae, a settlement small in the historical age[2] but according to Homer the palace, "rich in gold,"[3] of Agamemnon. The monumental Lion Gate stood above ground for all to see, and Schliemann's excavations found a powerful citadel and rich burials with golden death-masks and jewelry. Schliemann, a man of fertile imagination, is said to have

---

[1] For Schliemann, Troy and Mycenae were the two major parts of one story: he was excavating Homer. As research has progressed, it has become clear—as Homer himself would have indicated—that Troy was not part of the Mycenaean culture at all; and Troy, whatever its archaeological interest, would not today be considered a part of Mycenaean studies.

[2] Mycenae sent small contingents to Thermopylae and Plataea (Hdt. 7.202, 9.28), but was later destroyed and then resettled before petering out entirely in the Roman period.

[3] πολυχρύσοιο Μυκήνης, Hom. Il. 7.180, 11.46.

exclaimed, "I have gazed on the face of Agamemnon."[4] Later excavations at the sites where Homer and the mythographers had located the main centers of power in the heroic age revealed palaces of wealth and intricacy, quite unlike anything known from classical Greece. To the Greeks themselves these buildings had been marvels of mythical dimensions, "cyclopean" walls and a "labyrinth," built by people greater than themselves for purposes shrouded in mystery. The excavations found frescoed walls, storehouses that had once held stores of food, highly worked golden jewelry, and well-painted ceramics. As scholars came to grips with the discoveries, it was widely doubted whether the ruined palaces had been built by Greeks at all.

The Texts

The clue was found by Sir Arthur Evans at Knossos, where he found a number of clay tablets, written in a script that he could not read, and preserved by the accident of having been baked into ceramic by the fire that destroyed the palace. Evans was sufficiently perspicacious to demonstrate that the tablets used two different scripts, which he called, unimaginatively, "Linear A" and "Linear B." They bore an obvious relationship to a syllabic script that was still used in Cyprus in historical times, but the relationship was not close enough to allow Evans to read the tablets he had found.

The story of the decipherment of Linear B has been told elsewhere and told well,[5] and this is not the place to rehearse it. It was the work of many people, chief among them Evans, Carl Blegen (the latter, in his excavations of Pylos, found more than five hundred more Linear B tablets), Emmett Bennett, Jr., Alice Kober (who claimed from the first that the tablets could be deciphered even without a bilingual text, unlike every previous decipherment, by careful attention to the language structure, and whose demonstration of case inflection in the tablets was arguably the crucial discovery), and the final decipherer Michael Ventris, whose co-worker and

---

4 In fact Schliemann may have been in some doubt as to which mask was Agamemnon's, though he does not seem to have doubted that one of them was: see the correspondence quoted in Dickinson, "The 'Face of Agamemnon.'"

5 A brief account is given in DMG[2], 3–27; John Chadwick's original account, *The Decipherment of Linear B*, recaptures some of the romance of the original decipherment and of the decipherer, who died in an automobile accident at the age of 34 while *DMG* was still in press.

advisor on Greek language, John Chadwick, was the one who fashioned a story out of published and unpublished scholarly papers. For our purposes it is important to say what the tablets contained and what they did not. They are almost entirely inventories: inventories of items held at various places, inventories of assessments to be paid, inventories of personnel and livestock. They are written in a script that fits Greek most inadequately, one that would leave room for enormous ambiguities had the contexts not been so restricted and had the scribes not added ideograms to clarify their meaning. There are no poems, no letters, no narrative of any type. Archaeology, paradoxically, can show us more about the thoughts and fantasies of the Mycenaeans than can their own writings.

But the tablets themselves, unglamorous though their contents may be, have opened up a window on a world of which neither archaeology nor literature had given us any intimation. The excavations, indeed, had indicated that the palaces commanded a good deal of the wealth of their territory; the tablets have revealed the procedures and the bureaucracy—no other word is appropriate—by which the wealth was appropriated and managed. We learn from the tablets the names of the gods and of men and women, the titles of the kings and nobles, the methods of taxation, the management of land and of manpower, and none of these matters turn out to be quite what we would have expected—a cautionary note for the reconstruction of other societies that we know only from archaeology. The silences of the tablets are also informative: the number of inscriptions is large enough to give us a reasonable confidence that those matters which are not treated in them fell outside of the palatial system.[6] The language of the tablets is itself of interest, being both recognizably Greek and considerably different from the Greek we know; some of the words, moreover, seem not to be Greek at all, and hint at broader cultural ties than we had known.

What makes Mycenaean studies a separate subfield of classics is not so much the Mycenaean age as the Dark Ages that followed it. The language of the Mycenaeans survived, with changes, into the classical period; their pottery underwent drastic changes, though certain continuities can be traced; but their political organization, their economy and their writing system collapsed almost entirely, so that Greeks of the archaic period, aware only in the vaguest way of what had existed in what they considered the heroic age, had to reinvent these aspects of their lives on their own, influenced by their neighbors but not by their ancestors. For people raised

---

[6] On this see the perceptive article of Halstead, "The Mycenaean Palatial Economy: Making the Most of the Gaps in the Evidence."

on classical Greece, the Mycenaean world is a different world, a world of whose workings the classical Greeks were unaware but about whose people they continued, and continue today, to tell larger-than-life stories. For some the foreignness of the Mycenaean world means that it can be ignored with impunity; for others precisely that foreignness is its fascination.

OUTSTANDING PROBLEMS

The generations that saw the discoveries of Schliemann and of Ventris saw a world open before them in which everything was new and unknown; for those two generations, Mycenaean studies were by far the most promising and exciting field for new research. The basics of those two discoveries have by now been assimilated; as with the field of classics itself, we have passed the time when new editions of important unknown texts were appearing all the time and moved into the longer time when our job is to see what more there is to be learned from the information we have. The most important questions are undoubtedly those that nobody has yet thought to ask; these are the ones that have the potential to revolutionize the field. But there are also some well-established questions for whose answers we are still waiting.

When Was the Palace at Knossos Destroyed?

In about 1400 BCE, according to its excavator, Sir Arthur Evans; but Carl Blegen, who excavated Pylos, placed that palace's destruction about 1200 BCE and noted the close similarity between the artifacts and the tablets found in the two places. This has led to a long and acrimonious controversy, based chiefly upon the examination of Evans' excavation notes, over the question of whether the date of the Knossos conflagration must be brought down to 1200;[7] the basic lines of the controversy were set out in Palmer and Boardman, On the Knossos Tablets, and other solutions to the problem have since been suggested.[8] The controversy has not, as of this

---

[7] One might have thought that further excavation could resolve the question, but Evans' excavation and reconstruction left little if any area for further uncontaminated excavation.

[8] See, inter alia, Driessen, "Le palais de Cnossos au MR II–III: Combien de destructions?"; for a recent overview see Preston, "Late Minoan II to III B Crete."

writing, been authoritatively resolved, and archaeologists generally refer, where possible, to events and findings in the period not by absolute date but by the relative dates that were first established by Evans. This system divides the Minoan period into Early Minoan, Middle Minoan and Late Minoan; each of these is in turn divided into three periods indicated by Roman numerals, and those periods are further subdivided into periods indicated by capital letters, so that, for example, the earlier part of the third phase of the Late Minoan period will be denoted as LM III A. The periods and sub-periods are established by the dominant pottery styles. This general division was employed by Blegen and Wace for the Mycenaean world; in order to avoid using the same abbreviation they called their periods Early Helladic, Middle Helladic and Late Helladic. These divisions, which are internally consistent, allow scholars to discuss the periods involved within an agreed framework, raising the question of absolute dating only when it is relevant.

Linear A

The decipherment of Linear A remains an open challenge. Although Linear B turned out, to many people's surprise, to be Greek, the decipherment has if anything made it even more certain that Linear A is not Greek. The Linear B syllabary fits Greek very poorly—it does not distinguish b from p, g from k, or r from l—and the simplest explanation of the fact is that it is an adaptation of some other syllabary, presumably Linear A, which was invented for a language with a radically different phonology. This challenge, however, is probably a chimera: there are many fewer documents in Linear A than in Linear B, and those there are do not offer sufficient basis for a reliable decipherment. Potential decipherers should at least be warned that working on this puzzle, intriguing though it may be, is not a promising way to academic advancement. Bennett and Kober, whose work turned out to have been of fundamental importance, got little recognition at the time; and Ventris was not an academic at all, but an architect who was attracted to the problem as a puzzle.[9]

---

[9]   In fact, once he had worked out the decipherment, Ventris indicated that he had no further interest in the Mycenaeans: Robinson, *The Man Who Deciphered Linear B*, 147.

Synthesizing the Archaeological and the Textual Evidence

It was the great palaces that made the Mycenaeans so intriguing, but by now those palaces are only a part of the archaeological record. Remains from the Mycenaean period have been found throughout Greece, and the techniques of the "new archaeology"[10] have revealed many details of the life of the period that were not hinted at by the palace excavations. The reasons for a regime's strength are never to be found exclusively at the center; it is on the people of the realm that every ruler, however autocratic, ultimately depends. Our picture of the Mycenaean world will be much more interesting as the connections between the palace, the smaller settlements and the countryside are elucidated.

A parallel challenge is the synthesis of the archaeological and the textual evidence. The original decipherment took account, of course, of what archaeology had taught us about the Mycenaeans, and it was the Linear B documents that made it finally clear that the heroic model of kingship we see in Homer had little if anything to do with the power of the Mycenaean kings. But as archaeology and textual analysis progress, there is always a challenge of keeping the two abreast of each other, so that our general picture takes account of all the information we possess—a meager enough sample, even with the wonderful discoveries.

The Absorption of Mycenaean Studies into the Classics

As the classical world forms the basis for our own, the Mycenaean world formed the basis for the classical Greek world that followed it almost a thousand years later. The classical language was directly descended from the early Greek of which the tablets preserve one dialect; the Greek gods were mostly those whom the Mycenaeans had worshiped; the heroes about whom they told their stories were thought to have lived in the age that we call Mycenaean. Nevertheless, the history of Greece for most of us still starts in the archaic period; and bridging the gap that historians call the Dark Ages remains a task that has been fulfilled only partially.

The Mycenaeans and Their Neighbors

The Mycenaeans are apparently depicted in Egyptian wall-paintings and mentioned in Hittite records. The Philistines are now generally recognized

---

[10] See above, pp. 186–8.

as a people with significant Greek connections, or even, perhaps, transplanted Greeks themselves.[11] Linear B itself includes many words that are not identifiably Greek, and some, at least, are certainly loanwords. There is little to recommend claims that Greek civilization was "copied" or even "stolen" from its near Eastern neighbors,[12] but much remains to be done in elucidating the connections of the Mycenaeans with the world around them.

MAJOR RESOURCES

The twin pillars of Mycenaean studies are archaeology and the study of the Linear B texts. The basic documents of the first were Schliemann's famous volumes: *Troy and Its Remains*, *Mycenae*, *Ilios*, *Troja*, and *Tiryns*, but, for all their romance and historical importance, these can no longer be read today without the greatest of care; see on this Traill, *Schliemann of Troy* and the considerable scholarly discussion since. The names of Wilhelm Dörpfeld, Sir Arthur Evans and Carl Blegen are no less basic to the Minoan and Mycenaean periods, though they are only the most famous of the many who contributed. Even had Schliemann been a source of the utmost reliability, Mycenaean archaeology has progressed vastly since his days, not only in the excavation of the great sites but in the discovery of Mycenaean remains from all over mainland Greece, Crete and the Aegean islands. Mylonas, *Mycenae and the Mycenaean Age* was an excellent summary and has not been surpassed, though it has aged considerably (it devoted only ten pages to the Linear B documents, which were then still hot news). Many serviceable books of a slightly less scholarly nature can serve as a good introduction, but a new synthesis is greatly to be desired. In the meantime we have a new "companion," Shelmerdine, *The Cambridge Companion to the Aegean Bronze Age*.

The basic document of the second pillar is Ventris and Chadwick, DMG², a book that has weathered its first fifty years (the first edition was in

---

[11] For a recent summary of the evidence see Killebrew, *Biblical Peoples and Ethnicity*, 197–245.

[12] The extreme statement of this claim was Bernal, *Black Athena*, for which cf. Levine and Peradotto, eds., *The Challenge of Black Athena* and Bernal, *Black Athena Writes Back*; for a negative account of the extremes to which this hypothesis has been taken see Lefkowitz, *Not Out of Africa*. A more scholarly catalogue of near Eastern influences on Greek culture is West, *The East Face of Helicon*. Neither Bernal nor West is dealing particularly with the Mycenaeans; both are interested in making claims about the roots of classical Greek culture.

1956) quite well and remains the best summary of what the tablets are, how they appear and what sorts of information are contained in them. This, however, is only a selection; the complete documents are printed, though not translated or discussed, in Bennett, *The Pylos Tablets Transcribed*, Killen and Olivier, *The Knossos Tablets*, Aravantinos, Godart and Sacconi, *Thèbes: Fouilles de la Cadmée* and Melena and Olivier, *Tithemy*. We now have a Mycenaean dictionary, Aura Jorro, *Diccionario Micénico* (DMic); a Mycenaean grammar, Bartoněk, *Handbuch des mykenischen Griechisch*; and even a primer for beginners, Hooker, *Linear B: An Introduction*. Mycenaean Greek, unknown to the editors of LSJ[9], was included in the *Revised Supplement*; DGE restricts itself to giving cross-references to DMic, which itself forms part of DGE. For an overview there is a companion here, too: Duhoux and Davies, *A Companion to Linear B: Mycenaean Greek Texts and Their World*. The bibliographical journal *Studies in Mycenaean Inscriptions and Dialect* is an ongoing project that appeared from 1953 to 1978 and was revived in 1994; admirably complete for the years it covers and available online as SMIDonline, it has not yet succeeded in the Sisyphean task of catching up to date.

16

NUMISMATICS

COIN COLLECTING AND NUMISMATICS

Numismatics, more than any other subfield of classical studies, intersects with a field whose interest in the ancient world is only tangential: that of coin collecting. Coin collectors may be hobbyists, investors or speculators, but they are scholars of the ancient world only insofar as it is the ancient world that produced the coin in which they are interested, and that gives it its distinctiveness. Much of the technical writing for collectors is interested in the market value of particular coins, a question that may have little if any connection with the scholarly interest of the coin. Numismatists are interested not only in the coin's weight, composition, condition and origin, but also in questions that may have little effect on its value: where and in what context was it found? Why did the moneyer choose the particular design that appears on the coin? What other coins were found with it? According to what weight standard was it made, and how accurately was the weight controlled? What, if anything, can it tell us about the people who authorized it, the people who produced it and the people who used it?

HOW COINS WERE MADE

Most coins in the ancient world were made of gold (Aʋ), silver (Aℛ) or bronze (Æ); the signs in parentheses are generally used in numismatic publications to refer to these three metals. Other metals were used: electrum (an alloy of gold and silver), billon (8 percent copper and 20 percent silver) or sometimes simply a silver-plated copper piece.[1] These last were often counterfeits, but in some places they were legal currency.

Ancient coins were normally struck: that is, the *flan* (the pre-weighed disk of precious metal) was placed between two *dies* (hard metal disks with an intaglio pattern) and then struck with a hammer, transferring the (reversed) image on the dies to the coin. The more important image[2] is called the *obverse*, the less important the *reverse*; the chief image on either side is called the *type*, and any lettering is called the *legend*. In Greek coins the obverse was generally the form on the lower die (the one on the anvil, not the one struck by the hammer); once it became customary to put the head of the ruler on the coin, the side with the head was the obverse, and that is why the sides are distinguished colloquially as "heads" and "tails."

This method of production meant that the coin itself was always slightly irregular in shape: if you find one that is a perfect disk, it is a modern fake, and a poor one.

IDENTIFYING A COIN

A modern coin is relatively easy to identify: it usually bears the name of the government that issued it, its year of issue and its nominal value, written clearly for all to see. It may include other items whose meaning is less clear—not every American knows what *e pluribus unum* means on a dime, nor does every Briton know what the words *pleidiol wyf i'm gwlad* mean on the rim of some one-pound coins—but for a coin whose legend is written in a known alphabet, it is not difficult for the user, or even for a foreigner, to identify where it comes from and what its value is. Coins of recent decades, moreover, are generally made of base metal, which is less valuable than silver and gold but harder, so that the letters remain legible.

That is not, in general, the case for ancient coins; even when they are in good condition, they are not easily identified by an amateur. Greek coins have an image on each side, and often the name of the issuing city; but the

---

[1] The symbols El, Bi and Cu are sometimes used to indicate electrum, billon and copper issues respectively.

[2] This is, as far as I have been able to establish, the more common meaning of the terms *obverse* and *reverse*; some numismatists, however, always use the term *obverse* to refer to the lower die, *reverse* to the upper die. In ancient numismatics the two usages usually, but not always, coincide.

name may be abbreviated, written in an archaic alphabet or omitted entirely. From the Hellenistic period onward the name and image of the king will generally appear; the value of the coin is hardly ever written on it. Roman republican coins often, though not always, bear the name of the issuing magistrate, but, although you will be able to guess that M·CIPI·M·F refers to Marcus Cipius, son of Marcus, you will probably need a catalogue to inform you that he dates from the late second century BCE. If you take the trouble to consult MRR and RE you can discover what is known about him—nothing, except that he minted these coins. Imperial coins are somewhat easier, since the number of emperors was smaller than the number of republican officials; but imperial identifications have their pitfalls, too. The non-specialist will not feel too inadequate for being unable to date IMP C CARAVSIVS P F AVG,[3] but may require some help in recognizing which Faustina is meant on a coin whose obverse has DIVA FAVSTINA and whose reverse has AETERNITAS S·C,[4] and may be entirely surprised to discover that ANTONINVS PIVS AVG, further identified on the reverse of the coin[5] as PONTIF·TR·P·XI COS·III is not Antoninus Pius, but Caracalla.

For an amateur to identify a coin—assuming, as is not necessarily the case, that it is genuine[6]—will generally require finding an identical coin or a close parallel in a catalogue, whether printed or online. For this kind of search the indices at the end of a catalogue will generally steer you to the right place to discover what is before you.[7] The lettering on the coin is crucial, but it is not all: the pictures and the workmanship may mean as much or more, and the dimensions of the coin, both diameter and

---

[3]   M. Aurelius Carausius, who was proclaimed emperor and ruled over Britain and part of Gaul from 286 to 293 CE.

[4]   This Faustina was the elder one, wife of Antoninus Pius: Mattingly et al., RIC 3, p. 161 nos. 1099–1115.

[5]   Ibid. 4, Part 1, p. 228 nos. 100–06.

[6]   It is almost impossible for a beginner to recognize a well-made fake. The best guarantee for a collector is buying from a reputable dealer; a scholar, who does not have to buy coins to begin a career as a numismatist, will develop over time a better background than most forgers have, and will be able to see through their imitations. It must be remembered, too, that not every counterfeit is modern: the ancients, too, struck counterfeit coins, and an ancient counterfeit may on occasion be no less intriguing than a legitimate coin.

[7]   For Greek coins, Plant, Greek Coin Types and Their Identification was written with this in mind; Reece and James, Identifying Roman Coins is much briefer and restricts itself to the coins commonly found in Britain, but within its limits gives practical advice very accessible to the beginner.

thickness, are important information; so is the weight. For an amateur to identify a single coin, however, is a matter of coin collecting, not numismatics. The interesting part, from a scholarly point of view, is what we can find out from the coin once we recognize it.

PUTTING IT IN CONTEXT

We are accustomed to coins that are generally stable: a dime minted in 1972 differs from a dime minted in 2002 only in the date. Even modern coins, however, can offer telltale information about their history. The zinc pennies minted by the United States in 1944 tell a story about the difficulties of obtaining sufficient copper for the war effort; no such problem, apparently, existed with silver, from which dimes and quarters continued to be struck. In 1965, on the other hand, a sudden and acute shortage of silver[8] caused the United States to abandon entirely the use of silver in its coins. Designs, too, have their stories to tell. The francs of France's Vichy government kept the design of the coins of the third republic, but replaced the slogans *République française* and *liberté—égalité— fraternité* with *État français* and *état—patrie—famille*. The fasces, a central symbol of the Roman republic, had been the reverse type of American dimes since 1916; forever besmirched by Mussolini, they were replaced by a torch on the new Roosevelt dimes that appeared in 1946.

In the ancient world, where the intaglio had to be made by hand each time a die wore out, the opportunities for innovation were much greater than they are today. Events much more fleeting than revolutions and world wars were recorded on coins, and the choice of design and legend is often significant. Victories, celebrations, legal innovations and many other events were commemorated by the issue of special coins. The legend or the type may inform us about these events, or may help date them. On the Faustina coin we mentioned above, the word *diva* makes it clear that she was dead, for imperial figures were not deified in their lifetimes; this, in turn, explains the word *aeternitas* on the reverse.

DATING COINS

Since they were made by hand, no two ancient coins are precisely identical; since the dies were also made by hand, the designs on the coins

---

[8] For the extremity of the shortage, little remembered today, see Rickenbacker, *Wooden Nickels*, 13–22.

will be identical only if they were struck from the same die. This means that one can distinguish different issues of coins by the details of the design; many different dies may have been used even in a single year, so that distinguishing the particular issues can give us a remarkably detailed chronology—but only if we can tell which design came first and which came later.

For a long time chronologies of coins that had no clear indication of date were established, *faute de mieux*, by style, and it is indeed the case that styles vary not only according to the individual artisan but also with time and place. Letter-forms change; styles of building and costume change, and the designs on coins change accordingly; the level of workmanship may go up or down in accordance with economic or political events. But dating by style will always be impressionistic, and modern numismatists generally rely on other criteria as well.

There are a number of considerations that can help date a coin. Hellenistic or Roman coins, with the head of the ruler and/or the name of the issuing magistrate, often with accompanying titulature, in effect bear their date on their face almost as clearly as modern coins do. Hoards of coins are useful in indicating what sorts of coins circulated together: if we know the date of some of them, then we know the approximate dates of the others. Coins that are found in archaeological excavations can usually be dated by the level at which they are found, though of course an individual coin may simply have fallen into a place where it did not belong. If the coin bears an indication associating it with a historical event, that can date the coin. Finally, the condition of the coin is an indication: a coin found in very good condition probably did not circulate for long before it was deposited or lost.

Most of these clues (except, usually, for the dates of magistrates) will give us only approximate dates, and, indeed, coins generally circulate for a number of years; but accumulation of information can sometimes help us be more specific. A further technique can be helpful in establishing relative dating of many coins of a single issue; that technique is dating by die sequence.

Our ability to establish a die sequence is based on the fact that two dies were needed to produce a coin, and they did not generally wear out at the same time, so that when the reverse die wore out a new reverse would appear with the old obverse die; later, when the obverse die wore out, we would get a new obverse with the same reverse. Since the die develops imperfections as it wears out, we can often tell which of the different obverse dies that go with a particular reverse (or vice versa) was the earlier. Where enough coins are available, it is possible to make a sequence of the different issues by matching up each new die with its predecessor; and this will give us, in the ideal case, a full chronological sequence for the coins of a particular type. Unfortunately for this method, however, we never have more than a tiny fraction of any given issue of ancient coins, so that we may have no more than one coin for each die, or indeed we may be missing any number of dies. Where practical, however, die analysis has much to teach us.

METROLOGY AND METALLURGY

The value of most ancient coins was a function of their metal and weight and their fineness (that is, their precious metal content), so variations in either of these matters are of great interest. The weight will tell us not only what coin we are handling—is it a drachma, a didrachm or a tetradrachm?—but will also tell us something about the commercial environment of the issuing state, since various systems of weights were in use in the ancient world, and a state's choice of which measures to use presumably had to do with its real or desired commercial relations. The fineness would also vary either as the issuing authority found it easier or harder to provide the precious metal or as it chose to adjust the content of the coinage to its own fiscal advantage. Since there was a constant tension between two concepts—a coin might be a piece of metal whose stamp represented merely a guarantee of its weight and fineness, or it might be seen as a token whose value derived from the fact that it would pass in the marketplace—there was on the one hand a temptation for the government to decrease the percentage of precious metal and rely on the second concept to maintain its original value, and on the other a tendency for the first concept to reassert itself and bring the market value of the debased coinage into line with its lower metal value. Modern metallurgical techniques allow us to follow these developments with much greater accuracy than was possible even a few decades ago; we can also determine precise amounts of trace-elements, information that can sometimes identify the source of the metal that the government was using for its coins. In fact, the fineness of ancient coins was usually quite stable; it was a factor in the earliest gold/electrum coinages, and became significant again when the Roman emperors debased the coinage, particularly in the third century, when adulteration of silver got completely out of hand and led to inflation of modern dimensions and eventually required the establishment of an entirely new system of coinage to replace the old one that no longer commanded confidence. But in more normal times, most

Greeks and Romans accepted coins by denomination as we do, without worrying too much about their precise silver or gold content.

ICONOGRAPHY

The pictures on ancient coins at the very least identify the authority that produced (or, in the case of counterfeits, was pretended to have produced) them; but their identification was usually a matter of recognized symbols. A female head wearing a helmet was Athena to a Greek; two faces on a single head were Janus to a Roman; a man carrying a club and wearing a lion skin was Hercules.[9] Whether these divinities appear as mere symbols or whether their presence on a coin was in some way intended to invoke the divinity's protection must be a matter of conjecture. The two possibilities do not necessarily exclude each other: the thalers of Maria Theresa, Empress of Austria (1745–80), were popular in Europe for their high silver content, whereas their popularity in Africa seems to have been connected with the Empress's ample bosom, a readily recognizable sign of fertility in African iconography.[10]

Propaganda, true or false, is a common motivation. Although not every victory claimed is a victory won, Vespasian's famous IVDAEA CAPTA coins publicized a victory that he undoubtedly did win; his simultaneous LIBERTAS RESTITVTA coins should perhaps not be taken too literally. For that very reason, though, they may be interesting: although libertas on this coin cannot have meant what it meant to Brutus and Cassius, that Vespasian should use it as his slogan, and that his slogan should indicate that it was something that had been lost under his predecessors, indicates something that we otherwise might not have known about the narrative on which he based his legitimacy. Not only the words but the picture may carry a message. King Darius of Persia probably spent relatively little of his time shooting arrows on the run, but that is the way his coins portrayed him, since martial prowess was what he wanted his subjects to associate with him. Iconography and propaganda can go together, as when the coins of the emperor Commodus show him with Hercules' lion-skin, or those of Demetrius I of Bactria with an elephant-scalp to advertise him as the conqueror of India.

---

[9] The use of iconography for easy recognition of a character whose features may be unfamiliar, imaginary or simply too small is still common in editorial cartoons and in children's books (where the king always wears a crown, even in bed).

[10] On the remarkable history of the Maria Theresa thaler see Semple, *A Silver Legend*.

Every item in the type of a coin may tell us something. The choice of an emblem may have various motivations: as a simple matter of identification, a state may choose its patron deity, its major product (barley in Metapontum, silphium in Cyrene or, combining the patron deity with the product, Dionysus on the coinage of a number of wine-producing polities), a significant historical or mythological connection (Pegasus in Corinth, Dionysus or his cantharus on Naxos, where he rescued Ariadne) or even a simple pun (the seal, φώκη, on the coinage of Phocaea, or the apple, μῆλον, for Melos). The language chosen may be significant: the legends on Macedonian coinage were in Greek, whereas the Carians used their own letters on their coins. Which deity was chosen was significant: Julius Caesar's coins featured Venus, from whom he claimed to be descended; the coins of Sextus Pompeius, who continued the fight against Caesar in the name of his dead father, featured a female figure whom the coins' legend identified as *pietas*. Even the letter-forms could be a matter of propaganda: although the Jews had been writing with Assyrian letter-forms for centuries, the Hasmonean kings, the leaders of the Great Revolt, and Bar Kochba all used the old Hebrew script.[11] It must have been hard for many of the Jews themselves to read, but it made a point about the antiquity of the claims of a relatively new, or even revolutionary, government.

THE ANALYSIS OF GROUPS OF COINS

There is much that can be learned from looking at coins individually, but that is not the end of the story. Various kinds of analysis can give us more information than any single coin could give. In addition to die analysis, mentioned above, there is also a good deal to be learned from hoard analysis: many of the most interesting finds are not single coins, but hoards that were hidden in antiquity and may contain hundreds or even thousands of coins. In any hoard, of course, the coins must all have been minted before they were buried, so, if the hoard was found in an archaeological context that allows it to be dated, we have a *terminus ante quem* for all the coins in the hoard—and in view of the impressionistic nature of the evidence available for establishing absolute dates, this can be very valuable information. Paying attention to the details, moreover, may reveal more than just dates. A single hoard buried under the floor of a temple at

---

[11] The later Hasmonean kings issued bilingual coins, which are the only source of our knowledge of their precise names.

Ephesus, containing unmarked "blanks," coins with an image on one side only, and coins with an image on both obverse and reverse, is the source of most of our knowledge about the stages through which coins passed at the time of their invention; the date of the floor under which it was found gives us the closest thing we have to a firm date by which we can be sure that coins were circulating.[12] In India, a hoard that included more than a thousand well-worn Indian coins along with two coins of Alexander the Great and a single coin of Philip Arrhidaeus, his hapless successor, in near-mint condition put paid forever to the idea that the concept of coinage had been introduced to India by the Macedonian conquest.[13] Often the composition of the hoard—Are the coins of large or small denominations? Are they from a single place or many? Do they span a long period of time or a short one? Are they worn or new?—can at least suggest to us something about the purpose for which the hoard was assembled, or the circumstances under which it was hidden.

Much more can be learned by comparing or surveying the contents of various hoards. If every hoard that is found in a datable context allows us to draw conclusions about the dating of the coins in it, comparing the contents of various hoards allows us to draw up reliable tables as to when and where different forms of coins were in circulation. We are able, moreover, to do a certain amount of *mobility analysis* by noting how far abroad coins may wander from their place of issue. For a rudimentary mobility analysis, it suffices to track where individual coins have been found; the analysis of hoards allows us not only to see where they may have been found, but to form some idea—with a good deal of caution—about how large a proportion they were of the coins circulating in various places.

This brings us to another form of analysis, *volume analysis*: the attempt to discover how many coins of a particular issue may have been minted. It is obviously of interest to know, for example, that Athenian "owls" were issued in enormous numbers and traveled throughout the eastern Mediterranean; it is more interesting, and much harder, to know precisely when that happened. Earlier generations of numismatists made judgments

---

[12] Recent excavations changed the dating of the floor, and so suggested a considerable downward revision of the estimated date of the invention: see Bammer, "A Peripteros of the Geometric Period in the Artemisium of Ephesus," id., "Les sanctuaires des VIIIe et VIIe siècles à l'Artémision d'Éphèse," and Schaps, *Invention of Coinage*, 95–6; see now, however, Cahill and Kroll, "New Archaic Coin Finds at Sardis," 613–14.

[13] Walsh, *Punch-Marked Coins from Taxila*.

of volume of issue simply by tabulating the number of coins of a given type that were known; modern numismatists, aware of both the tiny percentage of coinage that has survived and the large effect that chance may have on its survival, try to get more reliable results by combining volume analysis with die analysis. Since it presumably takes a similar number of coins to wear out each die, tabulating the number of known dies can give us some idea of the total volume of coins issued. This is still a very rough analysis, but it can be illuminating.

READING NUMISMATIC PUBLICATIONS

Numismatists find coins interesting for themselves. An outsider, or even an insider to whose research this particular item has no relevance, may have little patience for reading a catalogue of every one of the 567 coins in a hoard, or for reading a discussion of how the folds of a goddess's robe changed from one issue to another, but these, of course, are the basis without which the discoveries that may interest others could never be made. The person whose interest in a particular article is only tangential will presumably skim the details, but should not skip them: no article is proof against the unwarranted inference, the overgeneralization, and the other pitfalls of scholarship, and so, before you rely on a particular claim, you will want to judge whether or not the claim is indeed supported by the evidence adduced.

The evidence is normally brought in the form of descriptions and pictures of individual coins, often presented in the form of a catalogue. The pictures used to be drawings; now they will almost invariably be photographs. The descriptions usually follow a more or less standard format, of which the following[14] is one example:

18 AE. 21–2 mm, 5.25 g (7). Axis: 6   [1]
    Vives 141–13, Gil 73–4, GMI 991, 993
    PERM CAES AVG; laureate head, l.
    C A E LE V X; Aquila between two signa
    1–2. Ba 14696, 23724, 5.16, 5.07; **3.** Calicó 6/1979, 576, 6.78; **4.** L 2125, 5.13; **5. M 10877** (= Vives 141–13), 6.36; **6–8.** M 10863, 10878–9, 4.81, 3.44, 3.76 (broken).

[14] RPC I 18.

The information contained in these seven lines is as follows:

1. **18.** In any publication that deals with more than one coin (and most do), each is given a number.
2. **AE** would normally mean that the coin is made of bronze, but that term can cover a large variety of alloys. RPC, from which this example is taken, tries to be slightly more specific, and so uses AE for an "uncertain copper-based alloy" (which is indeed what numismatists usually mean when they describe a coin as "bronze"), reserving the term "bronze" for those alloys that the editors know to include about 5–30 percent tin.
3. **21–22 mm.** is the diameter. Numismatic publications nowadays almost universally use the metric system.
4. **5.25 g** is the weight in grams.
5. **(7)** is the number of coins of this type whose weight is known to the editors.
6. **Axis: 6** indicates that the reverse is inverted ("at 6 o'clock") by comparison to the obverse. Sometimes the relationship of the reverse to the obverse is indicated by an arrow.
7. **[1]** is a mark introduced by the editors of this collection, indicating the number of specimens represented in the major museum collections of the world; the number is offered in the hope that it gives some rough idea of how common the coin was in antiquity.
8. **Vives 141–13, Gil 73–4, GMI 991, 993** are the major bibliographical references; the publications to which they refer are indicated in a list of abbreviations, generally at the beginning or end of the publication.
9. **PERM CAES AVG** is the obverse legend, perm(issu) Caes(aris) Aug(usti), "by permission of Augustus Caesar."
10. **laureate head, l.** is the type: a head crowned with a laurel wreath facing left. "Laureate" is one of a number of such expressions, usually transparent enough to a classicist, that are part of the numismatic shorthand. Occasionally even a beginner whose Latin is excellent will need one of the numismatic dictionaries to discover that, for example, "fulminating" means "wielding a thunderbolt." "Left" and "right" in numismatics mean the left and right of the viewer, not the left and right of the figure who looks out at you from the coin.
11. **C A E LE V X; Aquila between two signa** gives the same information for the reverse that was given above for the obverse. The legend, as can be discovered from Stevenson, Smith and Madden, *A Dictionary of Roman*

Coins s.v. V X,[15] means *Colonia Augusta Emerita, Legio XV* (the *colonia* of Augusta Emerita, 15th legion); and if you check RE under the entry "Emerita" you will discover that Augusta Emerita is the modern Mérida in Spain; since today it is a not inconsiderable town, any good map will show you where it is. An *aquila* is not just any eagle, but an eagle on a pike used as the standard of a legion; *signa* are other military ensigns.

12. **1–2. Ba 14696, 23724, 5.16, 5.07; 3. Calicó 6/1979, 576, 6.78; 4. L 2125, 5.13; 5. M 10877 (= Vives 141–13), 6.36; 6–8. M 10863, 10878–9, 4.81, 3.44, 3.76 (broken).** These are all the coins of this type known to the editors, eight in the current case; for each there is a bibliographical reference ("Ba 14696, 23724"—again you will have to refer to the book's bibliography to know what "Ba" is) and the weight of the specimen (5.16, 5.07—grams, of course).

This is by no means the only format in which you will find coins described in numismatic publications, but it is one that has been admired and imitated. Depending on the purpose of the publication the information may be presented in tabular form, some of the above information may be omitted, and some other (thickness, fineness, etc.) may be included as appropriate. The variations, once you have a picture of what sort of format is normal, are usually easily comprehensible.

COINS AND HISTORY

Coins will rarely rewrite history for us. Insofar as history is a narrative of the great events that occur to and among peoples, that narrative will rarely be established by numismatic evidence.[16] The numismatic evidence does, however, both illustrate and supplement our knowledge. It gives us a window into particular aspects of history that our narrative sources often neglect or distort: how rulers wished to be seen by their subjects, how wealthy they were, and how wide their influence; how long a commercial center may have operated, and how opulent its merchandise; how far a

---

[15] Having discovered from the article that the coin belonged to the fifteenth legion, I was intrigued by the surprising (to me) form V X for "fifteen"; and it was under the heading V X that I found the legend explained.

[16] There are, however, cases where it does happen: numismatics looms large in the reconstruction of the history of the Hellenistic kings of Bactria and India in Tarn, *The Greeks in Bactria and India.*

people's commercial relationships may have extended, or how wide the area served by a given market. Not to every historical question does numismatics have something to contribute; but where it does, it can be quite illuminating.

COINS AND ART

We may not be used to thinking of the design of coins as being a very high form of art, although in fact the production of a well-designed coin is a serious artistic undertaking; but ancient coins have the added advantage of being one of the least destructible forms of art. Painting from the ancient world, except for the painting of pottery, has rarely survived; even for most ancient buildings only the foundations survive, if that. Coins may occasionally recreate an important work of art or architecture that is now lost to us; more often, they reflect the artistic taste and practices of their period, and give us a valuable window into periods and peoples of whom little else may have survived. Both here and in historical questions, the tendency of coins to circulate near their place of origin may be a positive advantage, offsetting the tendency of our written sources to concentrate on what was happening in Athens, Rome and other places that seemed to them most important.

MAJOR RESOURCES

Handbooks

The most recent guide to the study of ancient coins is Nicolet-Pierre, *Numismatique grecque*; Alföldi, *Antike Numismatik* and Breglia, *Numismatica antica: Storia e metodologia* are still useful, and Christ, *Antike Numismatik* a brief but very useful introduction. Nothing like them exists in English, though Casey, *Understanding Ancient Coins* gives a short introduction to how they may be used by historians and archaeologists and Howgego, *Ancient History from Coins* is an accessible and popular introduction that focuses less on the way a historian should approach a coin and more on the historical problems on which they have or can shed light. Technical terms and basic concepts are available in Melville Jones, *A Dictionary of Ancient Greek Coins* and its companion Melville Jones, *A Dictionary of Ancient Roman Coins*; much larger and much older is Stevenson, Smith and Madden, *A Dictionary of Roman Coins*.

Catalogues

As in the case of inscriptions, the authoritative publication of coins is often the catalogue of the museum that owns them; the stupendous collections of the British Museum (*A Catalogue of the Greek Coins in the British Museum*, *Coins of the Roman Republic in the British Museum*, and *Coins of the Roman Empire in the British Museum*) are noteworthy, but there are many others, and the international series *Sylloge Nummorum Graecorum* now numbers more than 150 volumes in print. More useful to the outsider are collections of selected examples of coins. For Greece, the vast and learned Head, *Historia Numorum* is still incomparable, and the even vaster Babelon, *Traité*, though never completed, remains useful, but the more recent and less encyclopedic Kraay, *Archaic and Classical Greek Coins* will usually be more practical and reliable. For Rome, the essential collections are Michael H. Crawford, *Roman Republican Coinage* (RRC) and Mattingly et al., *Roman Imperial Coinage* (RIC); newer and more concise is Carson, *Coins of the Roman Empire*. For the provinces, though so far it covers only the years from 44 BCE to 96 CE, the catalogue is Burnett, Amandry and Ripollès, *Roman Provincial Coinage* (RPC). Excellent photographic reproductions can be found in Kraay, *Greek Coins* and its companion volume, Kent, *Roman Coins*. A group of Italian scholars has announced a project to produce a *Lexicon Iconographicum Numismaticae*, which if successful should be an enormously useful scholarly tool, and not only for numismatists.

The identification of a particular coin is a science in itself, and one that at some time or other concerns many people with no scholarly interest in ancient coins who may have come across an intriguing item in a tourist shop. The comprehensive printed catalogues are those of David R. Sear, *Greek Coins and Their Values*, *Greek Imperial Coins and Their Values*, and *Roman Coins and Their Values*. Alphabetical lists of coin legends can be found at the back of the volumes of RRC and RIC; for Greek coins Florance, *Geographic Lexicon of Greek Coin Inscriptions* is very helpful, but Icard, *Dictionary of Greek Coin Inscriptions*, if you can get your hands on a copy, includes all legends, not just ethnics, and has the advantage of being a reverse dictionary as well.

Innumerable websites offer reproductions of coins. *ANS Collections* is a good place to start; *Coin Archives.com: Ancient Coins*, a database of coins that have been offered at auction, is much better than most commercial sites.

Bibliography

Clain-Stefanelli, *Numismatic Bibliography* covers the entire field of numismatics, devoting more than three hundred pages to Greece and Rome. The more recent Daehn, *Ancient Greek Numismatics* limits itself to works on Greek numismatics published in English, and provides summaries of the contents of the works cited. Since 1967, the quinquennial International Numismatic Congresses have been accompanied by the publication of a *Survey of Numismatic Research*, which contains not only a list of articles but a geographically organized summary of the main developments over a five-year period; the first of them begins with 1960.

PART V

THE WRITTEN WORD

17

EPIGRAPHY

THE OLDEST WRITTEN TEXTS

Epigraphy is defined as the study of texts written on hard and durable surfaces (usually stone, but other materials occur).[1] These texts were in their time, as they are now, only a very small portion of what people wrote; they relate, moreover, only to certain matters, for most sorts of things that human beings say or write they would never inscribe on stone. But unlike the texts written on papyrus and other perishable substances, many of these texts remain, and they are the oldest Greek and Roman texts that we have in their original form, with the precise wording, spelling (including spelling errors), letter-forms and visual layout that they had when first written. Because they tell us the same story that they told the ancients, they are invaluable historical sources; because they tell it in the very form that the ancients used, they are invaluable linguistic sources. And lastly, because many more people are mentioned in stone inscriptions than are mentioned in history books, they are invaluable economic and sociological sources. They may be broken, eroded or erased; they may be unclear or indecipherable; they may refer to matters of which we have no knowledge in frustratingly impenetrable terms. But they offer us the

---

[1] That our inscriptions are usually on stone is simply a reflection of the fact that stone lasts longer; most inscriptions in ancient times, as in our own, were written on perishable materials, chiefly wood. See Eck, "Inschriften auf Holz."

opportunity to see aspects of antiquity that no other source will tell us, and new ones turn up all the time, with new stories to tell.

FORM OF PUBLICATION

Until the mid-nineteenth century, such inscriptions as were published were usually in travel books, often reproduced in line-drawings that attempted to give as good a picture as the traveler was capable of. Böckh in CIG imposed a uniform format on the inscriptions he published, and that format, refined by generations of epigraphers, has become standard practice. The form has four parts:

- the *lemma*, giving information about the physical nature of the inscription and its history since its discovery;
- the *transcription* of the text;
- the *apparatus criticus*, detailing variant readings; and finally
- the *commentary*, dealing with what we can learn from or about the text.

There are still variations of practice among editors, but an example from a recently edited corpus[2] will show the essentials of the form (see Figure 17.1).

1. **264**: In corpora or in any publication that deals with more than one inscription, each is given a number.
2. **Delphis. Inv. n. 3867, ibidem in Museo.** Where the inscription was found (its *Fundort*, in this case at Delphi) and where it is today (its *Aufbewahrungsort*: there in the museum, where it bears the inventory number 3867).
3. **Stela e marmore albo infra fracta, a. 0,40, l. 0,24, cr 0,035, ornata aëtomate cum acroteriis.** A description of the stone: its form (a stele), its material (white marble), its state of preservation (broken on the bottom), its dimensions (given in meters; this publication uses the European convention that puts a comma, not a point, between integers and decimal fractions: the stone is 40 centimeters high [a=*altitudo*, height], 24 centimeters wide [l=*latitudo*, width] and 3.5 centimeters thick [cr=*crassitudo*, thickness]), and any other relevant

---

[2] The stone is IG XII 6 1 264, edited in 2000 by Klaus Hallof and reproduced here by his kind permission.

264 Delphis. Inv. n. 3867, ibidem in Museo. Stela e marmore albo infra fracta, a. 0,40, l. 0,24, cr. 0,035, ornata aëtomate cum acroteriis. Litt. a. 0,009–0,01, dispositae στοιχηδόν (0,0190, 0,0189); interv. vv. 1–2 fere nullum, vv. 2–16 0,009.

Edd. Th. Homolle, *BCH* 23, 1899, 536–538 n. 24 ex apographo, quod confecerat Fournier (H. Pomtow, Syll.³ 276 A); J. Bousquet, *BCH* 83, 1959, 153–155 A c. phot. fig. 8 (SEG XVIII 200). Cf. Cargill, *Settlements* (1995), 21. 230 c. phot. tab. 3; G. A. Karla, Σαμιακές Μελέτες 2, 1995–1996, 9 (phot.). *Ect.* benigne misit F. Lefèvre a. 1995.

a. 334/3 a.   θ ε ο ί, τ ύ χ η·

ἐπὶ Κτησικλέο-   στοιχ. 12

ς ἄρχοντος Ἀθή-

νησι, ἐν Σάμωι δ-

5 ὲ Νεοκλέους, Ἀθ-

ηναίων ὁ δῆμος

ὁ ἐν Σάμωι χρυσ-

ὸν στέφανον ἀρ-

ιστεῖον τῶι Ἀ[π]-

10 όλλωνι ἀνέθ[ηκ]-

εν, σταθμὸν [τοῦ]

χρυσίου δ[αρει]-

κοὶ εἴκ[οσι, ἡμι]-

δαρε[ίκιον, ἡμι]-

15 ωβέ[λιον . . ? . .]

Suppl. Homolle ‖ 9 ['Aπ]– Homolle ‖ 10 ἀνέθ[ηκ]– Cargill ‖ 16 vestigia incertissima (⫶ Lefèvre), quae sintne litt. non constat; 'videntur nomina theorum secuta esse' (Pomtow).

V. 5 Νεοκλῆς· eundem atque Epicuri philosophi patrem (PA 10640, vide supra fastos p. 205) esse putavit Cargill n. 988.   12–13 Coronam, cuius pretium, ut solet, ad Dareorum normam redactum est, fere quadrin–gentarum drachmarum fuisse censuit Pomtow, quod pretium sane insolitum est. Eos quidem Dareos a nummis illis Persarum celeberrimis alienos esse voluit J. R. Melville–Jones, *Rev. Belg. Num.* 125, 1979, 25–26 (SEG XXIX 458), cui autem diffidit M.–F. Baslez, *Rev. ét. anc.* 91, 1989, 238. 242 (SEG XXXIX 1774).   14–15 De hemiobelio (argenteo), quod pondus tantum usui erat, cf. Bousquet, *BCH* 109, 1985, 229 adn. 16.

Statuit Pomtow cleruchos Samios a. 334 a. ad Pythia celebranda theoros Delphos misisse, qui simul coronam auream consecrarent.

Figure 17.1 The publication text of *IG* XII 6 1 264

information (it is decorated with a pediment [ἀέτωμα] with acroteria [ἀκρωτήρια], an ornament at the top of the pediment).

4. **Litt. a. 0,009–0,01, dispositae** στοιχηδόν **(0,0190, 0,0189); interv. vv. 1–2 fere nullum, vv. 2–16 0,009.** A description of the lettering: the height of the letters (9 to 10 millimeters); that the inscription is written *stoichedon* (on which see below, pp. 224–5) and that the dimensions of the rectangles in which each letter is placed are 19 × 18.9 millimeters; the space between the lines (practically none between the first two lines, 9 millimeters thereafter). Böckh and his immediate successors published sketches of the inscriptions that showed the form of every letter, but these sketches were so inaccurate that later editors have ceased the practice. Many, however, will insert at this point of the heading any unusual or noteworthy letter-forms appearing in this inscription, so that you may find at this point, with no further explanation, a list of letters such as (for example)

⊗ΖΓΣΦ. In recent publications, where photographs are regularly provided, the list of letter-forms is usually omitted, unless for some reason they are not clearly visible on the photograph. IG provides pictures, if at all, only of selected representative stones; the most recent volumes of CIL provide photographs, and often drawings, of every significant inscription for which they are available.

5. **Edd. Th. Homolle, BCH 23, etc.**: Bibliography; this will usually include every publication in which the inscription has been mentioned, except for those few inscriptions so famous that an exhaustive bibliography is impractical. Many recent editors consider it unnecessary to give every mention of the inscription, and limit themselves to the most important literature.

6. **ex apographo, quod confecerat Fournier**: How the editor knew the inscription. In this case the first editor, Théophile Homolle, had a written copy that one Mr. Fournier[3] had transcribed.

7. **(H. Pomtow, Syll.[3] 276 A)**: The current editor, Klaus Hallof, puts in parentheses editions in corpora that do not add new information.

8. **c. phot. fig. 8**: a bibliography will regularly note where a photograph of the stone can be found.

9. **Cf. Cargill, Settlements etc.**: After "cf." are listed places where the inscription is mentioned in the course of a publication that is not directly interested in the inscription itself.

10. **Ect. benigne misit F. Lefèvre a. 1995**: How the current editor has seen the inscription: in this case, F. Lefèvre sent him a squeeze of the stone in 1995.

11. **a. 334/3 a.** = *anno* 334/3 *ante* (Chr. *natum*): The date when the stone was inscribed, before ("a.") or after ("p.") the beginning of the Christian era.

12. **στοιχ. 12**: The inscription is written *stoichedon*—although that was stated in the heading with the size of the lettering, it is so important in determining the possible readings that it is regularly stated in the margin of the inscription. In those areas and periods where the *stoichedon* style was common, any other stone may be identified as "non-στοιχ.": the current editor considers that unnecessary, since

---

[3] So he is referred to by Homolle in the original publication, and in three "Communications" that he contributed to BCH 21 and 22 (1897–98); I have not succeeded in discovering his first name; perhaps he is the Dr. Eugène Fournier who contributed two signed articles to Daremberg and Saglio, eds., *Dictionnaire des antiquités*. The current editor wisely chose simply to mention him by surname; not every unresolved doubt is worth investigating.

very few of the inscriptions in this volume are *stoichedon*. "12" is the number of letters in each line.

13. **Suppl. Homolle**: Immediately after the text of the stone, usually in a paragraph by itself, is placed an *apparatus criticus* that mentions any alternative readings, conjectures, etc. This paragraph deals only with the question of what letters are (or once were, or were meant to be) actually inscribed on the stone; questions of content are dealt with in a separate paragraph. The expression *Suppl(evit) Homolle* means that the letters in brackets (those missing on the stone) are taken, unless otherwise noted, from the edition of Théophile Homolle, who first edited it.

14. **9 ['Aπ]– Homolle** means that in line 9 Homolle did not see any traces of the letters ΑΠ. Hallof, as can be seen in the text he prints, thinks that some remains of the first alpha are visible on his squeeze.

15. **5 Νεοκλῆς· eundem atque . . .**: In this paragraph come discussions, arranged line by line, of content arising from particular parts of the text.

16. **Statuit Pomtow . . .**: In a final paragraph the editor discusses whatever general matters may be relevant to the text: here Hallof quotes a conjecture as to what the circumstances may have been that induced the Athenian residents in Samos to dedicate this crown.

EPIGRAPHICAL SYMBOLS

For printing the text itself a system of signs and symbols was agreed upon at an international conference in Leiden in 1931 and has become standard, although it has since been revised. The details can be read in any of the more recent handbooks of epigraphy;[4] the most essential points are:

- | or / = beginning of a new line (the first line will not be so marked).
- || = beginning of a line divisible by five.
- [xxx] = letters that were once on the stone but are now totally illegible or lost.

---

[4] For a good summary see Woodhead, *The Study of Greek Inscriptions*, 6–11. The revisions are spelled out in Dow, *Conventions in Editing*, and further revisions in Krummrey and Panciera, "Criteri di edizione" and in Panciera, "Struttura dei supplementi e segni diacritici dieci anni dopo."

- (xxx) = letters intentionally not written on the stone (as in abbreviations).
- <xxx> = letters accidentally omitted or miswritten on the stone.
- {xxx} = letters inscribed by accident (as when the mason repeated letters by mistake).
- [[xxx]] = letters visible on the stone where previous letters have been erased.
- xxx = partly legible letters, whose traces on the stone might be the letter printed or might be some other letter (as where all that is legible on the stone is the bottom of a vertical stroke that might belong to an I or a T).
- . . . = letters missing on the stone whose number is certain (the number of missing letters will equal the number of dots). Often the number will be written for convenience: . . .⁶. . .
- - - - = an uncertain number of letters missing on the stone.
- v (for *vacat*) = an empty space on the stone in the middle of the inscribed area.

At the time when these conventions were first adopted, there was an effort to change the conventions of line numbering, printing in the margin every number divisible by four rather than five. The rationale behind this was that it made the number of any line obvious at a glance: either the line was numbered, or was just before or after a numbered line, or, if neither of those was the case, was precisely in between the two nearest numbered lines. This practice can be found in some publications, but it did not catch on.

LETTER-FORMS

The forms of the Latin letters as used for inscriptions are more or less the same forms we use today for majuscules, but they underwent a good deal of development from the earliest inscriptions to the latest. A certain stability was introduced with the *scriptura monumentalis* that was used from the Augustan era onward, and is still imitated today;[5] but at no period did this style efface the others entirely, or stop the development of letter-forms on stone, which underwent changes parallel to the ones we find in

---

[5]   Not least by the typefaces known as "Roman," from which the style will be familiar to almost any reader who pays attention to typefaces.

palaeographic book-hands.[6] There are some telltale variations that can be mentioned: the presence or absence of serifs (the short ornamental lines at the beginning or end of each line that makes up the letter: A has serifs, A does not), the tendency to use straight lines (monumental), curved lines (uncial) or tall and narrow forms (rustic capitals). These, however, are general terms; each of the styles changed from era to era and from mason to mason.

Greek inscriptions show if anything yet greater variation in the forms of their letters, particularly in the early period. Each *polis* inscribed its letters in its own dialect until the advent of *koine* in the Hellenistic and Roman period slowly displaced the local ways of speaking. Even the number of the letters and the phonetic meaning of the signs was not uniform until the decision to employ the Ionic alphabet, a decision taken by the Athenians in 404/3, gradually caused that alphabet to be adopted throughout Greece, where it is still in use today. Even then, however, forms of letters continued to change so much that an Athenian of the fifth century BCE faced with an inscription of the Roman period would probably have found the letters quite peculiar. This great variation is a difficulty, though not a terribly great one, for the beginning student, but it is very useful for the professional epigrapher, for it makes it much easier

Figure 17.2 *Scriptura monumentalis*: an inscription of the first century CE
Photograph by the author.

---

6   See below, Chapter 19.

to establish the approximate place and time of an inscription's origin. In recent years Stephen Tracy has demonstrated that it is possible, at least in some cases, to recognize an individual mason's idiosyncrasies, just as one can recognize a writer's handwriting. On this basis he has done a good deal of work in identifying the work of Athenian masons—information that allows us previously unimaginable precision in our knowledge about the inscription's origin, and has greatly increased our awareness of the technical issues involved in a mason's work.[7] Although nobody has attempted to identify the style of an individual Roman mason, Susini, *The Roman Stonecutter* has organized what we know of the technical issues, and the work of Richard Grasby, himself a stonecutter, has shown that in Latin epigraphy as well there is a good deal to be learned from the form of the inscriptions and not just their content. The increasing availability of high-quality epigraphical photographs online will make the appearance of inscriptions much more accessible.

Not only the form of the letters but their arrangement on the stone may vary. The earliest inscriptions were written, like those of the Phoenicians from whom the Greeks had learned to write, from right to left, or else[8] in the style called *boustrophedon* (βουστροφηδόν, "ox-turned"), where the stonecutter, like an ox plowing a field, reaches the end of one line and then goes back in the other direction for the next one (Figure 17.3). By the classical period, however, practically all inscriptions were written from left to right.

In classical Athens a style called *stoichedon* (στοιχηδόν, "lined up") was popular for a while. In this style the letters were aligned vertically as well as horizontally, rather like the letters of a crossword puzzle, though they were still read from left to right. This style is very welcome to the epigrapher, since it allows us to be certain of the number of letters missing in places where the stone has been damaged (Figure 17.4).[9] Word divisions, which were very often marked in Latin inscriptions, were usually not marked in Greek ones. It was common for the mason to try to

---

[7] Tracy, *The Lettering of an Athenian Mason*; id., *Athenian Democracy in Transition*; id., *Athens and Macedon*; id., *Attic Letter-Cutters of 229 to 86 B.C.* The method was pioneered by Tracy's teacher (and my own), Sterling Dow, who contributed an introduction on the subject to the first book.

[8] Although it is often stated that retrograde (right-to-left) writing of Greek is older than *boustrophedon*, the archaeological evidence does not, as of now, indicate that: Jeffery, *The Local Scripts of Archaic Greece*, 43–6.

[9] The most complete study of *stoichedon* is still Austin, ed., *The Stoichedon Style*.

Figure 17.3   A *boustrophedon* inscription (the law of Gortyn)

end each line at a word-boundary, or at least a syllable-boundary; in *stoichedon*, even this was often ignored.[10]

SQUEEZES AND PHOTOGRAPHS

It would be nice if an epigrapher could always have the stone easily available while working; in practice that is rarely the case. Many stones are parts of buildings or monuments and cannot be removed. Even those that are found lying free are generally too heavy to move and too bulky to store conveniently in one's office, and in any event most countries today

---

[10] It could, of course, be done if the mason chose to; and word-boundaries could be indicated by interpuncts, as they are in Figure 17.4.

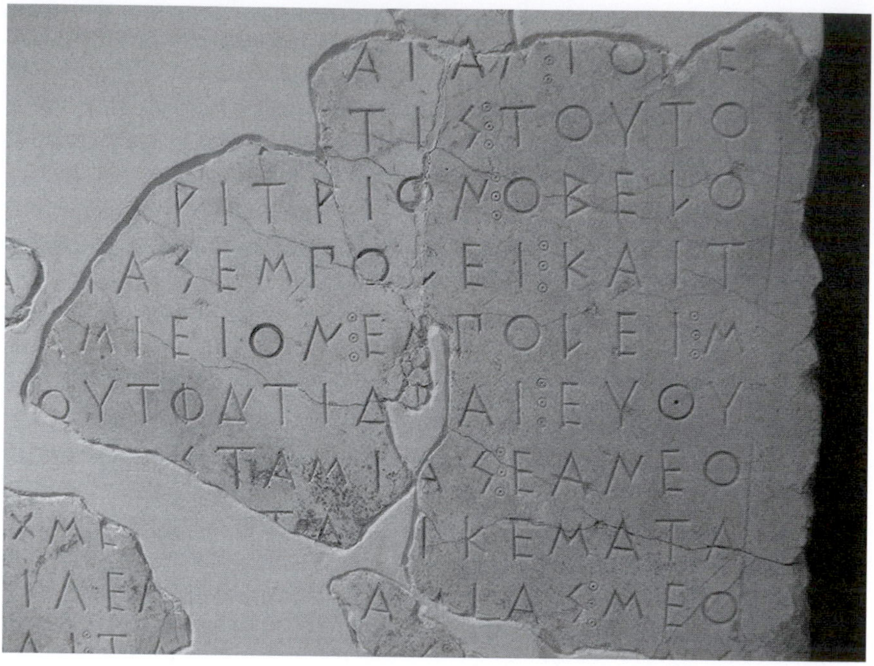

Figure 17.4 A *stoichedon* inscription (*IG* I³ 48)

consider it a criminal offense to remove antiquities. There are museums with large numbers of inscriptions, most notably the Epigraphical Museum of Athens and the Epigraphical Department of the National Museum in Rome, as well as the Vatican Museum; but it is a rare epigrapher who can spend most of a career in such a place. In the days when epigraphy was a matter for dilettantes, the traveler who found an inscription would draw up as good a copy as possible, but these were rarely very accurate. Modern epigraphers solve the problem by making what is called a "squeeze" (Lat. *ectypus*, Ger. *Abklatsch*, Fr. *estampage*, It. *calco*), usually made either by beating a wet piece of strong but not stiff paper over the stone or by spreading the stone with liquid latex; either method, when left to dry, will produce an image of the stone's surface much easier to carry and to store than the stone itself. A well-made squeeze, in fact, may reveal or clarify things that are hard to see on the stone: a squeeze can be held up to different angles of light, and does not reproduce misleading discolorations of the stone, and for this reason publications will some-times publish a photograph of a squeeze along with a photograph of the stone. Photographs themselves are also useful: once the limits of clarity and size meant that they could only be a secondary means of assistance, not a replacement for the stone itself, but today they often allow us to see things that we cannot see on the stone itself. Nevertheless, even with the best squeezes and photographs, autopsy—seeing it for yourself—always has the possibility of adding crucial knowledge that you would never have gotten at second hand.

RESTORING A TEXT

In the course of a few thousand years many things can happen to a stone, and most inscriptions that we find are partially or mostly broken or illegible. To the beginner it may appear the work of a fool or a genius to try to guess what may have stood in the missing space; but in fact there are things that can help. Measurement is the first: if it is possible to know how many letters are missing, that will put an important constraint on the possible reconstructions. Usually this will be possible only if we have both the left and right margins of at least one line (preferably more, since although right margins are often justified this is not always the case), though in some cases a restoration may be so certain that we can rely on it to indicate the length of the line even where the margin is missing. For a *stoichedon* inscription the number of letters will usually be fixed exactly, but even for a non-*stoichedon* inscription the number of letters will not vary greatly; and of course the shorter the lacuna, the less room there is for uncertainty.

Once we know how many letters are missing, the most reliable guide for what may have been there is a knowledge of the formulae used in inscriptions. Many forms of inscriptions are quite repetitive in the form in which they give their information: decrees often begin with formulae indicating the office-holders and the proposer of the decree; tombstones have various formulae of leave-taking that repeat from stone to stone; religious dedications generally have the name of the deity in the dative. Roman inscriptions used abbreviations very generously for such for-mulae, and are often incomprehensible to anyone unfamiliar with them; the main epigraphical handbooks, which we will mention under *Major Resources*, include lists of these abbreviations.

Besides the formulae that are common to many inscriptions, there are turns of phrase that recur in a single inscription: accounting inscriptions, for example, usually have standard ways of recording transactions, and what is found in one line may be a reasonable guide to what must have been present in another. Once we leave the realm of formulae, recon-struction becomes more and more treacherous as the length of the lacuna increases. Some epigraphers are more venturesome and some less; but in any event, when using information based on epigraphical evidence, make sure that the evidence you are quoting is something that really stands, or that must certainly once have stood, in the stone before you. Often there is no choice but to put a question mark next to your reconstruction.

Even formulae that are well known change over time; a preserved formula may help date an inscription, and before you restore one make sure it is not anachronistic. Similar care must be taken with matters of dialect and vocabulary, particularly in Greece, where dialect inscriptions were the rule, not the exception, until well into the Hellenistic period. And in the long run, the best guide is experience: with every new inscription you read, you become a better epigrapher.

MAJOR RESOURCES

Introductions to Epigraphy

By far the cheapest, shortest, clearest and most accessible introduction available in English for Greece is Woodhead, *The Study of Greek Inscriptions*; even shorter and newer, in German, is Petzl, "Epigraphik," but after either of these brief introductions a person who is interested in more will find huge amounts of information in the multivolume works of Larfeld, *Handbuch der griechischen Epigraphik*, now more than a century old, and Guarducci, *Epigrafia Greca*, a handbook that is also something of an anthology, considerably more recent than Larfeld but itself no longer up to date. For each of these there is a later, single-volume compendium, Larfeld, *Griechische Epigraphik* and Guarducci, *L'epigrafia greca dalle origini al tardo Impero*; more recent than either of them, though limited in chronological scope, is McLean, *Introduction to Greek Epigraphy of the Hellenistic and Roman Periods*.

For Latin epigraphy brief introductions are Gordon, *Illustrated Introduction to Latin Epigraphy* and Keppie, *Understanding Roman Inscriptions*; brief, clear and up to date is Eck, "Lateinische Epigraphik." The more complete disquisitions are René Cagnat, *Cours d'épigraphie latine* and Sandys, *Latin Epigraphy*. Very useful for finding the meaning of words and concepts occurring in inscriptions is Ruggiero, *Dizionario epigrafico di antichità romane*; unfortunately, it was completed only up to the word "Mamma." Nothing comparable exists for Greek epigraphy.

Rémy and Kayser, *Initiation à l'épigraphie grecque et latine* is not an introduction to epigraphy as such but a collection intended to introduce students to the use of inscriptions by a brief general introduction and a well-chosen set of inscriptions whose commentary is designed to demonstrate how they can be used to illuminate various aspects of the ancient world; Institut Fernand-Courby, *Nouveau choix d'inscriptions grecques*, although structured more like a collection, is designed with a similar purpose in mind.

Corpora

The complete corpora. The two great collections of inscriptions are *Inscriptiones Graecae* (IG) and the much larger *Corpus Inscriptionum Latinarum* (CIL), both imposing multivolume compilations without which it would be very hard for any but the most expert to make good use of the information that can be gathered from inscriptions. The corpora are divided geographically[11] into volumes, then by category within each volume, and finally by period within each category (there are too many inscriptions of uncertain date to allow an absolute chronological order). Without these corpora, only a professional epigrapher with the experience of Odysseus, the endurance of Atlas, and the memory of Nestor—and there have been such—could expect to know all the inscribed decrees of the Athenian *boule*, or all the gravestones of Roman Spain that list the deceased's *cursus honorum*. It is the corpora that collect the material and offer it all in a usable order to anyone who can read Greek or Latin. Neither IG nor CIL offers translations.

The chief goal of the corpora is to give the most reliable text available as of the time of publication and an ample bibliography; it is the user's responsibility to follow up the bibliography and find out what has been written. There is some minimal discussion of substantive matters, but to have offered even a moderately complete summary of what is worth knowing about every inscription would have inflated their volume, and the time and effort involved in their preparation, beyond even what their ambitious founders considered humanly possible.

Neither corpus is complete: there are fascicles of CIL, and even entire volumes of IG, that have never appeared. The inscriptions of Asia have never been included in IG; they do belong to Volume III of CIL, but the most recent fascicle was compiled more than a century ago, and it is in the nature of a corpus that the moment a volume appears it begins to age,

---

[11] The geographical principle is not a hard-and-fast one; volume XVI of CIL, for example, collects military diplomas.

since new inscriptions are being published all the time. There are periodicals that collect these new inscriptions, as we shall mention shortly, but when the problem becomes acute the corpus may commission a new edition of a volume that has already appeared, or a supplement to it. In the case of CIL, the regular issue of new fascicles covering periods and places already covered by earlier ones has resulted in a large number of inscriptions that appear more than once;[12] Fassbender, *Index numerorum* has now made it possible to trace the repeat appearances of a given inscription.

August Böckh's *Corpus Inscriptionum Graecarum* (CIG), the original Greek corpus, is even more thoroughly out of date than even the earliest volumes of IG, but it has two features that still make it worth consulting: it covers all of the Greek world, and it includes a Latin commentary on each text discussing the interpretation and significance of the inscription, matters that had already become impractical, for reasons of space, by the time of the publication of IG.

The need to keep IG and CIL up to date has been met by annual publications that do not entirely amount to a true updating—epigraphy has nothing like the looseleaf binders with which lawyers update every year their collections of laws and judicial precedents—but that can help fill you in on what has been found or written since the relevant volume was published. For Greek epigraphy there is the *Supplementum Epigraphicum Graecum* (SEG), begun in 1923 by a committee under the editorship of J. J. E. Hondius. SEG had the advantage of reproducing the texts of all new inscriptions, but the work was too much for those involved. Inaccuracies abounded and it proved impossible to produce a new volume every year: from 1938 to 1953 only two volumes appeared. In 1954 it was revived and continued through 1972, when the project foundered once more; but it was revived again in 1979 and has been appearing regularly since. Because of the difficulties of its publication, it is not exhaustive: by no means every inscription published since 1923 has appeared in SEG. For those that have, however, it is common practice to cite them by their SEG volume and number.

More regular and more precise has been the *Bulletin épigraphique* that has appeared annually in the *Revue des études grecques* since its inception in 1888, offering a catalogue and discussion—but not the text—of every inscription published or discussed during the year. From 1938 to 1984 it was edited by the redoubtable Jeanne and Louis Robert, whose high standards and blunt expression were the dread of editors and the delight of readers.

---

[12] There are such cases in IG as well, but for various reasons they are rarer.

The *Bulletins* have been published as a separate multivolume series. Since they do not include the texts of the inscriptions, the reader cannot simply scan them over to see if what is needed is in the inscription. The more valuable, then, the index volumes that have been published, which make it much easier to find the information you need.

For Latin epigraphy the task of updating the CIL has been carried out by *L'Année épigraphique* (*AnnEpigr*), a journal that has offered both texts and discussions since its foundation, also in 1888. Since *AnnEpigr* considers itself a journal of Roman, not only Latin, epigraphy, Greek texts of Roman relevance can also be found here. Of cardinal importance is the periodical *Supplementa Italica*, founded by Silvio Panciera, which publishes annual supplements to CIL for inscriptions from Italy; *Hispania Epigraphica* performs a similar function for Spain.

Select corpora. More compact are Dittenberger's *Sylloge Inscriptionum Graecarum* (SIG^3) and Dessau's *Inscriptiones Latinae Selectae* (ILS), each of which also covers the entire geographic field, offers a brief Latin commentary, and has the advantage of including only those inscriptions that their editors, men of rare erudition, considered to have some interest to those for whom the fact that it is there is not sufficient excuse for investigating an inscription.[13] These, unlike CIL and IG, are books that could once be browsed by people whose Latin and whose taste for epigraphy were up to the task, though today few students would dream of flipping through them for amusement. By now, too, they are a century or more old, and there is nobody today who would undertake so massive a task of selection and commentary on the totality of Greek or Latin inscriptions.

Somewhat easier to use are the topical collections of inscriptions. A few date from the time of SIG and ILS and have similar advantages and disadvantages: among these are *Orientis Graecae Inscriptiones Selectae* (OGIS), which was designed as a supplement to SIG^3 for the inscriptions of Asia Minor and points east; the *Sammlung der griechischen Dialekt-Inscriften* (GDI), a collection of inscriptions in non-Attic dialect which in addition to offering a wealth of literary information is also a rich source for the epigraphy of Greece outside of Attica in the years before the *koine* became the uniform dialect of all Greeks; *Inscriptiones Graecae ad Res Romanas Pertinentes* (IGRR), a collection of inscriptions whose language is Greek but whose subject matter is Roman; *Inscriptiones Latinae christianae veteres* (ILCV), and

---

[13] Where there exist (as in the case of the Athenian Tribute Lists, IG I^3 259–90, or the ephebic inscriptions, IG II–III^2 1006 *et passim*) a large number of inscriptions of similar content, a single example or a few representative ones (SIG^3 68 for the tribute lists, 717 for the ephebic inscriptions) is all that SIG^3 will provide.

others that anyone who deals with inscriptions will soon discover. *OGIS*, *IGRR* and *ILCV* have commentaries in Latin, *GDI* in German.

More recent topical collections tend to offer smaller collections and more copious discussion in a modern language: many a modern student will learn more from the few dozen documents edited with copious English commentary (though without translation) in Sherk, *Roman Documents from the Greek East* than from the thousands in *IGRR*. For Greek law, much of which is known to us only from inscriptions, the old *Recueil des inscriptions juridiques grecques (RIJG)*, can now be supplemented for the archaic period by van Effenterre and Ruzé, *Nomima*; for classical Greek history, Marcus Tod's wonderful *A Selection of Greek Historical Inscriptions* has been masterfully superseded for the fifth century by Meiggs and Lewis, *Greek Historical Inscriptions* (ML) and for the fourth by Rhodes and Osborne, *Greek Historical Inscriptions*. Other significant topical collections are Jeffery, *The Local Scripts of Archaic Greece*, a monograph that in its way is a mini-corpus of the oldest Greek inscriptions; Rhodes and Lewis, *The Decrees of the Greek States*, which is largely, though not entirely, based upon inscriptions; Maier, *Griechische Mauerbauinschriften*; Hansen, *Carmina Epigraphica Graeca* (CEG), which despite having been compiled in the 1980s offers its commentary in Latin; and Merkelbach and Stauber, *Steinepigramme aus dem griechischen Osten*. Topical collections of Roman inscriptions reflect the different subject matter of Latin epigraphy: Karl Georg Bruns, *Fontes Iuris Romani Antiqui*, now superseded by Riccobono et al., *Fontes Iuris Romani Antejustiniani* (FIRA); the military diplomas of *CIL* XVI and the milestones of the ubiquitous Roman roads, originally placed at the end of each volume of *CIL* but now to be collected in their own volume, *CIL* XVII. For the republic we have Degrassi, *Inscriptiones Latinae Liberae Rei Publicae* (ILLRP); early imperial history was treated in Rushforth, *Latin Historical Inscriptions*, whose general format has been retained in a number of more recent collections; and Christian inscriptions are collected in *ILCV*, mentioned above, and in *Inscriptiones Christianae Urbis Romae Septimo Saeculo Antiquiores* (ICVR) and *Inscriptiones Christianae Italiae* (ICI), three collections that give us a broader picture of early Christianity than we could ever squeeze out of literary sources alone. A few inscriptions, such as Augustus' *Res Gestae* or Diocletian's Edict on Prices, are sufficiently important to have been published on their own, with commentary and discussion.

More numerous than the topical collections are the geographical ones, organized either by their place of origin (*Herkunftsort*), such as Margherita Guarducci's *Inscriptiones Creticae* (IC) or *Tituli Asiae Minoris* (TAM) or, more commonly, by the place where they are currently found, such as Collingwood et al., *The Roman Inscriptions of Britain*; since stones do not travel

easily, there is little difference between these two principles of organization. Often a museum will undertake the publication of all the
inscriptions in its possession. Such was Hicks et al., *The Collection of Ancient
Greek Inscriptions in the British Museum*; such, more recently, is Lajtar, *Catalogue of
the Greek Inscriptions in the Sudan National Museum at Khartoum*. Special mention
must be made of the series begun by Reinhold Merkelbach, *Inschriften
griechischer Städte aus Kleinasien* (IK), which has made available to the public in
an orderly fashion a large area of epigraphy that previously was dispersed
through decades and decades of dozens of journals. The enormous range
of Latin epigraphy has given birth to a number of important collections.
The aim of *Inscriptiones Italiae* (II) has been to edit a corpus of all the
inscriptions from what is now Italy; although the ambitious plan has not
been realized in the three-quarters of a century since its beginning, the
volumes that have appeared give new life to the areas covered. Similar in
purpose, if smaller in scope, are such collections as *Die römischen Inschriften
Ungarns* (RIU), *Inscripţiile Daciei romane* and the forthcoming *Corpus Inscriptionum
Iudaeae/Palaestinae* (CIIP).

A great step forward in the ability to find what one needs has been the
advent of epigraphical databanks. One can mention, at the moment, the
ongoing *Epigraphik Datenbank Clauss-Slaby*, the *Epigraphic Database for Ancient Asia
Minor*, the international project *EAGLE* (*Electronic Archive of Greek and Latin
Epigraphy*), pioneered by Silvio Panciera (with which are associated the
Epigraphische Datenbank Heidelberg [EDH], the *Epigraphic Database Roma* [EDR] and
the *Epigraphic Database Bari* [EDB]), the online *Hispania Epigraphica*, the database
of Oxford's Centre for the Study of Ancient Documents (CSAD), and the
Searchable Greek Inscriptions of the Packard Humanities Institute (PHI); but
new and more ambitious projects can be expected.

Epigraphical Periodicals

Except for SEG and *AnnEpigr*, both of them inventories of inscriptions published elsewhere, there are no major journals dedicated entirely to the
publication and discussion of inscriptions, though there are important
local ones, as mentioned above.[14] Articles about epigraphy are generally
published in archaeological journals, and some of them (particularly
Hesperia, BCH and BSA) regularly devote much of their space to new
inscriptions; ZPE, which will be mentioned in the next chapter,[15] offers

---

[14] P. 231.
[15] P. 244.

the quickest publication. But in fact almost any classical journal may publish articles on epigraphy, and some of the most important have been published in journals that have no particular epigraphical slant.

Ancillae for Restoration of Texts

Lists of the abbreviations common in Latin inscriptions can be found in ILS, in Cagnat's *Cours d'épigraphie latine* and in Sandys' *Latin Epigraphy*, among other places; there is at least one list available online. For Greek abbreviations there is Oikonomides, *Abbreviations*. Prosopographies that can help you figure out a name (and can help you identify what bearer of that name is being spoken of) are mentioned in Chapter 13 of this book; retrograde dictionaries, helpful for figuring out the beginning of a word whose end is preserved, are found in Chapter 6. In general one must be careful about the use of dictionaries: not every word used by Aeschylus is likely to be found in an inscription, and on the other hand there are words quite common in inscriptions that never appear in literature—or never with this spelling. Only the most recent dictionaries give good coverage to epigraphical information: for Greek one must use Glare, *Revised Supplement* or, where available, the DGE, and for Latin, where available, Ruggiero, *Dizionario epigrafico di antichità romane*. For grammar, you are fortunate if you are dealing with an inscription from Attica: Threatte, *The Grammar of Attic Inscriptions* has no parallel for any other time or place.

Epigraphical Bibliography

A very welcome aid to the epigrapher has been Bérard et al., *Guide de l'épigraphiste*, a bibliographical guide with the great advantage of regular electronic updating on a site (*Guide de l'épigraphiste*) from which both the guide itself and its updates can be downloaded.

18

PAPYROLOGY

THE MEDIA OF WRITING

Papyrus is a reed found commonly in Egypt; the stalks were cut into strips and then stuck together in two layers at right angles to each other. It was customary (and easier) to write along the fibers, not across them, so that if only one side was written on, as would normally be the case in a papyrus roll, that side would have the text aligned with the strips, and the papyrus would be rolled in such a way as to have the writing on the inside. The inside is called the *recto*, the outside the *verso*. In those not-uncommon cases where we cannot recognize how the papyrus was rolled, the side where the writing is aligned with the strips is called the front, the other side the back. Although most commonly scribes wrote only on the front, there are papyri that contain writing on both sides, or even only on the back.[1]

Papyrus was perhaps the most common substrate on which people wrote and it was usually the only one appropriate for long texts,[2] but it

---

[1] Lewis, *Papyrus in Classical Antiquity*, with Lewis, *Papyrus in Classical Antiquity: A Supplement*, is the classic summary of what is known about the plant and the physical preparation of papyri. For *recto*, *verso*, front and back see Browne et al., "Note on the Terms 'Recto' and 'Verso.'"

[2] There were long texts that were inscribed on stone, but these required great expense, and were not everyday affairs.

was not the only one used. Wax-tablets were an extremely convenient medium: like a blackboard, they could be erased (by smoothing the wax) and reused indefinitely. Few of these have kept their wax intact for two millennia,[3] though sometimes the stylus made scratches on the underlying wood that may still be read.[4] There are also some wood and bark tablets that have survived. Potsherds, which because of their indestructibility were ubiquitous in the ancient world, were convenient for writing something short that did not have to be kept; this is presumably the reason that the Athenians used them for ostracism, which required only a single name and did not have to be kept any longer than it took to count the votes. Many inscribed potsherds (ostraca, the Greek term, is the one regularly used) have been published, though of course this is only a small fraction of the items that litter the ground of every ancient inhabited site. From the second century BCE onward, parchment—the dried and treated skin of an animal—was increasingly used as a substrate for the most important texts, but parchment was always a luxury item, and papyrus continued to be the most common substrate for writing well into the Byzantine period. In the medieval period the use of paper spread to the Muslim world from China, and eventually to Europe as well.

Papyrology as presently practiced includes rather more than the name implies: materials other than papyri, such as parchment, ceramic and wood, also fall within the purview of the papyrologist. The boundaries between epigraphy and papyrology are not entirely rigid. Graffiti tend to be treated by epigraphers, as do commercial seal-impressions on amphorae and bricks; the seals that made the impressions are the province of archaeologists. Papyrology once dealt almost entirely with Greek and Latin papyri, chiefly because those were the languages in which papyrologists were trained; in recent years the regular practice of publishing translations along with the papyri has allowed other languages, which were once treated as part of other fields (Egyptology, Semitics and such), to be increasingly integrated into the field.

Collections of papyri, whatever the name on their title page, are generally referred to by papyrologists by a standard system, the capital letter P followed by a period (a full stop) and a word or contraction

---

[3]   A photograph of one that did survive is available in Turner, *Greek Manuscripts of the Ancient World*, no. 4; it was originally published, without the photograph, by Kenyon, "Two Greek School-Tablets," at 39–40.

[4]   For two examples see Plate XVII of Birley, *Vindolanda's Treasures*.

indicating the collection.[5] Thus the book that, if it dealt with another subject, would be referred to as Bernard P. Grenfell and Arthur S. Hunt, *The Oxyrhynchus Papyri*, Part I is always referred to simply as P.Oxy. I, and vol. 7 of *Papiri della Università degli studi di Milano* is P.Mil.Vogl.VII. Editions of ostraca are indicated by an "O," of tablets by a "T": Brian P. Muhs, *Tax Receipts, Taxpayers, and Taxes* is O.Chic.Muhs, and Alan K. Bowman, *The Roman Writing Tablets from Vindolanda* is T.Vindol. Now that this system has become standard, many publications incorporate the appropriate contraction into the title, or give it as a subtitle.

THE LANGUAGES OF PAPYRI

Papyrus was used throughout the ancient Mediterranean, but it has only survived in the driest of environments. Practically all of our papyri come from Egypt, where the desert is only a short distance away from the heavily inhabited Nile flood-plain; and even in Egypt the papyri finds concentrate around particular areas that became desiccated during or after the ancient period.

The papyri themselves are mostly in Greek, the administrative language of Egypt at the time; but many are in Egyptian (either in the more formal hieratic or the more cursive demotic script—the hieroglyphics we associate with Egypt were only used for monumental inscriptions—or in Coptic, which is essentially Egyptian written in the Greek alphabet), some in Latin, and a few in other languages: Aramaic, Arabic, Pehlevi, Hebrew, and some languages so poorly attested at this time that the papyri form a major contribution to our ability to read the language at all. You, of course, can only read a language you know, so if you have no Egyptian or no Aramaic those papyri will not be immediately accessible to you, but it is worth paying attention to them, for others have read them, published them and—most importantly for you—translated them; and they speak of the same world that the Greek papyri speak of, often through the eyes of a different people.

---

[5]   This is the most common practice, followed by the *Checklist* and others; some, however, omit a period or two (P.Oxy, POxy) or put a space between the two terms (P. Oxy.)

LITERARY AND DOCUMENTARY PAPYRI

Papyrology shares with archaeology, epigraphy and numismatics the excitement, rare in most fields of the classics, of constant discovery of new material.[6] For scholars who like to deal with words, moreover, papyrology is the most exciting of all of these sciences. Unlike archaeology, it offers us texts; unlike numismatics, it offers us extended texts; and unlike epigraphy, it offers us almost the entire range of texts that were produced, not only those sufficiently important to be inscribed on stone.

Papyri are generally divided into two types, literary and documentary. Literary papyri are those that preserve a portion (very rarely the entirety) of a literary work. Sometimes, excitingly, it is a work that had hitherto been lost: by means of papyri we now possess the Aristotelian account of the Athenian constitution, a number of comedies of Menander, a satyr-play of Sophocles, a few poems of Sappho, Archilochus and Bacchylides, a history (the *Hellenica Oxyrhynchia*) of the fourth century BCE by an unknown author, some elegiacs by the Roman poet Cornelius Gallus, and others that appear from time to time. More often literary papyri contain texts already known to us from other sources, but even here they are not negligible, for the papyri are usually about a millennium older than our oldest manuscripts, and, although the oldest text is not necessarily the most accurate, it is certainly worthy of consideration. If there are new readings, they can throw new light on the text we have; and if there are none, that itself is a fact worth recording, for confirming our knowledge is not necessarily less valuable than contradicting it.

Documentary papyri include everything else that might be written: personal letters, contracts, receipts, records of transactions, census returns, magic formulae, bankers' orders, instructions from superiors to subordinates and accountings rendered by subordinates to superiors. The papyrologist is in a sense the spy master of classical scholarship. Modern military intelligence gathering is chiefly a matter of careful analysis of every bit of writing or speech our agents can collect from our enemies in

---

6   Not all of it is really "new"; much of the material has been in our hands for a century or more. There are hundreds of thousands of papyri scattered throughout the various collections of the world, of which, in the more than a century that papyrologists have been working on them, only a few tens of thousands have been published; so even if no new papyrus was ever discovered, the current supply would provide ample employment for new papyrologists for generations to come. Archaeology, moreover—both licit and illicit—continues to provide new and important papyrus finds.

the hope of building up an accurate prediction of their actions. The ancient Greeks, Romans and Egyptians are not our enemies, but documentary papyrologists work as intelligence agents do, building up an understanding of the people who interest them from whatever written material they may have allowed to reach our hands.

READING PAPYRI AND EVALUATING THEM

There are two essential tasks in papyrology: reading the texts and studying them. Reading a papyrus is a skill acquired by practice, but finding papyri to read is easier than you probably think. The papyri themselves are housed in the libraries of various institutions, many of which obtained them at the time of the great discoveries of the nineteenth century, and private individuals who bought them then or later. By far the largest collection is at the Sackler Library in Oxford, where the Oxyrhynchus papyri are housed; but many smaller collections exist, and almost anyone who owns an unread papyrus is interested in having it read. One way that beginners interested in reading papyri can gain access to them is to ask their teacher where papyri are available that someone will let them read. It is not considered ethical to publish the text of a papyrus to which some other scholar holds the "rights," and, since a few interesting papyri can make a scholar's reputation, it is not unprecedented for a scholar to hold on to the most interesting papyri, sometimes holding up their publication by decades. This practice, if understandable, is deplorable if continued for too long; in the worst cases, nothing significant is published until the responsible (or irresponsible) scholar dies. Many scholars are more generous, but don't be surprised if the first papyri you are given to read are small, scrappy and unremarkable. Now, furthermore, there is another approach. Many collections, including Duke and Yale, have put their entire holdings, or at least part of their unpublished texts, online. You still have to ask for permission to publish them, or at least should, but many collections will not normally refuse such a request. More collections will be going this route in the next decade.

Simply unrolling the papyrus is a matter for an expert; in the hands of a careless beginner the ancient reeds crumble. In recent years modern technology has been applied to papyrology, and proper application of this technology can make available papyri that were once too brittle to be opened and can read papyri that were once too faded or too charred to be legible. If a papyrus should ever come into your hand in an unopened state (once it is opened it will usually be preserved between two pieces of glass), make sure that you do not attempt to open it without the assistance of a professional.

Once the papyrus has been unrolled, the next step is reading it. Today it is easy to get an impression of what ancient Greco-Egyptian handwriting looks like from digitalized images available on the web; we shall have more to say in the next chapter about reading old scripts. Your first few glances will probably convince you that reading the handwriting is a more difficult matter than you might have expected; but as with any script, the secret of reading it with (relative) ease is to read a lot of it, and the web can be very helpful here.

As you read it, you will want to write out a transcription; the conventions for papyrological transcriptions are similar to the epigraphical conventions that we have already seen.[7] As in the case of inscriptions, it is very helpful if you know, or can plausibly deduce, the dimensions of the original column; this allows you to know something about what must have stood in the torn-away spaces if, as is usually the case, there were such. If the papyrus is burnt, erased or otherwise illegible in places where letters once stood, infrared photography and the more sophisticated multi-spectral imaging can often help. There are research centers that specialize in using these technologies for papyri, and they can be found on the web.

Once you have read what can be read you reach the interesting—or, depending on your temperament, the infuriating—part: figuring out what this document says and what we can learn from it. This is a matter of searching for parallels: if it is a document, what other known documents resemble it? Legal documents often follow a set form, and recognizing the parallels can turn a few scraps of text into an understandable piece of evidence. Literary texts are often known to us from other sources, and if you can find the source you will know what should have stood in the papyrus—and whether the papyrus confirms or challenges the texts we already have. Even for papyri that are relatively free in terms of form, such as personal letters, there are often formulaic elements (salutation, date and place, signature) and turns of phrase that can be paralleled. People mentioned in the document may be known from other sources. The handwriting may reveal something about the period when the document was written, and how formal a document it was: documents that are meant to last or that are considered important will usually be written more clearly and handsomely than ephemeral notes. The parallels that you

---

[7] Above, pp. 221–2.

find at this stage may send you back to the previous stage, by giving you a better idea of what must have stood in the lacunae. In extraordinary cases, you may be able to identify some other published papyrus as actually being a scrap of the same papyrus that you hold in your hand.

READING A PUBLISHED PAPYRUS

The conventions of papyrological publication are very similar to those that epigraphers use. Figure 18.1 is an example, courtesy of the Egypt Exploration Society:

1. **4895**: In papyri first publication in a corpus is the most common form of publication. This papyrus, published in P.Oxy. LXXII, will henceforward be known as P.Oxy. LXXII 4895 (some scholars omit the volume number when referring to a papyrus; the guidelines of the International Association of Papyrologists [AIP] recommend always including it).
2. **Loan of Money (Writing Practice)**: Papyri fall into a number of broad categories; giving the category as part of the heading makes it much easier for a papyrologist to know at a glance whether this document is relevant to the research in hand.
3. **28 4B.57/A(1–5)c**: This is the inventory number, which in the case of the Oxyrhynchus collection represents box number, season and folder. Institutions that have only a few papyri do not necessarily give each of them an inventory number, but Oxford's collection is immense.
4. **9.2 × 11 cm** are the dimensions of the document: 9.2 cm wide, 11 cm high.
5. **14 October 380** is the date given in the document, though the commentary raises the possibility that, being merely a school exercise, it was actually written later. (It cannot have been written earlier, since an earlier writer would not have known the names of the consuls for a future year.)
6. **On the back . . .** The discussion comes before the text. Since this is a first edition, there is no bibliography given.
7. Before the text itself many editors put an arrow indicating the direction of the papyrus strips: a vertical arrow indicates that the writing goes across the grain; a horizontal arrow indicates writing along the grain. The editors of P.Oxy. LXXII do not include these arrows, but the discussion makes it clear that we are dealing with writing on

4895. LOAN OF MONEY (WRITING PRACTICE)

28 4B.57/A(1–5)c   9.2 × 11 cm   14 October 380

On the back of the lower part of a document of 236–7 (**4892**), at 90° and along the fibres, someone penned the beginning of a loan. He stopped half-way through the main body, just before he would have run out of space. This is apparently a writing exercise, which may well be later than the date recorded in its text; another loan contract/writing practice is LXI **4117** (for another writing exercise, see below, **4905**). What is remarkable is the time gap between the two texts; see **4892** introd.

ὑπατείας τῶν δεσποτῶν
ἡμῶν Γρατιανοῦ τὸ ε// καὶ
Θεοδοσίου τὸ a// τῶν
αἰωνίων Ἀγούcτων,
5   Φαῶφι ιζ.
Αὐρήλιος Φιλόνικο[c
Διονυcοδώρου ἀπὸ τ[ῆc
λαμ(πρᾶc) καὶ λαμ(προτάτηc) Ὀξυρυγχ[ι]τ[ῶν
πόλεωc παρὰ Αὐρηλίου
10 Θεοδώρου Δημητρίου ἀπὸ
τῆc αὐτῆc πόλεωc
χαίρειν. ὁμολογῶ ἐcχηκέ-
ναι παρὰ cοῦ ἐν χρήcι δι-
ὰ χειρὸc ἐξ οἴκο cου εἰc ἰδί-
15 αν μου ̣ (vac.)

4 l. Ἀγούcτων   6 l. Αὐρηλίῳ Φιλονίκῳ   8 λαμʃ (bis)   13 l. χρήcει
14 l. οἴκου   ἰδι-

'In the consulship of our masters Gratianus for the 5th time and Theodosius for the 1st time, the eternal Augusti, Phaophi 17.

'To Aurelius Philonicus son of Dionysodorus, from the splendid and most splendid city of the Oxyrhynchites, from Aurelius Theodorus son of Demetrius, from the same city, greetings. I acknowledge that I have received from you on loan, by hand and out of your house, for my own ...'

1–4 For the consulship of Gratianus Aug. v and Theodosius Aug. 1 coss. 380, see *CLRE* 294–5; *CSBE*² 190. Its earliest occurrence in a papyrus dates from three days earlier (P. Flor. I 75 = W. *Chr.* 433).

6–7 Φιλόνικο[c] Διονυcοδώρου. The name Φιλόνικοc is not very common, and Διονυcόδωροc is rare in this period. It is a curiosity that the only other known bearer of the name Φιλόνικοc in Oxyrhynchus at that time is the son of Besammon (VII **1041** 6 of 381), another pagan theophoric name not common in this period.

15 ̣. The scribe wrote an upright, and then stopped. καί was intended.

N. GONIS

Figure 18.1 The publication text of P.Oxy. LXXII 4895

the back of an older document, and that the writing goes along the grain—that is, at right angles to the text on the *recto*.

8. **λαμ(πρᾶς) καὶ λαμ(προτάτης)**: In papyri not only abbreviations but also conventional symbols for common terms are very common; curved brackets may indicate either.

9. **4 l. Αὐγούστων**: Immediately after the text comes the *apparatus criticus*. Since this is a first edition, there are no opinions of other scholars to mention; the *apparatus* includes only corrections of misspellings (l. stands for *legendum*, "you should read") and one other:

10. **8 λαμ∫ (bis)** indicates that the papyrus twice has a symbol for suspension (omitting the end of an easily supplied word, as we write "Prof." or "c.") where the editor has supplied the full word in the text.

11. **'In the consulship . . .'**: First editions of papyri—and for that matter, first editions of inscriptions, though the example we gave above did not illustrate it—regularly have a full translation.

12. **1–4 For the consulship . . .**: As in epigraphical publications, discussion of matters of substance comes at the end, separate from the *apparatus criticus*, which is limited to textual matters.

MAJOR RESOURCES

The general introduction to papyrology of Mitteis and Wilcken, *Grundzüge und Chrestomathie der Papyruskunde*, has not been superseded, but the beginner, and particularly the English-speaking beginner, will find Turner, *Greek Papyri* or Pestman, *New Papyrological Primer* much more convenient. For an outsider trying to get a general picture of how papyri are read and used, Bagnall, *Reading Papyri, Writing Ancient History* is approachable. Bagnall, *The Oxford Handbook of Papyrology*, though not available as I write these words, is scheduled to appear before this book, and should provide English non-papyrologists with an excellent general background to the field. There is no beginners' handbook to the study of ostraca or tablets—they are usually subsumed under the category of papyrology—but the first volume of Wilcken, *Griechische Ostraka*, though more than a hundred years old, includes a good deal of useful information about the kinds of ostraca found and what can be learned from them.

The papyri themselves are distributed in more than a thousand different collections throughout the world; the best list of collections is at the website *Trismegistos*.

Papyri are published in various publications, most of them books containing the papyri currently housed in a particular collection; each publication or series has a unique name, as described below. The largest collection, the Oxyrhynchus Papyri (P.Oxy.), has been being published since 1898, and as of this writing includes almost five thousand published papyri; it will not be exhausted soon. The authoritative list of editions of papyri was Oates et al., *Checklist*; this has now been superseded by its online successor, Sosin et al., *Checklist of Editions of Greek, Latin, Demotic, and Coptic Papyri, Ostraca and Tablets*.

In addition to the collections, there are a number of journals specializing in papyrology, among them *Aegyptus, Analecta Papyrologica, Archiv für Papyrusforschung (Archiv* or *APF)*, the *Bulletin of the American Society of Papyrologists (BASP)* and the *Journal of Juristic Papyri (JJP)*. It is worth making particular mention of the *Zeitschrift für Papyrologie und Epigraphik (ZPE)*, which is still one of the fastest journals in getting an article into print, although it no longer does so in a few months as it used to. Papyri from Egypt that are published in periodicals are republished, with text and bibliography, in the *Sammelbuch griechischer Urkunden aus Ägypten (Sammelbuch)*; as is usual in corpora, each papyrus has a unique number, and papyri are often referred to by their *Sammelbuch* number.

An admirable scholarly aid, which could be profitably imitated in other fields, is the *Berichtungsliste der griechischen Papyrusurkunden aus Ägypten (Berichtungsliste)*, an ongoing list of all published corrections to papyrus texts that allows the scholar who has found a papyrus in a corpus or collection to be able to quote the most accurate text available.

The major collection of photographs and discussion of the palaeography of the papyri is Seider, *Paläographie der griechischen Papyri*. Older and briefer but with somewhat more discussion is Schubart, *Griechische Palaeographie*; newer, in English, and designed for the non-specialist is Turner, *Greek Manuscripts of the Ancient World*.

The study of published papyri has been revolutionized by the digitalization of many collections. These are available and searchable through the *APIS* website of a consortium of universities; *APIS* will also refer you to other such sites. A *Papyrological Navigator*, still in development as I write, will allow simultaneous search of the major databases. Heidelberg has an important searchable collection at the *Heidelberger Gesamtverzeichnis der griechischen Papyrusurkunden Ägyptens (HGV)*, and the Oxyrhynchus papyri are available at Oxford's POxy site. The texts of documentary papyri are included in the *Duke Databank of Documentary Papyri (DDbDP)*; a list (the technical term is "repertory") of non-documentary papyri can be found at the website of Mertens–Pack[3], which although it has no texts or reproductions can significantly reduce the time it takes to find what you need.

The Greek of the papyri is generally *koine*, and requires its own linguistic aids. Its dictionary is Preisigke, *Wörterbuch*, kept up to date by a number of supplements; for personal names used there is Preisigke, *Namenbuch* and for toponyms Calderini, *Dizionario dei nomi geografici e topografici dell'Egitto greco-romano*. The grammar of the papyri is the subject of Gignac, *Grammar of the Greek Papyri*, but this includes only phonology and morphology; for syntax it is still necessary to refer to Mayser, *Grammatik der griechischen Papyri aus der Ptolemaërzeit*. Needless to say, new words, new names and new grammatical phenomena are turning up all the time as new papyri are published.

19

PALAEOGRAPHY

PALAEOGRAPHY AND CODICOLOGY

Before we can judge the alternatives offered by the various manuscripts we have to read them, and that is not a trivial matter, as you can discover by a few moments spent trying to read a medieval manuscript. Palaeography, the study of the different forms of writing over the centuries, and codicology, the study of books and the ways they are put together, allow you to build on the experience of others. Photographs in particular are invaluable: though they do not reproduce all the characteristics of a manuscript, they allow a beginner to become familiar with the varieties of scripts that have been common in different places and times. Many important libraries are now in the process of digitalizing their manuscript collections and uploading them to the internet; where high-quality imaging is used, these images will allow students to familiarize themselves easily with various scripts, save palaeographers quite a bit of airfare, and make it possible for other scholars, who would never travel for the purpose, to check a reading with their own eyes.

VARIETIES OF HANDWRITING

The most basic distinction, of course, is that of alphabet: classicists usually deal with two alphabets, the Greek and the Latin, and each has its own

Figure 19.1 Greek uncials, third century CE (Ambros. F. 205 inf., Thompson 43)

[ως] φατο γήθησέν δε βοὴν αγαθος Διομήδης
[εγχ]ος μεν κατέπηξεν επι χθονι πουλυβοτείρη
[αυτα]ρ ο μειλιχίοισι προσηυδα ποιμενα λαῶν

Figure 19.2 Latin rustic capitals, fifth century CE (Vat. Palat. 1631, Thompson 84)

SCALAE IMPROUISO·SUBITUSQUE APPARUIT IGNI·
DISCURRUNT ALII AD PORTAS·PRIMOSQUE TRUCIDANT·
FERRUM ALII TORQUENT·ET OBUMBRA`N´T AETHERA TELIS·

Figure 19.3 Greek cursive, 295 CE (Brit. Mus. pap. 748, Thompson 35)

αυρηλιος σωτηρ σαραπιωνος βουλ(ευτης) παραληφα
ως προκειται αυρηλιος σωτηρ σαθοθρακος
βουλ(ευτης) παρειληφα αυρηλιος συρος φιλαδελφου
βουλ(ευτης) παρειληφα αυρηλιος σαραπιων σαραπιωνος
βουλ(ευτης) παρειληφα
τοις υπο ενβαριν πρεποσιτον λι(τραι)

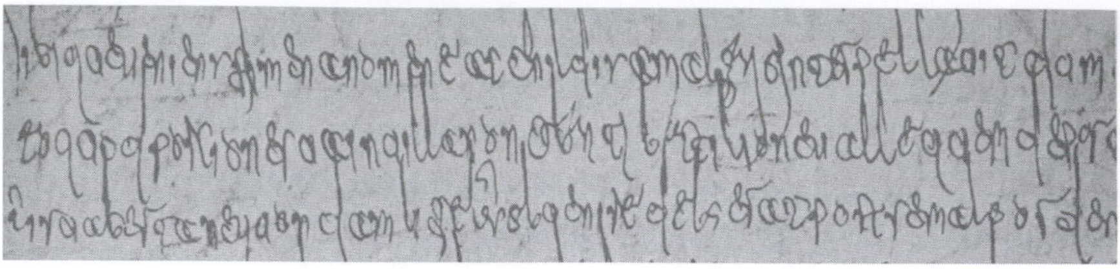

Figure 19.4 Latin official cursive 679–80 CE (Paris, Archives Nationales, K. 2, no. 13, Thompson 218)

Ibique veniens fimena nomene acchildis amalgario interpellavit dum [dicerit] eo quod porcione sua in villa noncobanti bactlione valle quem de part[i genetri-] ci sua bertane quondam ligebus obvenire debuerat post se malo orden[e retini-]

tradition of handwriting. Within the alphabet, on the other hand, language is not a major factor: in the Middle Ages as today, the various languages written in the Latin alphabet would all be written with more or less the same lettering, although there developed, as we shall see, different scribal traditions in different countries.

Within each tradition, the major division is between that of book-hands (Figures 19.1 and 19.2) and cursive writing (Figures 19.3 and 19.4). Everybody who writes balances the desire to write quickly with the need to write legibly, and obviously that calculation will work out differently for a person copying a book than from a person writing a receipt or a personal letter, or even a person writing a document of state. Book-hands, moreover, are designed not only to be legible but to be aesthetically pleasing, so the handwriting used for books is quite different from cursive writing, though of course there is a certain amount of seepage between the two, where a literary scribe through carelessness, habit or design adopts a cursive form, or a cursive writer may use a form that is usually restricted to literary texts; and in the long run, the two forms have a great tendency to influence each other.

Within literary texts, the next major division is between majuscule ("capital") and minuscule (small) letters. In Greek there are two majuscule alphabets: the "square" capitals that resemble those used in inscriptions (Figure 19.5), and uncials, a script in which most of the straight angles have been replaced by curves (Figure 19.1). In Latin in addition to square capitals (Figure 19.6) and uncials (Figure 19.7) there are also "rustic capitals," a script whose cross-strokes are usually narrower and often thin and/or wavy, somewhat less formal than the square capitals but still clear, the individual letters separated from each other (Figure 19.8). In every script, of course, some scripts are more elegant or legible

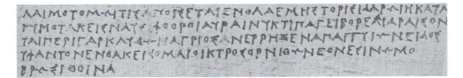

Figure 19.5 Greek square majuscules, fourth century BCE (Berlin Museums, Thompson 1)

ΛΑΙΜΟΤΟΜΩΙ ΤΙΣ ΑΠΟΙΣΕΤΑΙ ΕΝΘΑΔΕ ΜΗΣΤΟΡΙ ΣΙΔΑΡΩΙ Η ΚΑΤΑ–
ΚΥΜΟΤΑΚΕΙΣ ΝΑΥΣΙΦΘΟΡΟΙ ΑΥΡΑΙ ΝΥΚΤΙΠΑΓΕΙ ΒΟΡΕΑ Δ' ΙΑΡΑΙΣΟΝ–
ΤΑΙ ΠΕΡΙ ΓΑΡ ΚΛΥΔΩΝ ΑΓΡΙΟΣ ΑΝΕΡΡΗΞΕΝ ΑΠΑΓ ΓΥΙΩΝ ΕΙΔΟΣ
ΥΦΑΝΤΟΝ ΕΝΘΑ ΚΕΙΣΟΜΑΙ ΟΙΚΤΡΟΣ ΟΡΝΙΘΩΝ ΕΘΝΕΣΙΝ ΩΜΟ–
ΒΡΟΣΙ ΘΟΙΝΑ

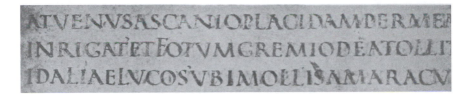

Figure 19.6 Latin square majuscules, fourth or fifth century CE (Cod. Sang. 1394, Thompson 82)

AT VENVS ASCANIO PLACIDAM PER MEM[BRA QUIETEM]
INRIGAT' ET FOTVM GREMIO DEA TOLLIT [IN ALTOS]
IDALIAE LVCOS' VBI MOLLIS AMARACV[S ILLVM]

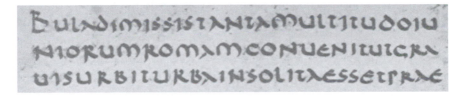

Figure 19.7 Latin uncials, fifth century CE (Vienna Imperial Library Cod. Lat. 15, Thompson 89)

Bula dimissis tanta multitudo iu-
niorum Romam conuenit ut gra-
uis urbi turba insolita esset prae-

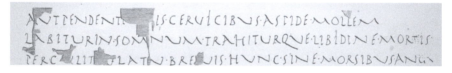

Figure 19.8 Latin rustic capitals, before 494 CE (Florence, Laur. Plut. xxxix.1, Thompson 86)

> AREA CUM PRIMIS INGENTI AEQUANDA CYLINDRO·
> ET UERTENDA MANU ET CRETA SOLIDANDA TENACI·
> NE SUBEANT HERBAE·NEU PULUERE UICTA FATISCAT·

Figure 19.9 Latin rustic capitals, before 79 CE (Naples, Museo Nazionale, Thompson 83)

> AVT PENDENTE [SV]IS·CERVICIBVS·ASPIDE·MOLLEM
> LABITUR IN·SOMNUM·TRAHITURQVE·LIBIDINE·MORTIS
> PERCVLIT [AD]FLATV·BREVIS·HVNC·SINE·MORSIBVS·ANGV[IS·]

(the two do not necessarily coincide), others less so (compare, for example, Figure 19.2 and Figure 19.9).

Both in Greek and in Latin the uncials dominated for a considerable time but were eventually superseded by minuscule book-hands (Figures 19.10 to 19.13; Figure 19.14 belongs to an intermediate "half-uncial" script, with minuscule forms mixed with uncials), based upon the cursive scripts but much clearer and much more stylized. In the later Middle Ages these scripts developed their own characteristics; in Europe after the Carolingian age, each country tended to develop its own "national" script, clearly recognizable to one who has spent a good deal of time with manuscripts (Figures 19.10 and 19.12, and Figure 19.15).

Cursive texts were always written in minuscule. For ephemeral documents these could be rather carelessly written (Figure 19.16, Figure 19.3 above), though they do not, to my knowledge, descend to the level of illegible scrawls except for such things as personal signatures: they were generally produced either by professional scribes or by people trained in penmanship, an ability much more essential in days when typewriters (much less computers) were not available. Most documents, however,

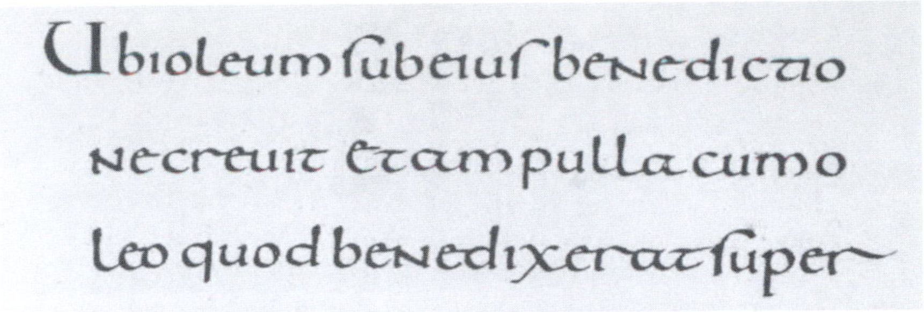

Figure 19.10 Latin minuscules, early ninth century CE (Quedlinburg, Thompson 132)

Ubi oleum sub eius benedictio-
ne creuit et ampulla cum o-
leo quod benedixerat super

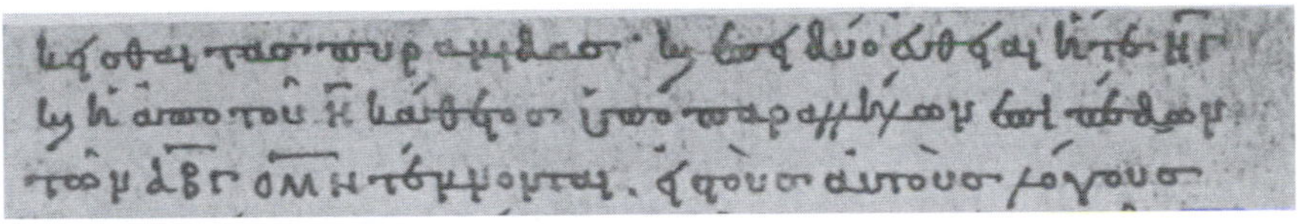

Figure 19.11 Greek minuscules, 888 CE (D'Orville MS 1, Bodleian Library,
Thompson 53)

κεῖσθαι τὰς πυραμιδας · κ(αι) επει δύο ἐυθειαι ἥ τε $\overline{HΓ}$
κ(αι) ἡ ἀπο τοῦ $\overline{H}$ κάθετος ὑπο παραλλήλων ἐπιπέδων
τῶν $\overline{ABΓ}$ $\overline{OMN}$ τέμνονται. ἐις τοὺς ἀυτοὺς λόγους

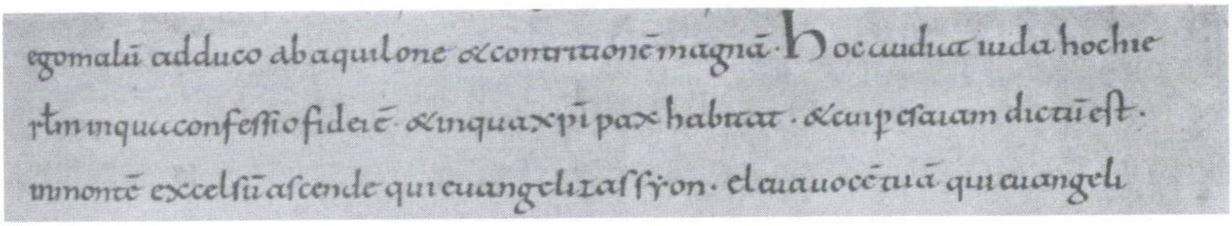

Figure 19.12 Latin minuscules, after 948 CE (Brit. Mus. Add. MS 22820,
Thompson 165)

ego malum adduco ab aquilone et contritionem magnam·
Hoc audiat iuda hoc hie-
rusalem in qua confessio fidei est·et in qua christi pax
habitat·et cui per esaiam dictum est·
in montem excelsum ascende qui evangelizas
sẏon·eleva vocem tuam qui evangeli-

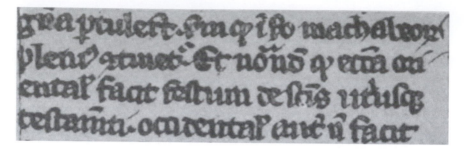

Figure 19.13   Latin minuscules, 1312 CE (Brit. Mus. Add. MS 11882, Thompson
190)

genera pertulerunt . secundum quod in secundo machabeorum
plenius continetur. Et notandum quod ecclesia ori-
entalis facit festum de sanctis utriusque
testamenti . occidentalis autem non facit

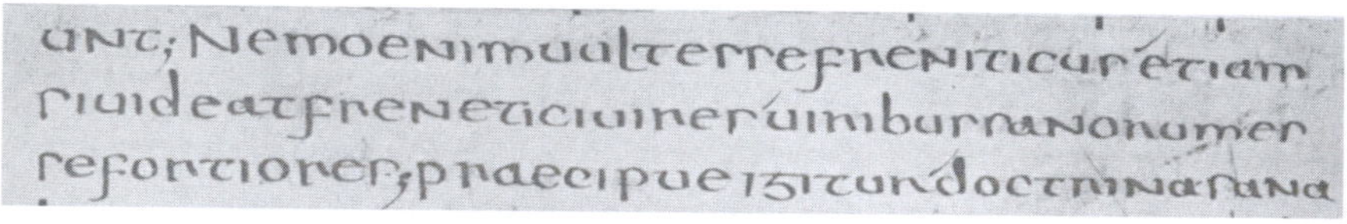

Figure 19.14   Latin half-uncials, sixth century CE (Paris, Bibl. Nat., MS Lat. 13367,
Thompson 99)

unt; Nemo enim uult esse freniticus´ etiam
si uideat frenetici uires´ uiribus sanorum esse fortiores; praecipue igitur´ doctrina sana

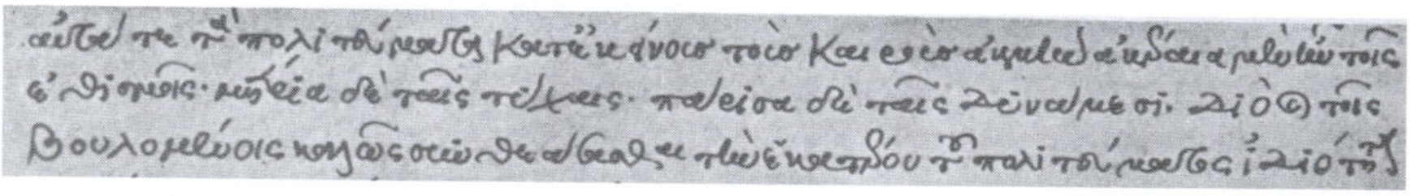

Figure 19.15   Greek minuscules, 1416 CE (Brit. Mus. Add. MS 11728, Thompson 78)

αὐτά τε τὰ πολιτεύματα κατ᾽ ἐκείνους τοὺς καιροὺς ἀκμὴν ἀκέραια
μὲν ἦν τοῖς
ἐθισμοῖς· μέτρια δὲ ταῖς τύχαις· πάρισα δὲ ταῖς δυνάμεσι. διὸ (καὶ) τοῖς
βουλομένοις καλῶς συνθεάσασθαι τὴν ἑκατέρου τοῦ
πολιτεύματος ἰδιότητα

were made to last, and these had to be produced in a script clear enough to be legible in a courtroom decades after they had been written; so the minuscule scripts developed, alongside the more negligent cursive, stylized and handsome versions; and it was from these that the minuscule book-hands of the Middle Ages descended. Nevertheless, there remained a distinction between "chancery script" (Figure 19.4 above, Figure 19.17) and book-hands, so that the palaeography of charters is a field of expertise not quite identical with that of literary palaeography.

The observant reader will have noticed one distinction that I did not mention: the distinction between texts written on papyrus and those written on parchment or paper. There is indeed something of a difference: any change in the implements of writing is likely to produce certain changes merely by virtue of the characteristics of the new medium. Nevertheless, the continuity is much more pronounced than the differences. The palaeography of parchment manuscripts is a direct continuation of the palaeography of the papyri.

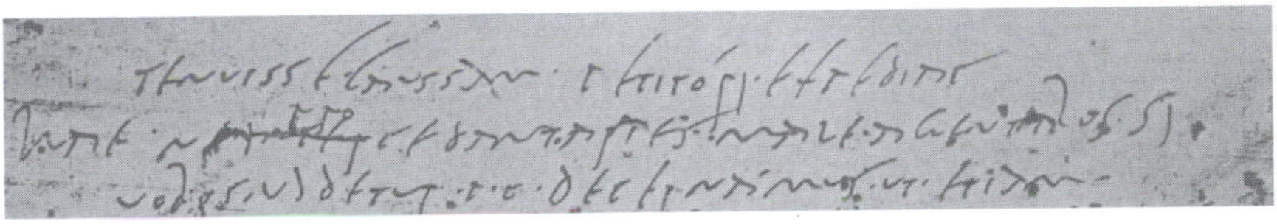

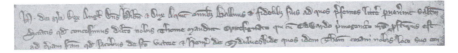

Figure 19.16 Latin cursive, 41–54 CE (Berlin Museums Pap. 8507, Thompson 106)

tenuisse·causam·petitóri·expediat
hae·ne·~~inter~~procedant·artes·male·agentibus·si
vobis·videtur p(atres)·c(onscripti)·decernámus·ut·etiam
prólatis·rebus·iis·iúdicibus·necessitas·iudicandi

Figure 19.17 Latin official cursive, England 1270 (Brit. Mus. Add. Ch. 19828, Thompson 233)

Henricus.dei gratia Rex Anglie·Dominus Hibernie et Dux Aquitanie·omnibus
Ballivis et fidelibus suis ad quos presentes littere pervenerint salutem
Sciatis quod concessimus dilecto nobis Thome Maudut Crucesignato qui cum
Edwardo primogenio nostro profecturus est
ad terram sanctam quod Iacobus de sancto victore et Henricus de Tyduluehside
quod idem Thomas coram nobis loco suo con-

SHORTHAND AND ABBREVIATION

Writing is a way of making words stand still, an almost magical power that can hold the ephemeral and enshrine it for centuries. But in order to record spoken words the scribe must either have a phenomenal verbatim memory, or get the speaker to speak very slowly, or write very quickly. Since the first two are not always possible, systems of shorthand were already developed in antiquity—possibly for Greek, certainly for Latin. The most famous shorthand[1] was the Tironian *notae*, ostensibly the invention of Cicero's slave Tiro, whose use in antiquity was relatively widespread. Some of the symbols used survived into the Middle Ages and are known to us; but entire documents written in shorthand are rare and late. More common was the practice of abbreviation, a practice helped by the Hebrew custom of not writing out divine names, a custom that was imported into Greek and Latin. In Latin, particularly, abbreviation was very common, generally in combination with some shorthand symbols; and part of learning to read manuscripts is developing a familiarity with the various abbreviations, contractions, shorthand signs and ligatures that were commonly used by scribes, often even for books, and that together with a general unity of concept showed a great deal of variation over time and place.

THE STUDY OF MANUSCRIPTS AND CODICES

Merely recognizing the script is just the beginning of getting to know a manuscript. Not only the style of writing, but every physical aspect of the manuscript may give information about its date and provenance[2]— valuable information when you are trying to establish its relationship to other manuscripts. Marginal corrections or notes at the beginning or end may indicate where else the manuscript has been before it reached your hands; and this information may not only give us hints as to the value of some of these later comments, but may also indicate the relationships among the various monasteries, humanists and collectors through whose

---

[1] A true shorthand does not simply abbreviate, but uses special non-alphabetic symbols for common words.

[2] The ideal indication, of course, is the case, not at all uncommon, where the scribe is identified in the manuscript, usually at the beginning or the end, but even here caution is in order, since one scribe may copy another's signature, just as both of them copied the original author's words.

hands the book has passed. How the sheets are lined and how they are bound are also items that change over time and that may have something to teach us; I was once able to demonstrate by examining photographs of the prickings that guided the lines along which the letters were written that two texts supposed to be independent of each other had actually been produced together.[3] Researchers whose interests are in the broader fields of epic poetry, political and social history, and such like may find this kind of investigation far from the great civilizations that fascinate them; but most of what we know about those civilizations has come to us through the people and the activities that are the palaeographer's province, and to learn about them is to learn about how we know and, if we know, what we think we know.

MAJOR RESOURCES

Introductions to Palaeography

The standard introduction to Greek palaeography is still Devreesse, *Introduction à l'étude des manuscrits grecs*; for Latin Clemens and Graham, *Introduction to Manuscript Studies* is now the best available. Older but also good are Bischoff, *Latin Palaeography* and the much older Thompson, *An Introduction to Greek and Latin Palaeography*. Thompson's yet earlier *A Handbook of Greek and Latin Palaeography*, much less liberally illustrated, is cheaper but less useful; if money is a consideration, the *Introduction* is now available for free on the web.

Palaeographical Photographs

In addition to the volumes already mentioned in connection with papyrology,[4] a good collection of photographs is Barbour, *Greek Literary Hands A.D. 400–1600*; much more copious are the volumes of Lake and Lake, *Dated Greek Minuscule Manuscripts to the Year 1200*. For Latin Lowe, *Codices Latini Antiquiores* goes up to the ninth century, and later examples may be found in Brown, *A Guide to Western Historical Scripts*. The palaeography of early

---

[3] Schaps, "The Found and Lost Manuscripts of Tacitus' Agricola." Many scholars have disagreed with the broader conclusions I drew from the observation—a salutary warning that our logic is no less subject to criticism than our observations.

[4] Above, p. 244.

charters, abundantly illustrated in Bruckner et al., *Chartae Latinae Antiquiores*, is of more interest to medievalists than to classicists. Many websites now offer at least sample pages of manuscripts; *Digital Scriptorium* is a cooperative effort to offer access to many collections at a single site; many other libraries (*Gallica, Codices Electronici Ecclesiae Colonensis, Parker Library on the Web, St. Laurentius Digital Manuscript Library* are just a sample) have uploaded their manuscripts or are in the process of doing so. The *Vatican Library* is, as of this writing, closed to the public for refurbishing; but an important project is underway to digitalize its manuscripts as well.

For help with Greek abbreviations, there is Oikonomides, *Abbreviations*. For Latin, where the use of abbreviations was much more widespread, Lindsay, *Notae Latinae* is a wide-ranging discussion covering manuscripts from 700 to 850, with a *Supplement to Notae Latinae* covering the next two hundred years, and it is available (without the supplement) online; but its organization by word, rather than by abbreviation, means that its chief use is for people who know what an abbreviation means and are interested in knowing what other forms could be used for the same word. Cappelli, *Lexicon abbreviaturarum* and its supplement by Pelzer, *Abbréviations latines médiévales*, on the other hand, arrange the abbreviations in alphabetical order, and show each in the hand in which it occurs, making it much easier for a person to decode an unfamiliar abbreviation when faced with one. (Cappelli's introduction has been translated into English: Cappelli, *Elements of Abbreviation in Medieval Latin*.) Even easier to use is the online Pluta, *Abbreviationes*, where you simply enter the legible letters and get back all the appropriate answers that the database has. This resource, however, is available only by paid subscription. An internet copy of Cappelli is available for free, not as a searchable text but as a set of photographic images.

Bibliographies

An indispensable bibliography for further study is Boyle, *Medieval Latin Palaeography*, which can direct the budding palaeographer to the published resources available, including catalogues, facsimile editions, studies of local scripts and scriptoria, and much more, thoughtfully arranged and collected with a very broad view of what you might need. The Italian translation (Boyle, *Paleografia latina medievale*) included a supplement with 484 more entries, and Boyle's colleagues have continued to update the information on the website *Electronic Palaeography*. The authoritative list of what manuscripts are where is Kristeller and Krämer, *Latin Manuscript Books*, to which an *Ergänzungsband* has now been added.

20

EDITING CLASSICAL TEXTS

THE EDITOR'S GOAL

The job of the editor of an ancient work is to try to print, as far as possible, what the author wrote. The stages of establishing this are three:[1] *recensio*, establishing what the texts in our possession say (in the terms that critics use, establishing what the "tradition"—the technical term is *paradosis*—is); *examinatio*, examining the paradosis to decide whether or not it is likely to preserve the author's actual words; and since no manuscript is without errors, the final stage is *emendatio*, proposing what the author may originally have written that was corrupted into what we have received.

RECENSIO

Assembling the manuscripts is not a negligible task. Among ancient authors, as among modern ones, some are more popular than others, and the more popular ones are more commonly copied; but the beginner is likely to be flabbergasted by the number of manuscripts of ancient works that exist in Italy, and in many more out-of-the-way places. Account must also be taken of papyri and of quotations or references in other authors:

---

[1] Maas, *Textual Criticism*, 1; other divisions have been suggested.

sometimes a later author will quote an earlier one in a form different from the one we find in the earlier author's manuscripts.

If you are reading a manuscript of a work that has never been published—a stroke of luck that happens to very few—you will, of course, have to record every letter; but if the work you are reading has been published, you will have with you a copy of it, and will record every case where the manuscript you are reading differs from the text in front of you.[2]

Up to this point the job of editing is essentially the job of the palaeographer; from here on, it becomes the job of the textual editor. The editor is not necessarily the person who has read all the manuscripts; in most cases, the editor will have examined the most important ones, but will rely on published or unpublished editions ("collations") of others, perhaps checking them (or their digitalized photographs) at critical places. An editor will also take account of the first edition ever published (*editio princeps*), since the manuscripts from which the first publisher derived his texts may not be those available to us today. Other editions, from then till now, will be examined not as independent sources for the text but for the observations, judgments and suggestions that they make about the text as we have received it.

An essential part of *recensio* is to establish, if possible, a stemma—a "tree" that shows which manuscripts derive from which. There is no infallible way to know this, but it is of great importance, for it allows us both to ignore manuscripts copied from originals that we possess and to recognize which variations are likely to be conjecture, with no older manuscript authority behind them. The stemma is established not by comparing true readings, but by comparing false ones: these are the ones, if they are not errors so simple that they are likely to have been repeated more than once, that show us that one manuscript has copied from another, or that both have copied from an earlier manuscript that already contained that error. Establishing a stemma is thus something of a circular process: first we see which manuscripts share false readings, then on that basis we determine their relationship to each other, and lastly we judge among other readings on the basis of the stemma we have built. There is no way out of this circularity; the best we can do is begin from those shared errors that give the most certain evidence of a shared tradition, and

---

[2]   It might seem simplest to simply record variant readings in the margins of your printed edition, but in practice that is rarely convenient. Editors often have a separate notebook in which they record every variant; but it is still desirable to have a single text against which you compare the manuscript.

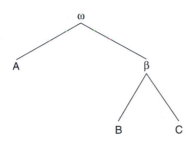

Figure 20.1 In this simple stemma, manuscript A and the lost manuscript β both stem from a lost prototype ω; manuscripts B and C derive from the lost β

on the basis of those argue to other cases. The stemma, like every stage of textual editing, depends more upon good judgment than upon any set of rules that can be followed mechanically.

The stemma, however, is based on the presumption that each manuscript is copied from one other—a presumption that obviously is not always the case. There may have been more than one manuscript before the scribe; more commonly, a later reader may have corrected the source of this manuscript according to another one, so that in the manuscript before us we can no longer tell which reading came from which source. This sort of copying, which is undoubtedly more scholarly but which palaeographers refer to as *contaminatio*, is in fact not uncommon. Where it can be established, it is indicated by a dotted line in the stemma; when the contamination is so widespread, or the connection among the documents so unclear, that none of them can be shown to be dependent upon any other, we cannot reduce their relationship to a stemma at all, and we speak of an *open recension*.

The stemma is only a means to understand better how the various readings of the manuscripts arose; the essential work is the establishment, word by word, of the text. Where we can build a stemma, it will often allow us to recognize what was in the manuscript (the *archetype*) from which the ones in front of us were copied (they are called *apographs* of the prototype), and thus to recognize what is the real paradosis and what is a

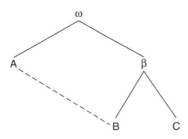

Figure 20.2 A simple stemma with *contaminatio*: although manuscripts B and C derive from the lost β, some of the readings of B (but not of C) stem from manuscript A

mere copyist's error or conjecture. When we know this, we have finished the *recensio*.

EXAMINATIO

What usually interests us in an ancient text is not what the last monk to copy it wrote, but what the ancient author wrote; and there will inevitably be differences. Sometimes they are obvious: sentences that don't parse, verses that don't scan, words that have no meaning. These errors, however, are fewer than you might expect; even where they occurred in the archetype they may have been "corrected" by a later copyist—making the original reading all the harder to recognize. Often the paradosis offers more than one plausible reading, and it is necessary to choose among them. There are guidelines—other things being equal, one prefers the reading of the manuscript that is less prone to error ("manuscripts should be weighed, not counted"); one prefers the more difficult reading, since it would be more likely to be corrupted into the simpler one than vice versa (*difficilior lectio praeferenda est*); but in fact every case must be addressed on its own terms, and, after absorbing the principles that can be gleaned from guidebooks, the editor must rely on judgment in each case. I am sorely tempted to give examples, but, since there would be no end to them, I must stand firm against temptation.

EMENDATIO

Often enough the paradosis offers no plausible reading at all; what can have been the original? Here editors for centuries have tried their hand at emendation, proposing an idea of what may have stood in the text in the first place and by what error or conjecture it was corrupted into the text in front of us. An emendation, by definition, has no manuscript support; it rests only on its own plausibility. Often a suggested emendation is so obviously correct that the problem is solved; much more often it is not, and the way is open for future editors, yourself included, to try to find a better suggestion. Be warned, however, that *emendatio* can be habit-forming, and after a while editors can become sufficiently sure of their own taste to offer emendations, and sometimes even plausible emendations, of a text that was perfectly comprehensible as it stood.

COMMON ERRORS

When faced with a problematical text, one of the most helpful questions to ask is: how did it get that way? Textual critics over the years have identified a number of common causes of error, and it helps to be aware of them:

- Similar letters: In many medieval Latin minuscule hands, the letters i, m, n and u were made up of one, two or three lines, connected by a thin cross-stroke at the top (n, m) or bottom (u). Distinguishing vi from in, or either of them from the letter m, is not impossible, but it is very easy to misread, particularly since the copyist is usually working more or less mechanically, not paying close attention to the meaning of the text. Similar things happen to other letters, depending on the script: praedarum could easily be read as praeclarum in a minuscule script; the same mistake would be very unlikely in majuscules. Knowing which kinds of letters are likely to be mistaken for each other is a matter of knowing the scripts in which the work was transmitted; conversely, recognizing characteristic errors can help establish the script of now-lost manuscripts that lie behind the one with which we are dealing.

   Similarity of letters may also be a matter of phonetics. When, from the Byzantine period onward, the pronunciation of Greek οι was the same as υ and rough and smooth breathings were no longer distinguished, a scribe may perhaps be forgiven for having written about a pig (ὗς) where the text being copied spoke of a sheep (ὄις).
- Similar words: A scribe who writes a text may also think about it, though this is not necessarily the case, and so may simply write one word where a word of similar meaning but entirely different shape appears in the text. A word of similar shape that is unfamiliar to the copyist may be replaced by a similar-looking but more familiar word; this kind of error (which can also be true of unfamiliar grammatical constructions) is the source of the principle that we should prefer the more difficult reading.
- Homoeoarchon, homoeomeson, homoeoteleuton: Sometimes a scribe's eye simply skips from the beginning, middle or end of one word or sentence to a similar group of letters or words in a later or earlier passage. If the passage to which the scribe has skipped is a later one, there will be a lacuna, a space where words have been lost from the text; if the passage is an earlier one, there will be a repetition, which is of course much easier to identify and correct.

- *Haplography, dittography, omission*: Sometimes a scribe writes once what should have been written twice (*insere* for *inserere*) or writes twice what should have been written once (the opposite). And sometimes, of course, a letter or group of letters or a word is simply omitted.
- *Abbreviations*: Abbreviations are common in manuscripts, but they vary from place to place and from time to time, or may simply not be noticed or understood by the scribe. When the abbreviated letters are merely omitted they can usually be restored; when the abbreviation has been incorrectly expanded it may require more alertness to realize that the original problem was a misunderstood abbreviation.
- *Wrong division*: Sometimes two consecutive words can be divided in more than one way: should we read *inflexu* or *in flexu* in Juv. 3.237? Since ancient texts were so often written without word division, re-dividing the words in a different way hardly counts as a correction; it is simply suggesting a different way to read the letters that have been transmitted.
- *Transposition*: A scribe reading a few words in the source text may accidentally transpose them before writing them in the new text.
- *Anticipation and perseveration*: Sometimes a word or concept that has just been mentioned or is about to be mentioned slips into the scribe's mind at the wrong point, causing a similar word to be read as if it were the anticipated or remembered one.
- *Intrusive glosses*: Readers in the ancient and medieval period, like many readers today, often wrote in the margins corrections, explanations or comments; and a later scribe, taking an explanation or a comment for a correction, might write the comment into the text.
- *Assimilation*: In a series of words of similar form—in Latin and Greek, this will usually mean words agreeing in gender, number and case—a word that has a different form may be miswritten to fit the others, causing confusion that is not always easy to clear up: even if it is clear that one of these words should be in another case, which word is it?
- *Correction*: The hardest of all to correct is the corruption that enters a text when a scribe, recognizing (rightly or wrongly) an error, tries to correct it. This is particularly common in verse, where many mechanical mistakes will cause the line to scan incorrectly, demanding correction. The better the scribe's Latin, the more likely the result is to be a plausible reading—and the less likely we are ever to discover it.
- *Multiple errors*: ὅπως ἐπιστέωνται οἱ Ἕλλανες τάν τε Ἀθαναίων ἀρετὰν καὶ τὰν Βυζαντίων καὶ Περινθίων εὐχαριστίαν wrote the Byzantines in a decree quoted in Dem. 18.91. A scribe misread the first tau of τάν τε for a pi and wrote πάντε, which does not mean anything but remains in one manuscript; and a later scribe corrected it

to πάντες, which is plausible enough as a beginning: ὅπως ἐπιστέωνται οἱ Ἕλλανες πάντες . . . . If it hadn't been for the parallelism τάν τε . . . καὶ τὰν, Porson might never have guessed the correct text.

This is a partial list, but there is no complete list, for there is no limit to human fallibility. Every reading is a new challenge, and imagination, good judgment and a good command of the language are required to discover what may plausibly have given rise to the text before us. If you are a person with imagination and good judgment—linguistic knowledge can be acquired—and you are not averse to using it in a field that will bring you little money and less fame, you will never lack for challenges in the field of textual criticism.

MAJOR RESOURCES

Introductions to Textual Criticism

The basic principles of editing texts can be found in West, *Textual Criticism and Editorial Technique*, an extremely readable and informative essay that was itself written as a successor to the essay of Maas, *Textual Criticism*. These books are strikingly brief for the reason that West gives: textual criticism has a few essential principles, but beyond that it is a matter of observation, practice, and a sense for language and for possibilities. The classic of Pasquali, *Storia della tradizione e critica del testo* will give the reader a wider background and deeper understanding of what editors and copyists have done with texts over the ages. Renehan, *Greek Textual Criticism* offers a wide variety of passages to illustrate the various ways of approaching problems. Willis, *Latin Textual Criticism* includes not only discussion of the common causes of corruption of passages but actual exercises on which budding editors can cut their critical teeth.

The basic principles of evaluating manuscripts are generally associated with the name of Karl Lachmann and with his editions of Lucretius, *De rerum natura* and *Novum Testamentum Graece et Latine*, though Timpanaro, *The Genesis of Lachmann's Method* has demonstrated that the principles were in fact worked out by many scholars over the first half of the nineteenth century. The greatest critic of Lachmann's method was A. E. Housman, known to non-classicists for his poetry but to classicists for his witty but chronically dyspeptic invective. His editions of Juvenal, *Satires* and Lucan, *Civil War* (both edited "for the use of editors") both state and exemplify his principles, a brief statement of which can also be found in Housman, "The Application of Thought to Textual Criticism."

History of Texts

For most authors the history of the text must be culled from the introductions to the chief editions, and often from monographs or articles that are referred to in those introductions or can be found by the usual bibliographical methods; but it would be unfair to you not to mention Reynolds, *Texts and Transmission*, a *Festschrift* for Sir Roger Mynors that offers "short and readily accessible accounts in a modern language"[3] of the textual transmission of almost all the major Latin authors.

---

[3] Reynolds, ed., *Texts and Transmission*, vii.

PART VI

THE CLASSICS AND RELATED DISCIPLINES

21

ART

ART HISTORY

A sensible, sensitive and intelligent young person once told me why she had never taken a course in art history: "There's only so long," said she, "that I can sit and listen to the teacher tell me to notice the dominant greens and blues." Artistic details—the folds of a dress, the tree at whose foot the shepherd is sitting, the dominant greens and blues—are to art history what dates are to general history, the picayune items, meaningless in themselves, that discourage the student who does not see past them to the larger story. Every art class is full of such details, and every student of art must learn to pay attention to them. The subject would not exist without them. But they themselves are not the subject.

The subject is most easily seen by a few comparisons. Figure 21.1 is an Egyptian relief[1] of Merenptah, a pharaoh of the late thirteenth century BCE, thrashing his enemies. The picture is propaganda, and its message is clear: the king is larger than life, larger than his enemies, and will punish them mercilessly. He holds them by their hair and his right arm is raised to strike. Their knees, on which they have fallen, are still facing to flee, but

---

[1] A "relief," if the term is unfamiliar, is a sculpture whose figures protrude from a wall behind them, as opposed to "free-standing" sculpture, which can be seen from all sides.

Figure 21.1 Pharaoh Merenptah thrashes his enemies

their faces are turned to Pharaoh and their arms try vainly to fend off the blow. They have fallen not only before Pharaoh, but before his dog as well.

Now look at a scene from the Treasury of the Siphnians at Delphi (525 BCE), depicting the gigantomachy, the battle of the gods and the giants (Figure 21.2). The missing right hand must be raised to strike; but this is a very different picture. The victorious warrior is the same size as his defeated

Figure 21.2 Battle scene from the Treasury of the Siphnians at Delphi

enemy, and he is punishing him not in a stylized way, but in a very practical way, holding him down with his knee and his shield as he prepares to strike the fatal blow. The picture is not necessarily devoid of message: the principals are all mythological, but it surely reflects and reinforces the ideal of manly prowess in battle that every Greek state wanted to instill in its citizenry. It is, moreover, descended directly from the sculptural traditions of Egypt, as can be seen from the earliest surviving examples of Greek sculpture. Nevertheless, the way the sculptor shows a victorious soldier is not the way that Merenptah's sculptor showed him. The archaic Greek sculptor showed a similar scene, but showed it very differently from what we see in Merenptah's tomb.

More than half a millennium later, Trajan's Column depicts the emperor's conquest of Dacia (Figure 21.3). There are soldiers here, but on Trajan's Column they do not only fight. Here they are building a camp: on the left mixing mortar, in the center hauling baskets of earth, on the right a soldier carries a beam. Only Trajan himself, inside the corner of the wall, strikes a heroic pose, and he is doing nothing: he is directing, as an emperor should. Emotion is absent: unlike the previous two pictures, where the postures of the victors and the vanquished (though not necessarily their faces) showed clearly their extreme emotions, Trajan's soldiers go about their work almost expressionlessly. When Trajan wanted to show the glory of his conquest, his

Figure 21.3 Scene from Trajan's Column: Roman soldiers build a fort

sculptors did it in a way very different from the way the Egyptians of the New Kingdom or the archaic Greeks would have done it. Battle scenes are present on Trajan's Column, but they are relatively few. Merenptah's triumph was presented as a triumph of a superior being over inferiors; the Siphnians showed victory as a matter of martial prowess of man against man. The Roman triumph, as Trajan's artists portrayed it, was a victory of civilization and organization over brave but wild barbarity. Again, something has changed, and the art both reflects it and displays it.

We can take another example from pottery painting (Figure 21.4). The background is reddish; the figures themselves—Apollo and Heracles fighting over the Delphic tripod—are painted on in black.[2] The figures would be mere silhouettes if the painter had not scratched off the paint in numerous lines. The painter of this pot, apparently the Taleides painter of about 520 BCE, shows a considerable amount of detail: the texture of Heracles' lion skin and cloak, the knobs on his club, and the border decoration of Apollo's chiton are all scratched in, as well as a few lines to indicate muscles and joints. All of these are indicated more telegraphically

---

[2] In fact the black color is not paint, but a secondary coating of clay that turned black in the end of the firing process by a technique that required some sophistication in the matter of temperature control.

Figure 21.4 Heracles and Apollo fighting over the Delphic tripod

than realistically—small dots and angles for the lion's hair, four wavy lines for Apollo's—and there is no attempt to show folds or drapery in the clothing. Nevertheless, the painter is obviously in control of the style, and the figures are far beyond the level of mere silhouettes.

Figure 21.5 shows another pot, from perhaps a generation later. In this picture of Achilles bandaging Patroclus' wound the black paint covers the entire background; the figures themselves are left unpainted so that the red background shows through. This technique allows the painter to paint details onto the figures with a very fine brush: the painter is generous with detail in the hair, the armor, the hands and feet, and the expression. Clothing folds are indicated around Patroclus' shoulders and at the bottom of both figures' chitons. The first kind of pottery is called "black figure," the second "red figure." The new technique is not necessarily better, and did not immediately put the old one out of business; but it doesn't take much looking to realize that the difference in technique will produce

Figure 21.5 Achilles bandaging Patroclus' wound

different kinds of drawing. Again, something has happened; this time it is not in the way the figures are portrayed but in the technique that is used for painting them—and the new technique entails a new style of painting.

A third example is shown in Figure 21.6. This relief from the Arch of Titus shows Titus' triumphal procession after the destruction of the Temple; the menorah and the other holy vessels are being carried into slavery.[3] It is a picture reproduced in practically every book of Jewish history, and is surely familiar to every Israeli. It is not a pleasant picture for a Jew to look at: it symbolizes more than any other the destruction of Israel's greatness and the beginning of a bitter two-thousand-year exile.

Figure 21.7 is a photograph from a flyer put out by a Jewish school that had been forcibly removed along with its settlement as part of the

---

[3]   The laurel garlands on their heads make it clear that it is the victorious soldiers who are carrying the spoils, but many Jews, not noticing this, think of the people passing in the procession as their captive ancestors.

Figure 21.6 Triumphal procession on the Arch of Titus

Figure 21.7 The evacuation of the synagogue at Netzarim, 2005

Israeli–Palestinian disengagement of 2005. Perhaps you have opinions about that particular item of recent history (I certainly do), but put them aside and consider the picture. The picture was taken almost two thousand years after the Arch of Titus, but the symbolism is unmistakable: the evacuation of the settlement is presented as a new destruction, a new exile. Here again, something has happened: not a new focus or a new technique, but the recollection of an old work of art for a contemporary purpose.

Art changes. In art as in other aspects of life, new styles, new emphases, new tastes and new meanings do not spring up spontaneously, but grow out of the old. Art has a history; and in the history of art perhaps more than any other sort of history it is the Greeks and the Romans who built the basis on which later centuries have built, and to which they have constantly harked back.

Art history is not linear, progressing from the primitive to the sophisticated in an unbroken, triumphal procession: as in other forms of history, the question of the relative values of different stages is open to question, and the progression from one to another is not a simple matter of things getting better and better, or even—to remove the value judgment—more and more like the later forms. Each artist has a particular way of working. One may be obsessively careful with details while another treats them cavalierly with a few brushstrokes; one may show the strain in the muscles of a warrior's thigh while another may, from lack of ability, lack of interest, or a desire to make a different point, make do with a thigh of the proper proportions, or perhaps not even that; one may show all faces smiling or handsome while another may show them frowning, crying or ugly. And for all that, every artist works in a certain context of time and place, a context that is constantly changing and developing. "Say cheese," says a photographer today, always wanting to show the subject smiling;[4] in the early days of photography smiles were not considered a universally, or even commonly, appropriate expression. Similarly archaic Greek art tends to show all its characters smiling, while classical Greek art gives them a serene, almost emotionless expression; Hellenistic and Roman faces, on the other hand, offer wide varieties of emotions. The art historian, by looking carefully at each individual work, comes to know the work in its context, and to trace the development by which one kind of art gives way to another.

---

[4] This convention is observed so absolutely that it can occur even when ghoulishly inappropriate, as in the case of a soldier smiling in a picture intended to document a serious crime: Morris, "The Most Curious Thing."

ART AND LITERATURE; ART AND CULTURE

Not all art tells a story. The statue of Augustus from Prima Porta (Figure 21.8) presents an image of the *princeps*—young, strong, standing firm, arrayed in the symbols of the Roman past—that undoubtedly has a strong propagandizing purpose, but it does not tell a story about him.[5] The picture of Achilles and Patroclus, on the other hand, is very much a part of a story, and it is only because of our familiarity with the story that we recognize who the two characters are. Much of Greek and Roman art is narrative art, and as such it offers new aspects of mythology: sometimes illustrating the myths we know from literature (and showing us how a Greek or a Roman envisioned them), sometimes showing a different story entirely. Some great works of antiquity are almost entirely narrative: Trajan's Column shows the course of his conquest of Dacia as clearly and as directly as a modern slide presentation.

Figure 21.8 The statue of Augustus from Prima Porta

[5] The armor he is wearing does not itself tell a connected narrative, but includes numerous scenes recalling Augustus' most glorious moments.

Whether or not it tells a story, art reveals a good deal about the person who made it. It also tells us something about the person who commissioned it, or the customers who were expected to buy it; and it may tell us something about the culture in which it was created. One form of Greek pottery decoration was a picture of a young man, often elegantly clothed, with the inscription *Handsome Leocrates*, or whatever his name was: compare this with the pinup girls of World War II or the centerfolds of the later twentieth century and you have food for thought about the collective subconscious of the cultures that created them. If the Prima Porta Augustus is a propaganda picture, it nevertheless bears comparison with the portraits of Commodus as a gladiator or as Hercules, no less propaganda, but with a very different focus.

Also significant in considering the relationship between art and culture is the particular purpose for which the item was intended. Saucers intended for use at a symposium would have a different kind of decoration from kitchen frying pans, and funeral urns had yet another aspect. In understanding the Greco-Roman world, a picture may indeed be worth a thousand words; and the words and the pictures combined are surely worth more than the sum of their parts.

ICONOGRAPHY

I have already noted above[6] the use of symbols to identify a character. I gave a few famous examples: Athena's helmet, Janus' two faces, Hercules' lion skin. These well-known examples by no means exhaust the list; nor, for that matter, are they invariable. Athena has other indications, chief among them the aegis and the owl; and people other than Hercules may appear with a lion skin. Iconography also gives an opportunity for subtler messages: Commodus with a lion skin is both the emperor and Hercules. A famous statue made by Kritios and Nesiotes depicted the supposed Athenian tyrannicides, Harmodius and Aristogeiton, about to strike the tyrant dead; depictions of Theseus, the mythical unifier of Attica and as such the founding hero of the Athenian state, in a similar position assimilate him to the tyrant-slayers, and put the suppression of tyranny at the basis of Athenian political life.[7] It may not be the case that every single item in a work of art is a symbol of something else; but the iconographical

---

[6] P. 206.
[7] Taylor, *The Tyrant Slayers*, 78–146.

world of the Greeks and the Romans was the world of ideas in which they worked, played and thought, and it is something of which an observer should always be aware.

ART AND POLITICS

"Art for art's sake" was an idea of the nineteenth-century Romantics; it was unknown to the Greeks and the Romans. The temples, sculptures and paintings that captivate the modern viewer were produced not by starving artists with dreams of aesthetic grandeur, but by workmen hired by the state or by wealthy patrons and presumably given clear instructions about what they were to produce. Many of these workmen, particularly those whose reliefs adorn the temples, are unknown to us, and were not famous in their time; others won fame and sometimes even fortune, but they nevertheless produced their art on commission, not under the inspiration of an entirely untrammeled Muse.

Of course much modern art is produced to order and according to specification, so this contrast can be overstated. In the ancient world as in the modern, to produce whatever one pleased and then try to sell it was presumably a more reasonable procedure for a potter than for a sculptor or an architect. But much ancient art, and perhaps all of the architecture and sculpture, reflects the interests of the people who ordered it, usually the rulers and always people of wealth or power: the propagandistic aspect of the art cannot be ignored. This does not mean, however, that the artist was merely a living tool for the ruler's intentions. Perhaps the most famous story about the interplay of artist and patron is that told by Pliny[8] about Praxiteles, from whom the citizens of Cos ordered a statue of Aphrodite. Praxiteles produced two, one clothed and one nude; the respectable citizens of Cos took the clothed statue, whereupon the Cnidians bought the nude one. The Cnidians got a work of art that was admired and imitated throughout the ancient world, and the modern world as well;[9] the Coans got an undying reputation as Philistines.

---

[8] Plin. *Nat.* 36.20–1.

[9] In fact, it was only much later, beginning in the first century BCE, that the Aphrodite of Cnidus became a figure of fascination and legend (Havelock, *The Aphrodite of Knidos*, 134–6)—a fine example of the vicissitudes of classical reception, with which we shall deal in Chapter 27.

HIGH ART AND LOW ART

A good deal of argument takes place over the question of what deserves to be treated as art. Recent years have seen an attack on the art value of painted pottery as critics have come to realize that the wealthiest citizens used vessels of gold, silver, copper and bronze, vessels most of which have long since been melted down and reused. The wall-paintings of Pompeii, our best and almost our only examples of Roman painting, are after all only the wall-decorations of a provincial suburb, not the paintings of the *Domus Aurea*. Not every museum piece was produced by the greatest of artists.

At the same time as that opinion has been taking hold, however, another and unrelated attitude has started to turn scholarly attention to popular art: if the pottery of Athens was not made for its wealthiest and most elegant citizens, that does not rob it of its interest. It may even add to its interest. Where earlier scholars would speak about "high" art and "debased" art, modern scholars tend to try to evaluate every piece of art on its own terms. An earlier generation thought that the Greeks had improved vastly on the sculpture of the Egyptians; a newer generation suggests that perhaps the Egyptians were never trying to do what the Greeks did—a suggestion very welcome in a postcolonial age.

This is a healthy attitude, but there is another side to the question. It is undoubtedly true that artists are often criticized unjustly for not achieving what they did not set out to do; but it is also true that an artist rarely— Plato would say never, and I think he was right—succeeds in producing exactly the work that had first been conceived in the mind's eye. Not every architect was trying to produce the Parthenon; but undoubtedly many would have liked to do so, if their talents had been up to it. It is often difficult to distinguish between a change in style and a decline in ability.

FORMS OF ART

Different forms serve different purposes and impose different constraints. Putting black paint on a red slip[10] allows a certain amount of detail, but one will not find much shading of color on a red-figure pot. When we looked at the relief of Merenptah above I would have liked to show what

---

[10] "Slip"—the word is cognate with "slop"—is the term for a suspension of fine clay and water used to coat the unfired pot in order to produce the desired finish.

a Greek stone relief looked like before the archaic age, when close contact with Egypt had allowed the Greeks to absorb the Egyptian techniques and styles; but the fact, as far as we know it, is that the Greeks did not cut many stone reliefs for almost half a millennium before the archaic period. The outstanding exception, the Lion Gate at Mycenae, is indeed executed in a style that an Egyptian would find understandable, if provincial. The poor, small and isolated communities of the Dark Ages had no use for, or perhaps no interest in, monumental wall sculptures. We have, on the other hand, a good deal of their decorated pottery, and many small bronze figurines. Every age has its characteristic art forms.

What this means for us is that each art form has to be studied, to a certain extent, on its own; we cannot simply put a Pompeian wall-painting next to a Flavian statue and expect to see the same characteristics in each. But no art form exists in a vacuum, and each form is influenced by the others. Coins may depict temples, and their iconography is the same as that of statues and paintings. When stone carving is becoming more realistic, it is probable that something similar is happening with bronzes as well. Pottery painters never carved statues, and probably never could have; but looking at their paintings we should have in mind, insofar as we can see them, the statues among which they moved.

ARCHITECTURE

The orders of Greek architecture—Doric and Ionic; the Corinthian order came later—were the absolute rule for temple construction in the archaic period, allowing of neither mixture nor substitution; but within the confines of the orders each temple had its own elaboration of the chosen style, so that the study of archaic Greek temple architecture offers a striking example of the interplay of individual genius with strict rules of implementation. There was more than one way to build a Doric temple. Architects in the classical period might allow themselves more leeway in introducing elements of another order, but a classical Greek temple was still clearly recognizable as Doric or Ionic; elements of the Corinthian order first begin to be seen in this era.

The fact that the orders contained elements that lent themselves to sculptural elaboration offered the architect an unparalleled opportunity for narrative art: the temple could show various scenes of a single theme, or a single long scene; and a good deal of inventiveness went into the blending of these sculptures into their architectural context, leaving us artwork interesting both in its own right and for the images that its creators wanted to have before the eyes of the worshipers in the centers of public cult.

Temple architecture was by no means the only architecture. Public buildings included governmental buildings and the buildings essential for everyday life: fountain-houses, colonnades, gymnasia, theaters and, in the Roman world, circuses and baths. Each of these had its particular form, dictated partially by function and partially by aesthetics. None are as imposing as the temples, and many are architecturally negligible; but there is a good deal to be said about Greek architecture beyond the description of the temples.

The cosmopolitan Hellenistic and Roman worlds were never restricted to the three canonical orders; the more striking is the survival and transformation of the elements inherited from classical Greek architecture, blended and reused in new styles that an observer might see, dependent upon viewpoint and upon which building was being observed, as decadent or as majestic. The arch, the dome and the use of concrete, three great architectural innovations of the Romans, opened up new possibilities of height, of light and of ornamentation. The Romans no less than the Greeks built magnificent buildings, and they did so in an eclectic style that tried to harmonize elements that might have quite disparate origins: the arches of the Colosseum are separated by Doric columns on the bottom story, Ionic on the middle and Corinthian on the upper. None of these are true columns; they are half-columns appearing in relief. Any one of these items might be paralleled elsewhere, but the imposing structure in its entirety is both utterly unlike anything the classical Greeks ever built and unthinkable without its Greek predecessors. Again, something has happened in art. And again, the Greco-Roman precedent never entirely dies: the sense that a column should be topped by a block (Doric), a scroll (Ionic) or a burst of leaves (Corinthian) is very much alive in the twenty-first century.

Numerous inscriptions deal with the construction of public buildings; these are of economic interest in illuminating the organization and financing of the work, and, although they are less interested in giving architectural information, they do on occasion offer details of construction that are not available (or are no longer available) from simple observation. But they are not our most important source, for in architecture we have what we lack for every other art form, a detailed manual. The works of Vitruvius, after their rediscovery in the fifteenth century, sparked the birth of a new classicizing architecture in Europe. It will be a rare person today who will use Vitruvius as an architectural textbook; but we have in his ten books an organized and clear account, at least from the view of one very educated Roman, of the theory and technology that lay behind the achievements of Roman architecture.

SCULPTURE

Greco-Roman sculpture has a number of survival advantages. It was made largely in non-perishable material, stone and bronze. It could be moved, so unlike a building it could survive the decision that the space where it was standing would be better used for something else. Stone sculpture was often of little use for other purposes: the silver of which a chalice was made could easily be melted down for any other purpose, and a stele might serve well as a paving-stone, but a free-standing torso wouldn't make a particularly good part of anything, except a sculpture. For all that, most of ancient sculpture has perished; but enough of it has remained to give us a very good idea not only of the styles current at various times and places, but of many celebrated works, their originals long lost but copied so often and so well that we can form a very good idea of them even at this distance.

What has not remained of ancient sculpture—nor, for that matter, of ancient architecture—is the color. The solid white—or more often, off-white—that we see in ancient sculpture was not the appearance that it originally gave.[11] Both literary sources and traces of paint that are occasionally found on statues and reliefs indicate that the Greco-Roman world was much more gaily colored in antiquity than its remains are today; but in most cases our attempts to reconstruct the colors must be based on imagination. Work has been done recently to try to remedy the lack, but it still requires a good amount of guesswork. Now, however, that archaeologists and art historians are more aware of the importance of color, and modern techniques make it possible to find traces of paint where earlier excavations failed to see it and washed it off, one can hope that more progress will be made in understanding the use of color in ancient architecture and sculpture.

Another loss is the loss of most of the works of the great sculptors of antiquity. The tyrannicides of Kritios and Nesiotes, the chryselephantine statue that stood in the Parthenon, Praxiteles' naked Aphrodite of Cnidus, the Colossus of Rhodes—all are lost, and the list could go on and on. Despite some remarkable survivals, bronze statuary, so easily melted down

---

[11] Unlike its modern imitations, which were normally bare stone in imitation of the modern appearance of the ancient sculpture.

and reused, is almost entirely gone. Here we are in some sense better off than in the question of color, for almost all of these great works were copied so often that we have a very good general idea of what they looked like; depictions on coins and literary descriptions also help. For art-historical purposes, that is almost good enough; for aesthetic appreciation, it is hard to believe that the works of imitators can really replace what we have lost. Much work was done in the past to reconstruct what the originals must have looked like; the modern age often finds itself no less interested in the varied ways that later generations copied, imitated or borrowed from works that were already classical then.

Very different from the great statues that get pride of place in museums are the smaller figurines, in bronze or in terra cotta, that were produced at all periods, even during the Dark Ages. Some of these are what we should call bric-a-brac; others are significant artistic or cultic items. It is not always easy to tell which is which.

WALL-PAINTING AND MOSAIC

From ancient Athens most of our surviving painting is painted pottery; from ancient Rome, the walls of Pompeii have given us an inkling, at least, of what wall-painting was like. For neither Greece nor Rome do we have many paintings executed on wood or other perishable media, the *tabellae pictae* that we know from literature; the situation is somewhat improved by the art from Hellenistic and Roman Egypt, where wood was better pre-served and mummy masks were sometimes painted. This gives us a very limited view, but still more than enough to keep a lover of painting occupied for life.

Wall-painting is known chiefly from Pompeii, where it has been divided into four styles. Pompeii is by no means the only place where wall-paintings have been found, and we can trace their continued development down to the Christian empire and into Byzantium; but Pompeii offered such a wealth of examples that it made classification, and hence understanding, much more reasonable than it could be in cases where we had a few fragmentary items.

Wall-painting was usually fresco: that is, the paint was applied while the plaster was still wet, so that when it had dried the color was absorbed into the surface and could survive abrasion and slight chipping. This implies, of course, that the wall-paintings we have could not have been produced in other media: a wooden wall required a different technique, and the coloring of limestone and marble, if they were not left in their natural coloring, would also have involved techniques entirely different from those we find in Pompeii and elsewhere.

The painter faces technical problems different from those of the sculptor. On the one hand, the painter does not have to represent the figure from all sides; on the other hand, the figures represented are three-dimensional figures being represented in a two-dimensional medium. A sculptor shows texture by imitating the texture itself; a painter must develop a way of indicating the texture by line, color or convention. A sculptor molds the figure and the viewer sees it in three dimensions; a painter must use shading, color and variations in scale to give the picture depth. Perspective, by which distant figures appear smaller, is an obvious thing to observe but a difficult one to imitate. The composition of a painting—what forms are depicted and how they are placed relatively to each other and relatively to the painted space—is a cardinal factor in the effect a painting has on the viewer. The history of ancient painting shows an interesting progress as painters invented and mastered the techniques that could turn a drawing into a scene.

Another popular medium from the Hellenistic period onward[12] was the mosaic, which even more than a fresco could maintain its original coloring indefinitely. The relationship between painting and mosaic is a close one, though each has its own features: mosaic is limited in its ability to depict detail, and by the nature of its technique relies on a more "impressionistic" manner of building up a scene or a figure from components that are not themselves intended to reproduce the original: a painted circle may have been made with a compass, while a mosaic circle can never be quite round. One cannot blend colors in a mosaic; there is a wide palette to choose from, since stones come in many colors, and they do not fade as dyes do, but the entire picture must be made from the colors available and no others. Since the ability to show detail is so limited, it is a rare mosaic that will show perspective. Painting, on the other hand, makes it easier to show facial expression,[13] a matter that the Roman wall-paintings developed much further than the Greek potters ever did; it allows background, and, where the landscapes we find in Roman murals have undoubted Hellenistic predecessors, we can observe the development of landscape only in the

---

[12] The mosaic technique itself was much older, but did not become popular in Greece until the Macedonian era.

[13] Showing facial expression is not impossible in mosaic; in fact any face, however primitively expressed, is seen as having an expression, and sometimes mosaic faces can be strikingly expressive, as anyone who has seen the Alexander mosaic in the Museo Nazionale di Napoli will recognize.

Roman examples; and the development of mood by use of color, background and details shown more or less distinctly is a powerful technique that was available to the painter more than to any other ancient artist.

POTTERY PAINTING

The basis of the history of pottery is connoisseurship, a term that in classics means the ability to distinguish the individual styles of different painters and different workshops. It was Sir John Beazley (1885–1970) who put connoisseurship on a firm foundation by the technique, pioneered for other areas before he applied it to ancient Greece, of concentrating on the treatment of anatomical details: how a given painter paints an ear, or a nose, or a foot. Many of Beazley's attributions have been challenged, and he himself sometimes changed his mind, but the general picture that he built up has not been radically modified. The identification of individual painters, even if they are often anonymous and we speak of "the Achilles painter" or "the Cleveland painter," is a great help both in dating pottery and in understanding the development of the painter's art.

Another item essential to the study of ancient pottery is an understanding of the process of pottery production. Much of a pot's decoration is determined by the technology of its manufacture; much of the talent of a good painter is a matter of overcoming the difficulties and exploiting the opportunities that this technology offers. I noted above the difference in technique between black-figure and red-figure pottery; examples could be multiplied. The tendency, which increased with time, for Athenian potters to restrict the use of pottery with a white background to vessels for funeral libations may have had something to do with a connection, attested in other cultures, of white with death; but it is plausibly explained by the fact that the white color tended to chip and even to flake off, and so was most appropriate for vessels that would be used once and broken or abandoned. The more you understand how a pot is made—and it will be very helpful if you make some yourself, despite the fact that much has changed in pottery production since antiquity—the better you will appreciate what was being done in ancient pottery.

No less significant than the process by which it was made was the purpose for which a pot was intended. All ancient pottery was made to be used, and the decoration on it was often determined by its use. Drinking cups for a *symposion* might be decorated with scenes of wine, women and/or song, water vessels for the bridal bath with wedding scenes, funeral urns with scenes of death and mourning. The vessels that held the oil given to victors at the Panathenaic games showed essentially the same scenes for more than a century.

Another area that has been attracting more attention is the relationship between the pottery painters and their customers. We mentioned above the interplay between what the artist wanted to create and what the public wanted to buy. It is possible, too, that foreign tastes were taken into account; Athenian decorated pots traveled widely—their greatest market, and their greatest imitators, were the Etruscans—and the buyers whom the painter wished to please need not have been the buyers of Athens.

The question of "potter and patron" is in reality only a small aspect of the wider question of the interaction of culture, economy and society, a theme that has cropped up more than once in this book. Here again, what we find in the restricted field of ancient pottery may illuminate and be illuminated by the framework in which these developments took place.

There are more areas of ancient art: gems, cameos and coins all have their distinctive aspects, and form a part of art history—as, indeed, does any way in which human beings attempted to reproduce visually the impressions they had of the world around them, or of the world they imagined.

MAJOR RESOURCES

Encyclopedias

Bandinelli, Becatti and Carratelli, *Enciclopedia dell'arte antica* is a collection of truly encyclopedic proportions, updated in the 1990s by a second supplement almost as large as the original encyclopedia itself. Of particular interest are the *Atlante dei complessi figurati e degli ordini architettonici* collecting architectural group-figures (friezes, metopes, figured columns, etc.) and elements of the architectural orders (chiefly capitals of Doric, Ionic and Corinthian columns) from the Greek and Roman world, and the *Atlante delle forme ceramiche* cataloguing, with illustrative drawings for each, the various forms of ceramics found in classical sites. More compact, more recent, and written in English is Campbell, *The Grove Encyclopedia of Classical Art and Architecture*, a good place to look for an unfamiliar term, person or place, but dealing at length where length is necessary: the article on architecture takes 108 pages, that on sculpture 104.

Western art has always been built about the names of individual artists. This was true to a large extent of ancient art as well, but since, except in the case of pottery, ancient works were rarely signed and are generally found by archaeologists in contexts that can tell us something of their time and place but not the name of the artist, we are less well informed about the oeuvre of individual artists. Now, however, there is Vollkommer, *Künstlerlexikon der Antike*, which offers a convenient source for what is known about individual artists, and a basis for further investigations of the impact of individuals.

The exhaustive account of iconography is the multivolume, polyglot LIMC, which offers thorough accounts of the varied signs of meaning associated with classical figures; for a briefer account of mythological references one can use Reid, *The Oxford Guide to Classical Mythology in the Arts* or Rochelle, *Mythological and Classical World Art Index*.

For pottery, the *Corpus Vasorum Antiquorum (CVA)*, founded in 1919 by Edmond Pottier, has by now produced more than three hundred volumes from all over the Greco-Roman world. Those that are out of print have been digitalized and made available online, along with much else, by the *Beazley Archive*, an important resource for Greco-Roman art, in particularly pottery, gems and sculpture. The *Perseus* website also contains a considerable collection of ancient art; an excellent selection of pottery in book form, with first-class reproductions and discussion of each item, is Simon, *Die griechischen Vasen*.

Introductions to ancient art are many and varied in their purposes. More than two hundred years ago Winckelmann, *History of Ancient Art* founded not only the discipline of art history but arguably the classicizing movement of the eighteenth century and the intense German identification with ancient Greece; it is striking how long Winckelmann's ideas have remained influential. Some very serviceable volumes are Richter, *A Handbook of Greek Art*, organized by genre, a book whose clarity and organization have kept it in use for a generation since its authoress died at the age of 90; Boardman, *The Oxford History of Classical Art*, and Boardman, *Greek Art*; Henig, *A Handbook of Roman Art*; and Kleiner, *A History of Roman Art*. In general, the more recent books pay more attention to the social and historical context of art.

A good set of handbooks of architecture are the Pelican History of Art series: Lawrence, *Greek Architecture*, Boëthius, *Etruscan and Early Roman Architecture* and Ward-Perkins, *Roman Imperial Architecture*; the recent editions of these manuals are much more generously illustrated than the early editions. Also popular for Rome is Sear, *Roman Architecture*; and Wilson Jones, *Principles of Roman Architecture* is a fascinating effort to learn from the monuments themselves what were the principles that the Romans put into practice—not always the ones that Vitruvius enunciated.

The indefatigable Sir John Boardman has done his share for illuminating Greek sculpture in three volumes, *Greek Sculpture: The Archaic Period*, *Greek Sculpture: The Classical Period* and *Greek Sculpture: The Late Classical Period*; for the Hellenistic period there is Smith, *Hellenistic Sculpture*, and for the Romans Kleiner, *Roman Sculpture*.

For vase-painting and pottery production in general it is again Boardman, *The History of Greek Vases* who provides the background; Schreiber, *Athenian Vase Construction*, by a practicing potter, provides a very useful point of view that no mere classicist would have been likely to provide. For wall-painting Ling, *Roman Painting* gives a detailed picture.

Lastly, of course, just as a budding student of literature must read a lot of literature, anyone intending to understand art should look at as much of it as possible. Many excellent art books are essentially catalogues of a museum's holdings or of a particular exhibition; and a well-planned and well-financed exhibition is often a non-negligible work of scholarship. A good deal is available on the internet, and undoubtedly more and more will be so; but it is also necessary, where possible, to see the works of art on their own. Time spent in museums or at archaeological sites is not time wasted. I had seen many pictures of the Lion Gate at Mycenae, but pictures in books, where an aquamarine and an aqueduct are the same size, left me entirely unprepared for the impression its monumental scale made *in situ*. Seeing artworks and thinking about them is the beginning of art criticism and art history; and to a large extent it is also the middle and the end.

22

MUSIC AND DANCE

MUSIC AND DANCE IN GREEK AND ROMAN LIFE

Music and dance were not quite ubiquitous in Greece and Rome: ancient artisans did not dance through their workshops, though workers might sing, and the discussions in the Senate were not accompanied by music. But most of the cultural forms that define classical culture for us had an important musical and often choreographic component, and that component is all but lost to us. The singers in Homer, and probably Homer himself, sang poems to the accompaniment of a *phorminx*, Sappho to a lyre, Solon very possibly to a pipe. Both in Greece and in Rome, music and dance were an essential part of religion; hardly any festival lacked them. Our own modern life is suffused with music that is electronically reproduced: background music accompanies us as we shop, as we drive and even as we walk in the street. The Greeks and Romans had only the music they made themselves, but they made much more of it than we do.

For the most part, the loss is irretrievable: a library of musical theory a hundred times larger than we possess could not give us the experience of hearing a song of Sappho, much less of seeing the performance of a Pindaric chorus. But in fact what we know is quite considerable; and like mathematicians who can prove propositions about the fourth dimension without being able to visualize it, we can understand a good deal about Greek and Roman music and dance without being able to hear it or to see it.

PERFORMANCE OF SONG

Different forms of poetry that have come down to us were accompanied by different forms of music. Some verse was spoken with instrumental accompaniment; some was sung by a single performer to the accompaniment of an instrument, played either by the performer or by somebody else;[1] some was sung by a chorus, generally accompanied by dance. The chorus itself might be composed of men, boys, women[2] or girls—one of the rare cases in which women performed in public, though it was sometimes for an all-female audience—and it might perform its song in unison or in a give-and-take dialogue between the chorus and one or more of its members. There were also popular songs that would be sung while working or while drinking, and songs with special purposes, like the paean that was sung after a meal or while advancing towards battle. It is worthwhile for modern readers to keep in mind the kind of performance that was envisioned for the text we are reading: we have neither the tunes nor the steps, but we can generally know who was singing and dancing.

The theater in particular was suffused with song and dance. The tragic and comic chorus, and for that matter the dithyrambic chorus, sang and danced; the actors in Roman comedy sang *cantica*, and in fact acted most of the play to musical accompaniment[3]—not quite opera or operetta, but a good deal more musical than a modern musical comedy. Try reading the libretto of an opera that you like, or the lyrics of a song you enjoy, without running the tune through your mind, and you will have an idea of what we have lost. It is amazing that what remains is still so good.

RHYTHM AND MELODY

The one part of ancient song that we possess almost entirely is its rhythm. There were characteristic meters for each kind of poetry, and they give us

---

[1] Whether the performer was also the instrumentalist depended chiefly on the sort of instrument used: stringed instruments could be played while singing but wind instruments could not.

[2] Although choruses of adolescent girls were much more common, there were occasions when adult (i.e., married) women would perform. For details see Calame, *Choruses of Young Women*.

[3] Moore, "When Did the Tibicen Play?"

some indication of what sort of melody may have lain behind them. The dactylic hexameter of epic and the iambic trimeter of spoken theater could be and were strung together indefinitely; the elegiac meter naturally divided verse into two-line units, making it particularly appropriate for epigrams, though it, too, was used for connected verse of indefinite length; the more irregular-sounding Aeolic rhythms were appropriate to songs, and for that they were used, sometimes in stanzas (usually for monody) and sometimes, like dactylo-epitrite, in freer compositions (usually for a chorus); and there is still a good deal of uncertainty as to how the dance reflected and reinforced the metrical pattern of strophic verse, which can hardly have been comprehensible without the dance that went along with it. Unfortunately, undergraduates often are not taught how to scan verse adequately, and are left in the unfortunate position that we would all be in if we had to read our epics, our sonnets and our limericks in prosaic prose paraphrases.

Very little, on the other hand, remains of ancient melody, though the little that does and the discussions of the writers give us some meager indication; at the very least, it is clear that in ancient Greece, as in modern Europe, the rules underwent a development by which musicians introduced practices that once would have been rejected as irregular or unaesthetic, widening the area of the permissible.[4] It is also clear that accompaniment was not a matter of simply playing along the same notes that the singer sang; both the writers on music and, if West[5] has interpreted them correctly, a few papyri give indications of heterophony, where the instrument plays an accompaniment that complements but does not duplicate the singer's melodic line. I am not aware of any indication that the Greeks or the Romans ever used choral harmony or counterpoint, in which different voices sing different tunes (or even different texts) at the same time. This would seem to make their music extremely simple in our terms; but as in their poetry, which used no rhyme but developed metrics to an intricacy and variety far beyond what later generations in Europe used, the ancients varied other aspects of music far beyond the practice of musicians in the later tradition.

[4]   [Plut.] De Mus. 1133b.
[5]   West, Ancient Greek Music, 206–7.

MODES, SCALES AND THEORY

The twelve-tone[6] diatonic scale that we refer to with the letters C-D-E-F-G-A-B-C or the syllables do-re-mi-fa-sol-la-ti-do is of great antiquity.[7] The intervals between tones in the diatonic scale are not equal; two of the intervals (E-F and B-C) are "half-tones," half as great as the intervals between the other notes.[8] The placing of these half-tones in a scale composed mostly of full tones is not arbitrary, but there are many possibilities of where to place them. Western music of the last few centuries regularized the tone system and restricted itself to two modes (the so-called *major* and *minor* modes). Ancient Greek music permitted scales (*genera*) other than the diatonic and, as a consequence, intervals smaller than a half-tone; the "enharmonic genus" dominated classical Greek music, with the "chromatic genus"[9] becoming—scandalously, to some ears—more acceptable in the late fourth century, and the diatonic genus becoming common in the Hellenistic period and dominant in the Roman. In addition to distinctions of genus, however, there were also differences in mode, differences that involved various characteristics of the music that seem later to have been simplified in restricting their difference to differences of key.

If the previous paragraph seems bewildering, it is because I have compressed perhaps one one-hundredth of Greek musical theory into one ten-thousandth of the space required for a proper exposition. The musical

6   "Twelve tone" including the half-tones C#, D#, F#, G#, A# (=D♭, E♭, etc.).
7   The claim of Bob Fink ("Neanderthal Flute: Oldest Musical Instrument's 4 Notes Matches 4 of Do, Re, Mi Scale," based upon the find described in Kunej and Turk, "New Perspectives") that the diatonic scale can be traced to Neandertal times has been challenged, among others, by Chase and Nowell, "Taphonomy of a Suggested Flute"; but there is no doubt that this scale was well established long before the earliest Greeks. The modern names of the notes ("do-re-mi") have their origin in names given by Guido of Arezzo in the eleventh century from the initial syllables of hemistiches in the hymn "Ut queant laxis," each of which began on the note to which it gave its name. Guido's scale began with "ut" and ended at "la": "do" and "si"/"ti" are later developments.
8   The definition of an interval, and much else, is omitted here for purposes of brevity; a clear description, comprehensible to a layman and essential for any exposition of the ways in which ancient music differed from our own, can be found in West, *Ancient Greek Music*, 8–12.
9   This term in Greek music does not mean what it does in modern music, a twelve-note scale in which all the intervals are half-tones; but again for reasons of space I refrain from further detail, and refer the reader to West, 160–4.

theory of the Greeks was comprehensive and heavily mathematical: from the Pythagoreans, who first established the correspondence between mathematical ratios and pleasing harmonies, the ancients attempted to put the aesthetic experience of music on a scientific basis. The effort produced a tension between the empirical sense of what they found pleasing and the art that gifted musicians produced, on the one hand, and the mathematical theory on the other hand that explained what the possibilities should be and what sorts of things should be pleasing. Similar tensions in modern music led to the developments of the twentieth century, developments that devotees of the older music found as scandalous as Aristophanes claimed to find the music of Euripides.

The theory and its application will necessarily remain a relatively marginal part of the classical canon as long as our ability to reconstruct real ancient music remains as limited as it is; if, on the other hand, more substantial transcribed texts should come to light—a very real possibility, as new papyri are constantly being read and published—the study of ancient music may become one of the most exciting aspects of the ancient world.

ANCIENT DANCE

For ancient dance we have much less than we have for ancient music. The archaeological material is perhaps no less valuable here, for, although there is no notation of ancient dance to match the notation of ancient music, pictures of people (or satyrs and maenads) dancing are much more informative than pictures of people singing or playing a pipe. Theoretical material from the Greeks and the Romans, however, is almost entirely lacking. The work that has been done has been done by people for whom dance was a natural expression and even an obsession: the art of any serious artist is, or becomes, something of an obsession, and the artist sees the world through the glasses of art. People who look at ancient pictures through these eyes have quite a bit to teach us. Maurice Emmanuel did a great deal of theoretical work on ancient dance at the end of the nineteenth century: working with modern dancers, he compared their movements and positions to what he found on Greek vases to try to distinguish and classify the parts of Greek dance; Isadora Duncan, slightly later, studied Greek paintings meticulously for information about a kind of dance that she considered more natural and more beautiful than the ballet that then dominated the world of the dance. Her innovations began the tradition that we now know as modern dance. I have no idea how close or how far they were from ancient dance; but I am confident that they were not the last thing that modern dancers could learn from the ancients.

In the century that has passed since Emmanuel and Duncan were doing their pioneering work, the study of ancient dance, like that of other cultural forms, has moved from reconstruction towards integration, trying to understand the function of dance within the society, where it was used and what it meant in its context; for this both textual studies and comparisons with other cultures have been helpful.

Roman dance pervaded its society less than Greek, and the elite authors whom we read affected an attitude of disdain; famous is Cicero's defense of Lucius Murena against the unbelievable calumny that he was a dancer.[10] Modern authors until recently tended to reflect the bias of our sources; in the age of popular culture, this bias is disappearing. Pantomime, the art form that filled the theaters of late antiquity, is now the subject of serious study, and the entire world of gesture on which it is based is attracting new attention. Dance for the Romans was more a matter of spectacle than of participation, but it held a place in the culture that all the moralists could not dislodge.

MAJOR RESOURCES

The resources we want for ancient music and dance—to hear the music and to see the dance or, better, to play and sing the music and to dance the dance—are not available. We have to make do with the treatises and the pictures that have been left to us. West, *Ancient Greek Music* is a masterly exposition of what is known and what is not. Mathiesen, *Apollo's Lyre* describes the material from the point of view of a musicologist, a point of view that a classicist interested in the subject will want to take seriously.

A significant collection of Greek musical texts was edited by von Jan, *Musici Scriptores Graeci*; to the authors published there can be added Wallis, *Claudius Ptolemaeus: Harmonika*, Macran, *The Harmonics of Aristoxenus*, Winnington-Ingram, *Aristeides Quintilianus: De Musica*, Pearson, *Aristoxenus Elementa Rhythmica* and Delattre, *Philodème de Gadara: Sur la musique*. Most of these, and others as well, are translated in Barker, *Greek Musical Writings*.

A number of texts have come to light with actual Greek musical notation. Those that were found earliest were published in Jan, but much

---

[10] Cic. Pro Mur. 6.13.

has been found since then; the currently authoritative text and discussion is Pöhlmann and West, *Documents of Ancient Greek Music*.

There is now a general account of ancient musical instruments, Di Giglio, *Strumenti delle Muse*; this does not go into great detail, but defines and organizes the known instruments according to the classification systems of the Greeks, with illustrations and texts. For the strings we have Maas and Snyder, *Stringed Instruments of Ancient Greece*, and for the reed pipe Schlesinger, *The Greek Aulos*. An undertaking called the Astra project is attempting to reconstruct by computer modeling the sound of ancient instruments; whether the sound you will hear from your computer when you click on its website is indeed the sound of ancient Greek instruments is not a question that any living person can answer authoritatively.

A bibliography of research into ancient music for the years 1957–87 is appended to Wille, *Schriften zur Geschichte der antiken Musik*, and, if you read modern Greek, a general lexicon[11] of musicians and musical terminology is available in Michaelides, *The Music of Ancient Greece*.

On rhythm the handbooks mentioned above (p. 127) can be supplemented with Chapter 5 of West, *Ancient Greek Music* for an indication of how the various meters worked out musically.

You will have noticed that most of the material deals with Greek music; for Rome Wille, *Musica Romana* is voluminous but deals chiefly with the part music played in the life of the Romans rather than the nature of the music itself; Tintori, *La musica di Roma antica* is briefer but clear and well organized.

For ancient dance we are even less well informed. The classic Emmanuel, *La Danse grecque antique*, a work of exceptional professionalism and influence (Emmanuel was a student of Delibes and a classmate of Debussy, and wrote with the cooperation of a ballet troupe at the time when modern dance was first being invented on the basis of supposed Greek models) has been translated into English (Emmanuel, *The Antique Greek Dance*) and reissued in French. Emmanuel's book is generously illustrated with drawings of modern dancers; Louis Séchan's book of the same name, a generation later, added chronological considerations and a view of the development of modern dance since Emmanuel's time; Germaine Prudhommeau, still with the same name, turned Emmanuel's technique on its head, using more modern techniques of animation to produce pictures where the Greek figures themselves appear to dance. Lawler, *The Dance in Ancient Greece* concerned itself less with the mechanics of the dance and more with its

---

[11] It calls itself an encyclopedia, and is indeed such in that the information it gives is more than is necessary simply to define its terms; but its entries are shorter than one might expect of an encyclopedia.

historical and social context. Most recently the two books of Marie-Hélène Delavaud-Roux attempt to synthesize what her predecessors have done and to put it in a wider ethnographical perspective, and Naerebout, *Attractive Performances* offers a survey of western study of ancient dance since the Renaissance and a challenge for further research.

On Roman pantomime see now Garelli, *Danser le mythe*; Hall and Wyles, *New Directions in Ancient Pantomime* and Ruth Webb, *Demons and Dancers*.

23

SCIENCE AND TECHNOLOGY

A NEGLECTED FIELD

Modern science developed from ancient science. After centuries when the authority of a few ancient authors—Aristotle, Ptolemy, Galen—was such that study of the natural sciences was more an effort to understand their meaning than to judge their accuracy, scientists of the Renaissance and after began testing their theories, often against other ancient theories that had not been canonized. The results are well known: Ptolemy's geocentric universe is held today to be false, and Aristotle's four elements and Galen's four humors not only false but almost meaningless. Science has progressed in new directions, and even those ancient authors whose ideas prevailed have been left behind: if we possessed all the works of Democritus, nobody would turn to them to learn atomic science.

The study of ancient science has not been a major concern of classical scholarship. Few classicists find it interesting; had they been interested in science they would not have spent all those years studying Greek and Latin. Scientists are no more interested: they want to discover what is, not what somebody once thought might be. Historians of science, a not inconsiderable band, generally do not have the linguistic capabilities needed for the serious study of Greek texts, though Latin is necessary for the history of any but the most modern or the most ancient science. The science of the Greeks and the Romans, the seed from which modern science grew and the backdrop against which its development must be understood, is perhaps the most neglected field of classical study.

ANCIENT AND MODERN SCIENCE

The ancients did not have a word for "science" in our sense; the study of the physical world was a part of philosophy, in which physics, meta-physics, ethics, astronomy and astrology lived comfortably together. Modern science restricts itself to those matters that allow of experimental proof or disproof, but the ancients never made wide use of experiments. They observed the world about them, and those who were interested often observed it carefully and minutely,[1] but the idea of a controlled experiment, the idea that under conditions that nullified all factors but one bodies would behave differently than they do under normal conditions, was not an essential part of their way of thinking; for this reason their scientific inquiry did not take place in laboratories.[2] Their speculations about the nature of the physical world were judged by the same kind of logical arguments that they used on speculations about the moral or the divine world, and the distinction between those forms of knowledge that are subject to experimental proof or disproof and those that are not—the distinction, in the contemporary world, between science and philosophy—was not a distinction that they made.

When we speak of ancient science, then, we are necessarily imposing a modern framework on ancient thought. The temptation is great to take the baby and throw out the bathwater, to take Democritus' atoms and disparage or ignore Aristotle's four elements, to look, albeit with con-descension, at Ptolemy's *Almagest*, the basic work of pre-Copernican astronomy, but ignore his *Tetrabiblos*, the basic work of astrology. To a certain extent, perhaps, we cannot help this; but it is a mode of investigation that seriously misrepresents, and underestimates, ancient scientific thought. To take the example of astrology, we, too, believe that celestial phenomena affect our lives: that sunspot cycles may affect the weather, or that cosmic rays may cause cancerous mutations. But because the develop-ment of science over the past few centuries, in discovering what was true, has demonstrated many other possibilities to be false, many ideas that were perfectly reasonable to the Greeks—that, indeed, they would have

---

[1] See Ar. *Nub.* 184–94, where the students of Socrates' Thinkery appear with eyes down, peeping through the dark of Tartarus.

[2] A further problem was the difficulty of precise measurement, particularly the measurement of time, and the lack of a universal standard of measurement; but the ancients in fact were capable of remarkable accuracy when they found it necessary, and it is not impossible that if they had felt the need for greater precision they would have been able to achieve it.

had no justification for rejecting—are no longer reasonable to us. To us, the stars are not fixed in a single sphere, but scattered throughout space, and the stars in a constellation are not really closer to each other than to stars of other constellations; they merely seem that way from the particular angle from which we earthlings view them. On this premise, the idea that the particular stars that seem to form a backdrop to a given planet at a given time should have any special effect on us is no longer a reasonable one. To understand the science of the Greeks and the Romans we must think ourselves back to a time when this possibility was still an open one, as reasonable to explore as any other possibility.

When we do that, we find that they were not only thinking about possibilities that we exclude, but they were thinking in terms that we do not use. The air of which they spoke is not necessarily a mixture of various separable gases like our air, and a geometrical length may not be as easily described in numerical terms as it is today. For us, the fact that the length of the diagonal of a unit square cannot be expressed as the ratio of two integers indicates that there are numbers like that, and we call them "irrational"; for the Greeks it seems to have indicated that there simply was no number that could express that length. We not only have to open our minds; we have to redefine our terms.

It might be thought, in this circumstance, that "not knowing much modern science can be an advantage, for then you do not have to unlearn what you have been taught in order to comprehend ancient science."[3] But this can only be true in a very limited sense. Ignorance does not make us better judges of ancient science; on the contrary, knowing—as best we can, for modern science is itself neither omniscient nor free of error— what really happens in the physical world is what gives us the information from which to judge what it was that the ancients saw and how they reached their conclusions. A person not interested in modern science is not that likely to be interested in ancient science; and indeed, much of the literature on ancient science has been written for, and sometimes by, scientists, not classicists. But once we know something about modern physics, we can only begin to understand the Greeks by an effort of will, putting ourselves back in the time when many possibilities were still open, and when people had not yet decided that number and experiment were the keys to all real knowledge. Much of what we find in ancient science now seems to us ill conceived or flat-out wrong; but it was from ancient science that modern science took its beginnings, and indeed the

---

[3] Rihll, *Greek Science*, x. Rihll herself recognizes the limits of this statement: ibid., xi–xii.

great experimenters of the early scientific revolution would hardly have conceived their experiments except from within the framework of ancient science with which they started. The Greeks and the Romans, however imperfect their ideas, were the giants on whose shoulders modern science stands.

MATHEMATICS AND GEOMETRY

The one field in which the Greeks succeeded in building a lasting scientific structure was mathematics.[4] Unlike the principles of Aristotle, Ptolemy and Galen, Euclid's *Elements* remain valid today, and were still used as a school text in the nineteenth century. It was from questions based on Euclid himself that modern mathematicians developed alternative geometries, geometries that complemented that of Euclid rather than replacing it.[5] Modern geometry has indeed refined the work of Euclid, but the basis is clear enough, and courses in Euclidean geometry are still taught in university mathematics departments. No physics department would teach Aristotelian physics.

The study of the development of Greek mathematics—and it did not end with Euclid—is in a sense the study of the birth of science itself. Its two parents were the speculative freedom of Greek philosophy and the empirical sophistication of Egypt and Babylonia, but mathematics as the Greeks studied it was a new birth, an abstract theory based on a limited number of assumptions from which results of great complexity were derived. It would be two millennia before the other exact sciences could approach this kind of deductive purity.

The elaboration of Greek mathematics was a major force behind the technological development of the ancient world. The mechanical devices

---

[4] For the much-debated question of what makes theories scientific I accept here the three characteristics stated by Russo, *The Forgotten Revolution*, 17: (1) their statements are not about concrete objects, but about specific theoretical entities; (2) the theory has a rigorously deductive structure; (3) applications to the real world are based on correspondence rules between the entities of the theory and concrete objects. The curious reader can see Russo's fascinating book for further explanation.

[5] Geometry is not all there is to mathematics, and in the centuries since Descartes even geometry has come to include matters of vastly more complexity and abstraction than anything Euclid dealt with, or indeed could have found the words to speak of. This does not detract from the greatness of Greek mathematics; on the contrary, the achievements of the younger generation only emphasize how firm was the basis they received from their forebears.

with which Archimedes defended Syracuse against the Roman navy[6] are an interesting anecdote, but the aqueducts of the Romans, the massive stones that were lifted to create their buildings, and the martial success of their artillery are all achievements repeated many times over that would not have been possible without the mathematical foundations built up before them. When the mathematics of the ancients had been all but forgotten, people did not merely marvel at these achievements; they could no longer understand how ordinary people could ever have accomplished them.[7]

For all that, mathematics did not define science for the Greeks and the Romans as it does for us,[8] and recent work has reflected the questioning of basic principles that in the humanities has been a feature of postmodernism but in mathematics began much earlier and constituted one of the major strands of twentieth-century research. The way in which mathematical concepts were grasped, the development of the system of deduction, and the place of mathematics and mathematical concepts within the culture of the Greeks[9] have become major subjects of interest in recent years.

[6] Polyb. 8.5–7, Liv. 24.34, Plut. *Marcellus* 14–18. The more famous story of Archimedes burning the fleet with mirrors does not occur in the early sources, but it is not, as has been claimed, impossible, and moderns have been able to reproduce similar phenomena (Modiano, "How Archimedes Stole Sun," cf. Kreyszig, "Archimedes and the Invention of Burning Mirrors"). Mills and Clift, "Reflections of the 'Burning Mirrors'" hold that such a plan would have been so poor a use of manpower as to be unlikely.

[7] Anglo-Saxon poetry regularly refers to Roman buildings as *enta geweorc*, "the handiwork of giants": Marsden, *The Cambridge Old English Reader* 33.2 (*Maxims II*), 37.2 (*The Ruin*), 38.87 (*The Wanderer*), cf. *giganta geweorc*, 31b.71 (= *Beowulf* 1562).

[8] "While we attempt to transform the world into an abstract mathematical entity which transgresses the boundaries of the inorganic universe and infiltrates into biology and the realm of man, the Greeks saw the cosmos as a living organism, as a projection of man into the distances of the outer world." Sambursky v. But cf. Augustine's statement that six is not a perfect number because the world was created in six days, but rather the world was created in six days because six is a perfect number (Aug. *de Gen. ad lit.* 4:14).

[9] In mathematics as in the rest of ancient science, the focus has traditionally been on the accomplishments of the Greeks, but this is now changing, and at least one major research project on *Science and Empire in the Roman World* has been undertaken; details are available at the project's website.

ASTRONOMY AND METEOROLOGY

It is hard to know the stars in a modern city, where light pollution obscures all but the most brilliant of them; it is hard not to know them in a small village where tens of thousands of them can be seen on a moonless night. The earliest Greeks had names for certain stars and for the constellations, and theories about their nature; they knew the procession of the sun through the sky through the year, and the moon through the month. In time many theories would be propounded, not excluding the idea that the constellations are stationary while the earth rotates, and that the earth itself revolves around the sun.[10] Because, however, of the difficulties in measuring celestial distances accurately, it was centuries before a reliable map of the heavens was produced. The elaboration of a mathematical model that would account for the phenomena was a work of tremendous erudition and extraordinary meticulousness, and it was not for nothing that the *Almagest* of Ptolemy was admired and relied upon for a millennium. The physical explanations on which the *Almagest* was based—a series of concentric spheres and epicycles revolving around a stationary earth—have long been rejected, but the method that produced it—increasingly meticulous observation of celestial phenomena and the elaboration of mathematical models to explain them—has only been strengthened in the course of the centuries.

The most obvious connection of the heavens with human life is the weather. Here, too, modern ideas have separated astronomy from meteorology,[11] but popular beliefs among farmers persist to this day in trying to predict a season's weather from phenomena both celestial and terrestrial. The Greeks produced *parapēgmata*, boards[12] with holes for a peg that a farmer would move each day, perpetual almanacs that provided astronomical and meteorological information. As long as ancient science was studied only as the beginning of modern science, items like this, which have no scientific descendants, got little attention; as ancient science has come to be studied as a matter of interest in its own right, ancient meteorology, too, has become a subject of interest.

---

[10] On these hypotheses, for which our attestation is quite late and fragmentary, see Neugebauer, *A History of Ancient Mathematical Astronomy*, 693–8.

[11] Not, of course, completely; the seasons still follow the revolution of the earth (the motion of the sun, as the ancients would have said), tides follow the moon, and the influence of sunspots on climate is still a subject of active research.

[12] In fact the ones we have are flat stones; it seems reasonable to presume that there were wood *parapēgmata* as well, but they have not survived.

PHYSICS

It is the study of inanimate objects, oddly enough, that produced the most extravagantly original theories in the ancient world and that continues to produce them today. When we study more complex phenomena—the motion of the heavens or the generation of animals—it is enough to describe them in terms of simpler phenomena: the heavens whirl around like a wheel; animals grow like plants. But when we get down to the simplest phenomena—why a rock, no matter how hard or how high we throw it, falls to the earth, or why it skips on the surface of the water instead of falling in—we can only begin to answer the questions when we are able to describe what the most basic characteristics of nature are; and in these the ideas of the ancients were no less bold, and no easier to comprehend in depth, than the modern theories of relativity, quanta, quarks and strings. If matter is continuous, as Aristotle thought, how does anything move? If it is made up of discrete atoms, as Democritus thought, whatever caused two of them to meet and interact? If matter tends toward a given state—if, for example, it wants to fall toward the earth—why has it not reached that state long ago? If, on the other hand, it is in constant flux, as Heraclitus thought, why do objects appear to stand still? If everything flows from the Infinite, as Anaximander said, or the One, as Xenophanes held, why do things look so different? Modern physics has despaired of finding a fundamental explanation, for a reason based in modern logic: since every logical description must start from undefined terms and unproven propositions (otherwise its definitions and proofs would be circular), modern physicists no longer expect to be able to explain *why* energy comes in discrete packets, *why* space seems to curve around physical objects, or *why* our knowledge of a physical system must always have a clearly defined level of uncertainty;[13] it is enough to know that that is the case, and to be able to describe how those principles affect the physical world. Modern philosophy finds the ancient theories of physics no more satisfying: in the end all of them, consciously or not, reduce to principles that can be asserted but not really explained. But the variety of these theories can be an eye-opener for a modern, trained in a tradition of physical science that silently takes a certain view of the

---

[13]   To be more precise, we might be able to explain any of these principles, but only by describing them on the basis of more essential principles, the most basic of which will always be matters that defy explanation. Modern philosophy of science has accordingly moved in different directions to explain the nature of scientific explanation.

universe for granted and indeed puts it out of the realm of scientific discussion. Studying ancient theories of physics is not likely to cause us to reject modern physics in favor of one of the ancient theories;[14] but it does make us aware of how little we understand the solid ground on which we seem to stand.

BIOLOGY

Living beings come in bewildering variety, from the cedar of Lebanon to the hyssop in the wall, from the blue whale to the mite. It is obvious to the most casual observer that any given living thing has some that are its close relatives and others that are more distant: a horse is obviously more like a donkey than like a tiger, more like a tiger than like a pine tree. Modern biology has succeeded to an astounding extent in systematizing these relationships and reducing them to the variations of base pairs in strands of DNA; ancient biology never reached any such systematic view of all living beings, though it did give a rough organization on the basis of increasing "perfection" of the natural parts of an organism. Aristotle and Theophrastus, the earliest researchers whose works have reached us, worked in that direction; later writers tended more to the accumulation of facts, many of them interesting, but not leading to a grand synthesis that could offer a unified explanation for the variety of living beings.

From the first the animal and the vegetable were distinguished; Aristotle's writings concentrate on the first, Theophrastus' on the second. Aristotle, in fact, offered a taxonomy of living beings whose broad outlines survive to our day, and a wealth of systematic thought on the subject that must command respect. But theoretical study of biology did not flourish in the ancient world thereafter. Unlike the speculation about physics, which was in its basis a theoretical inquiry into the nature of reality, and unlike ancient mathematics, which was so thoroughly systematized as to deal only with ideal forms, ancient biology became the handmaiden of practical uses: chiefly of medicine, but also of agriculture and of cosmetics. The great

---

14 Though this, too, is not out of the range of possibility, at least according to Kuhn, *The Structure of Scientific Revolutions*, who traces Galileo's theories of movement to a view of nature that preferred Plato over Aristotle. Kuhn's analysis, both of Galileo and of scientific progress, remains controversial: Lakatos and Musgrave, eds., *Criticism and the Growth of Knowledge* and McTighe, "Galileo's Platonism." For a more recent and less revolutionary example of modern enquiry informed by ancient controversy see Rabinowitz, "Falling Bodies."

theoretical discussions of the ancient world after Theophrastus were about what constituted the healthy state of an organism, and what disturbances to that state produced disease.

Because of this practical tendency, the biology of the later period, thin in theory, had relatively little to offer modern biology. Aristotle was another matter. Vesalius and Linnaeus harked back explicitly to what the ancients themselves had done. Their work and that of their successors soon built up a new structure, based on new observations, that put ancient theories into the dusty intellectual storeroom of old ideas, still available but rarely visited; but when Darwin, late in his career, received a translation of Aristotle's *Parts of Animals* he was impressed. "Linnaeus and Cuvier have been my two gods," he wrote, "though in very different ways; but they were mere school-boys to old Aristotle."[15]

Certain aspects of ancient biology are discredited; but as with all branches of science, the way that the ancients looked at problems before the sciences were institutionalized can open up avenues that current approaches neglect. Moreover, the observations themselves are of interest: although modern evolutionary theory considers the time from antiquity to today to be little more than a moment, there are matters (like the age of menarche, or the flora and fauna of given areas) where the ancient literature offers valuable comparative evidence. Even when the ancients preserve for us "facts" that are patently wrong—that eels are generated spontaneously from mud, or that a woman's womb may become displaced to various places in her body—consideration of how they came to these errors can on occasion reveal to us something of themselves, or something of the facts they were observing, or even, most interestingly, something about ourselves.

MEDICINE

Ancient medicine was a theoretical free-for-all, with comprehensive theories competing with each other for the allegiance of practitioners and of patients. The major sources that have come down to us are those attributed to Hippocrates, actually the works of various authors of the Hippocratic school, and those of Galen, six hundred years later, so voluminous as to constitute 10 percent of all surviving literature in

---

[15] The praise was apparently sincere: Gotthelf, "Darwin on Aristotle."

ancient Greek—and new fragments, usually translations into other languages of material whose original is lost, continue to be found.[16]

The works of Galen dominated medical practice for a thousand years, eclipsing other ancient theories and inhibiting more modern ones. Nobody today mourns the passing of the theory of the four humors, nor have even the most marginalized of medical theorists tried to revive it; but the ancient medical lore holds a wealth of practical medical history, unparalleled, to my knowledge, in any ancient culture, and little read precisely because there is so much of it.

Various subjects have attracted the attention of modern researchers. A perennial favorite is the attempt to identify the diseases of the ancient world, particularly those of which we have clear accounts: the plague at Athens described by Thucydides, the death of Alexander the Great, the chronic illness of Aelius Aristeides. Other approaches encourage us to broaden our perspective. What were the underlying concepts of the various medical theories? How effective were the procedures? Recent work on contraception and abortion suggests that they were more effective than had been thought.[17] The misconceptions of ancient medicine may themselves be of interest, and feminist researchers have elucidated both the attitudes that affected the treatment of women and the non-negligible place of women in ancient medical treatment. The place of doctors in society, and for that matter the place of doctors in medical treatment, is a subject of considerable interest. The ancient world had no licensing for doctors and no clear distinction between professional healers and amateurs; people with health problems turned to various remedies and purveyors of remedies, not excluding the religious and the magical.[18]

GEOGRAPHY AND ETHNOGRAPHY

The Greeks were traders before they were conquerors; in the course of time, the Romans became both. As such, they were in constant contact with foreign civilizations; but their curiosity about those civilizations

---

[16] "Since 1945 a new fragment of Galen, and often a whole work, has been announced or published on average every two years, and there is every prospect that this will continue for a few years yet. It has added another 25 per cent to the already enormous mass of the Corpus Galenicum, and represents the largest accession of writings to any classical author since the Renaissance." Nutton, The Unknown Galen, vii.

[17] Riddle, Contraception and Abortion; Kapparis, Abortion.

[18] "As, indeed," David Sansone points out to me, "they do today."

went far beyond anything we know of in other ancient nations, even those who traded and conquered. Description of foreign lands and foreign peoples was a matter of practical value, but the success of geographical and ethnographical writers from Herodotus to Strabo to Tacitus shows that the subject was of interest to many more people than those who expected one day to meet the peoples of whom they wrote.

The ethnographical literature of the Greeks and Romans is in many cases our main source for the history of other nations. The early history of the Persians, the Germans, the Britons, the Gauls and the Armenians, and almost all the history of the Scythians and Bithynians—to offer a very partial selection—are known almost entirely from Greco-Roman sources. It is from these sources that we know not only their king-lists and their battles, but a good deal of their customs and their culture: that the Lydians had the custom of prostituting their daughters[19] and that among the Germans men fought for their chief and would be ashamed to survive a battle in which he fell[20] are bits of anthropological information owed to ancient ethnographers that are still influential today. They are mere tidbits out of a wealth of information.

It may be objected that the information is only third-hand, and the Greek and Roman sources were relating foreign customs that they may have misunderstood or fabricated. This objection is not to be taken lightly: if we did not have the writings of the Jews themselves, we should believe Tacitus that they worshiped an ass in the Holy of Holies[21] and Justin that they fasted on the Sabbath.[22] It is quite certain that the characteristics of Aeschylus' and Herodotus' Persians and Tacitus' Germans are to a certain extent an inversion of the Greeks and the Romans,[23] and, although that is not the entire story, it is difficult, when so little other material is available, to judge the reliability of what we are told. That said, we can add that this is a problem of anthropology in general: though modern field-workers are better trained in recording the details of the society in which they work, they are nevertheless members of a different society and can never entirely escape the universal tendency to see others through one's own world-view. Our ancient ethnographical sources have to be treated with

---

[19] Hdt. 1.94.1.

[20] Tac. Germ. 14.1.

[21] Tac. Hist. 5.4.2.

[22] Just. Epit. 36.2.14.

[23] I am simplifying by referring to the representation of foreign or enemy cultures as inversions; the characterization of what is today called "the other" is a more complex phenomenon. See Hall, *Inventing the Barbarian* and Cohen, *Not the Classical Ideal.*

caution and with a critical eye, but they remain the best information we have about scores of nations, some that have perished and some that have survived, and valuable additions to our sources for many others.

The ancient geographers have left us their works almost entirely in the form of texts: although maps were both made and consulted,[24] very few have survived. The geographical texts, like the ethnographic ones, are a mine of information, for geography, too, can change over the centuries. The Alps, surely, are still there, but coastlines change: the coastline at Thermopylae is not what it used to be, and many an ancient port is today located miles inland, while others, less commonly, are under water. Places once inhabited are now wilderness, and vice versa. Occasionally ancient observations can add vital information to modern. The ancient descriptions of the eruption of Vesuvius in which Pliny the elder lost his life were so widely at variance with what is known of modern volcanoes that they were generally discounted until 1980, when the eruption of Mount St. Helens taught modern vulcanologists how hot and how swift a pyroclastic flow can be. More attention to Pliny might have saved the life of some of the fifty-seven people, one of them a vulcanologist, who died in the eruption.[25]

The interest of ancient geography is not limited to differences in detail; as scholars of the late twentieth century realized, geographical concepts in the ancient world were not necessarily the same as they are today. Geographical history is also intellectual history. In certain cases this may be seen as simply culture-dependent; in other cases it is a matter of progress. We know the world much more precisely, and in much more detail, than the ancients did; but the progress that they themselves made was striking. They were able to describe a point on the globe by its latitude and longitude, though they had no agreed-upon fixed point from which to measure the latter; and it is this very precision that often allows us to ascertain when they are in error. Eratosthenes, famously, computed the circumference of the earth in the third century BCE, and obtained a result not far from the truth. In geography as in other fields of science, the Greco-Roman period was a time of immense progress, unparalleled until the most recent centuries.

We do not have the maps of the ancients, but from their written information it is possible to draw our own. This is not as simple a process

---

[24] The first world map (γεωγραφικὸς πίναξ) was made, according to Eratosthenes ap. Strab. 1.1.11, by Anaximander in the sixth century BCE.

[25] The vulcanologist was David A. Johnston, who lived long enough to cry over the radio "Vancouver! Vancouver! This is it!" His body has never been found.

as it seems. Rome and Athens are not hard to identify, but in most cases the identification of an ancient site requires a good deal of scholarship, which we, brought up on ready-made maps, generally take for granted. The modern historical atlases are prodigious achievements based upon centuries of observation, correlation and discussion. The user of historical atlases should be warned, however, that every historical atlas is to a certain extent anachronistic. Although ethnic and political boundaries existed in the ancient world, they were not always defined with the precision of modern boundaries, and did not always mean what a modern boundary would mean: not every political unit defined itself geographically. Even where a boundary existed, it is often unattested; even if nobody today knows precisely where the boundary between the Milesians and the Carians fell—and the Milesians and the Carians may themselves have disagreed about this question—the mapmaker must draw it somewhere. We are greatly indebted to the mapmakers, without whom we should have little idea of where the great events of history took place and how their geographical setting affected them, as it always did; but when we look very carefully at what happened on the boundaries of city-states or on the boundaries of empire, we discover matters that may teach us something about modern boundaries as well.

TECHNOLOGY

It was the opinion of Sir Moses Finley that the ancient world was one of technological stagnation, a state of affairs that he attributed to the easy availability of slave labor.[26] This opinion has now been challenged,[27] and there is still quite a bit to be said on the subject. The ability of archaeology to adjudicate this subject is limited. Most ancient machinery was made of wood, and leaves little if any trace in the archaeological record; nor, when we find an improvement in health, in productivity or in technique, can archaeology be counted on regularly to tell us whether it was caused by technological innovation, by social change or even by changes in the physical environment. Nevertheless, there is no doubt that the Greco-Roman period produced marvels that were not seen again in the world for many centuries: the monumental Greek buildings, the Roman roads and aqueducts, the Greek trireme that ruled the seas until it was displaced by

---

[26] Finley, "Technological Innovation."
[27] Greene, "Technological Innovation."

more powerful warships—all of these were built on a scale and with a precision that continue to arouse admiration and even wonder today, and they were not produced without a good deal of technical analysis, some of it preserved, much of it, surely, passed down orally among artisans and professionals or recorded in books that have not survived. The study of the technology of the Greeks and Romans has suffered from a divorce between technologists, who know little of the ancient world, and classicists, who know little about technology. For an enterprising researcher, there is a gold mine of information in putting together the dots of the archaeological evidence, the parallels with other societies and the reasons for innovation or for conservatism, and the socio-economic framework of antiquity in which these technologies developed or failed to develop, from which they drew their origin and to whose nature they themselves contributed.

CIVIL ENGINEERING

I do not find this topic mentioned in any general discussion of science or technology, and perhaps it belongs more properly under the heading of history or the heading, which this book does not contain, of politics; but the civil engineering of the Greeks and Romans is a subject that has drawn some attention and is worthy of more. Neither the Greeks nor the Romans had a term for what we now call city planning, but they practiced it, and they were not the first to do so: the great cities of Mesopotamia and the Levant were not mere anarchic collections of houses. A good deal of information is preserved both in literature and in archaeology about matters that we should consider matters of civil engineering. Greek cities had zoning laws restricting certain activities in certain areas; the building of city walls was an enterprise whose details are known to us by large numbers of inscriptions;[28] the provision of an agora, first (as the derivation from ἀγείρω indicates) as a place of gathering, later as a marketplace, was often a state initiative, as were the public and cult buildings. The building of Roman cities was often entirely a state-planned process, based upon the uniform rules by which the Roman army built its camps in such short order; and the main roads of a camp, the *cardo* and *decumanus*, can still be identified in many cities two thousand years after the Roman planners left their mark; the city's hinterland was measured off by surveyors

---

[28] Collected for the Greek world in Maier, *Griechische Mauerbauinschriften*.

(*agrimensores*) and apportioned among the settlers. Drainage, "which every-one agrees is the greatest need,"[29] was a civic responsibility from the beginning: the first archaeological indication of the unification of the city is the drainage of the forum, and the *cloaca maxima* dates from the period of the kings. The public baths and latrines of Rome remained a permanent institution in the east even after the fall of the Empire; the west would not reach this level of water-supply and sanitation until the nineteenth century. The organization of all of this is relatively well attested for the Roman Empire, and much can be learned from it about how and for whom the Romans managed their cities. In particular, archaeology can teach us, as single works rarely do, the dynamics of the process: what succeeded and what failed, what lasted, what languished, what perished, and why and how the cities of the Roman Empire became the very different cities of its Christian and Muslim successors.

MAJOR RESOURCES

Many if not most articles about ancient science appear not in classical journals but in journals of the history of science or of the sciences themselves. An important resource is the current bibliography published each year as a supplement to *Isis*, the journal of the History of Science Society: publications dealing with ancient Greece and Rome are conveniently collected under a single rubric, and periodically compre-hensive bibliographies are issued covering longer periods.

There is no encyclopedia of ancient science, though we are now closer than we ever were with Keyser and Irby-Massie, *The Encyclopedia of Ancient Natural Scientists*; there is no series of texts in ancient science, no lexicon of ancient scientific terms. Until recently, the only general accounts of particular subjects were woefully out of date, but two recent series, the Routledge *Sciences of Antiquity* and the German *Geschichte der Mathematik und der Naturwissenschaften in der Antike* (GMN) have done much to remedy the situation. For a general background to ancient science in English, Lloyd, *Early Greek Science* and Lloyd, *Greek Science after Aristotle* give a good and thoughtful brief account, and Rihll, *Greek Science* is a very short but lively survey of scholarship; and Lloyd, *Methods and Problems* offers not only a number of penetrating essays but a well-stated explanation in the preface of the importance of the study of ancient science. A number of sourcebooks have been edited: Cohen and Drabkin, *A Sourcebook in Greek*

---

[29] *Opus omnium dictu maximum*, Plin. *Nat.* 36.24.104.

Science, Irby-Massie and Keyser, *Greek Science of the Hellenistic Era*, Heath, *Greek Astronomy*, Bulmer-Thomas, *Greek MathematicalWorks*, Panessa, *Fonti greche e latine per la storia dell'ambiente e del clima nel mondo greco*, Longrigg, *Greek Medicine*, and the various sourcebooks of the early philosophers. These can give the beginner some inkling of what is available, but the history of ancient science remains, as Rihll called it, "a land of opportunity for adventurous scholars."[30]

Introductions to Individual Fields

For mathematics there is the compendious, if old, Heath, *A History of Greek Mathematics*, which summarizes the contributions of all the great mathematicians in the terms that a modern would use. Very different is the recent Cuomo, *Ancient Mathematics*, which deals with what he calls "lower" mathematics—counting and measuring and such—and treats the more advanced mathematics discursively: Cuomo quotes actual mathematical texts, but sets them off clearly from his main text so as not to frighten off the non-mathematician. As is common in more recent discussions, Cuomo is interested not only in the theory itself, but in the place that mathematics held in the world of the Greeks. Intriguingly, he divides each discussion into "evidence" and "questions"—the latter being questions that he himself raises, and generally does not answer definitively. "Hopefully," he writes, ". . . people will ask their own questions, and give their own answers."[31] More specific but very basic problems are dealt with by Fowler, *The Mathematics of Plato's Academy*; by Reviel Netz in a number of works, and by the essays in Tuplin and Rihll, *Science and Mathematics in Ancient Greek Culture*. Postcolonialism might have been expected to explore more thoroughly the relationship of Greek mathematics to its Egyptian and Babylonian predecessors, but that can only be done by a scholar willing to tackle the documents of those three very different languages and cultures. Such a scholar was Otto Neugebauer, whose *The Exact Sciences in Antiquity*, though half a century old, can still offer a firm basis for further research.

For astronomy Neugebauer, *A History of Ancient Mathematical Astronomy* is not likely to be surpassed in the near future, but the less mathematically sophisticated will prefer Evans, *The History and Practice of Ancient Astronomy*. For

---

[30] Rihll, *Greek Science*, xii; Rihll uses this term of the history of Greek science, but that does not mean that the Romans are better served.

[31] Cuomo, 3.

both mathematics and astronomy new volumes are promised by GMN. For astrology, which was part and parcel of ancient astronomy, Barton, *Ancient Astrology* or Beck, *A Brief History of Ancient Astrology* can give an introduction; the latter, on pages 2–3, gives a good summary of the disadvantages of studying ancient astronomy and astrology independently of each other. Taub, *Ancient Meteorology* has given the subject its first general treatment; for parapēgmata see Lehoux, *Astronomy, Weather, and Calendars*.

Ancient physics has generally been treated in the context of ancient philosophy, but now Schürmann, *Physik/Mechanik* offers an overview.

Moderns consider the study of animals and plants to be a part of biology, the study of all living organisms; ancients considered it a part of natural history, the study of natural phenomena. The first is treated by Wöhrle, *Biologie*, the second by French, *Ancient Natural History*. Neither zoology nor botany has a general treatment, though Pellegrin, *Aristotle's Classification of Animals* and Lennox, *Aristotle's Philosophy of Biology* have put Aristotle's zoology in a new and more understandable light, and for botany Suzanne Amigues' copiously annotated Budé Theophrastus, along with the articles collected in her *Études de botanique antique*, give a good idea of what can be done. The identification of the species referred to by particular Greek or Latin words, a tricky problem on which the standard dictionaries are unreliable, is made possible by such works as Thompson, *A Glossary of Greek Fishes*; Arnott, *Birds in the Ancient World from A to Z*, which builds on Thompson, *A Glossary of Greek Birds*; Beavis, *Insects and Other Invertebrates in Classical Antiquity*; Davies and Kathirithamby, *Greek Insects*; and Baumann, *Greek Wild Flowers*, which offers beautiful color photographs but no footnotes and little argumentation.

Nutton, *Ancient Medicine* is careful, closely argued and complete; a practicing physician would have produced a different book, but to my knowledge none has. Phillips, *Greek Medicine*, and Cruse, *Roman Medicine* are more readable, if much less complete. Diseases, classified under their modern names, received a thorough treatment in Grmek, *Diseases in the Ancient Greek World*; articles both in classical and in medical journals continue to debate the issues summarized there. The practice of medicine is described in Jackson, *Doctors and Diseases in the Roman Empire*, and the different concepts of ancient medicine in Gourevitch, *Le triangle hippocratique* and Grmek, *Western Medical Thought*; its technical language is the subject of D. R. Langslow, *Medical Latin in the Roman Empire*. The pioneering work on women's issues in medicine was Danielle Gourevitch, *Le Mal d'être femme*; the subject has been broadened and deepened by Dean-Jones, *Women's Bodies in Classical Greek Science*, King, *Hippocrates' Woman* and Flemming, *Medicine and the Making of Roman Women*. A good bibliography of articles is available at the Diotima website, an excellent place to start for all matters involving women in antiquity. For ancient veterinary medicine, a matter on which we are better informed than one might think, the collection of essays in Cam, La médecine vétérinaire antique can offer an idea of recent work. For source texts of ancient medicine, the Corpus Medicorum Graecorum/Latinorum is now freely available in online facsimile. Other important editions exist: in addition to the Hippocratic corpus, Celsus, and Galen, the exemplary edition of Heinrich von Staden, Herophilus, and Burguière, Gourevitch and Malinas, Soranos d'Éphèse deserve mention, as does Évelyne Samama's collection of epigraphical sources, Les médecins dans le monde grec. An international Society for Ancient Medicine provides contact among researchers; the Wellcome Trust, a British charity whose main function is biomedical research, interprets its mandate broadly and has done quite a bit to encourage research into ancient medicine.

For geography the English general works Bunbury, A History of Ancient Geography and Thomson, History of Ancient Geography are quite outdated; Hübner, Geographie gives a much better picture of the current state of the subject. Ancient cartography became a matter for systematic treatment with Dilke, Greek and Roman Maps and much more with Harley and Woodward, The History of Cartography; for the current status of the subject see Talbert, "Greek and Roman Mapping." For the fragments of the ancient geographers, almost all consigned by Strabo to oblivion, Müller, Geographi Graeci Minores and Riese, Geographi Latini Minores remain what we have until Part V of F Gr Hist (for which see below) is published.

Historical Atlases

The authoritative historical atlas for the current generation is Talbert, Barrington Atlas of the Greek and Roman World, which covers the ancient world from modern Morocco to western China and from Norway and Sweden to Kenya. The maps are large and detailed, including topographical features and, best of all, a "Directory" that includes discussion of difficulties—all included not only in two beautifully produced volumes but in a searchable CD-ROM that comes with them. Despite the magnitude of the achievement represented by this work, for many purposes a set of smaller maps describing particular historical moments or events will be more convenient; for this the best are the handy Bengtson and Milojčić, Grosser historischer Weltatlas and Hammond, Atlas of the Greek and Roman World in Antiquity. Far more ambitious, if you can afford it, is Wittke, Olshausen and Szydlak, Historischer Atlas der antiken Welt, many of whose maps offer more precision and explanation than earlier efforts did; in due course it will presumably be available in English as part of *Brill's New Pauly*. Other historical atlases are available, but no recent one is up to the level of these. There is still a good deal to be done. Historical developments, which could once be shown by superimposed transparencies, can now be shown digitally, as a few examples are at the *Mapping History Project* site; we shall presumably see more of these. Another use of digital technology is to facilitate study of what we have: the *Stanford Digital Forma Urbis Romae Project* holds out hope of the reconstruction of part of a marble map of Severan Rome of which we have over a thousand fragments.

Technology

The wide-ranging Oleson, *Oxford Handbook of Engineering and Technology in the Classical World*, although organized as a collection of articles, fulfills the function of an encyclopedia better than anything that has hitherto been available, and its articles provide both a survey of the field and an introduction to the various uses of technology; previously there had been no comprehensive treatment. This collection will be useful not least for its bibliography. Earlier important studies were Forbes, *Studies in Ancient Technology*, a mine of material, and K. D. White, *Greek and Roman Technology*, who put technology into its cultural and economic framework. Burford, *Craftsmen in Greek and Roman Society* described the life of a craftsman, a subject not dealt with in Oleson's *Handbook*, and Meißner, *Die technologische Fachliteratur der Antike* described the transmission of technological knowledge. The bibliography in Oleson, *Bronze Age, Greek and Roman Technology*, although updated (very selectively), with a brief description of each item, in Humphrey, *Ancient Technology*, 195–212, is presumably now superseded by the bibliographies in the articles of the *Handbook*. The series *Technology and Change in History* has produced Wikander, *Handbook of Ancient Water Technology*, Wright, *Ancient Building Technology*, Curtis, *Ancient Food Technology* and Thurmond, *A Handbook of Food Processing in Classical Rome*. A sourcebook, Humphrey, Oleson and Sherwood, *Greek and Roman Technology*, is available. Land surveying has been particularly well served by the collection of texts, edited, translated and with commentary, in Campbell, *The Writings of the Roman Land Surveyors*; a brief but expert general account had already been offered by Dilke, *Roman Land Surveyors*. For other areas, a well-produced series of texts and a lexicon of technological terms continue to be desired.

On civil engineering Robinson, *Ancient Rome* gives an excellent account of the administrative situation as it appears in the legal sources; an archaeology-based account of the Greek city where city planning can best be studied is offered by Cahill, *Household and City Organization at Olynthus*. There are many articles based on individual sites, and a general treatment could contribute quite a bit to our understanding.

24

ANCIENT RELIGION AND MYTHOLOGY

THE STUDY OF RELIGION

When virtually all of the scholarly world adhered to a single religion, the study of religion was, like any other study, the study of something whose existence does not depend upon ourselves: what we know and what we can know about G-d (or, in antiquity, the gods) and the consequences that that knowledge has or should have for our lives. This is what today is called theology. In times when religious beliefs become a subject of widespread controversy—at the time of the first spread of Christianity, or the Protestant reformation—the nature of this inquiry becomes more polemical, with a tendency for presupposed conclusions to determine the evidence rather than the opposite. When a generally skeptical attitude towards religion is widely adopted—as in Epicurean philosophy, or in the materialist theories of the nineteenth century—the study of religion ceases to be a study of anything outside of ourselves and becomes a study of people: scholars do not seek to understand gods (whose existence they consider unprovable, debatable or irrelevant or deny completely),[1] but to

---

[1] This does not mean that a modern student of religion must be an atheist, agnostic or universalist, considering all religions equally false or equally true: it is possible to compare people's behavior towards a presumed divinity without reference to the question of whether their presumption is true. But this is not the form that the study of religion has taken in ages of faith.

understand why people believe in gods, and what effect this has upon them. The study of religion ceases to be study of G-d or of the gods and instead becomes a study of human psychology and society.

As such, it is treated with entirely different tools. If we believe that phenomena have objective existence, we study the phenomena that demonstrate them: physicists study moving objects, biologists study plants and animals, and the study of "comparative physics," looking for unifying motifs in, shall we say, Aristotelian, Newtonian and Buddhist explanations of physical phenomena, would be of peripheral interest at best. For a physicist, false beliefs are to be discarded, not considered as evidence; and that was the attitude of the Hebrew prophets, who asked contemptuously what the straw had to do with the wheat (Jer. 23.28). If, on the other hand, the phenomena are the productions of human minds, then the comparative method is as reasonable for religion as it is for language or for literature.

Since we do not believe that the gods of the Greco-Roman pantheon really existed, our study of ancient paganism is necessarily psychological and sociological: we are interested in what the ancients believed about those gods, why they believed it, and how that belief affected them. The first phrase, *what the ancients believed about their gods*, includes a good deal of mythology (though tales about the gods are by no means the only myths of the Greeks and the Romans) as well as a certain amount of geographical and social information about the spheres of influence of the various deities. *Why they believed* it is the subject of most comparative religious study, looking into the psychological and sociological contexts that are reinforced or challenged by religion. *How that belief affected them* entails the cults and rituals through which they related to the gods, rituals that left their stamp on their daily behavior, on their political institutions, on their literature and on their physical surroundings. It is hard to read very far in an ancient text, to look at very many ancient buildings or to investigate in detail the history of the ancients without encountering their religious beliefs and practices; and that being the case, a certain understanding of ancient religion is necessary for almost everyone who deals with the classics.

MYTHOLOGY

As long as the myths of the ancients are remembered there will be an audience for new retellings of the old myths; it is precisely their Protean ability to mean different things to different people that both accounts for their fascination and assures that no one person's retelling will ever be quite the same as another's. Slightly more scholarly than mere retelling of the stories is their harmonization: the variations of the stories are legion and often contradict each other, a problem that has bedeviled every mythographer since Hesiod, who for all his efforts at consistency occasionally has the same god born twice or even three times. Modern scholars, however, do not generally make any effort to enforce a false consistency on stories that were obviously told in different ways at different times by different people—or even by the same person.

More intriguing to modern researchers are the questions that arise out of the place of myths in society and in psychology. The Greeks and Romans used their myths for literary purposes, but also on occasion based political action upon them. We find cities quarreling about the relics of a mythological hero, or offering mythological connections as bases for alliances or enmities. Reenactment of the myths was often a part of religious ritual; on other occasions a myth might be cited to make a moral or a psychological point. The social world of the Olympian gods seems at first glance a transparent transposition of the social world of the Greeks, but it had its differences—the goddesses had more explicit institutional power than they would have had in most Greek *poleis*—and the ancients themselves were occasionally aware of the incongruousness, as when Pisthetaerus in Aristophanes' *Birds* lectures Heracles on his rights of inheritance or when Ovid informs us that the Milky Way, if he dares say so, might be called the Palatine quarter of heaven.

If mythology manipulated people, it was no less true that people, then as now, manipulated mythology, both by inventing new mythical stories (Alexander's divine parentage, the lock of Berenice, the comet of Julius Caesar) and by manipulating the ones that existed (Augustus as the new Romulus, or Commodus as the new Hercules). The Trojan War could offer examples for (*Iphigenia in Aulis*) or against (*The Trojan Women*) the sacrifice of the individual to a nation's military goals; a woman who acted like a man might be admirable (Sophocles' Antigone) or monstrous (Aeschylus' Clytemnestra). The interplay between myth-making, myth-telling and myth-interpretation is as active today as ever, but it is more readily detected in ancient Greece and Rome, whose myths were clearly designated as such and in whose "correct" interpretation we have no vested interest.

Not all the stories we call "myths" are of the same sort. Some deal with gods, and with the particular actions or genealogies of the various deities; these obviously have a religious aspect, and are often suspected of hiding a significant element of symbolism. Stories of heroes are another sort of myth; although we cannot bring certain proof of the existence of any of the figures of the Greek heroic age (nor, for that matter, of the primitive heroes of ancient Rome), parallels from other societies indicate that such stories are often told about real historical figures, such as the Song of Roland about Charlemagne; and for that matter, the undoubtedly historical figure of Alexander the Great collected about himself enough mythical material for a number of epics. A third sort of myth is the folktale (mythologists often prefer the German term Märchen): these, as the Brothers Grimm were the first to demonstrate, are archetypical stories that appear in various different civilizations, and many of the ones known from the ancient world can be paralleled from other societies far removed.

Theories of the origins of myths were already proposed in the ancient world. Livy, to take one example from hundreds, offered an etymological reason for the myth of the wolf who suckled Romulus and Remus,[2] and Euhemerus claimed to have visited an island where all those who were held to be gods had once been human beings.[3] Modern theories seem more sophisticated to us, and they can base themselves on much broader anthropological, sociological and psychological bases of information. Their starting-point is with the Cambridge ritualists, a group of early-twentieth-century theoreticians centering around Jane Ellen Harrison, who first tried to explain myth as a form of literary expression of rituals surrounding a cycle of annual renewal involving the death of the old and the birth (or rebirth) of the new. This particular approach is no longer in fashion, but the essential idea that myths deal with deeper issues than their literary representations might suggest is an idea that has not disappeared. The question that has often been broached but never solved, however, is the question of what it was that the myths encoded, and what the nature of that encoding is. Do they represent archetypical psychological situations, of which Oedipus and Electra are the most famous examples proposed? Are they explanations ("teleological myths") of rituals whose origin had been forgotten or repressed? Is the iconographic apparatus of mythical figures—the beasts that surround the goddess of the hunt, the trident of the lord of the sea, the smile that adorns the face of the goddess of love and the god of wine even when they are most destructive and vindictive—an important indication of the figure's essential character, or a mere conventional label for easy identification? All theories that attempt to deal with such questions must necessarily base themselves on a theoretical grounding that is open to considerable debate. For some

[2]   Liv. 1.4.7.
[3]   Diod. Sic. 6.1.

that makes the discussion seem sterile; for others that is what gives it its interest.

WORSHIP AND RITUAL

Of the ancients' relationship with the supernatural, it is mythology that has left the clearest traces on our culture and our consciousness; but for the ancients themselves, religion was much more a matter of practice, the service of various gods, some universal, some local, some familial or even individual. The multiplicity of these practices may seem at first sight amazing—a Greek could worship a god by throwing a pebble on a heap, by running a relay race or even by parodying the god himself—but in another sense it is the uniformity that is striking: sacrifice, incense, temples and sacred localities are the basic building-blocks of Greek and Roman worship, and they are by no means without influence on more modern forms of worship.

For the study of ancient religious practice a huge amount of material is available. There are literary descriptions, of course, but these only scratch the surface: they usually do not describe the universal aspects that, though alien to us, were absorbed by the ancients from babyhood. Archaeology offers a great deal. The temples themselves show us the environment in which at least certain aspects of cult were practiced; the temple decoration may be merely decorative, but may equally well indicate aspects of the cult that the builders wished to hold in the worshipers' mind. Items found in the temple may indicate what sort of things were considered appropriate gifts to the deity; inscriptions often tell us the circumstances of the dedication and some basic facts (gender and nomenclature, and thus, often, ethnicity) about the dedicator. Accounting inscriptions tell us of the day-to-day administration of the temple, or at least of special projects undertaken. More modern archaeological techniques, by examining animal bones and vegetable remains, can often elucidate the way in which the victim was sacrificed or the ritual meal prepared; and comparing these results with those at other sites can often identify cult localities, of which there were many, that did not include a temple or altar. Statuary and vase paintings depict many scenes of cult performance, and document innumerable mythological variants that have left no trace in the literary record.

Anthropology is helpful, too. We can never, in this life, interrogate an ancient Greek or Roman, but we can interrogate modern polytheists, and, although it is no longer widely believed that all societies pass through the same stages of development, comparative anthropology gives us some tools by which our knowledge of modern pagans can illuminate the practice of the ancients.

STATE RELIGION AND DIVINATION

Good relations with supernatural powers were essential to the community no less than to individuals, and every ancient community had public festivals and rites in which all citizens, and often even non-citizens, were expected to participate; this was, in fact, the one area of public life in which women participated more or less fully.[4] State religion was if anything even more closely associated with politics than are modern state religions; Julius Caesar began his political career by capturing the office of Pontifex Maximus at a young age. Religious transgressions were punished by the state, often as capital offenses; festivals took precedence over all state business, even the most urgent, and a general who initiated a battle without performing the proper sacrifices ran the greatest of dangers— from the people no less than from the gods.

Even better than requesting the gods' favor would be knowing in advance what their intention was; and a good deal of ancient religion was bent toward this purpose. The flight of birds and the entrails of sacrifices were common indicators, but not the only ones; an ill-omened word or an unlucky day were no less significant. In Rome, apparently under Etruscan influence, divination was essential to almost every public act. The year was divided into days of good and ill omen (fasti and nefasti); on the latter no business could be transacted. At any point the appropriate official could end any public proceedings by announcing that he was watching the skies—he did not even have to have seen anything. There was always a strain of skepticism around divination, from Hector's famous dismissal ("One omen is the best: to defend the country"[5]) to Cato's wondering how one haruspex could pass another without laughing;[6] but divination as a state practice did not disappear as long as paganism remained, and as a

---

[4]   This is not to imply that ancient religion was gender-blind—it was anything but— but rather that women had a clearly defined and important role in it, as is testified, among other facts, by the large percentage of dedications that were made by women. Some cults and some observances were reserved for men, others for women; but most included both sexes.

[5]   Hom. Il. 12.243.

[6]   Cic. Div. 2.51.

private practice it remains, on a much smaller scale and much less respectable, in our own day. Like religion itself, the practice of divination and the institution of state religion suffused the ancient world in a way that must necessarily color any effort to understand the people who lived by it.

MAGIC

The boundary between religion and magic is heavily disputed today. In times when one system of religious belief is generally accepted, the distinction is clear: religion is a way of relating to the true gods, the good gods or the most powerful gods, magic a way of manipulating the world by means of false gods, evil gods or subordinate gods. The distinction to us is harder to define, but it was unquestionably present: the young witch so affectingly portrayed in Theocritus' Second Idyll would never be mistaken for the good-hearted young girl of Plautus' *Aulularia* who is always careful to sprinkle a bit of meal in front of the family's household god. Most ancients believed in magic (so, for that matter, do many moderns), and they have left us many relics of the fact. Again, it is literary texts that are the most explicit, but we have other items: curse texts, voodoo dolls, amulets and texts of pseudo-mystical gibberish. For many years these items were relegated to the margins of classical scholarship, as their practitioners were marginalized in their world; but as scholarship has become less focused on the elite and on those practices that the elite sanctioned, magic has come more and more to the foreground of scholarship.

FOREIGN CULTS

The study of those cults that the Greeks and Romans considered "foreign" is not qualitatively different from the study of the religion of the Greeks and Romans themselves; the varieties of pagan worship in the ancient world were many, and some foreign cults eventually found their way into the religious world of the conquerors. Some were entirely "naturalized"; others, like the worship of the *Magna Mater*, retained a certain aura of exoticism even when their devotees had become legion. Two issues, however, present themselves in particular with respect to foreign cults: what the attitude of the dominant culture was in general, and what it was that caused their increasing popularity in the early centuries of the present era until it eventually brought about the conversion of the Roman Empire to Christianity.

JUDAISM

To a certain extent one may consider the relative importance attributed to Judaism in the classical world to be a matter of hindsight colored by the eventual triumph of its daughter religion, Christianity; but it is also true that we possess far richer sources for the Judaism of antiquity than we possess for any other one of the religions that competed for the allegiance of the ancients. The Greek translation of the Bible that goes under the name of the Septuagint, though of varied authorship and stemming from various periods, nevertheless preserves a good deal of information about how the Bible was read in the Hellenistic diaspora; it also preserves the Apocrypha and the Pseudepigraphica, various books that were not canonized in the Hebrew Bible and not preserved by the Jews. More information, no less intriguing for its heterodoxy, is offered by the philosophical works of Philo, and the historical works of Josephus give us a good picture both of contemporary Jewish history and of contemporary Jewish polemic; for history the libelous account in Tacitus' *Histories* shows us what we should nowadays call the anti-Semitic tradition, and other Roman historians give us an outsiders' view of Judaism that is in certain respects unlike anything that a Christian source would produce.

The sources preserved by the Jews, almost entirely in Hebrew and Aramaic, show—not surprisingly—a picture quite different from what we would have drawn from the pagan and Christian sources. The difference is partly due to the deep sectarian cleavages among Jews of the time, disputes well attested in both Jewish and non-Jewish sources, though for some reason scholars often write as if their existence were a surprising modern discovery. Another reason for the difference between the picture drawn from Hebrew and Aramaic sources and the one that emerges from the Greek and Latin texts is geographical: Judaism in Judaea, where the Jews were the dominant (though not the only— another well-attested fact that is sometimes presented as being somehow subversive) element in the population, was different from Judaism in Rome, in Sardis or in Alexandria.

And here, again, the literary texts are not all that we have. Archaeology, both in Israel and elsewhere, has produced much of interest in terms of the development of synagogues, their administration, and the size and significance of many communities that would otherwise be unknown; papyrus discoveries, most famously the Dead Sea Scrolls but also other documents stemming from Egypt and from the Judaean desert, have given us first-hand knowledge of sectarians whom we had known only from their opponents' descriptions, and of Jews whose religion was not the central fact in their lives (or at least their lives as documented). Perhaps emblematic was the discovery of the name of the leader of the second-century rebellion, which turned out to be neither Bar Kochba (as the pagan tradition called him) nor Bar Koziba (as the rabbinic tradition called him), but Ben Kosiba: in the polemical deformations of the two sides, the great leader's actual name had been forgotten by everybody.

CHRISTIANITY

There is a good deal of controversy about the conversion of the Roman Empire to Christianity: how it happened, why it happened, how long it took, how much it changed politics, economy and society, and other questions too numerous to mention. What cannot be doubted is that it amounted in the end to one of the great cultural revolutions of history—perhaps the greatest. The culture and history of at least a thousand years after this event cannot be spoken of without reference to Christianity, and it is very hard to conceive what the late antique world and medieval would have been like had the conversion of the Empire never taken place. From Constantine onward, religion became one of the central issues in the Roman world, and remained so after that world had crumbled.

No less striking than the victory of Christianity is the disappearance of paganism; as Gibbon noted, the total disappearance of a religion without the physical destruction of its believers is a very rare thing in the history of the world.[7] The last days of paganism, and the efforts made by the more devoted of its adherents to preserve it and to restore it, are an interesting story that was once ignored at the margins of the Christian triumph.

Since Christianity is still very much alive, a good deal of the scholarship on Christianity falls under the category of theology rather than the classics; but since its impact is impossible to ignore, it forms a necessary background to any discussion of late antiquity. The structure and growth of the church into a power paralleling, sometimes reinforcing and sometimes competing with, the Empire itself is a question for ancient historians no less than for ecclesiastical historians; questions of influence

---

[7] "The ruin of Paganism, in the age of Theodosius, is perhaps the only example of the total extirpation of any ancient and popular superstition, and may therefore deserve to be considered as a singular event in the history of the human mind." Gibbon, *Decline and Fall*, Chap. 28.

by and upon the pagan world—questions which were the subject of lively controversy among the early Christians themselves—can only be properly dealt with by scholars familiar with the ancient languages and with their literatures. Parallels between the triumph of Christianity and the triumph of other religions (notably Buddhism and Islam) that acquired similarly wide dominion would seem to demand scholars as much at home in Arabic and in the Indic languages as they are in Greek and Latin. Such scholars are hard to find.

OUR RELIGION AND THEIRS

Still harder to find, if such a being can be found at all, is the scholar who is able to approach religion without preconceptions. Since all of us have religious opinions, whether positive or negative, well before we begin an academic career, it is practically impossible for a modern scholar to approach ancient Christianity in a sterile and objective manner. Less obviously but no less truly, our approach to paganism is affected by our religious opinions: we may see in it an illegitimate opponent, an intriguing alternative, a primitive predecessor or an enlightening parallel to modern religion, but we cannot generally escape the fact that some ways of understanding ancient religion are more agreeable to our own religious ideas than others. There is probably no way of overcoming these prejudices completely; in all fields, works that seemed to their authors and their contemporaries to be objective and scientific are often seen by a generation with different inclinations to be embarrassingly subjective, and that is particularly the case with religion. We must be aware, however, that the more our scholarship reflects our prejudices, the less it deserves the name of scholarship.

Many people are attracted to the study of religion because they are attracted to religion itself. There is nothing inherently wrong with this, but if you enroll as a religion major in order to strengthen your own faith you will probably be disillusioned. The reason is not, as it is sometimes portrayed, that the study of religion in any way proves that some religions or all of them are false, but rather that the demands of scholarly discourse make it impossible for a person of faith to express that faith in scholarly research. If one person believes that a certain text is divinely given and infallible, the fact that other people disagree does not disprove the assumption; but it does mean that discussion with them is impossible unless the believer either excludes the belief from discussion or—what is hardly likely—convinces them of it. Scholarly debate, as long as it is being held among people of different beliefs, must necessarily exclude all of those beliefs as a basis for discussion; and talking as if you were an unbeliever is not a promising way to strengthen your faith.

MAJOR RESOURCES

There is not, and never was, any authoritative statement of the beliefs of the ancient pagans, but many people, from antiquity onward, have attempted to collect and categorize, or at least retell, the myths that the ancients told about their gods and their heroes. These are usually referred to as "Greek mythology," in keeping with the common belief—a belief that many Roman authors shared—that most of the stories, or at least the most interesting ones, are of Greek origin, and were at best adapted, retold or augmented by the Romans. There are innumerable guides to mythology, some designed for reference and ordered alphabetically, others designed for reading and ordered by subject. Among the alphabetical encyclopedias of mythology, by far the most complete is Roscher's multivolume *Lexikon der Mythologie*, exhaustive but long out of date; the most popular is Grimal, *The Dictionary of Classical Mythology*, originally published in 1951 but still very usable and attractively published; an abridgement is published by Penguin, with the usual tradeoff between price and portability on the one hand and completeness on the other. Many newer encyclopedias exist, each with a slightly different focus; which one is appropriate to you will depend on the use you are likely to make of it.

The narratives of Greek mythology are still represented in the popular paperback world by the three old standards, Rose, *A Handbook of Greek Mythology*, Hamilton, *Mythology* and Graves, *The Greek Myths*, all of them serviceable for a general retelling of the stories but very out of date and not to be relied upon in their interpretations. Hard, *The Routledge Handbook of Greek Mythology* is two generations more recent, readable, and sparsely but usefully illustrated; but it is not, as of this writing, available in a cheap paperback edition. The sources, both literary and artistic, for early Greek myth are handled in an exemplary fashion by Gratz, *Early Greek Myth*.

Those Roman stories that are traditionally considered myths—Aeneas, Romulus, Horatius at the bridge, and the geese that saved the capitol—are retold in Grant, *Roman Myths*, available in a Pelican paperback; very different is Wiseman, *The Myths of Rome*, which presents Roman stories that are myths in the modern sense—archetypical tales through which a society defines its past and its self—with lavish illustration and abundant quotation from later literature to show how these myths were understood and manipulated in Rome, and have continued to supply a kaleidoscopically varying mythical background to poets, thinkers and statesmen ever since.

The popularity of mythology means that it is treated by innumerable websites; precisely this popularity means that many of these websites are created and maintained by people whose knowledge of the classics, and indeed of mythology, is far from perfect. The web is undoubtedly the most accessible way for most people to get a quick bit of background, but it is worth finding out how trustworthy a given site is before relying on its information. The quickest (though not infallible) indication is the institution sponsoring the site.

A taste of various theoretical approaches to ancient mythology can be found in Edmunds, *Approaches to Greek Myth* and Csapo, *Theories of Mythology*.

When LIMC[8] was finally and successfully finished, its creators began a new project that resulted in the *Thesaurus Cultus et Rituum Antiquorum* (ThesCRA). This provides a stupendous amount of information about the various cult practices of the ancient world (Greek, Etruscan and Roman), though the organization of the articles is not uniform and the absence, at least at present, of a topical index makes it somewhat difficult to use as a reference work. Johnston, *Religions of the Ancient World* offers articles on all aspects of ancient Mediterranean religions, both Greco-Roman and not, as far east as Iran, but not Celtic or Germanic religion. For a readable one-volume account of the practices of Greek paganism the standard work is Burkert, *Greek Religion*, and for the Romans it is Beard, North and Price, *Religions of Rome*. A quick alphabetical reference for Greek and Roman religion in general is Price and Kearns, *The Oxford Dictionary of Classical Myth and Religion*; for Rome there is Adkins and Adkins, *Dictionary of Roman Religion*. Whatever is known about the priests and priestesses of the various deities, notably including the holders of the priesthoods at any given time, can be found in Rüpke, *Fasti Sacerdotum*.

A good and accessible book of sources on ancient magic is Luck, *Arcana Mundi*. The curse-tablets of ancient Athens were published in Wuensch, *Defixionum Tabellae*, and those of other localities in Audollent, *Defixionum Tabellae*. Such religious legislation as has been recovered by epigraphy has been collected in Prott and Ziehen, *Leges Graecorum Sacrae e Titulis Collectae* (LGS), Sokolowski, *Lois sacrées de l'Asie mineure*, *Lois sacrées des cités grecques* and *Lois sacrées des cités grecques: Supplément*, and Lupu, *Greek Sacred Law: A Collection of New Documents* (NGSL): each of these updates the earlier ones, so that no single one of them gives all the texts.

---

[8] Above, p. 286.

Christianity, which supplanted paganism as the religion of the ancient world, and its mother-religion, Judaism, are both subjects with a vast literature, little of which properly belongs in the field of classical studies but much of which is relevant to our field. The text of the Septuagint generally in use is Rahlfs, *Septuaginta*; the most comprehensive source for the other Greek translations of the Old Testament is still Field, *Origenis Hexapla*, though quite a bit of new material has been discovered in the many years since it was published. The critical edition of the Greek New Testament is Nestle–Aland, *Novum Testamentum Graece*. Concordances are Hatch and Redpath, *A Concordance to the Septuagint* and Clapp, Friberg and Friberg, *Analytical Concordance of the Greek New Testament*. There is also a dictionary of the New Testament, Danker, *A Greek–English Lexicon of the New Testament*. The texts of the Christian fathers are to be found in *Corpus Christianorum* and in PCC, mentioned above, pp. 108–9; the interaction of Christianity with the ancient world is the subject of a vast encyclopedic enterprise, the *Reallexikon für Antike und Christentum*, about half-finished at its twentieth volume.[9] The literature on early Christianity, and on Hellenistic and Roman Judaism, is much too large to be summarized here.

---

[9] An associated journal, the *Jahrbuch für Antike und Christentum*, publishes articles and occasionally monographs on all subjects related to the subject of the encyclopedia— which includes, among other things, almost anything connected with Greece and Rome.

25

LAW

ROMAN LAW AND GREEK LAW

Throughout this book, when it has been necessary to treat the Greeks and the Romans separately, the Greeks have come first, since the high point of their culture preceded that of the Romans, and the Romans in many respects learned from the Greeks and copied them. In law, however, I shall treat the Romans first, because their law was much closer to what we take the law to be: a matter for professionals, based upon legislation but also upon a body of legal scholarship, with basic principles, constantly developing through interpretation and through new cases. Since classical Greek law was much less elaborate, and as such will be less familiar to us, I will leave it for the later part of the chapter.

THINKING LIKE A LAWYER

Some people claim that all human beings have in them a certain aspect of their psyche that thinks like a lawyer. Certainly children playing games develop very early a sense of rules that must be kept, and can get into very lawyerlike arguments over whether or not a certain action is valid if the proper words were not used, or if the action was performed in a way that seems incomplete or irregular. This mode of thinking pervaded the discourse of the Romans, and I will offer one example out of thousands.

Not all foreigners had *conubium*, the ability to contract a legitimate marriage with a Roman citizen. If a foreigner had such an ability and lived with a wife who was a Roman citizen, then, since the marriage was legitimate by Roman law, the status of the children followed that of their father, and they were foreigners as their father had been. But if he had no such right, the marriage was not legitimate, and the "law of the nations" applied: the children followed their mother's status, and they were Roman citizens.[1] That a child would be a non-citizen if the parents' marriage was legitimate but a citizen if it was not is peculiar, and it seemed odd to the Romans as well, who eventually corrected the situation and made the child a foreigner in any event; but if you cannot imagine how such a situation could ever have arisen, or why people would ever have behaved this way—if your reaction to the anomaly is something like "But that's just silly," and that undeniable fact seems to you to dismiss the matter— you are not thinking like a lawyer. To a lawyer the law is a set of principles that are real, that have a right interpretation and many possible wrong interpretations, a set of principles that can be manipulated, bent and reinterpreted, but must not be violated.

What turns a set of laws into a system of laws is the successive definitive working out of basic principles. Controversies that arise over the meaning of a law or of a principle are decided, and the decisions become binding in the future. By this method what started as a relatively straightforward list of rules becomes an enormously complicated list of headings and subheadings, details and details of details, that require years of study to master. When this happens, law becomes a matter for professionals; and the Romans, who were trained in law from childhood,[2] went further down this road than any other ancient people known to us, perhaps excepting the Jews.

THE SPECIALIZED VOCABULARY OF LAW

Every specialty has its own vocabulary, but the vocabulary of lawyers is particularly difficult for a number of reasons: it is highly developed, having had millennia in which to develop its specialized terms; it is very old, so that many of the terms are in dead or foreign languages, or bear meanings that are no longer current in our everyday speech; it speaks

---

[1]   Gaius I 78. The law that changed the matter was the *Lex Minicia*, near the beginning of the first century BCE.

[2]   Cic. *Leg.* 2.9.

about everyday matters, and so we often find the lawyers speaking about something we ourselves speak about, but using different terms; and some of its terms are still used in everyday speech—but with different meanings. It is not hard for us to understand that I may sell my neighbor the right to build a wall that will obstruct the view from my window; but if we had not learned Roman law we would never guess that I had sold my neighbor an *urban praedial servitude*. It is not obvious to a non-lawyer that I may not possess what I own: that if, for example, you grab my wallet, I still *own* it but you now *possess* it. It will no doubt seem even odder that, if I find you living on my land and evict you by force, you can bring an action to have me evicted without having to show that you own the land. This is called a *possessory interdict*, but that is only because we are dealing with Roman law; English law used the term *novel disseisin*, though the procedure is no longer in use. (In Roman law I can eventually get my land back by *vindicatio*.) When I speak of a *conveyance* I usually think of a bus or a train; but a lawyer who speaks of a *conveyance* means a legal act that transfers ownership of a thing.

This vocabulary, like every technical vocabulary, is designed not to obfuscate—though of course, like every technical vocabulary, it lends itself easily to that purpose—but on the contrary to make sure that our discussion proceeds in terms that are well defined and that we agree on their meanings. There is no way to speak meaningfully about Roman law without being clear about the difference between ownership and possession, and we cannot follow what is happening unless the distinction between a possessory interdict and *vindicatio* is kept clear. There are, then, no terms in which the law can be discussed except its own, and the beginner has no choice but to learn the vocabulary. But once you have learned it, you will have at your command the terms for much more precise thought and discussion; and many matters that you come across in Roman history and literature will take on a new and more interesting aspect.

THE PROGRESSIVE STABILIZATION AND ARTICULATION OF LAW

Difference of opinion makes horse races, and it makes law cases as well. No law can ever be free of ambiguity, nor can any law predict every new case that will some day arise. Questions arise about the meaning and the ramifications of a law, and different opinions are stated. Once a question has arisen, a court must decide what the proper answer is. The answer is always addressed to the case before the court; but the question may arise again, and if we want a person to be able to keep within the law, the person must know what a court is likely to decide if the question comes up again: we want, that is, a definitive answer, one that not only tells us who wins the case, but also tells us what interpretation of the law will henceforward be considered correct. In English law the definitive answers come about chiefly by way of judicial precedent: a decision, usually of a high court, is issued with a legal exposition of the reasoning behind it, and that reasoning itself becomes a part of the law. In Roman law, these definitive answers came about not by judicial precedent—a Roman court was composed of laymen, whose decision did not bind any future court—but by interpretations by professional jurists, and later by pronouncements of various kinds by the emperor enunciating or implementing particular interpretations of the existing law. By this method the law, like a tree, became more and more solid and fixed around its center, but developed more and more intricate branches as each question that was decided raised new questions, which in turn would themselves be decided, raising new questions, in a self-perpetuating cycle. The law became ever more detailed, ever clearer in its basic principles and ever more arcane in its details. This progressive articulation of the law continued throughout the classical period of Roman law, until it became too unwieldy even for its masters. In the post-classical period, the principles tended to become vague and were often dropped.

HOW LAW WAS MADE IN ROME

The Romans knew they had laws before they had written any of them down. The laws were the *mos maiorum*, ancestral custom that throughout the republican period was a stronger force than legislation in the shaping of law.

The first written laws of Rome were the Twelve Tables that were published—to give the traditional date—in 451–450 BCE; up to that time the laws were unwritten, and we can only guess at what their nature may have been. New laws could be made by the popular assemblies, the *comitia curiata* or the *comitia centuriata*, in both of which every male Roman citizen was a member but neither of which voted according to the principle of one man, one vote. From 287 BCE onward, *plebis scita*, that is, decisions of the *concilium plebis*, of which only plebeians were members, were also recognized as laws. Neither the *comitia* nor the *concilium plebis* could originate legislation; their role was limited to approving or rejecting laws proposed by magistrates (*comitia*) or tribunes (*concilium plebis*). Laws were generally known by the name of their proposer: the *Leges Liciniae Sextiae* of 367 BCE, for example, were proposed by the tribunes C. Licinius Stolo and L. Sextius Lateranus.

The senate could not make laws; it had originated in the days before the republic as an advisory body to the kings, and its decisions were always phrased as *senatus consulta*, "advice" of the senate to the magistrates; but when Sullan legislation required magistrates to abide by the "advice" of the senate, the decisions of the senate received in effect the force of law. Beyond the laws themselves, the opinions of *iurisconsulti*, legal experts who might be asked for their opinions on particular points of law, were of great weight, though it is not clear to what extent they actually bound anyone; commentaries on existing law also made a great difference in how the law was interpreted, and thus in how the law was implemented. But no less important than the *ius civile*, the Roman citizens' law as legislated by the people, advised by the senate and interpreted by the jurisconsults was the *ius honorarium*, the practical law made by the office-holders.

In practice every law depends upon the way it is carried out by the officials in charge, and the *ius civile* was supplemented by decisions of officials (chiefly the praetor) as to how the law would be implemented—specifically, what kinds of "actions" (in English law a layman would call them "suits," a lawyer "remedies") he would allow. From the *lex Aebutia* of about 125 BCE the law recognized the right of the praetor to allow new forms of actions for claims not covered by the existing forms. The incoming praetor would issue an edict announcing what sorts of actions he would grant, and from this arose a new form of law, the *ius honorarium*. In a particular lawsuit, the praetor would hold a preliminary hearing and would issue a "formula" to the judge: if the facts are such and such, you must find in favor of the plaintiff, but if they are otherwise you must find in favor of the defendant. The praetor thus became an effective source of law, as long as the formulaic system remained; and the praetor's edict, once dependent upon the decision of each praetor upon entering office, eventually became a permanent, standardized document.

In the imperial period, the pronouncements of the emperor (*constitutiones*) were recognized as having the force of law. These might be *edicta*, statements of how he intended to administer the law; *mandata*, orders to officials about how the law should be administered; *decreta*, judicial decisions that, by virtue of coming from the emperor, had a binding force not unlike that of precedent in English law; and *rescripta*, answers to questions of law that were put to the emperor by lower judges or petitioners.

By the time the Empire was centuries old, the law—particularly the law that was based upon the *constitutiones* of the emperors—was an imposing if incoherent mass; and to deal with this problem Theodosius II in 438 authorized a collection of the imperial constitutions since Constantine, a period of somewhat more than a hundred years. Much more significant than the Theodosian Code, however, was the work of Justinian, a number of collections published from 529 to 534. These works were collections of the existing law, but by imperial order they became the only authoritative statement of that law; all previous law was explicitly annulled. It was these works that constituted the basis of Roman law for the centuries that came after them, long after the Empire itself had ceased to function.

CORPUS IURIS CIVILIS[3]

The juristic work of Justinian is composed of four parts.

The *Institutions*, patterned after the earlier work by Gaius, is a general law-book putting forward the basic principles of the law in a systematic order—that is, it is an introductory textbook. Its divisions have come to be seen as the four basic parts of Roman private law: the law of persons (Book I), of things (Book II), of obligations (Book III) and of actions (that is, of legal remedies, Book IV). Public, criminal and penal law is not treated.

The *Codex* is a collection of imperial constitutions, the earliest cited being from Hadrian.

The *Digest* or *Pandects* are a collection of excerpts of the works of jurisconsults and commentators. By Justinian's edict, these, too, now became law—the exclusive law of the Empire, in fact: he forbade writing commentaries upon them or even referring to the original works from which the pandects were excerpted, to make sure that only the precise words of the pandects were accepted as law. This prohibition, unsurprisingly, was soon ignored.[4]

The *Novellae* were additional imperial constitutions issued after 534.

Justinian's collection was intended to be the final and authoritative statement of the law of an eternal empire; in fact it gained its authority precisely from the fact that the Latin empire had already collapsed, so that it was indeed the last word as far as the west was concerned.

---

3   This name for Justinian's collection is in fact modern; the ancient collection had no single title, but a separate title for each of its four parts.

4   If indeed it was ever meant to be a blanket prohibition: see Scheltema, "Das Kommentarverbot Justinians."

Unmentioned in the early Middle Ages, it was rediscovered in the late eleventh century, beginning a new legal tradition—a tradition that moderns call *civil law* (English law is called *common law*)—that was superseded only in the nineteenth and twentieth centuries, when most European states followed the lead of the *Code Napoléon* in replacing the ancient Roman sources with modern codes, largely (though not entirely) based upon the Roman law but, from the moment of their adoption on, independent of it. Today there are few states, most of them former Dutch colonies, where Roman law can still be cited in a courtroom.[5]

THE CONTENT OF THE LAW

To begin to describe the content of Roman law, even in outline, would go far beyond the confines of this chapter; for that the interested reader must pick up one of the introductory texts available, or search the web for a good outline. But a few well-known items may give something of the flavor:

- *Ius civile* and *ius gentium*: The Romans understood from the beginning that their own law was exceptional, differing in many basic aspects from the laws of other nations. The true Roman law applied only to Roman citizens, and was therefore called *ius civile*, "citizens' laws"; to other groups the Romans applied another set of laws: a set that they themselves had formulated, but that they considered to be the *ius gentium*, the law that applied to all other nationalities.
- *Res mancipi* and *res non mancipi*: How you transferred ownership depended upon what was being transferred. For certain types of property—slaves, beasts of burden, Italic land, and various sorts of partial rights over such land—merely delivering the item did not transfer ownership; one had to perform a ceremony called *mancipatio*, in which one person held bronze scales, five others witnessed, and in their presence the buyer or receiver grasped the object, made a statement, and struck the scales with a piece of bronze that was then passed to the seller or giver as payment.[6] These items were called *res mancipi*; the ownership of any other items (*res non mancipi*) could be transferred by simple delivery.

---

[5] Those states of which I know are San Marino, South Africa, Lesotho, Swaziland, Namibia, Zimbabwe, Indonesia and Sri Lanka.

[6] These items could also be transferred by *in iure cessio*, a fake judicial procedure in which the receiver claims the item and the grantor does not contest the claim, whereupon the judge decides in favor of the receiver.

- *Patria potestas and the emancipation of a son*: A Roman father had total power over his descendants: their property belonged to him, and in the early period he, rather than the courts, would judge them for their offenses, no matter what their age. In the archaic period he could also sell them into a sort of servitude; and although they would revert to him if freed, an ancient law deprived him of his power over a son whom he had sold into slavery three times. This law thereby became a device by which a man who so pleased could make his son an independent person: he would sell his son to a friend, who would immediately free him; and when this charade had been performed three times, the son was no longer under his father's power.

These three examples can give a slight flavor of the universal outlook of Roman law, which from the very beginning presumed to include law appropriate for every human being; of the attachment to formal acts that made Romans require five witnesses and bronze scales long after sales had become quite ordinary transactions paid for with coins; and of the willingness to use a legal form, once it existed, for a purpose for which it had never been intended. They are just a few examples of the ways in which the law worked. As one looks into the law in more detail, it becomes less alien, more understandable and, for a person who thinks like a lawyer, more interesting.

GREEK LAW

Since ancient Greece was never a single political entity, there was nothing in the classical period that could properly be called Greek law; each *polis* had its own law and its own forms of procedure. In the Hellenistic world, the expression "Greek law" applied to those principles of law by which the Greek and Macedonian subjects, as opposed to the natives, were governed. There were many principles that were common to Greeks everywhere, and it was presumably from these that the Hellenistic "Greek law" was derived.[7]

The classical law of Greece is known to us chiefly from the Athenian orators, that of the Hellenistic period from the papyri. We have sporadic knowledge of other Greek laws: the basic rules of Spartan education were

[7] On the appropriateness of the term see Gagarin, "The Unity of Greek Law."

much admired during the short period when Sparta dominated Greece, a large inscribed wall has maintained for us a large number of private laws from the Cretan city of Gortyn, and over a thousand manumissions inscribed on the stones of Delphi give us some picture of the laws of slavery and enfranchisement in north-western Greece. None of these, however, competes with the rich material from the main sources, and when scholars speak of "Greek law" they are usually speaking either of Athenian law of the classical period or of the Greek law of Ptolemaic Egypt. These laws are not entirely identical, though they are similar enough to allow a good deal of comparison. For neither Athens nor Egypt do we possess a law-book; our knowledge of the law comes from reading accounts of cases that appeared before courts, from the laws that are quoted in connection with those cases, and from various mentions here and there in literature, in inscriptions and in papyri.

THE ABSENCE OF PRECEDENT

A hallmark of the Athenian democracy was the *heliaea*, a court wherein a magistrate presided but decision rested with a group of a few hundred[8] citizens chosen by lot and voting by placing pebbles in an urn. Such a group could make no precedent, since it was not required to explain what its reason was for deciding the case as it did; nor was there any requirement that all of the judges agree upon the same argument. The judges were not necessarily ignorant or arbitrary; they were sworn to uphold the laws. But for their decision they simply dropped their pebble in whichever urn they considered right, and nobody could tell which reason persuaded them. Nor were there jurisconsults in the Roman sense, although there were Athenians better versed in the law than others. In the court itself each speaker could offer any explanation he wished of the law; the procedure allowed only for the text of the law itself and the text of whatever depositions witnesses might have given to be read out to the judges. What this meant was that no interpretation ever became authoritative: the hardening and articulation of law that happened in Rome never took place in Athens,

---

8   There were six thousand members of the *heliaea* (Ar. *Vesp.* 662, [Arist.] *Ath. Pol.* 24.3), but only one case is known when they all sat on a single case (Andoc. 1.17). Normally a case was judged by a few hundred judges; how many would depend, perhaps among other things, upon the seriousness of the offense (see [Arist.] *Ath. Pol.* 53.3).

and law in Athens remained, for the most part, a matter for the judgment of intelligent laymen.[9]

There is a consequence of this absence of authoritative interpretation that scholars sometimes forget: it is impossible to say what the "real" principles of Athenian law are. Only the words of the law were "real"; the opposing speakers could, and regularly did, offer opposing arguments as to what principle lay behind the law, and at no point did one argument become legally binding. The Athenians themselves recognized that the laws could not cover every case. They spoke not of *ius* ("the law") as the Romans did, but of *hoi nomoi*, "the laws"; and the judges' oath included the provision that, where there was no applicable law, they would apply the most honest principle.[10] This does not mean that the laws were meaningless; the judges presumably took seriously their oath to judge according to the laws. But it does mean that, although we can speculate (as the Athenians did) about the reason why a law was first passed, we can never truly enunciate as a principle of Athenian law anything that was not explicitly written in a statute.[11] This can be very frustrating to a person who thinks like a lawyer; every law is as flexible as a persuasive speaker can make it, or as rigid as a lay citizen may want to take it.

GREEK LAW AND GREEK SOCIETY

For all that, we can observe some general trends running through Greek law. Constitutional authority, in the classical period, belonged to the people; although it was not necessarily clear which people (oligarchies held that only those who expended their resources on the state had a right to manage it, whereas democracies were more inclusive), even tyrants derived their power from the real or pretended good will of the people, not from the gods or from custom immemorial, however weighty

---

[9]　See the comment of MacDowell, *The Law in Classical Athens*, 9: "By profession I am a classicist, not a lawyer, and any lawyers who read this book may find my discussion of law unsophisticated. But I do not regard this as a serious handicap, since the Athenians themselves were not professional law-makers and had no knowledge of Roman or modern jurisprudence."

[10]　This observation was made by Sealey, *The Justice of the Greeks*, 51–8.

[11]　It was illegal to judge on the basis of an unwritten law (Andoc. 1.85); but this term applied to alleged laws of the state that were not included in the official archive. The Athenians recognized divine law and social convention as a form of "unwritten law": see MacDowell's commentary on the Andocides passage, and see Harris, "Antigone the Lawyer."

considerations of religion and custom might be in determining the law itself. The family was the basic unit, consisting of a man, a woman, an ox[12] or a slave to provide for them, and eventually their children; the man was the head of the family, but in no case was his authority as absolute as that of a Roman *paterfamilias*. All male children inherited equally; if there were only daughters, they married the deceased's next of kin, and the children thus produced inherited the estate. These principles worked out differently in different places, and it is quite likely that the same phenomenon was understood to embody one principle in one *polis* and an entirely different principle elsewhere.

Because of the relative paucity of sources and the uncertainty about legal principles, the study of Greek law goes hand in hand with the study of Greek society. The principles that the law embodied were presumably those of the society at large; and only by understanding the underlying sociology can we understand the law itself.

Hellenistic Greek law did not have the same democratic, almost revolutionary spirit that pervaded the Athenian *heliaea*; but as here, too, we have no law codes, our knowledge comes from the myriad legal and commercial documents that we find in papyri. Athenian law provides a background, but is not necessarily the same: in Athens, for example, a marriage was contracted between the groom and the father (or other male relative) of the bride, whereas in Egypt the bride might be given away by her mother, by both parents or even, in rare cases, by herself.[13] From Egypt we have many marital agreements, a document unknown for classical Athens. The laws governing commerce were not the same. Most intriguingly, we can still look forward to much new legal information from Egypt as papyri continue to be published; but the legal sources for Athenian law remain pretty much the same today as they were two hundred years ago.

MAJOR RESOURCES

We have no legal textbooks from ancient Greece; such laws as we know are gleaned chiefly from the orators, from inscriptions and from papyri.

---

[12] Hes. *Works and Days*, 405 as interpreted by Aristotle, *Politics*, 1252b 10–12, who explains that the ox was the poor man's slave. In our text of Hesiod, line 406 makes it clear that his basic household consists of a man, a female slave and an ox. Which text Hesiod wrote is debatable; see West ad loc. Neither Hesiod nor Aristotle, apparently, considers the children an essential part of the minimal family.

[13] Yiftach-Firanko, *Marriage and Marital Arrangements*, 43–4.

Woefully out of date are Beauchet, *Histoire du droit privé de la république athénienne* and Lipsius, *Das attische Recht und Rechtsverfahren*, but only one attempt has been made since then to produce a comprehensive account of Athenian law, and Harrison (*The Law of Athens*) died before completing the work. Much more useful as an introduction to the subject are MacDowell, *The Law in Classical Athens* and Todd, *The Shape of Athenian Law*, but they make no effort to explore the law in all of its details. An excellent introduction to the major issues as they are now being addressed is Gagarin and Cohen, *The Cambridge Companion to Ancient Greek Law*. Wolf, *Griechisches Rechtsdenken* is not properly a book about law at all, but a book about how the various Greek writers, from Homer and Hesiod to Plato, thought about law; Triantaphyllopoulos, *Das Rechtsdenken der Griechen* gives a more recent account, extremely concise but clear and well documented (its endnotes are nine times as long as the text).

The law of Hellenistic Egypt,[14] as revealed in the papyri, has received its most thorough treatment for now in Taubenschlag, *The Law of Greco-Roman Egypt*; the two volumes of Erwin Seidl, *Ptolemäische Rechtsgeschichte* and *Rechtsgeschichte Ägyptens als römischer Provinz*, are also helpful, though even they are by no means up to date. Of major importance are the two volumes of Hans Julius Wolff, *Das Recht der griechischen Papyri*.

The original textbook of Roman law, from which almost all subsequent textbooks are derived, is Gaius, *Institutiones*. Of this two major editions exist: Seckel and Kuebler, *Gaius: Institutiones* and Krueger and Studemund, *Gai Institutiones*; the latter is older but more complete in its coverage of textual matters. From each respectively an English translation has been prepared, the more readable Gordon and Robinson, *The Institutes of Gaius* and the more precise de Zulueta, *The Institutes of Gaius*. The Theodosian Code was edited by Mommsen and Meyer, *Theodosiani Libri xvi* and translated into English by Pharr, Davidson and Pharr, *The Theodosian Code and Novels*. The legal collections of Justinian were edited by Mommsen et al., *Corpus Iuris Civilis*. A translation of the *Digest* is available in Watson, *The Digest of Justinian*; Watson's earlier edition, Mommsen, Krueger and Watson, *The Digest of Justinian*, contains the Latin text as well. The earlier translation by Scott, *The Civil Law*, though covering all of Justinian (and much else), is not reliable. There is a collection of earlier sources of law in Riccobono et al., *FIRA*, which completely supersedes the earlier Karl Georg Bruns, Mommsen and Gradenwitz, *Fontes*

---

[14] Egypt is not the only area for which we have papyrological evidence—see, for example, Katzoff and Schaps, eds., *Law in the Documents of the Judaean Desert*—but it dominates the world of juristic papyrology even more than Athens dominates the world of classical Greek law.

Iuris Romani Antiqui. For the early jurisconsults we have Bremer, *Iurisprudentia Antehadriana* and collections of legislation in M. H. Crawford, *Roman Statutes* and Elster, *Die Gesetze der mittleren römischen Republik*. Much of this material, including the entire *Corpus Iuris Civilis*, both in Latin and in translation, is available on the internet, generally in older editions; the excellent site *Roman Law Library* is a good place to start any search, though the English translation of Justinian is Scott's.

The chief comprehensive textbook in English is still Buckland, *A Text-Book of Roman Law*. Less comprehensive, with both the advantages and disadvantages of greater concision, is Thomas, *Textbook of Roman Law*, and even simpler (and more user-friendly for the non-classicist) is Borkowski and Plessis, *Textbook on Roman Law*; but if a person trained in law is to read only one book about Roman law, that book should be Nicholas, *An Introduction to Roman Law*.[15]

There are also important studies of various sections of the law: Kaser, *Das römische Privatrecht* (translated into English as Kaser, *Roman Private Law*, if you can get a copy); Kaser and Hackl, *Das römische Zivilprozessrecht*; Zimmermann, *The Law of Obligations* (written for law students, with an eye to showing Roman law's relation to civil and common law); and for the law of the very early classical period, Watson, *The Law of Persons* and Watson, *The Law of Succession*, to name a few. The most original and insightful work on Roman law in the English language in recent decades was that of David Daube. His more specialized articles, mostly in English, some in German, are in *Collected Studies*.

On the history of the law, the basic book in English is Jolowicz and Nicholas, *Historical Introduction to the Study of Roman Law*, and much briefer, Robinson, *The Sources of Roman Law*. In German there are many famous studies, of which a relatively recent one is Wieacker, *Römische Rechtsgeschichte*.

For classicists wanting to know more about Roman law in its historical and social setting the book to read is Crook, *Law and Life of Rome*. Once Crook has whetted your appetite, you will probably be interested in Daube, *Roman Law*, a series of lectures addressed to classicists not specialists in Roman law. The most useful aid to decoding technical vocabulary is Berger, *Encyclopedic Dictionary of Roman Law*.

The later development of Roman law, which was revived in the eleventh century and remained the basic law of most of continental Europe until the nineteenth, is traced in outline in Watkin, *An Historical Introduction to*

---

[15] Ernest Metzger has now published a revised edition (Nicholas and Metzger, *An Introduction to Roman Law*), which I have not seen.

Modern Civil Law; Zimmermann, *Roman Law, Contemporary Law, European Law* discusses its continued development in modern European law. A much briefer account, from the Twelve Tables to the European Community in 132 pages, is Stein, *Roman Law in European History*.

26

SOCIOLOGY, ANTHROPOLOGY, ECONOMICS AND PSYCHOLOGY

THE CLASSICS AND THE SOCIAL SCIENCES

In the nineteenth century, the Greek and Roman classics were an important part of all scholars' backgrounds, even of those who chose to study other fields. Karl Marx's doctoral thesis was entitled *The Difference between the Democritean and Epicurean Philosophy of Nature*;[1] Max Weber, on his thirteenth birthday, presented his parents with two original essays, one of which was entitled "About the Roman Imperial Period from Constantine to the Migration of Nations,"[2] and his *Habilitationsschrift*—the post-doctoral work required of a German who aspires to a university position—was entitled *Roman Agrarian History and Its Significance for Public and Private Law*. David Hume wrote that, although he studied law, and his family "fancyed I was poring over Voet and Vinnius, Cicero and Vergil were the Authors which I was secretly devouring."[3] In those days, the pioneers of the young sciences whose names are the title of this chapter applied their knowledge of classical antiquity to their work, and applied their own work to the understanding of classical antiquity. The study of Roman agrarian history was not qualitatively different from the study of German agrarian history:

[1] Marx and Engels, *Collected Works*, I, 25–105.
[2] Told by his widow in Weber, *Max Weber: A Biography*, 45.
[3] David Hume, *My Own Life*, published as Appendix A of Mossner, *The Life of David Hume*, p. 611.

both were a matter of careful reading and analysis of what could be gleaned from the literature of the various ages.

In the twentieth century, each of the social sciences developed its own methodology and its own vocabulary. Few of the great social scientists of the twentieth century were well grounded in the classics, and the methodologies and theories developed were not easily applicable to the ancient world. Modern sociology is based upon studies of various strata, classes and groups in society; our ancient sources are overwhelmingly from a single group, elite males. Modern anthropology is based, where possible, upon protracted residence among the natives of the societies studied and interviews with them; we cannot live among the ancient Romans or ask them questions. Modern economics is based upon statistics, but the ancients left us almost no statistics, nor did they leave us the raw material from which we might compose our own. Modern psychology is based upon experimentation or psychoanalysis; we can do neither to the ancients. Unable to apply the accepted methodologies of the social sciences, most classicists continue to use the philological method that has served them well over the generations, and deal with the questions of social relationships within the framework available.

But classicists have not remained oblivious of what is going on in the social sciences. Partly because of the increased prestige of the social sciences themselves and partly through the influence of the American tradition of liberal education that exposes every student to a variety of disciplines, many classicists have adapted methodologies and theories developed in other fields to the study of the ancient world. Indeed, once a person has been exposed to the concepts of other fields, it is hard not to ask similar questions about the ancient world. Ferdinand Tönnies, one of the fathers of modern sociology, distinguished between *Gemeinschaft*, a "community" whose members generally give precedence to the goals of the community as a whole, and *Gesellschaft*, "society," whose members give precedence to their individual self-interest but structure their relationships in such a way that they can cooperate efficiently while doing so.[4] Each of these is a theoretical type, and any historical society partakes to a certain amount of both; but which of the two most nearly describes archaic Sparta? Classical Athens? Early republican Rome? Late republican Rome? The answers are complicated, but thinking in these terms can help clarify the issues involved.

---

[4] Tönnies, *Community and Civil Society* (the book *Gemeinschaft und Gesellschaft* was originally published in 1887).

Questions like this arise in every one of the social sciences. An anthropologist cannot discuss Athenian men parading with *phalloi* or the young Romans who ran almost naked on the Lupercalia, striking bystanders (and particularly women) with goatskin straps, without comparing it to the fertility rites of cultures separated from the ancients by thousands of years and thousands of miles. An economist cannot help but ask to what extent ancient Athens or ancient Rome was a capitalist economy. A psychoanalyst cannot read the comedies of Plautus and Terence without seeing Oedipal elements in the relationship of the *adulescens* to the *senex*. All of us approach classical texts from the point of view of our own experience and our own interests, but when a person's approach is informed by professional expertise it may put these texts in a new light whose significance goes beyond that of a mere personal reading.

The meeting of the social sciences and the classics can take different forms. The simplest is the study that applies a social-scientific theory to a classical subject: a Marxist reading of Thucydides, a feminist reading of Ovid, or such. This kind of study is by no means useless; since most classicists are well read in the classics but not in the social sciences, a study like this can expose the classical world to important work that has been done in other fields. It is, however, unlikely to advance the other field: insofar as it takes the given theory for granted, it will generally do no more than to show how the classical subject studied can be understood in terms of the theory.

In fact, however, when you choose to write a study like this, you are not merely "applying" the theory; you are testing it. Perhaps, indeed, Marxist theory provides invaluable insights for understanding Thucydides; but it is also possible that Thucydides may offer insights that challenge or revise some of Marx's ideas. The best kind of interdisciplinary study keeps an open mind towards both the evidence and the theory, and so gives the opportunity of deepening our understanding of both.

While classicists are debating a topic, however, social scientists do not stand still. Often classicists find themselves debating a theory that has been superseded or deeply modified since the classicists first discovered it—and the classicists themselves are unaware of the newest development. This book, I am sure, is not free of such problems, but that does not mean that yours cannot be. It is worth taking the time—if your professional masters will allow you to—to familiarize yourself with the newest professional literature in the broader field with which you are working before coming to apply it to a classical subject.

For whom, in fact, are you writing? Most people who write about the ancient world write for classicists. Classicists, for one thing, are familiar with the information on which their studies are based; for another, a subject like "the sociology of ancient Rome" is likely to seem central to a classicist and peripheral to a sociologist. For this reason, classicists generally import from the social sciences more than they export to them. This is understandable, but unfortunate: if our subject has insights worth knowing, they are probably worth knowing in the modern world no less than the ancient. But since our methodologies will necessarily differ from the methodologies of those studying more modern societies, it will always be necessary to be very clear about the justification of our methodological basis if we hope to have an influence on social scientists in general.

SOCIOLOGY

The social structure of the ancient world has been a matter of interest to classicists for as long as the science of sociology has existed. In 1864, when the word *sociology* was still a rare neologism,[5] Numa Denis Fustel de Coulanges published his famous study on the importance of religion and social institutions in accounting for the growth and structure of the ancient city-state.[6] The various institutions that intrigue sociologists in other societies are popular subjects for research in the classics. To give just a taste of the sorts of things that have intrigued scholars:

- *The family*, including both the nuclear family (*oikos, familia*) and the extended "family" (*genos, gens*); included in this are many matters peculiar to the ancient world, such as the power of the Greek *kyrios* and the much more extensive power of the Roman *paterfamilias*; the living arrangements in Greek and Roman houses; the place of men, women, adolescents, children and slaves within the family; political connections among families; the inheritance both of property and of family connections; relationships among in-laws.
- *Marriage*, in terms of both how marriages were contracted and how the affairs of married couples were arranged; what constituted legitimate

---

[5] "The new science of sociology, as it is barbarously termed": OED[2] s.v. sociology, from *Fraser's Magazine* 44 (1851), p. 452. The "barbarism" involved in the mixture of the Latin *societas* with the Greek *logos* is the sort of thing to which moderns, and even classicists, have long since become inured. Fustel de Coulanges himself was a historian, not a sociologist; the first university department of sociology was established at the University of Kansas in 1890.

[6] Fustel de Coulanges, *The Ancient City*.

marriage in Greece and in Rome; by whom, with whom and for what reasons marriages were contracted; dissolution of marriage, by whom it could be initiated, and what its consequences were for each party and for their children; management of the property of a married couple; who provided and who controlled the dowry; the various forms of marriage available in Roman law; liaisons outside of or in violation of formal marriage.

- *Gender*: once this meant "the role of women," but it is now generally recognized that the role of a Greek or Roman man was also circumscribed (as, for that matter, is the role of a modern man) by gender-determined expectations; and beyond the obvious fact of the heavily patriarchal structure of both Greek and Roman society, increasing attention has been paid to how men and women negotiated their own status within that structure.
- *Social status*: aristocracy and masses in Greece; patricians and plebeians, *nobiles* and *plebs* in Rome; the institution of *clientela* that pervaded Roman society; legal and political effects of status distinctions; the status of household slaves, of "industrial" slaves and of former slaves; foreigners and resident non-citizens; the role of the army in society, and the social status and rights of soldiers.
- *Social organizations*: tribes, phratries and *genē*; *hetairiai* and *orgeōnes*; professional organizations (there were such, at least in the Hellenistic and Roman periods) and organizations of charity and of mutual assistance.
- *Ethnicity*: ethnic self-definition and definition by others; language, religion and genealogy as ethnic determinants; ethnic pride and ethnic prejudice; ethnic loyalty versus political loyalty; ethnic divisions and subdivisions.
- *Demography*: life expectancy; population estimates (the sources are never full enough for us to speak of "population figures"); distribution by age, by gender, and by wealth; distribution between rural and urban environments.
- *Religion*, with which we dealt in Chapter 24.

Under each of these headings, and many others that might have been offered, the society of the Greeks and the Romans had its own aspects, many of them fundamentally different from our own and of interest both to students of other areas of the classics and to students of sociology. When you read a Roman love elegy and the poet describes flirting with his married girl-friend, what family expectations lay behind that? What was likely to happen to him, or to her, if they were discovered? What kinds of social interaction with another man's wife were legitimate? How much of a difference did it make if the lover was married: when a poet seems to ignore the matter, does that mean that he is assuming the *persona* of a bachelor, or that the man's marital status didn't make much difference? How common is it, and how significant, for this kind of literature to flourish precisely under a ruler who promulgated legislation designed to foster what we should call family values?

Modern sociology relies heavily upon statistical methods that are rarely if ever practical in dealing with the ancient world. Statistics, to be useful, have to be based on a sufficiently large sampling of comparable pieces of information. A modern sociologist can count the number of marriages in a group and count how many of them end in divorce; can interview divorced and non-divorced couples, asking each the same questions, to try to find the differences; and can investigate archives to find the legal reasons alleged for divorce at various periods. On the basis of any of these, the researcher will be able to compile statistics that can suggest, corroborate or disprove theories about marriage and divorce in the group in question. A classicist has none of these tools at hand. Even such a simple source as a regularly maintained registry of marriages is not available to us from any ancient city. The sociological description of the ancient world is necessarily more impressionistic and less numerically based than similar descriptions of modern societies. But we are not entirely without resources. Besides such information as can be gleaned from the literature—and there is a good deal that can be gleaned, particularly when we venture beyond the canon of "great authors" to explore works of small inherent interest that nevertheless preserve information that the greater authors may not have mentioned—papyrology has revealed personal letters of the ancients, and not only of the elite; rescripts of Roman emperors and opinions of jurists often preserve information that illuminates details of personal relationships; archaeology shows us the physical environment in which people lived, and which left its imprint upon their social relationships. Most of the field-work of the ancient sociologist will generally take place within a library; but that does not mean that there is no field-work to do.

ANTHROPOLOGY

Anthropology deals particularly with comparisons among societies and establishing typologies that help us understand what sorts of societies human beings inhabit. Some of the application of anthropological theory to the classics is simply a matter of adopting theories and concepts developed elsewhere and applying them to the ancient world: Was ancient Greece at any point more of a shame-culture than a guilt-culture? If so, did that change, and when, and why? Can early Roman religion be considered animist, a form of belief that endows inanimate objects with souls that can be hostile or benevolent? Are gladiatorial spectacles comparable to blood-sports in other societies, to bullfighting, to cockfighting, or to public executions? Are they comparable to our own athletic competitions? If so, in what sense, and in what way was the Roman institution different?

There is a certain amount of anthropology that we can do on our own. For one thing, the ancient world held many societies besides those of ancient Athens and ancient Rome. The Greeks were organized into many different *poleis*, and many Greeks were not organized into *poleis* at all; and they lived among other nations—Pelasgians, Carians, Lydians, Phoenicians, Persians—with whom they interacted, and about whom we can collect information both from the writings of the Greeks and from the archaeological and epigraphical remnants of those nations. The early Romans had dealings with Oscans, Umbrians, Samnites, Gauls and the perennially fascinating Etruscans, and their descendants met and conquered peoples from the outlandish Britons to the swarthy Moors and Indians. Both the Greeks and the Romans produced ethnographic literature that can be seen as a sort of proto-anthropology. Of all of these people we have only spotty and generally anecdotal evidence, but the very breadth of scale, the large variety of nations with whom the ancient Greeks and Romans came into contact, opens up the opportunity of seeing them in the context of their own times, two particularly successful societies among many competitors, offering two particular forms of society from among many alternatives.

Lastly, the approach of applying anthropological insights to the ancient world can be turned on its head. The Greeks and the Romans were exceptionally aware of the fact that there were many possible forms of law, of custom and of government. They discussed, and often changed, their own ways of doing things; and they were very open about the considerations that led them to do so. We can often understand the ancient Greeks and Romans at least as well as a modern anthropologist can understand the people among whom a field-worker has spent a few months or a few years; in particular, we have the advantage of being able to observe them talking to each other, without the consciousness of our presence. Just as we can use the insights of the anthropologists to illuminate the ancient world, we can use our own insights from the ancient world to illuminate other societies, both the modern and the less modern.

This will no longer be what it once was, a matter of classically educated westerners seeing all other societies as if they were necessarily passing through the same stages that the Greeks and the Romans did; but it is probably a mistake to presume that the societies we study are any less revealing of human nature and human culture than the societies that concern more traditional anthropologists.

ECONOMICS

Modern economics is such a statistic-laden field that it may seem hard to imagine how it can be applied to the ancient world. Apparently it is indeed hard to imagine, at least for those economic historians who begin their economic histories of Europe in the medieval or early modern periods. But of course people in the ancient world faced the basic problems with which economics deals: they had to provide food, clothing and shelter for themselves, and they had to have some mechanism for determining or distributing rights to what they owned or produced. Although the ancient authors in general did not consider the gaining of one's livelihood a proper study for literature, enough information found its way into their books to give us a good basic understanding of ancient farming and production methods, of market trade and interstate commerce, of credit and banking. Epigraphy has made significant contributions to the picture, and papyrology much more. Even without statistics, there is a good deal of interest in the ancient economy.

But in fact the lack of statistics is not as complete as all that. The Zenon papyri give us considerable information about the way estates were managed in Ptolemaic Egypt, and the expenses involved. A number of significant temples inscribed on stone the expenses of particular construction projects, or even—in the case of Delos—simply the annual expenses of the temple managers. The emperor Diocletian promulgated an edict specifying the maximum price permitted for each commodity; whether or not the edict was ever really observed (scholarly opinion differs on the matter), it shows a good deal of information about prices of commodities relative to each other. Roman census reports from Egypt can allow us a reasonable picture of how family composition differed over the years; somewhat less reliable as a source of statistics are counts of tombstones, since only certain people in certain circumstances inscribed tombstones. All of these sources have to be used with a good deal of caution: none of them preserves a totally objective record of the information it is passing on, and each of them offers information peculiar to the circumstances of the institution, state or individual that ordered it or compiled it. But when due caution has been exercised, there is no reason why we should not make use of the information we have; and as of this writing scholars have barely begun to tease out of it all the information that is there to be gotten.

For many years the greatest controversy in ancient economics was the question of the "modernity" or "primitiveness" of the ancient economy: whether the commerce and industry that undoubtedly existed in ancient Athens and Rome were an essential driving force in an economy that was in general terms comparable to the modern one, though on a smaller scale, or whether the societies over which Athens and Rome presided were essentially peasant agricultural societies, with a certain amount of commerce and industry that was more visible for being centered in the cities and dealing with elite customers but still almost negligible in the larger scheme. The disagreement began in the early twentieth century[7] and continued for at least two generations; although more recent scholars urge us to put the argument behind us, the question of how far modern economic theory offers an appropriate instrument for understanding the ancient world remains basic to the approach we take to it.

PSYCHOLOGY

Unlike sociology, anthropology and economics, psychology has hitherto had little effect on studies of the society and history of the ancients. Most psychological research and theory deals with the workings of an individual's mind; since one person's thoughts are not available to another except insofar, and in such a manner, as the thinker chooses to make them so, it is hard enough to gain access to a living person's thoughts, much less those of a person dead for millennia. The question, moreover, of how much any individual determines society or history is a subject of considerable contention, so that psychological explanations of famous people must compete with theories according to which those people's behavior and achievements were largely determined by factors other than their own personal psyche. There have been provocative psychologically based studies of ancient figures, but at least so far it has not been in the description of ancient history that psychology has made its mark.

In the understanding of literature, however, a certain amount of psychology can hardly be avoided. How can one discuss Euripides' *Bacchae*

---

[7]   Finley, ed., Bücher–Meyer.

or *Orestes*, or Aeschylus' *Libation Bearers*, in which the central characters are driven to insanity, without some attention to psychology? Vergil explains Dido's infatuation with Aeneas, and Aeneas' abandonment of her, by divine intervention; is there really no psychology active here? Were that the case, the epic would be much less intriguing than it is. This does not mean that one must read Freud or Lacan or the every-increasing literature of neuropsychology before reading Euripides or Vergil; most classicists who write about these works are not well read in modern psychology. Nevertheless, they do, and must, use their own understandings of the workings of the mind in order to explain what is happening; and it is obvious that a more informed understanding of human psychology can have something to contribute to the analysis of works like these.

Even deeper is the relationship between ancient mythology and psychology, a relationship that goes in both directions. If the subconscious mind of individual Greeks and Romans is only dimly available to us, the communal fantasy world is an open book, described in fascinating detail in scores of ancient texts and at least mentioned in almost every one. It is precisely because we do not believe these stories literally that they are so revealing to us about the ancient mind; our own myths, insofar as we believe in them, are less revealing, since our beliefs may be based on real perceptions or historical facts, and are in any event harder for us ourselves to distinguish from our perceptions of the real world. Ancient mythology has offered a fertile field for psychological speculation, and psychology in its turn has offered a good deal of theoretical basis for understanding ancient myths. There is, however, a serious stumbling-block: much more than the other social sciences, psychology is divided into competing schools, none of which has succeeded in building a base of evidence sufficient to convince the others. A person attempting a psychological explanation of a myth—or, for that matter, of a literary work—will generally have to decide which psychological theory to follow before much progress can be made.

The Greeks and Romans had their own theories of psychology, and, although the relevant works are generally subsumed under the headings of philosophy or medicine, it is here that the beginnings of western psychological speculation are to be found. Ancient psychology is of interest not only for the light it sheds on the way the ancients themselves perceived the world and themselves, but also because it reflected phenomena that are still imperfectly understood, and continued to influence psychological thought (and thereby also religious thought) throughout the Middle Ages and the early modern period. Modern experimentalism, which seems to be increasingly successful in connecting psychological states with physical states of the brain and the hormonal system, promises to build up a new basic structuring of psychological phenomena that will be as unconnected with ancient psychology as modern physics is with ancient physics. So far that promise is only partially fulfilled, and it remains to be seen whether, in the coming decades, ancient psychology will continue to offer illuminating insights into the human mind.

MAJOR RESOURCES

The major resources of sociology, anthropology, economics and psychology are not to be found on the shelves of classical seminar libraries. All of these disciplines are founded upon large and ever increasing bodies of data in which the ancient world plays little if any part; no classical librarian can allow the expense of a complete and constantly updated collection of books and articles on domestic violence, initiation rites, monetary theory and schizophrenia. The best I can offer is a sampling of important works involving the intersection of these fields with the classical world, with a repetition of the warning already given that the relevant fields have continued to change since these works were produced. If your knowledge of other fields is derived from earlier classicists you run the danger of discovering that the concepts underlying your work are outmoded or even discredited.

The people who introduced anthropology to the classics were the Cambridge ritualists;[8] their work was based on an evolutionist view that saw all societies as passing through similar stages from primitivism to civilization, and, because that view is no longer held, their most important works (Frazer, *The Golden Bough* and Harrison, *Themis*) are rarely cited by classicists today. A better idea of the intersection of anthropology and classics can be had from Humphreys, *Anthropology and the Greeks* or from the more recent but more polemical Detienne, *The Greeks and Us*. The first real classical sociologist was Louis Gernet, a student of the great sociologist Émile Durkheim. Gernet's *Droit et société* and the articles in *The Anthropology of Ancient Greece* can still be read with profit. The French have maintained a strong interest in the sociological and anthropological study of the ancient world, and Gernet's student Jean-Pierre Vernant (a hero of the *Résistance* before he began his academic career) and his colleagues Pierre Vidal-Naquet, Nicole Loraux and Marcel Detienne have been among

---

[8] On whom see above, p. 319.

the most influential writers on ancient society, extending the investigation from the social institutions of the society to "mentalities"—how the society conceived the terms in which it thought of itself, and how those terms arose from within the society and influenced its later development. In the English language it was Moses Finley, who had worked in his early years with the great anthropologist Franz Boas, who introduced socio-logical analysis to the discussion of ancient history with his seminal work *The World of Odysseus*. Finley's thesis—that the society described in the Homeric poems, although he does not consider it a reflection of Mycenaean society, is a consistent one from a sociological viewpoint—placed the question of how a society's institutions relate to each other in the foreground of an entire generation of ancient historians; and as social institutions have increasingly taken pride of place in discussions of ancient history[9] and the broadening of archaeology has increasingly required classical archaeologists to become familiar with a wide spectrum of societies,[10] the study of the Greco-Roman institutions both in their own right and in the light of other societies has moved from the periphery to the mainstream of classical research.

Two great surveys, Rostovtzeff's *Social and Economic History of the Hellenistic World* and Tenney Frank's *An Economic Survey of Ancient Rome*, seemed to form the basis for a comprehensive economic history of antiquity, but it was Finley who put the study of ancient economics on an institutional footing, examining the economy not in the terms used by modern economists but in terms that he took to be appropriate to the ancient world (Masters/ Slaves, Town/Country and such). His *The Ancient Economy*, adopting an essentially primitivist viewpoint, became the basis for the studies of a generation of scholars and is now becoming increasingly the target for new studies that have in some respects broadened enormously and in other respects undermined his discussion. In addition to opening up new areas of investigation such as ecology,[11] demography and gender, newer studies have assimilated a good deal of information, much of it originating in archaeology and in epigraphy,[12] into the economic picture.

---

[9] See above, p. 169.

[10] See above, pp. 177–9.

[11] Here the seminal work was Sallares, *The Ecology of the Ancient Greek World*. For demography and for gender in economics it is not possible to point to a single all-encompassing work; on demography the studies have been numerous, on gender numberless.

[12] Papyrology, on the other hand, had been mined as a source of economic information since its beginnings, and well before Finley much of our picture of ancient economic practice was based on papyri.

A good place to start for the current state of scholarship is Scheidel, Morris and Saller, *Cambridge Economic History*.

For all of the subjects mentioned above—anthropology, sociology and economics—Horden and Purcell, *The Corrupting Sea* has changed the terms of the debate by raising the view of a general Mediterranean society whose peoples all shared certain characteristics and certain problems by virtue of the sea that both divided and connected them and by virtue of their continuous interaction with each other. A new field of Mediterranean studies has grown up, offering a new and challenging viewpoint on Greco-Roman society and institutions.

The effect of psychology on classics is less easy to define. Plato, Aristotle, Cicero and Augustine all discussed the soul in considerable depth and detail. Their opinions continue to be discussed by classical scholars, and recent works have investigated their influence on modern psychological theories.[13] Feminism in particular has encouraged engagement with psychological theory, an engagement that is generally antagonistic.[14] Occasionally authors whose background is in psychology have contributed illuminating insights.[15] But at least as of now one cannot really speak of a subfield of ancient psychology as we speak of ancient sociology or ancient economics.

---

[13] Leonard, *Athens in Paris*; Miller, *Postmodern Spiritual Practices*.

[14] See du Bois, *Sowing the Body*.

[15] Slater, *The Glory of Hera* was generally ignored by classicists, who considered the author's treatment of his sources to be too unsophisticated to be useful; the less ambitious Shay, *Achilles in Vietnam* was generally welcomed as providing real insights that stemmed from the author's clinical practice.

PART VII

THE CLASSICS SINCE ANTIQUITY

27

THE CLASSICAL TRADITION AND CLASSICAL RECEPTION

THE CLASSICAL TRADITION AS A SUBJECT OF STUDY

The appearance of a cultural phenomenon as a subject for university study is not necessarily a good sign. Sometimes it is a sign that the phenomenon itself has become so alien that people who in a different time or place would have absorbed it from their parents, their environment or their school teachers must be taught it in a classroom. This is what happened with the classical tradition, a subject that appeared in university syllabi around the middle of the twentieth century. Earlier generations of students, who had learned Caesar, Horace and Vergil (at least) in school, would recognize on their own many classical allusions, forms and imitations, and would recognize many more if they were pointed out. That Shakespeare drew on Plutarch for his knowledge of Julius Caesar was of interest to students of Shakespeare, but not particularly to students of Plutarch.

When the Greek and Latin classics lost their dominant position in school curricula, many students who knew Dante or Milton might not know Vergil, and many who knew Shakespeare and Racine might not know Euripides. Classics teachers, once secure in the knowledge that their subject was basic to any study of literature, began to be interested in teaching about the classical tradition, to show the new generation how much of the vernacular literature that they knew came about by a reshaping and reworking of the old. In many places courses on the classical tradition were simply survey courses for undergraduates intended to show the importance and continuing vitality of the classics: scratch Goethe or Shelley, or for that matter Anouilh or T. S. Eliot, and you find that the Greeks and Romans have not really been as dead for two thousand years as you might have thought. But along with the general surveys came a good deal of interesting scholarship as people traced the way various classical works, genres, themes and stories had been dealt with through the ages.

STUDIES OF THE AFTERLIFE OF A SINGLE AUTHOR OR WORK

One approach to reception studies is to take a single author, work or character and follow what the Germans call the *Nachleben*, the "afterlife." One may follow Odysseus from the Odyssey's brave trickster to the careful but eventually noble Odysseus of Sophocles' *Aias*, the mean trickster of the same author's *Philoctetes*, the evil genius of the Aeneid, the mad adventurer of Dante's *Inferno* who sails out beyond Gibraltar to an unknown, limitless sea where he dies, down to James Joyce's Leopold Bloom and further. Each new Odysseus/Ulysses reflects the earlier ones, determines the later ones, and the examination itself will almost always show you new sides of Homer's Odysseus that you may not have seen yourself. Who gets included in a survey like this may also require some thought, for many characters who are not directly modeled upon Odysseus incorporate some of his traits: the Aeneid presents Ulysses himself as the evil genius who doomed Troy, but his presence is much more pervasive in Aeneas, who follows journeys that parallel those of Ulysses through the first six books. A history of the *Nachleben* of Medea may be a history of retellings of the myth itself, or a history of murderous mothers, or a history of dangerous witches; each will show up a different aspect of the character. The *Nachleben* may be traced in various media: in painting, in literature, even in scholarship.

GENRE STUDIES

The literary genres with which we grew up—tragedy, comedy, history, novel, epic—are not determined by any logical necessity; there are quite literate societies whose literary genres are entirely different. What this means is that each genre has a history of its own. The later scholars of literature divided Greek comedy into old, middle and new comedy, but of course comedy did not stop there. When new comedy was translated and reworked by Plautus and Terence, the resulting *comedia palliata* was not quite the same kind of thing as Menander and Diphilus had produced; the style of the early Roman mimes and the farces, of which we know next to nothing but their name (*fabulae Atellanae*), must have been responsible for some of the differences, and the different social milieu in Rome surely made its impression, too.[1] When Shakespeare and Molière produced their comedies, although they are undoubtedly in the Plautine tradition and occasionally even based on identifiable plays of Plautus, they were nevertheless very different again from the Roman originals—affected by an independent theatrical tradition (that of the medieval mystery plays), different circumstances of production, and a different social milieu. Modern situation comedies preserve some of the essentials of the genre, particularly a plot built about romantic difficulties and ending with a wedding or, more recently, a reaffirmed love relationship; but again the genre has been reshaped almost to the point of unrecognizability by new literary and social circumstances—as well as (and this should have been said in all the previous examples as well) by the particular genius of its authors.

STUDIES OF A RECEIVING AUTHOR

There is no need to point out that a copious book could be made out of the use of the Odyssey in Joyce's *Ulysses*: more than one such book has already been written about this novel, which would be read entirely differently did its title not reveal to us a parallel that is nowhere stated expressly within the text. Milton, Racine and countless others are easy topics for discussions of their attitude towards the classics. But precisely here one has to look beyond the obvious: it is no problem to find "classical allusions," but much more interesting is the question of how the author has shaped the classical models: what is rejected may be as telling as what is accepted, and how what was accepted was reworked in its new setting. That Homer began each of his epics with a topic word—*mēnin* in the Iliad, *andra* in the Odyssey—is well known, as is the way that Vergil combined them when he began the Aeneid with *arma virumque*. It is not

---

[1] The character of the soldier, for example, was developed differently by Plautus, writing for an audience at the end of a long and dangerous war in which many of the spectators must have taken part, from the way he appeared in Greek New Comedy: see Hofmann and Wartenberg, *Der Bramarbas in der antiken Komödie*.

surprising that Milton does the same, beginning "Of man's first disobedience. . . ." But the form of the imitation changes here. The verb is the second word of the Iliad, the third word of the Odyssey and the Aeneid; but *Paradise Lost* does not reach its main verb until the sixth line, despite the general rule that makes the verb the second element in an English sentence (and the first in an imperative sentence like Milton's). Homer and Vergil have influenced Milton, but it seems to have been the influence of Caesar, who habitually postpones his verbs to the end, that was decisive. Was this because Caesar was the author from whom every child learned how Latin should be written? Or did Milton have other reasons, in English or in Latin? I do not know. Maybe you will find out.

STUDIES OF A RECEIVING PERIOD, PLACE OR GENRE

The classics in Victorian England, in colonial America, in the Third Reich: any one of these or of a hundred similar topics reveals a good deal about the receiving culture—What did they like? What did they hate? What did they do with it?—and about the way that the culture saw the ancients. As mentioned before, the classics in Italy, which ruled the world in ancient times, hold a very different place from the place they hold in England, an outlying province of the Roman Empire that was abandoned well before the Empire's fall. Englishmen of a hundred years ago admired the Roman imperialists; Englishmen of today find them less congenial. Often a particular genre will show things that do not appear elsewhere: articles on classics in the cinema have become something of a staple, a pleasant occupation for classicists who enjoy the movies but also a window into how the classics function in a more lowbrow culture.

The classics continue to influence us. When his parents (whichever of them chose the name) named Cesare Borgia, the name may have been meant as a classical allusion; when Cesare himself chose for his motto *aut Caesar aut nihil*, he was certainly seeing himself as a new Caesar. George Washington, who saw himself as the Cincinnatus of America, drew a benign inspiration from the classics; Benito Mussolini, who saw himself as the restorer of the Roman Empire, drew a more dangerous one. The study of the classical tradition, like the study of the classics themselves, is a structure that helps us observe and analyze the whole spectrum of human thought and behavior.

RECEPTION STUDIES

The study of the classical tradition considered that tradition a unique or almost unique cultural phenomenon: it was the greatness of the Greeks and the Romans that made their legacy a matter of such abiding importance. But in the mid-twentieth century there arose a school of literary thought that put our relationship to the classics in a different light. Hans Robert Jauss[2] pioneered what he called "reception aesthetics," the idea that every literary work—the idea has since been broadened to include performance and art as well—is written for a presumed audience, and has its meaning only in terms of the way it is read by that audience, or whatever other audience may come to read it. Meaning, according to this view, is not inherent in the text; it is something that is negotiated, as it were, between the author and the reader. When looked at this way, all literature that is still read becomes a part of the background against which new literature is produced and understood; conversely, not only writers and students of literature but anybody who comes in contact with the literature, even indirectly, is a part of its reception, and a part of the meaning that the society attributes to that literature. The classics do not merely instruct us; we negotiate with them, interpret them and reinterpret them, appropriate them for our own purposes and understand them in our own terms—or perhaps the terms that they (and other books) have taught us to use.

In the classical tradition there had always been heroes, buffoons and a goodly number of bit players. Boethius, St. Thomas Aquinas, Dante, Shakespeare, Milton, Goethe—these were the heroes, great cultural figures who used and reshaped the classical tradition from generation to generation. People such as the author of *Ovide Moralisé*, who tried to make Ovid into a preacher, or the authors of centos, who strung together unconnected verses to make a new poem that did not include a single original word, may perhaps appear to later generations as figures of fun, although they were perfectly serious in what they were doing and were taken very seriously in their own times. The bit players were the schoolchildren who suffered through Latin, the students who dropped choice phrases into their vocabularies, the frauds who would string together bits of mumbo-jumbo with -us and -um on the end of some of the words to pretend to a culture that they did not possess, and innumerable others whose connection with Greek and Roman culture was not that of Dante

---

[2] Jauss, *Toward an Aesthetic of Reception*.

and Milton. Earlier studies of the classical tradition wasted little time on the buffoons and even less on the bit players. Modern reception studies, in keeping with the late twentieth century's generally broader definition of what counts as literature and what cultural phenomena are worth studying, consider all of the players interesting, and see in every one who has ever been affected by the classics a receiver, a reflector and a transmitter of the classical tradition; and they see in reception studies a two-way street, illuminating both the ancients themselves and the receiving culture.

In reception theory, the image of the ancient world in propaganda, in film and in advertising is quite as interesting as its image in poetry and sculpture; and the Doric columns on American banks are as intriguing for what they say about the impression the architects (or more properly, their employers) wanted to give—permanence, importance and even a bit of religious awe—as for their aesthetic qualities. And if that impression is at odds with the actual personalities and practices of the bankers for whom they were built, that just makes it all the more intriguing. We are still studying the classical tradition, but we are looking not only at the ways our culture learns from it or imitates it—after all, according to reception theory, the texts do not have a single correct message for us to assimilate—but at all the ways in which we use it, for good or for less so. Although reception studies can point up aspects of the classics that may have been ignored, and so affect our reading of the classics, their main focus is usually upon the receiving culture: what is fascinating to a classicist in the movie *Life of Brian* is not so much any insights it may give us into ancient Rome as the quirky way in which it exploits the classical world for its own purposes.

The attitude that sees meaning as something negotiated between the author and the reader also gives an opening for reading modern interests back into our texts. There is nothing new about this; modern books about ancient homosexuality or ancient racial prejudice, much as they may reflect modern interests, are not essentially different from the studies of a late-Renaissance Frenchman about the Gauls,[3] Machiavelli's *Discourses on Livy* or Marx's studies of the ancient class struggle. But reception theory offers the modern reader much greater freedom in understanding the texts as the reader wishes to understand them. It may be argued that we cannot gain much from a text if we are only willing to see in it what we wish; and the proper balance between restricting ourselves to what we

---

[3] On which see Dubois, *Celtes et Gaulois au XVI* siècle.

have been told the author means on the one hand and exploiting the author as an amplifier for our own opinions may require some amount of care and fair-mindedness on the part of the reader.

MAJOR RESOURCES

The classic English-language narrative histories of the classical tradition are Bolgar, *The Classical Heritage*, which deals with the Middle Ages and the Renaissance, and Highet, *The Classical Tradition*, a survey from the fall of Rome to the twentieth century. These works deal with the survival, influence and reaction to the classics in later culture; the meaning of the classics themselves is not at issue. More recent surveys take a different attitude: Finley, *The Legacy of Greece* is more a discussion of Greek culture itself, contrasted with its image as seen through the lens of its inheritors and imitators. Jenkyns, *The Legacy of Rome* takes the various authors and aspects of culture one by one, offering various viewpoints on their development in later cultures. Most recent, and most in tune with current trends in reception studies, is Kallendorf, *A Companion to the Classical Tradition*.

Studies of individual authors or works, of genres and in particular of recurring themes in literature are legion, as are studies of the reception of the classics in this or that later age or country. For the first type Steiner, *Antigones* or Ziolkowski, *Varieties of Literary Thematics* (for that matter, almost any of the works of Ziolkowski) can give you an idea of what sorts of things can be done; for the latter, one might mention Jenkyns, *The Victorians and Ancient Greece*, Reinhold, *Classica Americana* and Schmidt, *On Germans and Other Greeks*. Any who think that the classical tradition necessarily makes a person more broad-minded and humane may be interested to look at Demandt, "Klassik als Klischee: Hitler und die Antike" and Nelis, "Constructing Fascist Identity: Benito Mussolini and the Myth of Romanità."

A good place to start on the new wave of reception studies is Hardwick, *Reception Studies*; a fuller overview can be gotten from Hardwick and Stray, *A Companion to Classical Receptions* and Martindale and Thomas, *Classics and the Uses of Reception*. Studies more restricted in scope such as Edwards, *Roman Presences* are appearing all the time—a hot subject, as of this writing.

28

HISTORY OF CLASSICAL SCHOLARSHIP

SCHOLARSHIP ABOUT SCHOLARS

In the first chapter I commented on the anomaly that many people spend their careers as humanists, studying art, appreciating it, teaching it, but never creating it. Even more perverse, one may think, is not to study the art itself, but to study others who studied it—hoping, presumably, to do such fine work that a later generation will study how we studied those who studied . . . .

In fact, however, understanding any field of scholarship is a matter, to a certain extent, of knowing how we got there. As I hope this book has demonstrated to you, editing a text, writing a commentary or producing a dictionary is not a job whose rationale and methodology are self-evident. Each of those tasks, on which we rely daily, has undergone a good deal of development, and continues to do so now. The development of the field, moreover, is not divorced from the society around it. The *apparatus criticus* was introduced in imitation of the *Masorah* with which the rabbis had recorded all the variants in the text of the Bible; the discursive dictionaries of the elder and the younger Stephanus were the product of an age when printers had more access to ancient texts, and spent more time engaged with them, than almost anyone else; Nietzsche's theories about Dionysiac religion were part and parcel of the late Romantic movement as it moved towards what would eventually be called Decadence. None of these facts negates the scholarly achievement involved; even an anti-Semite can make good use of an *apparatus criticus*, and the Thesauri of the Stephani are still useful in an age when more texts are available to us, at arm's length in a library or at the touch of a button on the internet, than either Stephanus saw in his whole lifetime. But knowing the milieu in which these things were created helps us better understand what it is we are holding in our hands, what sort of help it can give us and what alternative ways there may be for achieving our aims.

The history of scholarship is not only a history of changing fashions; it is often, though not always, a history of progress. The increasing discovery of inscriptions has slowly filled out our lists of Athenian and Roman officials, allowing us to date securely events that were once uncertain, and they have taught us tomes about law and society—and not only of the Athenians. Archaeology, together with the decipherment of the Linear B tablets, has revealed to us a period of history about which scholars two hundred years ago knew nothing, and has shown us both how remarkably accurate and how hopelessly anachronistic Homer can be. The study of oral poetry, in turn, has so thoroughly revised our understanding of the mode of composition that lay behind Homeric epic that when we read works of a mere century ago—and many of them are still worth reading—we must recast their arguments into a form that will accord with what we now know. There are undoubtedly aspects of the classics in which recent years have seen a decline: hardly anybody nowadays reads the ancient languages with the facility and the grammatical acuity that were common in the nineteenth century, and that is a very serious loss. But in many aspects, not excluding the broader and deeper understanding of language and significance in general that has been achieved over the past century and a half, we stand on the shoulders of giants and see further than ever. The question of how we got here is one of some interest that can give us insight into both the successes and the failures of our field.

A brief sketch of the changing challenges that have faced and shaped the study of the classics was given in the first chapter;[1] I hope it gives some idea of the fact that scholarship itself is a changing phenomenon with a history of its own, a part of the reception of the classics and of the intellectual history of the western, and increasingly the non-western, world. This brief chapter will not attempt a fuller history of classical scholarship, but will offer a few ideas of what sorts of research the study of classical scholarship offers.

---

[1] Pp. 7–13.

THE CONTROVERSIES THAT HAVE SHAPED CLASSICS

Many a bitter controversy will seem to a later generation to be a tempest in a teapot; for the memory of them is forgotten, also their love, and their hatred, and their envy, is now perished[2] says King Solomon of the dead, and in most cases that is surely a good thing. But some controversies continue through the centuries. The dispute between the supporters of analogy and anomaly[3] continued throughout the Middle Ages and continues, in a changed but recognizable form, to this day. At the moment the anomalists have the upper hand, and believe the question to be definitively settled; a good account of the history of the debate might give cause for suspecting that the view of the analogists may still crop up in the future—and might make clearer why the dispute has had such a long life.

The question of whether the Iliad and the Odyssey were written by the same poet was already debated in antiquity. In the nineteenth century, in the wake of Friedrich August Wolf, *Prolegomena ad Homerum*, the question was widened to ask whether either of the poems was the work of a single poet or whether they were a conflation of various different ancient poems that had been stitched together without resolving the contradictions among the parts. The question became so basic that it was, and in many circles still is, known as "the Homeric question"; and even though the discoveries of Milman Parry in the 1920s about methods of oral composition have thrown the entire debate into a new light, a good deal of debate still remains among "oralists" who see the poems as a collation of oral performances, "neo-unitarians" who see in them the work of a single poetic genius reworking older oral material, and "neo-analysts" who, without necessarily taking sides between the others, identify contradictory themes and mythological traditions behind the text. Many scholars would find the history of the dispute itself interesting; it becomes downright sensational when traced together with the history of the documentary hypothesis of the Hebrew Pentateuch, the lynchpin of modern biblical criticism, which seems to have echoed each new development in Homeric scholarship.[4] The interrelationship of the two seemingly unrelated fields does not of itself discredit either, but it reveals an aspect that may put matters in quite a different light than they wore when examined individually.

---

[2] *Eccl.* 9:5–6.
[3] Above, pp. 82–3.
[4] On this see Cassuto, *The Documentary Hypothesis*.

Is the main purpose of classical studies their integration in the general culture or their more precise understanding by scholars? This was the subject of a major disagreement in the English universities in the nineteenth century.[5] In the short run, the first approach won out; in the long run, as the general culture lost interest in Greece and Rome, the second came to dominate the field; in recent years, as the general disinterest has become so great as to threaten the continued willingness of the society to support scholars researching the classics, classicists have begun desperate efforts to try to regain part of what the first approach had hoped to achieve.

These are three examples chosen almost at random. Some controversies seem to crop up again and again. And when they do, some research into the history of the controversy may often shed more light on it than either side is able to do on its own.

BIOGRAPHIES OF CLASSICISTS

Not everybody is a proper subject for a biography. A biography is a story, and, although everybody's life can be said to have a beginning, a middle and an end, for many of us the various parts of our lives are not easily worked into a single story-line, or even a complex one. Many people of great achievements have had very quiet and uninteresting lives.

But there are others. The career of Jane Harrison, one of the seminal figures in the study of mythology, is interesting for her pioneering intellectual work, for the interest of an influential woman in the still heavily male-dominated Cambridge of her time, for her pacifism, for her debunking of religion and her defense of it—there is plenty of interest here for a biographer.[6] And then comes the biographer of the biography and shows how the biography itself is a literary construct, a simplification of a life much more complex than the story-line allows.[7] But the fascination remains, and new biographers appear,[8] and each new approach gives us a new understanding of what is going on in her work, which means a new approach to a good deal of what is going on in current work in the fields that she influenced.

---

[5] Sparrow, *Mark Pattison and the Idea of a University*; cf. Brink, *English Classical Scholarship*, 128–33.

[6] Among them Peacock, *Jane Ellen Harrison: The Mask and the Self* and Ackerman, *The Myth and Ritual School*.

[7] Beard, *The Invention of Jane Harrison*.

[8] Robinson, *The Life and Work of Jane Ellen Harrison*.

Hundreds of years earlier, in the sixteenth century, was Joseph Scaliger, a person today remembered only by classicists and by many of them only vaguely; but he was one of the major forces in turning textual criticism from a loose conglomeration of guesses into a discipline with scholarly method and principles, and in placing the ancient Greeks and Romans in the context of the other ancient nations—the Persians, the Egyptians, the Babylonians—of whom a good deal was known that could give a broader view of the ancient world than the classical languages alone could provide. Moving from place to place, dealing with the greatest scholars of his time and not uninfluenced by the religious upheaval going on in Europe, he led a life that bears some interest for those of us who are his heirs even today.[9]

There have been classicists who were influential in other areas. Gilbert Murray was a revered professor and a prolific author on classical subjects; he was also an important mover in the foundation of the League of Nations and of Oxfam. Some people became so eminent in politics that their classical background has been mostly forgotten, but cognoscenti can tell you that James A. Garfield, the twentieth president of the United States, had been an instructor of classical languages before deciding against an academic life, and that W. E. Gladstone, the Grand Old Man of nineteenth-century British politics and four times Prime Minister of the UK, continued to write on Homer during intermissions from his political career.[10] The humanist Aeneas Silvius Piccolomini was pope from 1458 to 1464, taking the long-forgotten papal name Pius from the epithet of his ancient namesake.[11] For each of these, the interplay between their classical background and their public activities is an aspect that a classicist is uniquely qualified to evaluate.

HISTORIES OF SCHOLARSHIP

There are also histories of scholarship itself. What a lexicographer was doing in the ninth century was something very different from what a sixteenth-century lexicographer was doing; and both of them were pursuing goals very different from those of modern lexicographers. The

---

[9] His recent biographer is Grafton, *Joseph Scaliger*; the pioneering work was Bernays, *Joseph Justus Scaliger*.

[10] Bebbington, "Gladstone and the Classics."

[11] He was Pius II. Pope Pius I had reigned more than a millennium earlier, when the Roman Empire was not yet Christian.

history of texts passes from the history of how they were produced to the history of how they were copied to the history of how they were discovered to the history of how scholars began concentrating their efforts on recovering a more authentic text. Archaeology passes from the romance of Schliemann to the precision and the new vistas of modern science, with a number of important stages on the way, and with no ending; the history of the relationship of archaeology to the public that encourages it and uses it is a history in itself. Each of these histories—and again I have merely picked a few random examples—raises questions about what the field does, what it can do and what it should do. Regional histories may help connect scholars to each other and may make them more conscious of how different traditions of scholarship produce different approaches; often a few words can make clear a difference that would otherwise pass unnoticed:

> Americans do not believe what they read in ancient authors. Germans did. The distinction is telling . . . . During his most impressionable years Wilamowitz learned from his beloved teacher an intensely personal approach to a text, to find something there that would make him better. This means to judge morally what the ancients said.[12]

You may not agree with this observation, and indeed its author has to justify it by quoting from Niebuhr and from Wilamowitz himself; but once the statement has been made, the door has been opened to the possibility that books that we read as if they all came from the same source and sought the same goals may really be very different in their underpinnings. And once that door has been opened, it is not easy, and probably not desirable, to close it.

Many scholars became great by working under the tutelage of other great scholars. For those who did not have this advantage, and perhaps even more for those who did and can appreciate the depth of personality that can accompany great work, the study of the history of scholarship can be a way of hobnobbing with the great.

---

[12] Calder, "Ecce Homo," 23.

MAJOR RESOURCES

Histories of Classical Scholarship

Wilamowitz-Möllendorff, *History of Classical Scholarship* is, as its author's works generally are, concise, readable, opinionated and illuminating, though for the modern student no history of classical scholarship that does not include Wilamowitz himself can be complete.

Much longer and drier is Sandys, *A History of Classical Scholarship*. It has been to some extent superseded by Pfeiffer, *History of Classical Scholarship*, a work that was never properly finished: as his life neared its end, Pfeiffer dashed off the history of the eighteenth and early nineteenth centuries— the period that gave the study of the classics the structure and purpose that, more or less, they retain to this day—in a mere twenty-four pages, and did not even attempt the period after 1850.

Eckstein, *Nomenclator Philologorum* gives a brief identification of every significant philological scholar up to 1871, but, since it has no cross-references, you will not find Stephanus if you don't know to look under Estienne. For the modern period ("from the matriculation at Göttingen of Friedrich August Wolf, *studiosus philologiae* in 1777 up to the death of Arnaldo Momigliano in 1986") there are capsule biographies of fifty classicists in Briggs and Calder, *Classical Scholarship*. Biographical material for Britain up to 1960 was collected in Todd, *Dictionary of British Classicists*. For other classicists the first place to look for a summary of their work is usually the obituaries that are published in classical journals after their deaths. These obituaries were a regular feature of *Bursians Jahresbericht*, and the *Proceedings of the British Academy* regularly includes obituaries of its members.

Archaeology has some of its own historical accounts, among them Stiebing, *Uncovering the Past* and de Grummond, *An Encyclopedia of the History of Classical Archaeology*.

Probably the greatest contribution of the twentieth century to the history of classical scholarship is the many essays of Arnaldo Momigliano, published from 1955 to 1992 in collections of which the first was Momigliano, *Contributo alla Storia degli Studi Classici* and the rest were numbered serially: *Secondo Contributo*, *Terzo Contributo*, and so on until the posthumous *Nono Contributo*. Despite the Italian title, many of the essays are in English, the language of Momigliano's exile. Selected essays, some of them translated from Italian, have been published in Momigliano, *Studies in Historiography* and Bowersock and Cornell, *A. D. Momigliano: Studies on Modern Scholarship*. Valuable contributions to the history of nineteenth- and twentieth-century scholarship (particularly German) are the bibliographies and the essays of William M. Calder III; a selection of the latter is published in Calder, *Men in Their Books*.

The work of the first half of the twentieth century was summed up in the articles in Platnauer, *Fifty Years (and Twelve) of Classical Scholarship*. For a German summary of the current state of classical studies, see the articles in Schwinge, *Die Wissenschaften vom Altertum*. A brief survey of the situation in elementary and secondary schools of Europe, quite revealing as to the wide variety from country to country, is given in Bulwer, *Classics Teaching in Europe*; for Latin in America, see LaFleur, *Latin for the 21st Century*.

On the transmission of ancient literature to the west a brief and readable account is given in Reynolds and Wilson, *Scribes and Scholars*. More information about the transmission of the Greek classics can be found in Wilson, *Scholars of Byzantium* and id., *From Byzantium to Italy*. These works deal largely with the "scholarly" matter of the actual transmission of the works; the story of their absorption into western culture is the story of the classical tradition and reception, dealt with lightly in the previous chapter of this book. For the Arabic transmission, an absolutely essential phase in the preservation of Greek science and philosophy, a good place to start is Gutas, *Greek Thought, Arabic Culture*.

29

RECONSTRUCTING THE ANCIENT WORLD

Anyone who studies the ancient world must wonder what it was like to live there, and to an extent all study of the past is an effort to recreate it, at least in our own minds. Such a reconstruction is necessarily imperfect: even today, a visitor or even an immigrant to a foreign country can never erase the past entirely and begin to think quite the way the locals do. If, as L. P. Hartley wrote, the past is a foreign country, we can never really experience it the way the Greeks and the Romans did—even if a time-machine were actually to take us there and leave us there forever. But the wish to reconstruct the past remains, and many efforts have been made to do so, with various levels of success.

OPERA AND MODERN DANCE

The greatest effort of reconstruction, of course, was the Renaissance, when people wanted to read Latin and Greek, to write and even to speak Latin and Greek, to sculpt and to build in the classical style, to produce tragedies and comedies—the list could go on, and a number of examples have already been mentioned in the previous chapters. Perhaps the most striking effort at reconstruction of an ancient art form was the invention of grand opera in the late fifteenth century by people who thought that they were recreating Greek tragedy.[1] The new art form flourished—and as it did, scholars began to demonstrate how different it was from the Greek tragedy that it had ostensibly revived. This phenomenon of thesis and antithesis, whereby one person or group attempts to reconstruct some aspect of antiquity only to have the accuracy of the reconstruction impugned afterward, is one that recurs throughout the history of ancient reconstructions; it is most obvious today in classicists' generally skeptical reactions to movies set in ancient Greece and Rome.

If grand opera is not what Greek tragedy looked like, what is? The tragedies of Corneille and Racine? Of Shakespeare? The modern productions, often devoid of music, where the chorus chants but neither sings nor dances? It is easy to demonstrate the ways in which each of these efforts differs from what Aeschylus, Sophocles and Euripides were doing, but anyone who has ever worked on such a production will understand the ancient theater much better for the experience. Actors, directors and producers all have to deal with matters that must have been as problematic for the ancients as they are for us. What must you do to ensure that the audience understands the words? How can you focus the audience's attention on the significant actor and the significant gesture; how can you communicate emotion to spectators who, even if you do not wear a mask as the Greeks did, are too far away to see your face? A modern scriptwriter who finds it necessary to change the plot line of an ancient work for the screen or the stage is indeed falsifying the text, but that is precisely what the Greeks themselves did to Homer, and what the Romans did to the Greeks.

Opera shows us another phenomenon that continues in other places as well: a successful reconstruction develops a life of its own. Monteverdi may have been imitating the Greeks or the Romans, but later composers were imitating Monteverdi. So Plautus reworked Greek New Comedy into a form that bore some of the earmarks of Italian farce; Shakespeare then took Plautus' *Menaechmi*, added a double slave from his *Amphitruo*, and produced *The Comedy of Errors*, imitating not the Greeks (whose works by then were lost), but their Roman adapter. Hundreds of years later George Abbott, Richard Rodgers and Lorenzo Hart wrote *The Boys from Syracuse*, quite conscious that they were imitating Shakespeare, but blithely ignoring—if they knew it—the work of Plautus, much less of his still unknown Greek original.[2] Similarly Isadora Duncan gazed at Greek paintings and imitated

---

[1]   In fact, it has recently been argued that they were influenced by Rome more than by Greece: Ketterer, *Ancient Rome in Early Opera*.

[2]   If there was such; see Stärk, *Die Menaechmi des Plautus und kein griechisches Original*.

them in modern dance; but those who came after her were imitating Isadora. This, of course, is as it should be: the Greek genres themselves were not static, but changed with time, sometimes for better, sometimes for worse.

GREEK AND LATIN COMPOSITION

Another way of recreating the ancient world is the practice of Latin and Greek composition, forced for years on unwilling schoolboys and now practiced by a small coterie of brave and inventive classicists, enjoying the wordplay but frustrated by the lack of an audience to appreciate it. Latin and Greek composition fell out of favor in the last half of the twentieth century under the not unreasonable question "To whom will I ever need to write in Latin or in Greek?" The university at which I teach never dreamed of offering such a course until an elderly gentleman, whose Latin studies had been interrupted by the holocaust, joined our department and asked for it. Teach it we did—and I finally came to understand Latin grammar. Here, again, grappling with the problems that the ancients had to deal with (in this case, simply the problem of expressing oneself in their language) taught us a huge amount about the actual experience behind the texts we have inherited.

RECONSTRUCTION OF THE PHYSICAL ENVIRONMENT

The issue is truly joined in the case of archaeology. Excavators usually find ruins. A certain amount of restoration is always done: coins are polished, broken stones and broken pots are put back together. But when all the pieces we have are put back in place, what we have is usually still a ruin. What shall we do now? Should we leave the vase with a hole in it? Should we try to fill in the design that we think was there? If we have half a column, should we leave it standing at only half-height? And if we have the top and the bottom but not the middle, should we fill in the middle with concrete in order to put the parts of the column in their proper place? And if we do so, should we try to make the concrete look as much like the marble as possible, so that the viewer sees the column as much as possible the way the Romans saw it? Or should we, on the contrary, make a clear mark of where the genuine artifact ends and the reconstruction begins, in order not to deceive visitors? Though extreme answers, either leaving everything in ruins or rebuilding everything as we think it was,[3] are probably mistaken approaches, when we get into the details these are not questions that have a right answer and a wrong one; each approach has its advantages and its disadvantages, and the weight attached to each will differ according to the particular item being considered, its ancient and modern context, and the people making the decision.

Reconstruction can also be undertaken as a form of research; this is known as *experimental archaeology*. The most famous example was probably the voyage of the Kon-Tiki, a raft built and piloted by the Norse ethnographer Thor Heyerdahl to prove the possibility of prehistoric navigation from Peru to Polynesia. Perhaps the most strikingly original such project in recent years was the Trireme Project, in which a group of British scholars supervised the building and launching of an ancient Greek warship, proving that it was possible for a ship with three banks of oars to maneuver in the open sea.[4] Another lesson, no less important, was learned a few years later when an inspection revealed that some of its planking was diseased, and after being left out in the open for a long time its timbers were dry, and it was no longer seaworthy.[5] If the success of the project taught us much about Greek shipbuilding, its near-demise—it was later refurbished to participate in the ceremonial torch relay for the 2004 Athens Olympics— taught us something about the maintenance of Greek warships, and how short their lifespan would be in the absence of proper care.

Not every effort in experimental archaeology need be as elaborate as the reconstruction of a trireme. A few friends with mock-up shields, swords and spears can allow testing of various possibilities of phalanx fighting; an experienced cook can experiment with ancient recipes; and a home-made loom can be quite informative about how much of her web Penelope could produce in a day, how long it would take to undo it at night, and what it feels like to spend one's day weaving. We must be aware of unavoidable differences—an ancient diet would probably have different effects on a body brought up on modern food than it had on the ancients—but with a bit of ingenuity and enterprise there is a lot to be learned here.

The reconstruction of ancient music is another field in which practical reconstruction can be a handmaiden to research: building ancient instruments and learning to play them will teach us tomes about what ancient

---

[3]   One famously extreme example was the extensive reconstruction done by Evans at Knossos, described in Gere, *Knossos and the Prophets of Modernism.*

[4]   Morrison, Coates and Rankov, *The Athenian Trireme.*

[5]   Coates, "Historical & Technical."

music sounded like, the more so when we use our instruments to play the brief fragments of ancient Greek music scores that have come down to us. But again, things take on a life of their own: if the music is good—and if it isn't good, it probably isn't accurate—other musicians will begin to imitate it, building a new reality less and less dependent upon the ancients.

COMPUTERIZED RECONSTRUCTION

Not everybody has the manpower or the organizational ability to rebuild a trireme or a temple, but modern computer technology allows a good deal of simulation. The simplest of these are the computer games, in which the use of a classical backdrop can be used, if well researched, to allow the player to get some of the ambience of the ancient world. Those who have not played these games in recent times may be unaware of their sophistication: there are currently games involving thousands of people in open-ended international competitive simulations of problems facing ancient societies, games that involve serious dangers of internet addiction that may outweigh the fascinating insight they offer into how strategic choices may have played out.

Sounds can be synthesized on a computer, allowing an educated guess as to the sound that we would have gotten from an instrument that we are not capable of building. Drawings, and particularly scale drawings, are a specialty of computers. It has always been possible to create a picture of what the building whose ruins stand before us must have been like; now it is possible to produce a three-dimensional image, letting the visitor walk around the building, enter it and explore it from within, without actually having to disturb a single stone on the site.

Just looking and playing is not all that can be done with computer reconstruction. The *VRoma* project, designed as a tool for instruction in Latin, offers an interactive environment in which people from anywhere interact with each other and with programmed characters within a recon-structed image of Rome through which they move at will.

And finally, computers and stones can be brought together: in one striking project, Israeli archaeologists are using computers to identify every fragment of a ruined synagogue, and to put the puzzle back together again, piece by piece, out of its original stones.[6] Even a religious Jew who

---

6   Singer, "Rising Again."

prays in the reconstructed synagogue will not be experiencing what the original congregation felt: they were praying in their village prayer-house, not in an archaeological site of great antiquity. But the experience will be extraordinary, and the reconstruction is quite an achievement.

MAJOR RESOURCES

The state of experimental archaeology in the 1970s is described in Coles, *Experimental Archaeology*, and Graham, Heizer and Hester, *Bibliography of Replicative Experiments* lists was done before then. Mathieu, *Experimental Archaeology* is not a survey, but the articles there can give an impression of some newer developments. The website of EXARC, the international organization of Archaeological Open Air Museums, offers a calendar of current projects. For glossy pictures of what can be done with computer reconstruction see Forte and Siliotti, *Virtual Archaeology*; for a scholarly survey, Evans and Daly, *Digital Archaeology* will provide a beginning. None of these sources is restricted to classical archaeology.

Reconstruction of ancient theater, music and dance is inseparable from the study of those subjects themselves, each of which has been treated in its own place.

30

TRANSLATION

THE BASIC REQUIREMENTS

The classical languages are no longer the heritage of every educated person, nor are they likely to be so again. Most people in our world will get whatever direct knowledge they have of the classics through the translucent window of translation. Once the main purpose of a translation could be to help students work out the meaning of the original. Today, the quality of our translations is to a large degree the quality of the classics themselves as our generation will come to know them.

Yehuda Ibn Tibbon, who translated a number of the most important works of Jewish scholarship from Arabic into Hebrew in the twelfth century, made the point that a translator must know three things very well: the language in which the work is written (what we call the *source language*), the language into which it is to be translated (the *target language*) and the subject matter. If any one of these three is known imperfectly, the result is unlikely to be a success.

Let us presume, then, that you know Greek and Latin, you know your native language and you know pretty well the subject of the work you are to translate. You have the capability to be a competent translator; but there is nothing automatic about translating, and you will still have to deal with a number of basic issues.

THE FIRST RULE

The first thing that you must know is what was already mentioned in connection with lexicography,[1] that no word is ever the precise, unique and complete translation of any other word.[2] Where Cicero says that when Ennius praised Cato the elder *magnus honos* was added to the reputation of the Roman people,[3] we are surely entitled to translate *honos* as "honor"; but when Caesar reminds the senate that he had requested *nullum extraodinarium honorem*,[4] he means not that he had requested no special honor, but that he had requested no special *office*, waiting patiently until he could legitimately run again for election as consul. Nor is our word "honor" always translated by *honos*: when a rogue violates a woman's honor, it is not her *honos* but her *pudicitia* that he attacks.

It is not simply that *honos* is a difficult case; any word in the dictionary would have served as an example. Even concrete nouns cannot be relied upon: the planets were *stellae* to the Romans, but they are not stars to us; actors and athletes are stars to us, but would not have been *stellae*. It follows that you can never rely on a given English word to translate all occurrences of a Greek or Latin word; in each case, you have to consider what the author is actually saying. Dictionary entries for single words can often be quite long, and you have to be aware of the fact that every single translation offered in a given entry is there because, in some passage, it is the most appropriate translation. The passage in front of you may be that passage.

A particular problem is what translators refer to as *false friends*: words whose meaning is not that of the English word that sounds like them or is derived from them. *Servire* rarely means "to serve" in the modern sense; its usual meaning is to be a slave. *Servare*, even further, means "to watch over." It was a weakness for false friends that fooled Ezra Pound into thinking that he understood Propertius and Sophocles well enough to translate them; and it was his use of false friends that made him so easy a target for Robert Graves's ridicule.[5]

---

[1]   Above, p. 70.

[2]   This was first argued by Jakobson, "On Linguistic Aspects of Translation," and to my knowledge nobody has offered a convincing counterexample in the fifty years since then.

[3]   Cic. *Pro Arch.* 22.

[4]   Caes. *Bell. Civ.* 32.

[5]   Graves, "Dr Syntax and Mr Pound." Many, chief among them Sullivan, *Ezra Pound and Sextus Propertius*, have come to Pound's defense, accepting his claim that his *Homage to Sextus Porpertius* was not meant to be a translation at all and defending it on the grounds of Pound's greatness as a poet. What Graves demonstrates in his short and

What is true of words is true *a fortiori* for grammatical structures. By this stage you have presumably discovered the disappointing fact that you cannot count on every genitive to be a possessive genitive, or every accusative to be a direct object. You must first understand what the Greek or the Latin is saying and then think of how you would say it in English. But even that may not be enough. There are other questions that you have to have in mind when translating a text.

BASIC QUESTIONS

What Sort of Text Are You Translating?

Different kinds of texts require different treatment. A legal text has a particular sort of phrasing in Greek or in Latin, and legal English is likely to be the appropriate phrasing for a translation of a text like that. Aristophanes uses and even revels in dirty words; Menander never does. The way that Petronius' characters speak is part of their characterization; Vergil's shepherds, on the other hand, all[6] speak the same perfect Latin. Aeschylus is heroic and verges on the bombastic; Euripides uses simple language in contexts that verge on the sophistical. It is impossible to reproduce all the nuances of a text and, depending on your answer to the next question, it may not be necessary to try; but if you use Aristophanic vocabulary in a text of Sophocles, or even of Hippocrates, there is a problem with your translation.

Recognizing the differences in texts is not just a matter of reproducing their characteristic style; it may also affect the understanding of the text itself. Legal and philosophical texts are expected to use their terminology carefully and consistently; rhetorical texts, on the other hand, often achieve the desired effect precisely by using terms imprecisely, encouraging the

---

amusing piece for *Punch*, however, is not that Pound is inaccurate (which a poet may be excused for being), but that his inaccuracies are those that arise from not having understood the Latin in the first place.

[6]   Or almost all (or almost perfect); at Ecl. 3.1 Menalcas uses one archaic letter (*cuium* for *cuius*), and brought down upon Vergil the sarcasm of Numitorius (*Vita Donati*, 43). For the claim that the shepherds of this particular eclogue are indeed characterized by a Plautine coarseness see Currie, "The Third Eclogue and the Roman Comic Spirit"; but except for this one letter, which is not incorrect but archaic, the coarseness is not a matter of speaking incorrect Latin. Currie claims that *cuium* is a hint at Plautus, who used the form commonly.

listener to conceive one sort of action in terms more appropriate for another. Poets make careful use of the nuances and suggestions of a word: when Sophocles uses the verb *oide* about Oedipus, the similarity to Oedipus' name is presumably intentional, and a translator may want to try to produce a similar effect; the same phenomenon would be less likely to be intentional if the author were Thucydides, and unlikely in the extreme if it were Galen.

For What Purpose Are You Translating?

How a text should be translated depends not only upon the text but also upon the purpose for which the translation is intended—what translation theorists nowadays call the *skopos*.[7] If you are translating the *Corpus Iuris Civilis* for lawyers, it will be very important to make sure your translation will leave the reader with the same understanding of the law as the Latin would; its literary qualities will not matter much. If you are translating the same text for a discussion of legal style in ancient Rome, your priorities will be reversed. A translation of Homer designed for a commercial market will try to be as exciting and as moving as the original; a translation designed to help students understand the Greek will sacrifice some literary quality for the sake of literalness. A translation of drama designed for production will try to make sure that the translation will sound right on the stage, and will pay close attention to problems of staging; a translation designed for reading may give less priority to these matters. A few lines of text translated for use in a journal article will have to be meticulously accurate, in a way that both supports the point the author is making and indicates any ambiguity that might be in the original; and I take this opportunity to mention that editors generally request that you indicate whether you are using your own translation and, if not, which translation you are using.

For Whom Are You Translating?

Most of the answers to this question will have been given when considering the previous one, but, even when two translators' goals are similar, different

---

[7] See Vermeer, "Skopos and Commission" for a definition; there has been much discussion of the theory in recent decades.

target audiences may make their choices different. A translation designed for schoolchildren will obviously read differently from one designed for adults; and even one designed for adults will read differently if the adults in question are ones who can be expected to recognize the classical background or who need it indicated in the text. In his published translation of Euripides' *Bacchae*, William Arrowsmith translated the words ἴτω δίκα φανερός as "O Justice, principle of order, spirit of custom, come! Be manifest; reveal yourself," using seven English words to translate the Greek δίκα and four to translate φανερός. When speaking to scholars, he translated "this chilling refrain" with four words: "Let justice go openly."[8]

LITERARY TRANSLATION

Since no word exactly translates any other, and since the grammar of modern languages is quite divergent from that of Greek and Latin, there is no way that your translation can reproduce all the nuances of the original. If you are precise about the meaning you will miss the sound; if you try to get the sound right, you will have to make some sacrifices in transmitting the meaning; even if you should succeed at both, you will miss the echoes of other words used or hinted at elsewhere in this work or in others. There have been translators who went to extremes in one direction or another. Aquila's translation of the Bible into Greek had creation taking place "In the chapter" (ἐν κεφαλαίῳ), which was peculiar Greek, but kept the etymological connection between the word "beginning" (Heb. *reshit*) and the word "head" (Heb. *rosh*) that was in his source text. Two thousand years later Celia and Louis Zukofsky translated Catullus 50.1–4

> Ille mi par esse deo videtur,
> Ille, si fas est, superare divos,
> qui sedens adversus identidem te
> spectat et audit

with the English lines

> He'll hie me, par *is* he? The God divide her,
> he'll hie, see fastest, superior deity,
> quiz—sitting adverse identity—mate, in-
> spect it and audit[9]

---

8 Arrowsmith, *Bacchae*, 1011; id., "Teaching Euripides' *Bacchae*."
9 Zukofsky and Zukofsky, *Catullus*.

I am not sure that they entirely lost the meaning, but they surely pushed the English language into a difficult corner ("He'll hie me"), forced the meter, and took wide liberties with the meaning (*Si fas est superare divos*/"See fastest, superior deity") to preserve the sound pattern of vowels and consonants as best they could.

There is indeed no small controversy as to whether or not poetry should be translated by poetry at all. Few people would want to translate Catullus into prose except as an aid to translation; but for more than a century people have been translating Homer into prose, claiming that our generation has no feeling and no patience for epic and, if Homer were alive today, he would have written a novel. This is the attitude of what is called "familiarizing translation," which tries to make the foreign text seem as comprehensible as possible to the reader by playing down the differences in culture. The opposite opinion, variously called "alienating," "estranging," "distancing" or simply "defamiliarizing" translation, can also be defended: perhaps the whole point of translating Homer is to take the English reader somewhere that reader has never been before. When Richard Bentley famously damned Alexander Pope's best-selling translations of the Iliad and the Odyssey with the words, "It is a pretty poem, Mr. Pope, but you must not call it Homer," he was undoubtedly right in one sense, for Pope had taken great liberties in changing the style of Homer into a style unmistakably that of Pope. A critic with a different sensibility might have countered that nothing that is not a pretty poem can ever be called Homer. If you should ever have the temerity to translate Homer, you will have to decide where you stand on this issue; and even in translating lesser authors, the question remains.

Even assuming that we do translate Homer into verse, what kind of verse? On the face of it we would want to translate him into non-rhyming hexameters with a caesura, but most efforts to do so have been unsuccessful, chiefly because it is very hard to write a line of poetry that an English reader will read as a dactylic hexameter unless you make all the feet dactyls—something that Homer rarely did. A further problem is that the English language has a subordinate stress on every other syllable, so that writing dactyls usually means restricting yourself to short words—again unlike Homer, for whom πολυφλοίσβοιο θαλάσσης was a perfectly acceptable turn of phrase. But is Homer Homer without the hexameter? Is Catullus Catullus without the hendecasyllables? You will make your own choice and do the best you can to transmit as much of the original as possible.

One last problem with translation is perhaps the most intractable of all: how original can you be? One might say, not at all: originality is the enemy of fidelity, and, wherever you insert yourself, you are not giving over Homer, or Tacitus, or whoever it is that you are translating. It may seem reasonable—indeed, I myself suggested it above—that when translating Greek tragedy you should write something that would work well on the stage. It would undoubtedly nevertheless be *hubris* to think that you have as good a sense for stagecraft as Aeschylus, Sophocles and Euripides did, so at some point you will have to rein in your originality. Catullus and Sappho have suffered particularly at the hands of people who substituted their own poetic sensitivities for those of the ancient authors, but can Catullus and Sappho be translated without poetic sensitivity? If there is no originality in your translation, can it possibly give any of the experience that one gets in reading these extremely original poets?

THE LITERAL TRANSLATION

Literal translation is easier than literary translation not because it is obvious—on the contrary, it can be quite difficult to find a way to make your English enough like Greek or Latin for the student to recognize and enough like English for the student to comprehend—but because the decisions you must make have a single overriding consideration: to help the student understand the original text. Here, too, questions of judgment arise: how much like the original can it be and still be English? A particular problem occurs in the translation of a mutilated text: how can one show what is known and what is not? The simple answer is, one cannot; but translators have resorted to various methods for passing the information when necessary, by use of typographical means (parentheses, italics) or by footnotes.

TRANSLATION AND ADAPTATION

One possibility is to give up on translation entirely and offer an adaptation. Is *A Comedy of Errors* the same as Plautus' *Menaechmi*? By no means; but it could be argued that it captures the spirit of Plautus more than many translations. Novels on ancient themes, and movies derived from ancient works, are obviously adaptations; a chance papyrus find proved to us what Eduard Fraenkel had already demonstrated, that Plautus himself did not translate his Greek originals, but adapted them for his place, his time and his audience.[10] The controversy erupts anew every time an adaptation

---

[10] Fraenkel, *Plautine Elements in Plautus*; Handley, *Menander and Plautus: A Study in Comparison*.

plays fast and loose with the original. Here, you are probably constrained by your publishers or employers, who will generally not accept an adaptation if they asked for a translation, nor vice versa; but you yourself may want to consider which direction you are more interested in going.

SPECIAL PROBLEMS

As already mentioned, Greek and Latin are very different from English. The differences are constantly presenting themselves, whether or not you have expected them. It is probably worth giving them some general thought, rather than simply translating every word ad hoc. How do you translate a potential optative? A gerundive? A supine? Once you find the answer, you start discovering the exceptions (there always are exceptions); but you will be better able to deal with them when you have thought about the problem—and once you have thought about the problem, every case that does not fit the way you thought it should will teach you something new about the language from which you are translating.

A particular problem for the ancient languages is word order. Word order is not arbitrary in Latin and Greek; it simply follows rules different from those of English. In particular, its rules are semantic, not syntactic: to give a vast overgeneralization, the first thing in the sentence says what you are speaking about, and the second thing says what you have to say about it. Saying "Use the overpass to cross the railway tracks" is not ungrammatical, but it is not the way a Greek or a Roman would say it; to put it that way would imply that we are talking about what to do with the overpass, and there really aren't many possibilities other than crossing the tracks. A Greek or a Roman would say, "To cross the railway tracks, use the overpass."[11] There is a lot more to word order than this, but the essential matter is that a translation that ignores word order is missing a good deal of what is in the original, whereas it is hardly ever appropriate to transmit that information by means of English word order, which is not usually determined by the sentence's meaning, but by its syntax. Moreover, it may be impossible to transmit the information without losing something else. The author may have intentionally postponed a word that can only be postponed in English by wrenching the syntax or changing the construction, perhaps to the passive, where the original was fluent and active.

---

[11] This, with a slight Americanization, is the example of Simpson and Vellacott, *Writing in Latin*, 9.

Your translation cannot reproduce all of the characteristics of the original: which should you choose? The more you know, the deeper your problems; but in proportion as you solve them, the more you know, the better your translation.

MAJOR RESOURCES

The major resources for a translator are all items that have been mentioned in earlier chapters: a reliable text with an *apparatus criticus*; a good dictionary, of course; a comprehensive grammar book; a good commentary, and preferably more than one, to help you understand the text and to point out subtleties that may affect your choice of words; other translations, if there are such, whose felicities you will imitate and whose infelicities you will avoid; if you are translating Latin, you will want Krebs, *Antibarbarus der lateinischen Sprache*, and if you are translating Greek you will wish you had something similar to warn you against "false friends."

There is in fact an entire field of translation studies, which may have a good deal to teach a professional translator; and although that specialty lies beyond the purview of this book and the competence of its author, every classicist does a certain amount of translation, if only in the classroom and in professional writing, and should at least be aware of the fact that there is a good deal of theoretical discussion of issues that face everyone who tries to communicate in one language what was first said in another.

ABBREVIATIONS

In the nature of a broad-ranging manual, most books mentioned are mentioned only once, and it would perhaps have been possible to dispense with abbreviations; but since abbreviations are so commonly used in the classics, the reader may find it useful to have listed here the abbreviations of many commonly used works mentioned in this book.

Superscripts refer to the number of the edition: LSJ^9 = the ninth edition of Liddell–Scott–Jones.

The standard lists of abbreviations are the much more copious lists contained in LSJ^9 (for Greek authors), OLD or Lewis and Short (for Latin authors), OCD^3 and BNP (for secondary works), the *Checklist* (for papyri) and *APh* (for periodicals). Classical authors mentioned in this book are abbreviated according to LSJ^9, Lewis and Short, and OLD, though occasionally I have given a slightly longer form than those used in the space-challenged dictionaries.

AA	*Archäologischer Anzeiger* (periodical).
AD	Ἀρχαιολογικόν Δελτίον (periodical).
AE	Ἀρχαιολογική Ἐφημερίς (periodical).
AIP	Association Internationale de Papyrologues = International Association of Papyrologists.
AJP	*American Journal of Philology* (periodical).
AnnEpigr	*L'Année epigraphique* (periodical).
ANRW	Temporini, Hildegard and Wolfgang Haase, eds., *Aufstieg und Niedergang der römischen Welt: Geschichte und Kultur Roms im Spiegel der neueren Forschung* (de Gruyter, Berlin 1972–).
AO	Develin, Robert, *Athenian Officials, 684–321 B.C.* (Cambridge University Press, Cambridge 1989).

APF   Davies, John K., *Athenian Propertied Families, 600–300 B.C.*
                   (Clarendon Press, Oxford 1971).

APh   *L'Année philologique* (periodical). Website: http://www.annee-
                   philologique.com/aph/, access date 25 May 2009.

APIS   *Advanced Papyrological Information System* at
                   http://www.columbia.edu/cgi-bin/cul/resolve?ATK2059,
                   access date 20 April 2009.

Archiv   *Archiv für Papyrusforschung* (periodical).

BASP   *Bulletin of the American Society of Papyrologists* (periodical).
                   Website: http://quod.lib.umich.edu/b/basp/, access date
                   25 May 2009.

BCH   *Bulletin de correspondance hellénique* (periodical). Website:
                   http://cefael.efa.gr/result.php?site_id=1&serie_id=BCH,
                   access date 25 May 2009.

Berichtungsliste   Preisigke, Friedrich et al., eds., *Berichtungsliste der griechischen
                   Papyrusurkunden aus Ägypten* (Brill, Leiden/Boston/Köln
                   1922–).

BNJ   Worthington, Ian, ed., *Brill's New Jacoby* (Brill,
                   Leiden/Boston/Köln, forthcoming); access to an online
                   version is available for purchase at http://www.brill
                   online.nl, access date 25 May 2009.

BNP   Cancik, Hubert and Helmuth Schneider, eds., *Brill's New Pauly:
                   Encyclopaedia of the Ancient World* (Brill, Leiden/Boston 2002–);
                   access to an online version is available for purchase at
                   http://www.brillonline.nl, access date 4 July 2010.

BSA   *Annual of the British School at Athens* (periodical).

CAH   Bury, J. B. et al., eds., *Cambridge Ancient History* (Cambridge
                   University Press, Cambridge 1924–39; rev. ed., various
                   editors, 1963–71).

CEG   Hansen, Peter Allan, *Carmina Epigraphica Graeca* (Texte und
                   Kommentare 12, 15) (de Gruyter, Berlin/New York
                   1983–89).

Checklist   Print edition: Oates, John F. et al., eds., *Checklist of Editions of
                   Greek, Latin, Demotic, and Coptic Papyri, Ostraca and Tablets*, fifth
                   edition (Bulletin of the American Society of Papyrologists
                   Supplement 9) (American Society of Papyrologists,
                   Oakville, CT 2001). Website: *Checklist of Editions of Greek, Latin,
                   Demotic, and Coptic Papyri, Ostraca and Tablets* at
                   http://scriptorium.lib.duke.edu/papyrus/texts/clist.html,
                   access date 2 April 2009.

CIG	Böckh, August, *Corpus Inscriptionum Graecarum* (G. Reimer, Berlin 1828–77).
CIIP	*Corpus Inscriptionum Iudaeae/Palaestinae* (de Gruyter, Berlin forthcoming).
CIL	*Corpus Inscriptionum Latinarum* (Berlin-Brandenburgische Akademie der Wissenschaften [the name of the publishing institution has varied over the years according to political changes], Berlin 1867–).
CP	*Classical Philology* (periodical).
CQ	*Classical Quarterly* (periodical).
CR	*Classical Review* (periodical).
CRF	Ribbeck, Otto, *Comicorum Romanorum Fragmenta*, published in id., *Scaenicae Romanorum Poesis Fragmenta*, third edition (Teubner, Leipzig 1897–98).
CSAD	Centre for the Study of Ancient Documents at Oxford University. Website: http://www.csad.ox.ac.uk, access date 28 June 2009.
CVA	*Corpus Vasorum Antiquorum*, an international project with many publishers; details available online at *Corpus Vasorum Antiquorum* at http://www.cvaonline.org, access date 25 June 2009.
Daremberg–Saglio	Daremberg, Charles and Edmond Saglio, eds., *Dictionnaire des antiquités grecques et romaines d'après les textes et les monuments* (Hachette, Paris 1877–1919).
DDbDP	*Duke Databank of Documentary Papyri* at http://idp.atlantides.org/trac/idp/wiki/DDBDP, access date 20 April 2009.
DGE	Adrados, Francisco Rodríguez et al., *Diccionario Griego–Español* (Consejo Superior de Investigaciones Cientificas, Madrid 1989–). Website: *Instituto de Lenguas y Culturas del Mediterráneo y Oriente Próximo* at http://www.filol.csic.es/dge/, access date 7 April 2009.
DK	Diels, Hermann and Walther Kranz, *Die Fragmente der Vorsokratiker: griechisch und deutsch*, sixth edition (Weidmann, Berlin 1951).
DKP	Ziegler, Konrat and Walther Sontheimer, eds., *Der Kleine Pauly: Lexikon der Antike* (Alfred Druckenmüller, Stuttgart 1964–75).
DMG	Ventris, Michael and John Chadwick, *Documents in Mycenaean Greek* (Cambridge University Press, Cambridge 1956; second edition 1973).

DMic	Aura Jorro, Francisco, *Diccionario Micénico* (Diccionario Griego–Español Anejo I–II) (Consejo Superior de Investigaciones Cientificas, Madrid 1985–92).
DNP	Cancik, Hubert and Helmuth Schneider, eds., *Der Neue Pauly: Enzyklopädie der Antike* (J. B. Metzler, Stuttgart/Weimar 1996–2004); access to an online version is available for purchase at http://www.brillonline.nl, access date 4 July 2010.
EDB	*Epigraphic Database Bari* at http://www.edb.uniba.it/, access date 7 April 2009.
EDH	*Epigraphische Datenbank Heidelberg* at http://www.uni-heidelberg.de/institute/sonst/adw/edh/, access date 7 April 2009.
EDR	*Epigraphic Database Roma* at http://www.edr-edr.it/, access date 7 April 2009.
F Gr Hist	Jacoby, Felix, ed., *Die Fragmente der griechischen Historiker* (Weidmann, Berlin 1923–58), now continued by BNJ.
FHG	Müller, Karl Otfried, ed., *Fragmenta Historicorum Graecorum* (Firmin-Didot, Paris 1841–1938).
FIRA	Riccobono, Salvatore et al., *Fontes Iuris Romani Antejustiniani* (S. A. G. Barbèra, Firenze 1941–43, 1969).
FRP	Hollis, Adrian S., ed., *Fragments of Roman Poetry c. 60 BC–AD 20* (Oxford University Press, Oxford 2007).
GBD	Malitz, Jürgen, ed., *Gnomon Bibliographische Datenbank*, published on CD-ROM (Eichstätt, 1996–). Website: http://www.gnomon.ku-eichstaett.de/Gnomon/en/Gnomon.html, access date 25 May 2009.
GDI	Bechtel, Friedrich and Hermann Collitz, eds., *Sammlung der griechischen Dialekt-Inscriften* (Vandenhoeck & Ruprecht, Göttingen 1884–1915).
HCT	Gomme, A. W., A. Andrewes and Kenneth J. Dover, *A Historical Commentary on Thucydides* (Clarendon Press, Oxford 1959–81).
HGV	*Heidelberger Gesamtverzeichnis der griechischen Papyrusurkunden Ägyptens* at www.rzuser.uni-heidelberg.de/~gv0, access date 20 April 2009.
IC	Guarducci, Margherita, *Inscriptiones Creticae* (Libreria dello Stato, Rome 1935–50).
ICI	*Inscriptiones Christianae Italiae* (Edipuglia, Bari 1985–).
ICVR	de Rossi, Giovanni Battista, Angelo Silvagni and Antonio Ferrua, *Inscriptiones Christianae urbis Romae septimo saeculo antiquiores*

(Pontificale Collegium a Sacra Archaeologia/Regalis Societas Romana ab Historia Patria, Rome 1922–).

IG   *Inscriptiones Graecae* (Berlin-Brandenburgische Akademie der Wissenschaften [the name of the publishing institution has varied over the years according to political changes], Berlin 1873–).

IGRR   Cagnat, R., J. Toutain and P. Jouguet, eds., *Inscriptiones Graecae ad Res Romanas Pertinentes* (Ernest Leroux, Paris 1906–27).

II   Unione Accademica Nazionale, *Inscriptiones Italiae* (Libreria dello Stato, Rome 1931–).

IK   Merkelbach, Reinhold, ed., *Inschriften griechischer Städte aus Kleinasien* (Rudolf Habelt, Bonn 1972–).

ILCV   Diehl, Ernst, *Inscriptiones Latinae Christianae Veteres* (Weidmann, Berlin 1925–31).

ILLRP   Degrassi, Attilio, *Inscriptiones Latinae Liberae Rei Publicae* (La Nuova Italia, Firenze 1957–65).

ILS   Dessau, Hermann, *Inscriptiones Latinae Selectae* (Weidmann, Berlin 1892–1916).

Jenkins   Jenkins, Fred W., *Classical Studies: A Guide to the Reference Literature*, second edition (Reference Sources in the Humanities) (Libraries Unlimited, Westport, CT/London 2006).

JHS   *Journal of Hellenic Studies* (periodical).

JJP   *Journal of Juristic Papyrology* (periodical).

L&S Abridged   Liddell, Henry George and Robert Scott, *A Lexicon Abridged from the Greek–English Lexicon* (Clarendon Press, Oxford 1891).

L&S Intermediate   Liddell, Henry George and Robert Scott, *An Intermediate Greek–English Lexicon* (Clarendon Press, Oxford 1889).

Lewis and Short   Lewis, Charlton T. and Charles Short, *A Latin Dictionary* (Clarendon Press, Oxford 1879).

LfgrE   Snell, Bruno and Hans Joachim Mette, *Lexikon des frühgriechischen Epos* (Vandenhoeck & Ruprecht, Göttingen 1955–).

LGS   Prott, Hans Theodor Anton and Ludwig Ziehen, *Leges Graecorum Sacrae e Titulis Collectae* (Teubner, Leipzig 1896–1906).

LIMC   *Lexicon Iconographicum Mythologiae Classicae* (Artemis, Zürich/München 1981–99).

LSJ[9]   Liddell, Henry George, Robert Scott and Sir Henry Stuart Jones, *A Greek–English Lexicon*, ninth edition (Clarendon Press, Oxford 1940).

LXX   Rahlfs, Alfred, ed., *Septuaginta* (Bibelanstalt, Stuttgart 1935).

Mertens–Pack³	Website: Mertens, Paul and Roger A. Pack, CEDOPAL:The Mertens–Pack³ database project, access date 25 May 2009.
Migne, PCC	Migne, Jacques-Paul, Patrologiae Cursus Completus (J.-P. Migne, Paris 1844–58).
Migne, PG	id., Patrologia Graeca (J.-P. Migne, Paris 1857–58).
Migne, PL	id., Patrologia Latina (J.-P. Migne, Paris 1844–45).
ML	Meiggs, Russell and David M. Lewis, A Selection of Greek Historical Inscriptions to the End of the Fifth Century B.C. (Clarendon Press, Oxford 1969).
MRR	Broughton, T. Robert S., The Magistrates of the Roman Republic (Philological Monographs published by the American Philological Association 15) (Press of Case Western Reserve University, Cleveland, OH 1951–52).
Nestle–Aland	Nestle, Eberhard and Erwin, Kurt and Barbara Aland et al., eds., Novum Testamentum Graece, twenty-seventh edition (Deutsche Bibelgesellschaft, Stuttgart 1993).
NGSL	Lupu, Eran, Greek Sacred Law: A Collection of New Documents (Religions in the Graeco-Roman World, vol. 152) (Brill, Leiden/Boston 2005).
OCD	Cary, M. et al., eds., The Oxford Classical Dictionary (Clarendon Press, Oxford 1949; second edition N. G. L. Hammond and H. H. Scullard, eds., 1970; third edition Simon Hornblower and Antony Spawforth, eds., 1996).
OCT	Oxford Classical Texts (Scriptorum Classicorum Bibliotheca Oxoniensis).
OED	Murray, James A. H., ed., A New English Dictionary on Historical Principles: Founded Mainly on the Materials Collected by the Philological Society (Clarendon Press, Oxford 1884–1928; second edition J. A. Simpson and E. S. C. Weiner, The Oxford English Dictionary, 1989). Website: www.oed.com, access date 31 December 2009.
OGIS	Dittenberger, Wilhelm, ed., Orientis Graeci Inscriptiones Selectae: Supplementum Sylloges Inscriptionum Graecarum (S. Hirzel, Leipzig 1903–05).
OLD	Glare, P. G. W. et al., eds., Oxford Latin Dictionary (Clarendon Press, Oxford 1982).
PA	Kirchner, Johannes, Prosopographia Attica, second edition (de Gruyter, Berlin 1966).
PCG	Kassel, Rudolf and Colin Austin, eds., Poetae Comici Graeci (de Gruyter, Berlin/New York 1983–).
PHI	Packard Humanities Institute.

PIR	Klebs, Elimar, Paul von Rohden and Hermann Dessau, *Prosopographia Imperii Romani Saec. I. II. III.* (first edition Reimer, Berlin 1897–98; second edition Edmund Groag et al., de Gruyter, Berlin/Leipzig/New York 1933–).
PLRE	Jones, A. H. M., J. R. Martindale and J. Morris, *The Prosopography of the Later Roman Empire* (Cambridge University Press, Cambridge 1971–92).
P.Oxy	*The Oxyrhynchus Papyri* (Egypt Exploration Fund: Graeco-Roman Branch, London 1898–). Website: *Oxyrhynchus Online* at http://www.papyrology.ox.ac.uk/POxy, access date 20 April 2009.
PW	See RE.
RBLG	Boned Colera, P. et al., *Repertorio Bibliográfico de la Lexicografia Griega* (Diccionario Griego–Español Anejo III) (Consejo Superior de Investigaciones Cientificas, Madrid 1998).
RBLG Supl.	Website: *Repertorio Bibliográfico de la Lexicografia Griega: Suplemento* at http://www.filol.csic.es/dge/blg/blg-s.htm, access date 26 April 2009.
RE	Pauly, A., G. Wissowa and W. Kroll, eds., *Real-Encyclopädie der klassischen Altertumswissenschaft* (Druckenmüller, Stuttgart 1893–1980). Sometimes abbreviated PW.
REG	*Revue des études grecques* (periodical).
RhM	*Rheinisches Museum für Philologie* (periodical). Website: http://www.rhm.uni-koeln.de/inhalt.htm, access date 25 May 2009.
RIC	Mattingly, Harold et al., *Roman Imperial Coinage* (Spink, London 1923–).
RIJG	Dareste, R., B. Haussoullier and Th. Reinach, *Recueil des inscriptions juridiques grecques* (E. Leroux, Paris 1892–1904).
RIU	Barkóczi, László and András Mócsy, eds., *Die römischen Inschriften Ungarns* (Hakkert, Amsterdam 1972–).
RPC	Burnett, Andrew, Michel Amandry and Pere Pau Ripollès, *Roman Provincial Coinage* (British Museum Press/Bibliothèque Nationale, London/Paris 1992–).
RRC	Crawford, Michael H., *Roman Republican Coinage* (Cambridge University Press, Cambridge 1974).
Sammelbuch	Preisigke, Friedrich et al., eds., *Sammelbuch griechischer Urkunden aus Ägypten* (Trübner, Strassburg 1915–).
SEG	*Supplementum Epigraphicum Graecum* (periodical); access to an online version is available for purchase at http://www.brillonline.nl, access date 25 May 2009.

SIG³	Dittenberger, Wilhelm, ed., *Sylloge Inscriptionum Graecarum*, third edition (S. Hirzel, Leipzig 1915–24).
TAM	Österreichische Akademie der Wissenschaften, *Tituli Asiae Minoris* (Hoelder-Pichler-Tempsky, Vienna 1901–).
TAPA	*Transactions of the American Philological Association* (periodical).
TGF	Nauck, Augustus, ed., *Tragicorum Graecorum fragmenta*, second edition (Teubner, Leipzig 1889).
TGL	Stephanus, Henricus, *Thesaurus Graecae Linguae*, second edition (H. Stephani oliva, Geneva 1582).
TLG	*Thesaurus Linguae Graecae* at http://www.tlg.uci.edu, access date 27 April 2009.
TLG Canon	Berkowitz, Luci and Karl A. Squitier, *Thesaurus Linguae Graecae Canon of Greek Authors and Works*, third edition (Oxford University Press, New York 1990).
TLL	*Thesaurus Linguae Latinae* (Teubner, Leipzig 1897–). This abbreviation has also been used for Stephanus, Robertus, *Dictionarium seu Latinae Linguae Thesaurus* (Robertus Stephanus, Paris 1536).
TLS	*Times Literary Supplement* (of *The Times* of London). Website: http://entertainment.timesonline.co.uk/tol/arts_and_entertainment/the_tls, access date 4 February 2010.
TRF	Ribbeck, Otto, *Tragicorum Romanorum Fragmenta*, published in *Scaenicae Romanorum Poesis Fragmenta*, third edition (Teubner, Leipzig 1897–98).
TrGF	Snell, Bruno, Richard Kannicht and S. Radt, eds., *Tragicorum Graecorum fragmenta* (Vandenhoeck & Ruprecht, Göttingen 1971–2004).
ZPE	*Zeitschrift für Papyrologie und Epigraphik* (periodical).

BIBLIOGRAPHY

WEBSITES

Websites providing the text of a book or an article are listed under that publication in the main bibliography.

Abbreviationes (Olaf Pluta) at http://www.ruhr-uni-bochum.de/philosophy/projects/abbrev.htm, access date 11 May 2009.
AgoraClass at http://agoraclass.fltr.ucl.ac.be, access date 9 February 2010.
American Academy in *Rome* at http://www.aarome.org, access date 28 May 2009.
American Numismatic Society Collections at http://www.numismatics.org/Collections/Collections, access date 1 June 2009.
American School of Classical Studies at Athens at http://www.ascsa.edu.gr, access date 28 May 2009.
Ancient Commentators on Aristotle at http://www.kcl.ac.uk/schools/humanities/depts/philosophy/research/commentators, access date 30 December 2009.
L'Année philologique at http://www.annee-philologique.com/aph, access date 25 May 2009.
APIS: Advanced Papyrological Information System at http://www.columbia.edu/cu/lweb/projects/digital/apis, access date 25 June 2009.
Archäologischer Anzeiger at http://www.dainst.org/index_281_en.html, access date 28 May 2009.
Arts & Humanities Citation Index at http://thomsonreuters.com/products_services/scientific/Arts_Humanities_Citation_Index, access date 6 April 2009.
Aufstieg und Niedergang der römischen Welt at http://www.bu.edu/ict/anrw/pub/index.html, access date 29 April 2009.
Beazley Archive at http://www.beazley.ox.ac.uk/index.htm, access date 4 June 2009.
Bibliotheca Classica Selecta at http://bcs.fltr.ucl.ac.be, access date 5 May 2010.
Brepolis at http://www.brepolis.net, access date 9 December 2009.

British School at Athens at http://www.bsa.ac.uk, access date 28 May 2009.

British School at Rome at http://www.bsr.ac.uk, access date 28 May 2009.

Bryn Mawr Classical Review at http://bmcr.brynmawr.edu, access date 14 December 2009.

Centre for the Study of Ancient Documents at http://www.csad.ox.ac.uk, access date 28 June 2009.

Checklist of Editions of Greek, Latin, Demotic, and Coptic Papyri, Ostraca and Tablets (Joshua D. Sosin et al.) at http://scriptorium.lib.duke.edu/papyrus/texts/clist.html, access date 2 April 2009.

Codices Electronici Ecclesiae Colonensis at http://www.ceec.uni-koeln.de, access date 19 May 2009.

Coin Archives.com: Ancient Coins at http://www.coinarchives.com/a, access date 2 June 2009.

Corpus Vasorum Antiquorum at http://www.cvaonline.org, access date 25 June 2009.

Deutsches Archäologisches Institut at http://www.dainst.org, access date 28 May 2009.

Deutsches Archäologisches Institut (Abteilung Athen) at http://www.dainst.org/abteilung_264_en.html, access date 25 June 2009.

Deutsches Archäologisches Institut (Abteilung Istanbul) at http://www.dainst.org/abteilung_266_en.html, access date 25 June 2009.

Deutsches Archäologisches Institut (Abteilung Rom) at http://www.dainst.org/abteilung_263_en.html, access date 25 June 2009.

Digital Scriptorium at http://scriptorium.columbia.edu, access date 10 May 2009.

Diotima at http://www.stoa.org/diotima, access date 26 August 2009.

Duke Databank of Documentary Papyri at http://idp.atlantides.org/trac/idp/wiki/DDBDP, access date 20 April 2009.

EBSCO MegaFILE at http://web.ebscohost.com/ehost/search?vid=1&hid=6&sid=6ea7134d-c448-4cc5-8ade-bf3db68c94ff%40sessionmgr13, access date 22 December 2009.

École française d'Athènes at http://www.efa.gr, access date 28 May 2009.

École française de Rome at http://www.efrome.it, access date 28 May 2009.

Electronic Palaeography at http://geocities.com/Athens/Aegean/9891/palaeog.html, access date 14 May 2009.

Electronic Resources for Classicists at http://www.tlg.uci.edu/index/resources.html, access date 9 February 2010.

Epigraphic Database Bari at http://www.edb.uniba.it, access date 7 April 2009.

Epigraphic Database for Ancient Asia Minor at http://www.epigraphik.uni-hamburg.de, access date 29 April 2009.

Epigraphic Database Roma at http://www.edr-edr.it, access date 7 April 2009.

Epigraphik Datenbank Clauss-Slaby at http://www.manfredclauss.de, access date 7 April 2009.

Epigraphische Datenbank Heidelberg at http://www.uni-heidelberg.de/institute/sonst/adw/edh, access date 7 April 2009.

EXARC at http://www.exarc.net, access date 9 February 2010.

Gallica at http://gallica.bnf.fr, access date 24 April 2009.

Glossa at http://athirdway.com/glossa, access date 24 November 2009.

Glossary of Rhetorical Terms with Examples at http://www.uky.edu/AS/Classics/rhetoric. html, access date 28 April 2009.

Gnomon Online: The Eichstätt Information System for Classical Studies at http://www. gnomon.ku-eichstaett.de/Gnomon/en/Gnomon.html and http://www.gnomon. ku-eichstaett.de/Gnomon/gnomon-download.html, access date 6 April 2009.

Greek Lexicon Project at http://www.classics.cam.ac.uk/faculty/research_groups_and_ societies/greek_lexicon, access date 7 April 2009.

Heidelberger Gesamtverzeichnis der griechischen Papyrusurkunden Ägyptens at www.rzuser.uni-heidelberg.de/~gv0, access date 20 April 2009.

Hispania Epigraphica at http://www.eda-bea.es, access date 2 June 2009.

Introduction to Modern Literary Theory (Kristi Siegel) at http://www.kristisiegel.com/ theory.htm, access date 28 April 2009.

JSTOR at http://www.jstor.org, access date 22 December 2009.

LacusCurtius at http://penelope.uchicago.edu/Thayer/E/roman/home.html, access date 1 September 2009.

Latin Library at http://www.thelatinlibrary.com, access date 27 April 2009.

Mapping History Project at http://mappinghistory.uoregon.edu, access date 1 September 2009.

Papyrological Navigator at http://www.papyri.info, access date 20 April 2009.

Parker Library on theWeb at http://parkerweb.stanford.edu, access date 19 May 2009.

Periodicals Index Online at http://pio.chadwyck.com/home.do, access date 22 December 2009.

Persée at http://www.persee.fr/web/guest/home, access date 22 December 2009.

Perseus at http://www.perseus.tufts.edu/hopper, access date 6 April 2009.

POxy: Oxyrhynchus Online at http://www.papyrology.ox.ac.uk/POxy, access date 20 April 2009.

Project MUSE at http://muse.jhu.edu, access date 22 December 2009.

Prosopographia Imperii Romani at http://www.bbaw.de/bbaw/Forschung/Forschungs projekte/pir/de/Startseite, access date 27 May 2009.

Repertorio Bibliográfico de la Lexicografia Griega: Suplemento at http://www.filol.csic.es/ dge/blg/blg-s.htm, access date 26 April 2009.

St. Laurentius Digital Manuscript Library at http://laurentius.ub.lu.se, access date 19 May 2009.

Scholia Reviews at http://www.classics.und.ac.za/reviews, access date 14 May 2009.

Science and Empire in the RomanWorld at http://www.st-andrews.ac.uk/classics/science-and-empire/, access date 28 August 2009.

Searchable Greek Inscriptions at http://epigraphy.packhum.org/inscriptions, access date 6 April 2009.

SMIDonline at http://paspserver.class.utexas.edu/index.html, access date 28 May 2009.

Stanford Digital Forma Urbis Romae Project at http://formaurbis.stanford.edu, access date 1 September 2009.

Suda On Line at http://www.stoa.org/sol, access date 28 December 2009.

Thesaurus Linguae Graecae at http://www.tlg.uci.edu, access date 27 April 2009.
TOCS-IN at http://www.chass.utoronto.ca/amphoras/tocs.html, access date 6 April 2009.
Trismegistos at http://www.trismegistos.org, access date 17 April 2009.
Vatican Library at http://www.vaticanlibrary.va, access date 19 May 2009.
VRoma at http://www.vroma.org, access date 4 February 2010.
VRoma: Aufstieg und Niedergang der römischen Welt at http://www.cs.uky.edu/~raphael/scaife/anrw.html, access date 15 December 2009.
Website Attica at http://www.chass.utoronto.ca/attica, access date 27 May 2009.
Words (William Whitaker) at http://ablemedia.com/ctcweb/showcase/whitakerwords.html, access date 30 June 2009.
The Writing Site at http://www.thewritingsite.org, access date 6 April 2009.

BOOKS AND ARTICLES

Archaeologia Homerica (Vandenhoeck & Ruprecht, Göttingen 1967–90).
Cambridge Ancient History, second edition (Cambridge University Press, Cambridge 1963–71).
Chicago Manual of Style, fifteenth edition (University of Chicago Press, Chicago/London 2003).
Commentaria in Aristotelem Graeca (G. Reimer, Berlin 1882–1909).
Corpus Inscriptionum Iudaeae/Palaestinae (de Gruyter, Berlin forthcoming).
Corpus Medicorum Graecorum/Latinorum (Deutsche Akademie der Wissenschaften, Berlin 1927–), available on web at http://cmg.bbaw.de, access date 20 April 2010.
Enciclopedia Virgiliana (Istituto della enciclopedia italiana, Rome 1984–91).
Inscriptiones Christianae Italiae (Edipuglia, Bari 1985–).
Lexicon Iconographicum Mythologiae Classicae (Artemis, Zürich/München 1981–99).
Thesaurus Linguae Latinae (Teubner, Leipzig 1897–), available on web (for a small fortune) at http://www.degruyter.de/cont/fb/at/detail.cfm?id=IS-97831102 29561-1, access date 3 February 2010.
Ackerman, Robert, *The Myth and Ritual School: J. G. Frazer and the Cambridge Ritualists* (Theorists of Myth 2) (Garland, New York 1991).
Adams, J. N., *The Latin Sexual Vocabulary* (Duckworth, London 1982).
Adkins, Lesley and Roy A. Adkins, *Dictionary of Roman Religion* (Facts on File, New York 1996).
Adrados, Francisco Rodríguez, *A History of the Greek Language from Its Origins to the Present* (Brill, Leiden/Boston 2005).
Adrados, Francisco Rodríguez et al., *Diccionario Griego–Español* (Consejo Superior de Investigaciones Cientificas, Madrid 1989–). Its website is *Instituto de Lenguas y Culturas del Mediterráneo y Oriente Próximo* at http://www.filol.csic.es/dge, access date 7 April 2009.
Adrados, Francisco Rodríguez and Juan Rodríguez Somolinos, eds., *La lexicografía griega y el Diccionario Griego–Español* (Consejo Superior de Investigaciones Cientificas, Madrid 2005).
Alföldi, Maria R.-, *Antike Numismatik* (von Zabern, Mainz am Rhein 1978).

Allen, Joseph Henry and James Bradstreet Greenough, *Allen and Greenough's New Latin Grammar* (Ginn, Boston/London 1903), available on web at http://www.perseus.tufts.edu/hopper/text.jsp?doc=Perseus%3Atext%3A1999.04.0001, access date 26 May 2009.

Allen, W. Sidney, *Vox Graeca*, third edition (Cambridge University Press, Cambridge 1987).

id., *Vox Latina*, second edition (Cambridge University Press, Cambridge 1978).

Amigues, Suzanne, *Études de botanique antique* (Mémoires de l'académie des inscriptions et belles-lettres 25) (De Boccard, Paris 2002).

ead., *Théophraste: Recherches sur les plantes* (Collection des universités de France [Budé]) (Les Belles Lettres, Paris 1988–93).

Andresen, Carl, Hartmut Erbse, Olof Gigon, Karl Schefold, Karl Friedrich Stroheker and Ernst Zinn, eds., *Lexikon der alten Welt* (Artemis, Zürich/Stuttgart 1965).

Andronicos, Manolis, *Vergina: The Royal Tombs and the Ancient City* (Ekdotike Athenon, Athens 1994).

Aravantinos, Vassilis L., Louis Godart and Anna Sacconi, *Thèbes: Fouilles de la Cadmée* (Istituti editoriali e poligrafici internazionali, Pisa/Rome 2001–).

Armstrong, A. H., ed., *The Cambridge History of Later Greek and Early Medieval Philosophy* (Cambridge University Press, Cambridge 1970).

Arnott, W. Geoffrey, *Birds in the Ancient World from A to Z* (Routledge, London/New York 2007).

Arrowsmith, William, *Bacchae*, in David Grene and Richmond Lattimore, eds., *The Complete Greek Tragedies: Euripides V* (University of Chicago Press, Chicago 1959).

id., "Teaching Euripides' *Bacchae*," Bampton Lecture II delivered at Columbia University, 1984; to appear in S. Esposito, ed., *Euripides and the Dramaturgy of Crisis* (forthcoming), available on web at http://isc.temple.edu/ihfaculty/espofinal.pdf, access date 25 June 2009.

Asheri, David et al., *Erodoto: Le Storie* (Scrittori greci e latini) (Fondazione Lorenzo Valla: A. Mondadori, Milano 1978–2006).

Asheri, David, Alan B. Lloyd and Aldo Corcella, *A Commentary on Herodotus I–IV* (Oxford University Press, Oxford 2007).

Audi, Robert, ed., *The Cambridge Dictionary of Philosophy*, second edition (Cambridge University Press, Cambridge 1999).

Audollent, Augustus, *Defixionum Tabellae Quotquot innotuerunt tam in Graecis orientis quam in totius occidentis partibus praeter Atticas in Corpore Inscriptionum Atticarum editas* (Fontemoing et Cie, Paris 1904).

Aura Jorro, Francisco, *Diccionario Micénico* (Diccionario Griego–Español Anejo I–II) (Consejo Superior de Investigaciones Cientificas, Madrid 1985–92).

Austin, Reginald P., ed., *The Stoichedon Style in Greek Inscriptions* (Oxford Classical and Political Monographs) (Clarendon Press, Oxford 1938).

Autenrieth, Georg, *Homeric Dictionary*, tr. Robert P. Keep, rev. Isaac Flagg (Harper, New York 1877), reprinted University of Oklahoma Press, Norman, OK 1958, available on web at http://www.perseus.tufts.edu/hopper/text?doc=Perseus%3Atext%3A1999.04.0073, access date 17 June 2010.

Axelson, Bertil, Unpoetische Wörter: Ein Beitrag zur Kenntnis der lateinischen Dichtersprache (Skrifter utgivna av Vetenskapssocieteten i Lund 29) (H. Ohlsson, Lund 1945).

Babelon, Ernest, Traité des monnaies grecques et romaines (E. Leroux, Paris 1901–33).

Bagnall, Roger S., The Oxford Handbook of Papyrology (Oxford Handbooks in Classics and Ancient History) (Oxford University Press, Oxford/New York 2009).

id., Reading Papyri, Writing Ancient History (Approaching the Ancient World) (Routledge, London/New York 1995).

Bagnall, Roger S., Alan Cameron, Seth R. Schwartz and Klaas A. Worp, Consuls of the Later Roman Empire (Philological Monographs of the American Philological Association 36) (Scholars Press, Atlanta, GA 1987).

Bains, Doris, A Supplement to Notae Latinae (Abbreviations in Latin MSS. of 850 to 1050 A. D.) (Cambridge University Press, Cambridge 1936).

Baldi, Philip, Foundations of Latin (Trends in Linguistics: Studies and Monographs) (Mouton/de Gruyter, Berlin 1999).

Baldwin, T. W., William Shakespere's Small Latine and Lesse Greeke (University of Illinois Press, Urbana 1944).

Bammer, Anton, "A Peripteros of the Geometric Period in the Artemisium of Ephesus," Anatolian Studies 40 (1990), 137–60.

id., "Les sanctuaires des VIIIe et VIIe siècles à l'Artémision d'Éphèse," Revue archéologique (1991), 63–84.

Bandinelli, Ranuccio Bianchi, Giovanni Becatti and Giovanni Pugliese Carratelli, eds., Enciclopedia dell'arte antica classica e orientale (Istituto della enciclopedia italiana, Rome 1958–97).

Barbour, Ruth, Greek Literary Hands A.D. 400–1600 (Clarendon Press, Oxford 1981).

Barker, Andrew, ed., Greek Musical Writings (Cambridge Readings in the Literature of Music) (Cambridge University Press, Cambridge 1984–89).

Barker, Graeme, Companion Encyclopedia of Archaeology (Routledge, London/New York 1999).

Barkóczi, László and András Mócsy, eds., Die römischen Inschriften Ungarns (Hakkert, Amsterdam 1972–).

Bartal, Antonius, Glossarium Mediae et Infimae Latinitatis Regni Hungariae (Teubner, Leipzig 1901).

Barton, Tamsyn, Ancient Astrology (Sciences of Antiquity) (Routledge, London/New York 1994).

Bartoněk, Antonin, Handbuch des mykenischen Griechisch (C. Winter, Heidelberg 2003).

Baumann, Hellmut, Greek Wild Flowers and Plant Lore in Ancient Greece, tr. William T. Stearn and Eldwyth Ruth Stearn (Herbert Press, London 1993).

Bayerische Akademie der Wissenschaften, Mittellateinisches Wörterbuch bis zum Ausgehenden 13. Jahrhundert (C. H. Beck, München 1967–).

Beard, Mary, The Invention of Jane Harrison (Harvard University Press, Cambridge, MA 2000).

Beard, Mary, John North and Simon Price, Religions of Rome (Cambridge University Press, Cambridge 1998).

Beauchet, Ludovic, Histoire du droit privé de la république athénienne (Chevalier-Marescq et Cie, Paris 1897).

Beavis, Ian C., *Insects and Other Invertebrates in Classical Antiquity* (University of Exeter, Exeter 1988).

Bebbington, David W., "Gladstone and the Classics," in Lorna Hardwick and Christopher Stray, eds., *A Companion to Classical Receptions* (Blackwell, Oxford/ Victoria/Malden, MA 2008), 86–97.

Bechtel, Friedrich, *Die griechischen Dialekte* (Weidmann, Berlin 1923).

Bechtel, Friedrich and Hermann Collitz, eds., *Sammlung der griechischen Dialekt-Inscriften* (Vandenhoeck & Ruprecht, Göttingen 1884–1915).

Beck, Hans and Uwe Walter, eds., *Die frühen römischen Historiker* (Texte zur Forschung 76–77) (Wissenschaftliche Buchgesellschaft, Darmstadt 2000–04).

Beck, Roger, *A Brief History of Ancient Astrology* (Brief Histories of the Ancient World) (Blackwell, Oxford 2007).

Becker, Lawrence C. and Charlotte B. Becker, eds., *Encyclopedia of Ethics*, second edition (Routledge, London/New York 2001).

Beekes, R. S. P., *Comparative Indo-European Linguistics: An Introduction* (John Benjamins, Amsterdam/Philadelphia 1995).

id., *Etymological Dictionary of Greek* (Leiden Indo-European Etymological Dictionary Series 10) (Brill, Leiden 2010).

Bekker, Immanuel, ed., *Aristotelis Opera* (Preussische Akademie der Wissenschaften, Berlin 1831–70).

Bengtson, Hermann and Vladimir Milojčić, *Grosser historischer Weltatlas* (Bayerischer Schulbuch-Verlag, München 1954).

Bennett, Charles E., *New Latin Grammar* (Allyn & Bacon, New York/Boston 1918), available on web at http://www.thelatinlibrary.com/bennett.html, access date 26 May 2009.

Bennett, Emmett L., *The Pylos Tablets Transcribed* (Incunabula Graeca 51, 59) (Ateneo, Rome 1973–76).

Bérard, François et al., *Guide de l'épigraphiste*, third edition (Bibliothèque de l'École Normale Supérieure, Guides et inventaires bibliographiques 2) (Presses de l'École Normale Supérieure, Paris 2000). Regular supplements can be downloaded at http://www.antiquite.ens.fr/txt/dsa-publications-guidepigraphiste-en.htm, access date 17 April 2009.

Berger, Adolf, *Encyclopedic Dictionary of Roman Law* (Transactions of the American Philosophical Society, N.S. 43, Part 2) (American Philosophical Society, Philadelphia 1953).

Berkowitz, Luci and Karl A. Squitier, *Thesaurus Linguae Graecae Canon of Greek Authors and Works*, third edition (Oxford University Press, New York 1990). Updated version is the *TLG Online Canon of Greek Authors and Works* at http://stephanus.tlg.uci.edu/canon/fontsel, access date 27 May 2009.

Bernal, Martin, *Black Athena: The Afroasiatic Roots of Classical Civilization* (Rutgers University Press, New Brunswick, NJ 1987–2006).

id., *Black Athena Writes Back: Martin Bernal Responds to His Critics* (Duke University Press, Durham, NC/London 2001).

Bernays, Jacob, *Joseph Justus Scaliger* (W. Hertz, Berlin 1855).

Bickerman, E. J., *Chronology of the Ancient World*, revised edition (Aspects of Greek and Roman Life) (Thames & Hudson, London/New York 1980).

Bing, Peter and Jon Steffen Bruss, eds., *Brill's Companion to Hellenistic Epigram* (Brill's Companions in Classical Studies) (Brill, Leiden/New York/Köln 2007).

Birley, Robin, *Vindolanda's Treasures: An Extraordinary Record of Life on Rome's Northern Frontier* (Roman Army Museum Publications, Greenhead, Northumberland 2008).

Bischoff, Bernhard, *Latin Palaeography: Antiquity and the Middle Ages* (Cambridge University Press, Cambridge/New York 1990).

Blackburn, Simon, *The Oxford Dictionary of Philosophy* (Oxford University Press, Oxford/New York 1994).

Blackwell Companions, see under Bunnin; Erdkamp; Erskine; Hardwick; Kallendorf; Knox.

Blass, Friedrich, *Die attische Beredsamkeit*, second edition (Teubner, Leipzig 1887–98).

Boardman, John, *Greek Art*, fourth edition (The World of Art Library) (Thames & Hudson, London/New York 1996).

id., *Greek Sculpture: The Archaic Period: A Handbook* (The World of Art Library) (Thames & Hudson, London 1978).

id., *Greek Sculpture: The Classical Period: A Handbook* (The World of Art Library) (Thames & Hudson, London 1985).

id., *Greek Sculpture: The Late Classical Period and Sculpture in Colonies and Overseas: A Handbook* (The World of Art Library) (Thames & Hudson, London 1995).

id., *The History of Greek Vases: Potters, Painters, and Pictures* (Thames & Hudson, London/New York 2001).

id., ed., *The Oxford History of Classical Art* (Oxford University Press, Oxford/New York 1993).

Böckh, August, *Corpus Inscriptionum Graecarum* (G. Reimer, Berlin 1828–77).

Bodoh, John J., *Index of Greek Verb Forms* (Georg Olms, Hildesheim/New York 1970).

Boegehold, Alan L., *When a Gesture Was Expected: A Selection of Examples from Archaic and Classical Greek Literature* (Princeton University Press, Princeton, NJ 1999).

Boëthius, Axel, *Etruscan and Early Roman Architecture*, second edition (Yale University Press Pelican History of Art) (Yale University Press, New Haven, CT 1978).

Bolgar, R. R., *The Classical Heritage and Its Beneficiaries* (Cambridge University Press, Cambridge 1954).

Boned Colera, P. et al., *Repertorio Bibliográfico de la Lexicografía Griega* (Diccionario Griego–Español Anejo III) (Consejo Superior de Investigaciones Cientificas, Madrid 1998).

Bookstein, A. and M. Yitzhaki, "'Own-Language Preference': A New Measure of 'Relative Language Self-Citation'," *Scientometrics* 46 (1999), 337–48.

Borg, Barbara E., "Glamorous Intellectuals: Portraits of *Pepaideumenoi* in the Second and Third Centuries AD," in Barbara E. Borg, ed., *Paideia: The World of the Second Sophistic* (de Gruyter, Berlin/New York 2004), 157–78.

Borkowski, Andrew and Paul du Plessis, *Textbook on Roman Law*, third edition (Oxford University Press, Oxford/New York 2005).

Bowersock, G. W. and T. J. Cornell, eds., *A. D. Momigliano: Studies on Modern Scholarship* (University of California Press, Berkeley/Los Angeles/London 1994).

Bowman, Alan K., *The Roman Writing Tablets from Vindolanda* (British Museum Publications, London 1983).

Boyle, Leonard E., O.P., *Medieval Latin Palaeography: A Bibliographical Introduction* (Toronto Medieval Bibliographies) (University of Toronto Press, Toronto/Buffalo/London 1984).

id., *Paleografia latina medievale: Introduzione bibliografica* (Quasar, Rome 1999).

Boys-Stones, George, Barbara Graziosi and Phiroze Vasunia, eds., *The Oxford Handbook of Hellenic Studies* (Oxford University Press, Oxford 2009).

Breglia, Laura, *Numismatica antica: Storia e metodologia* (Feltrinelli, Milano 1964).

Bremer, F. P., ed., *Iurisprudentia Antehadriana* (Teubner, Leipzig 1896–1901).

Briggs, Ward W. and William M. Calder, III, *Classical Scholarship: A Biographical Encyclopedia* (Garland Reference Library of the Humanities 928) (Garland, New York/London 1990).

Brill's Companions, see under Bing; Rengakos; Roisman.

Brink, C. O., *English Classical Scholarship: Historical Reflections on Bentley, Porson, and Housman* (James Clarke & Co., Cambridge 1986).

Briscoe, John, *A Commentary on Livy, Books XXXI–XXXIII* (Clarendon Press, Oxford 1973).

id., *A Commentary on Livy, Books XXXIV–XXXVII* (Clarendon Press, Oxford 1981).

id., *A Commentary on Livy, Books 38–40* (Clarendon Press, Oxford 2008).

British Museum Dept. of Coins and Medals, *A Catalogue of the Greek Coins in the British Museum* (Trustees of the British Museum, London 1873–1927).

British Museum Dept. of Coins and Medals and Herbert A. Grueber, *Coins of the Roman Republic in the British Museum* (Trustees of the British Museum, London 1910).

British Museum Dept. of Coins and Medals, Harold Mattingly and R. A. G. Carson, *Coins of the Roman Empire in the British Museum*, revised edition (Trustees of the British Museum, London 1968–76).

Broughton, T. Robert S., *The Magistrates of the Roman Republic* (Philological Monographs published by the American Philological Association 15) (Press of Case Western Reserve University, Cleveland, OH 1951–52).

Brown, Michelle P., *A Guide to Western Historical Scripts: From Antiquity to 1600* (University of Toronto Press, Toronto/Buffalo 1999).

Browne, G. M. et al., "Note on the Terms 'Recto' and 'Verso,' 'Front' and 'Back' and the Use of Arrows (→, ↓)," in *The Oxyrhynchus Papyri, Volume XLI* (Egypt Exploration Society, London 1972).

Browning, Robert, *Medieval and Modern Greek* (Cambridge University Press, Cambridge 1983).

Bruckner, Albert et al., eds., *Chartae Latinae Antiquiores: Facsimile-Edition of the Latin Charters* (Urs Graf, Olten/Lausanne/Dietikon-Zürich 1954–).

Brugmann, Karl, *Kurze vergleichende Grammatik der indogermanischen Sprachen* (Trübner, Strassburg 1904).

Brugmann, Karl and Berthold Delbrück, *Grundriss der vergleichenden Grammatik der indogermanischen Sprachen*, second edition (Trübner, Strassburg 1897–1916).

Bruns, Karl Georg, Theodor Mommsen and Otto Gradenwitz, eds., *Fontes Iuris Romani Antiqui*, seventh edition (C. B. Mohr, Tübingen 1909–12).

Bubel, Frank, ed., Euripides:Andromeda (Steiner, Stuttgart 1991).

Buck, Carl Darling, Comparative Grammar of Greek and Latin (University of Chicago Press, Chicago 1933).

id., The Greek Dialects (University of Chicago Press, Chicago 1955).

Buck, Carl Darling and Walter Petersen, A Reverse Index of Greek Nouns and Adjectives (University of Chicago Press, Chicago 1945).

Buckland, W. W., A Text-Book of Roman Law from Augustus to Justinian, third edition (Cambridge University Press, Cambridge 1963).

Bulmer-Thomas, Ivor, ed., Selections Illustrating the History of Greek Mathematics (Loeb Classical Library) (Harvard University Press/Heinemann, Cambridge, MA/London 1939–41).

Bulwer, John, ed., Classics Teaching in Europe (Duckworth, London 2006).

Bunbury, E. H., A History of Ancient Geography among the Greeks and the Romans, from the Earliest Ages till the Fall of the Roman Empire (J. Murray, London 1879).

Bunnin, Nicholas and E. P. Tsui-James, The Blackwell Companion to Philosophy, second edition (Blackwell Companions to Philosophy 1) (Blackwell, Oxford 2003).

Burford, Alison, Craftsmen in Greek and Roman Society (Thames & Hudson, London 1972).

Burgière, Paul, Danielle Gourevitch and Yves Malinas, Soranos d'Éphèse: Maladies des femmes (Collection des universités de France [Budé]) (Les Belles Lettres, Paris 1988–94).

Burkert, Walter, Greek Religion:Archaic and Classical (Blackwell, Oxford 1985).

Burnett, Andrew, Michel Amandry and Pere Pau Ripollès, Roman Provincial Coinage (British Museum Press/Bibliothèque Nationale, London/Paris 1992–).

Bury, J. B. et al., eds., Cambridge Ancient History, first edition (Cambridge University Press, Cambridge 1924–39).

Butler, Samuel, The Authoress of the Odyssey:Where and When She Wrote,Who She Was, the Use She Made of the Iliad, & How the Poem Grew under Her Hands, second edition (Jonathan Cape, London 1922).

Cagnat, R., J. Toutain and P. Jouguet, eds., Inscriptiones Graecae ad Res Romanas Pertinentes (Ernest Leroux, Paris 1911–27).

Cagnat, René, Cours d'épigraphie latine, fourth edition (Fontemoing et Cie, Paris 1914).

Cahill, Nicholas, Household and City Organization at Olynthus (Yale University Press, New Haven, CT/London 2002). Available on web at http://www.stoa.org/olynthus, access date 2 September 2009.

Cahill, Nicholas and John H. Kroll, "New Archaic Coin Finds at Sardis," AJA (2005), 589–617.

Cairns, Douglas, ed., Body Language in the Greek and RomanWorlds (Classical Press of Wales, Swansea 2005).

Calame, Claude, Choruses of Young Women in Ancient Greece (Greek Studies: Interdisciplinary Approaches) (Rowman & Littlefield, Lanham, MD/Boulder, CO/NewYork/London 1997).

Calder, William M., III, "Ecce Homo: The Autobiographical in Wilamowitz' Scholarly Writings," in id., Men in Their Books: Studies in the Modern History of Classical Scholarship (Georg Olms, Zürich/NewYork 1998), 23–53.

id., *Men in Their Books: Studies in the Modern History of Classical Scholarship* (Spudasmata 67), edited by John P. Harris and R. Scott Smith (Georg Olms, Zürich/New York 1998).

Calder, William M., III and Daniel J. Kramer, *An Introductory Bibliography to the History of Classical Scholarship: Chiefly in the XIXth and XXth Centuries* (Georg Olms, Hildesheim/New York 1992).

Calder, William M., III and R. Scott Smith, *A Supplementary Bibliography to the History of Classical Scholarship: Chiefly in the XIXth and XXth Centuries* (Dedalo, Bari 2000).

Calderini, Aristide, *Dizionario dei nomi geografici e topografici dell'Egitto greco-romano*, with Supplemento by Sergio Daris (Cisalpino-Goliardica, Milano 1966–).

Cam, Marie-Thérèse, ed., *La médecine vétérinaire antique: Sources écrites, archéologiques, iconographiques* (Actes du colloque international de Brest, 9–11 septembre 2004, Université de Bretagne Occidentale) (Presses Universitaires de Rennes, Rennes 2007).

Cambridge Companions, see under Gagarin; Gerson; Long; Martindale; Preston; Sedley; Shelmerdine. Available and searchable on web to subscribers at http://cco.cambridge.org/public_home, access date 7 February 2010.

Campbell, Brian, *The Writings of the Roman Land Surveyors: Introduction, Text, Translation and Commentary* (JRS Monograph 9) (Society for the Promotion of Roman Studies, London 2000).

Campbell, David A., *Greek Lyric* (Loeb Classical Library) (Heinemann/Harvard University Press, London/Cambridge, MA 1982–93).

Campbell, Gordon, ed., *The Grove Encyclopedia of Classical Art and Architecture* (Oxford University Press, Oxford 2007).

Campbell, Lyle, *Historical Linguistics: An Introduction*, second edition (Edinburgh University Press, Edinburgh 2004).

Cancik, Hubert and Helmuth Schneider, eds., *Brill's New Pauly: Encyclopaedia of the Ancient World* (Brill, Leiden/Boston 2002–).

id., eds., *Der Neue Pauly: Enzyklopädie der Antike* (J. B. Metzler, Stuttgart/Weimar 1996–2004).

Capizzi, Antonio, *The Cosmic Republic: Notes for a Non-Peripatetic History of the Birth of Philosophy in Greece* (Philosophica 3) (J. C. Gieben, Amsterdam 1990).

Cappelli, Adriano, *Elements of Abbreviation in Medieval Latin* (University of Kansas Libraries, Lawrence 1982).

id., *Lexicon abbreviaturarum* = *Dizionario di abbreviature latine ed italiane* (Hoepl, Milano 1912), available on web at http://inkunabeln.ub.uni-koeln.de/vdib Production/handapparat/nachs_w/cappelli/cappelli.html, access date 19 May 2009.

Carden, Richard, ed., *The Papyrus Fragments of Sophocles* (Texte und Kommentare 7) (de Gruyter, Berlin/New York 1974).

Carlyle, Thomas, *On Heroes, Hero-Worship, the Heroic in History* (J. Fraser, London 1841).

Carson, R. A. G., *Coins of the Roman Empire* (Routledge, London 1990).

Cartledge, Paul, ed., *The Cambridge Illustrated History of Ancient Greece* (Cambridge University Press, Cambridge 1998).

Cary, M. et al., eds., *The Oxford Classical Dictionary*, first edition (Clarendon Press, Oxford 1949).

Casey, John, *Understanding Ancient Coins: An Introduction for Archaeologists and Historians* (Batsford, London 1986).

Cassuto, Umberto, *The Documentary Hypothesis and the Composition of the Pentateuch: Eight Lectures* (Magnes Press, Jerusalem 1961).

Chadwick, John, *The Decipherment of Linear B*, second edition (Cambridge University Press, Cambridge 1970).

id., *Lexicographica Graeca: Contributions to the Lexicography of Ancient Greek* (Clarendon Press, Oxford 1996).

Chandler, Henry W., *A Practical Introduction to Greek Accentuation*, second edition (Clarendon Press, Oxford 1881), reprinted A. D. Caratzas, New Rochelle, NY 1983.

Chantraine, Pierre, *Dictionnaire étymologique de la langue grecque* (Klincksieck, Paris 1968), reprinted with a supplement 1999.

Charles-Picard, Gilbert, ed., *Larousse Encyclopedia of Archaeology*, second edition (Larousse, New York 1983).

Chase, Philip G. and April Nowell, "Taphonomy of a Suggested Middle Paleolithic Bone Flute from Slovenia," *Current Anthropology* 39 (1998), 549–53.

Chassignet, Martine, ed., *L'Annalistique romaine* (Collection des universités de France [Budé]) (Les Belles Lettres, Paris 1996–2004).

Chomsky, Noam, *Language and Mind*, third edition (Cambridge University Press, Cambridge 2006).

id., *Syntactic Structures* (Janua Linguarum 4) (Mouton, 's Gravenhage 1957).

Christ, Karl, *Antike Numismatik: Einführung und Bibliographie* (Wissenschaftliche Buchgesellschaft, Darmstadt 1967).

Christidis, A.-F., ed., *A History of Ancient Greek: From the Beginnings to Late Antiquity* (Cambridge University Press, Cambridge 2007).

Cipolla, Paolo, ed., *Poeti minori del dramma satiresco: Testo critico, traduzione e commento* (Supplementi di Lexis 23) (Hakkert, Amsterdam 2003).

Clain-Stefanelli, Elvira E., *Numismatic Bibliography* (Battenberg, München 1985).

Clapp, Philip S., Barbara Friberg and Timothy Friberg, eds., *Analytical Concordance of the Greek New Testament* (Baker Book House, Grand Rapids, MI 1991).

Clarke, John, *Justini Historiae Philippicae: Cum Versione Anglica, Ad Verbum, quantum fieri potuit, facta, or, the History of Justin: With an English Translation, as Literal as Possible*, fifth edition (John Exshaw, Dublin 1754), available on web at http://books.google.com/books?id=9vIpAAAAYAAJ, access date 25 June 2009.

Clemenceau, Georges, *Demosthenes* (Houghton Mifflin, Boston/New York 1926).

Clemens, Raymond and Timothy Graham, *Introduction to Manuscript Studies* (Cornell University Press, Ithaca, NY 2007).

Coates, J. F., "Historical & Technical," *The Trireme Trust—Newsletter*, November 2000, available on web at http://www.atm.ox.ac.uk/rowing/trireme/tt19.html.

Cohen, Beth, ed., *Not the Classical Ideal: Athens and the Construction of the Other in Greek Art* (Brill, Leiden/Boston/Köln 2000).

Cohen, M. R. and I. E. Drabkin, eds., *A Sourcebook in Greek Science* (Harvard University Press, Cambridge, MA 1948).

Coles, John, *Experimental Archaeology* (Academic Press, New York 1979).

Collard, C. and M. J. Cropp, eds., Euripides VII and VIII (Fragments) (Loeb Classical Library) (Harvard University Press, Cambridge, MA/London 2008).

Collard, C., M. J. Cropp and K. H. Lee, eds., Euripides: Selected Fragmentary Plays (Aris & Phillips Classical Texts) (Aris & Phillips, Warminster 1995–2004).

Collingwood, R. G. et al., The Roman Inscriptions of Britain (Clarendon Press, Oxford 1965–94), first volume summarized at http://www.roman-britain.org/epigraphy/rib_index.htm.

Colomo, D. and N. Gonis, eds., The Oxyrhynchus Papyri, Part LXXII (Graeco-Roman Memoirs 82) (Arts and Humanities Research Council by the Egypt Exploration Society, London 2008).

Cooper, Guy L., III, Greek Syntax after K.W. Krüger (University of Michigan Press, Ann Arbor 1997–2002).

Corbeil, Jean-Claude, The Facts on File Visual Dictionary (Facts on File, New York 1986).

Cornell, T. J., ed., Fragments of the Roman Historians (Clarendon Press, Oxford forthcoming).

Cotton, Hannah M., Omri Lernau and Yuval Goren, "Fish Sauces from Herodian Masada," Journal of Roman Archaeology 9 (1996), 223–38.

Courtney, Edward, The Fragmentary Latin Poets (Clarendon Press, Oxford 1993).

Craig, Edward, ed., Routledge Encyclopedia of Philosophy (Routledge, London/New York 1998).

Crawford, Michael H., Roman Republican Coinage (Cambridge University Press, Cambridge 1974).

id., ed., Roman Statutes (BICS Supplement 64) (Institute of Classical Studies, London 1996).

Crook, J. A., Law and Life of Rome (Cornell University Press, Ithaca, NY 1967).

Cruse, Audrey, Roman Medicine (Tempus, Stroud 2004).

Csapo, Eric, Theories of Mythology (Blackwell, Oxford/Malden, MA 2005).

Cuomo, S., Ancient Mathematics (Sciences of Antiquity) (Routledge, London/New York 2001).

Currie, H. MacL., "The Third Eclogue and the Roman Comic Spirit," Mnemosyne 29 (4th ser.) (1976), 411–20.

Curtis, Robert I., Ancient Food Technology (Technology and Change in History 5) (Brill, Leiden/Boston/Köln 2001).

Daehn, William E., Ancient Greek Numismatics: A Guide to Reading and Research (Davissons, Cold Spring, MN 2001).

Danker, Frederick William, A Greek–English Lexicon of the New Testament and Other Early Christian Literature, third edition (University of Chicago Press, Chicago/London 2000).

Daremberg, Charles and Edmond Saglio, eds., Dictionnaire des antiquités grecques et romaines d'après les textes et les monuments (Hachette, Paris 1877–1919), available on web at http://dagr.univ-tlse2.fr/sdx/dagr/index.xsp, access date 4 February 2010.

Dareste, R., B. Haussoullier and Th. Reinach, Recueil des inscriptions juridiques grecques (E. Leroux, Paris 1892–1904).

Daube, David, Collected Studies in Roman Law, edited by David Cohen and Dieter Simon (Klostermann, Frankfurt am Main 1991).

id., *Roman Law: Linguistic, Social and Philosophical Aspects* (Edinburgh University Press, Edinburgh 1969).

Daviault, André, *Comoedia Togata: Fragments* (Collection des universités de France [Budé]) (Les Belles Lettres, Paris 1981).

Davies, Anna Morpurgo, *Mycenaeae Graecitatis Lexicon* (Incunabula Graeca 3) (Athenaeum, Rome 1963).

Davies, John K., *Athenian Propertied Families, 600–300 B.C.* (Clarendon Press, Oxford 1971).

id., *Wealth and the Power of Wealth in Classical Athens* (Ayer, Salem, NH 1984).

Davies, Malcolm, ed., *Epicorum Graecorum Fragmenta* (Vandenhoeck & Ruprecht, Göttingen 1988).

id., *Poetarum Melicorum Graecorum Fragmenta* (Clarendon Press, Oxford 1991).

Davies, Malcolm and Jeyaraney Kathirithamby, *Greek Insects* (Duckworth, London 1986).

Davis, Jack L., "Classical Archaeology and Anthropological Archaeology in North America: A Meeting of Minds at the Millennium?," in Gary M. Feinman and T. Douglas Price, eds., *Archaeology at the Millennium: A Sourcebook* (Kluwer Academic/Plenum Publishers, New York 2001), 415–37.

de Grummond, Nancy Thomson, ed., *An Encyclopedia of the History of Classical Archaeology* (Greenwood, Westport, CT 1996).

de Jong, Irene J. F., *A Narratological Commentary on the Odyssey* (Cambridge University Press, Cambridge 2001).

de Rossi, Giovanni Battista, Angelo Silvagni and Antonio Ferrua, *Inscriptiones Christianae urbis Romae septimo saeculo antiquiores* (Pontificale Collegium a Sacra Archaeologia/ Regalis Societas Romana ab Historia Patria, Rome 1922–).

de Ste. Croix, G. E. M., *The Class Struggle in the Ancient Greek World* (Duckworth, London 1981).

id., "Some Observations on the Property Rights of Athenian Women," CR 20 (N.S.) (1970), 273–8.

de Vaan, Michiel, *Etymological Dictionary of Latin and the Other Italic Languages* (Leiden Indo-European Etymological Dictionary Series 7) (Brill, Leiden/Boston 2008).

de Zulueta, Francis, ed., *The Institutes of Gaius* (Clarendon Press, Oxford 1946).

Dean-Jones, Lesley, *Women's Bodies in Classical Greek Science* (Clarendon Press, Oxford 1994).

Degrassi, Attilio, *Inscriptiones Latinae Liberae Rei Publicae* (La Nuova Italia, Firenze 1957–65).

Dekkers, Eligius, Dom et al., eds., *Corpus Christianorum* (Brepols, Turnhout 1953–).

Delattre, Daniel, *Philodème de Gadara: Sur la musique* (Collection des universités de France [Budé]) (Les Belles Lettres, Paris 2007).

Delavaud-Roux, Marie-Hélène, *Les Danses armées en Grèce antique* (Publications de l'Université de Provence, Aix-en-Provence 1993).

ead., *Les Danses pacifiques en Grèce antique* (Publications de l'Université de Provence, Aix-en-Provence 1994).

Della Corte, Francesco, ed., *Dizionario degli scrittori greci e latini* (Marzorati, Milano 1987–88).

Demandt, Alexander, "Klassik als Klischee: Hitler und die Antike," *Historische Zeitschrift* 274 (2002), 281–313.

Denniston, J. D., *The Greek Particles* (Clarendon Press, Oxford 1954).

Derrida, Jacques, "Structure, Sign, and Play in the Discourse of the Human Sciences," in *Writing and Difference* (University of Chicago Press, Chicago 1978), 278–94.

Dessau, Hermann, *Inscriptiones Latinae Selectae* (Weidmann, Berlin 1892–1916).

Detienne, Marcel, *The Greeks and Us: A Comparative Anthropology of Ancient Greece* (Polity, Cambridge/Malden, MA 2007).

Develin, Robert, *Athenian Officials, 684–321 B.C.* (Cambridge University Press, Cambridge 1989).

Devine, A. M. and Laurence D. Stephens, *Latin Word Order: Structured Meaning and Information* (Oxford University Press, Oxford/New York 2006).

Devreesse, Robert, *Introduction à l'étude des manuscrits grecs* (Imprimerie Nationale, Paris 1954).

Di Giglio, Anna, *Strumenti delle Muse: Lineamenti di organologia greca* (Femio 6: Collana di Didattica e di Manualistica) (Levante, Bari 2000).

Dickey, Eleanor, *Ancient Greek Scholarship: A Guide to Finding, Reading, and Understanding Scholia, Commentaries, Lexica, and Grammatical Treatises from Their Beginnings to the Byzantine Period* (American Philological Association Books) (Oxford University Press, Oxford 2007).

ead., *Greek Forms of Address from Herodotus to Lucian* (Oxford Classical Monographs) (Clarendon Press, Oxford 1996).

ead., *Latin Forms of Address from Plautus to Apuleius* (Oxford University Press, Oxford 2002).

Dickinson, Oliver, "The 'Face of Agamemnon,'" *Hesperia* 74 (2005), 299–308.

Diehl, Ernst, *Inscriptiones Latinae Christianae Veteres* (Weidmann, Berlin 1925–31).

Diels, Hermann and Walther Kranz, *Die Fragmente der Vorsokratiker: griechisch und deutsch*, sixth edition (Weidmann, Berlin 1951).

Diggle, James, *Euripides: Phaethon* (Cambridge Classical Texts and Commentaries) (Cambridge University Press, Cambridge 1970).

id., *Tragicorum Graecorum Fragmenta Selecta* (Oxford Classical Texts) (Clarendon Press, Oxford 1998).

Dik, Helma, *Word Order in Ancient Greek: A Pragmatic Account of Word Order Variation in Herodotus* (Amsterdam Studies in Classical Philology 5) (J. C. Gieben, Amsterdam 1995).

Dik, Simon, *The Theory of Functional Grammar* (Functional Grammar Series 20–1) (Mouton de Gruyter, Berlin/New York 1997).

Dilke, O. A. W., *Greek and Roman Maps* (Aspects of Greek and Roman Life) (Thames & Hudson, London/New York 1985).

id., *The Roman Land Surveyors: An Introduction to the Agrimensores* (David & Charles, Newton Abbot 1971).

Dimitrakos, Dimitrios V., *Μέγα Λεξικόν Ὅλης τῆς Ἑλληνικῆς Γλώσσης* (Domi, Athens 1964).

Dittenberger, Wilhelm, ed., *Orientis Graeci Inscriptiones Selectae: Supplementum Sylloges Inscriptionum Graecarum* (S. Hirzel, Leipzig 1903–05).

id., ed., *Sylloge Inscriptionum Graecarum*, third edition (S. Hirzel, Leipzig 1915–24).

Donlan, Walter, *The Classical World Bibliography of Greek and Roman History* (Garland Reference Library of the Humanities 94) (Garland, New York/London 1978).

id., *The Classical World Bibliography of Greek Drama and Poetry* (Garland Reference Library of the Humanities 93) (Garland, New York/London 1978).

id., *The Classical World Bibliography of Philosophy, Religion, and Rhetoric* (Garland Reference Library of the Humanities 95) (Garland, New York/London 1978).

id., *The Classical World Bibliography of Roman Drama and Poetry and Ancient Fiction* (Garland Reference Library of the Humanities 97) (Garland, New York/London 1978).

id., *The Classical World Bibliography of Vergil* (Garland Reference Library of the Humanities 96) (Garland, New York/London 1978).

Dornseiff, Franz and Bernhard Hansen, *Rückläufiges Wörterbuch der griechischen Eigennamen* (Berichte über die Verhandlungen der Sächsischen Akademie der Wissenschaften zu Leipzig, Philologisch-historische Klasse, Band 102, Heft 4) (1957).

Dover, K. J., *Greek Word Order* (Cambridge University Press, Cambridge 1960).

Dow, Sterling, *Conventions in Editing: A Suggested Reformulation of the Leiden System* (Greek, Roman and Byzantine Scholarly Aids 2) (Duke University Press, Durham, NC 1969).

Drerup, Engelbert, *Aus einer alten Advokatenrepublik: Demosthenes und seine Zeit* (F. Schöningh, Paderborn 1916).

Driessen, Jan, "Le palais de Cnossos au MR II–III: Combien de destructions?," in Jan Driessen and Alexandre Farnoux, eds., *La Crète mycénienne* (École française d'Athènes, Athens 1997), 113–34.

du Bois, Page, *Sowing the Body: Psychoanalysis and Ancient Representations of Women* (Women in Culture and Society) (University of Chicago Press, Chicago/London 1988).

du Cange, Charles du Fresne, *Glossarium ad scriptores mediae et infimae Graecitatis* (Anisson, J. Posuel, & C. Rigaud, Loudin 1688).

id., *Glossarium ad scriptores mediae et infimae Latinitatis* (G. Martin, Paris 1678), available on web at http://ducange.enc.sorbonne.fr, access date 10 June 2010.

Dubois, Claude-Gilbert, *Celtes et Gaulois au XVIᵉ siècle: Le Développement littéraire d'un mythe nationaliste (De Pétrarque à Descartes)* (J. Vrin, Paris 1972).

Duhoux, Yves and Anna Morpurgo Davies, *A Companion to Linear B: Mycenaean Greek Texts and Their World* (Bibliothèque des Cahiers de l'Institut de Linguistique de Louvain 120) (Peeters, Louvain-la-Neuve/Dudley, MA 2008–).

Eck, Werner, "Inschriften auf Holz: Ein unterschätztes Phänomen der epigraphischen Kultur Roms," in Peter Kneissl and Volker Losemann, eds., *Imperium Romanum: Studien zu Geschichte und Rezeption. Festschrift für Karl Christ zum 75. Geburtstag* (F. Steiner, Stuttgart 1998), 203–17.

id., "Lateinische Epigraphik," in Fritz Graf, ed., *Einleitung in die lateinische Philologie* (Teubner, Stuttgart/Leipzig 1997), 92–111.

Eckstein, Friedrich August, *Nomenclator Philologorum* (Teubner, Leipzig 1871).

Eder, Walter and Johannes Renger, eds., *Chronologies of the Ancient World: Names, Dates and Dynasties* (Brill's New Pauly Supplement 1) (Brill, Leiden/Boston 2007).

Edmonds, John Maxwell, "The Cairensis of Menander by Infra-Red," in Mary E. White, ed., *Studies in Honour of G. Norwood* (University of Toronto Press, Toronto 1952), 127–32.

id., ed., *Elegy and Iambus with the Anacreontea* (Loeb Classical Library) (Heinemann/ Harvard University Press, London/Cambridge, MA 1931).

id., ed., *The Fragments of Attic Comedy* (Brill, Leiden 1957–61).

id., ed., *Lyra Graeca* (Heinemann/Harvard University Press, London/Cambridge, MA 1922–27).

id., ed., *The Samia of Menander: The Augmented Text with Notes and a Verse Translation* (Deighton, Bell & Co., Cambridge 1950).

Edmunds, Lowell, ed., *Approaches to Greek Myth* (Johns Hopkins University Press, Baltimore 1990).

Edwards, Catherine, ed., *Roman Presences: Receptions of Rome in European Culture, 1789–1945* (Cambridge University Press, Cambridge 1999).

Edwards, Paul, ed., *The Encyclopedia of Philosophy* (Macmillan/Free Press, New York 1967).

Egghe, Leo, Ronald Rousseau and M. Yitzhaki, "The 'Own-Language Preference': Measures of 'Relative Language Self-Citation'," *Scientometrics* 45 (1999), 217–32.

Ellis, Linda, *Archaeological Method and Theory: An Encyclopedia* (Garland, New York/London 2000).

Elster, Marianne, *Die Gesetze der mittleren römischen Republik* (Wissenschaftliche Buchgesellschaft, Darmstadt 2003).

Embree, Lester et al., eds., *Encyclopedia of Phenomenology* (Contributions to Phenomenology) (Kluwer, Dordrecht/Boston/London 1997).

Emmanuel, Maurice, *The Antique Greek Dance after Sculptured and Painted Figures* (John Lane, New York/London 1916).

id., *La Danse grecque antique d'après les monuments figurés* (Hachette, Paris 1896), reprinted Slatkine Reprints, Geneva/Paris 1987.

Erdkamp, Paul, ed., *A Companion to the Roman Army* (Blackwell Companions to the Ancient World) (Blackwell, Malden, MA/Oxford 2007).

Erler, Tobias et al., eds., *Paulys Real-Encyclopädie der klassischen Altertumswissenschaft, Gesamtregister I, alphabetischer Teil; Gesamtregister II: Systematisches Sach- und Suchregister* (J. B. Metzler, Stuttgart/Weimar 1997–2000).

Ernout, A. and A. Meillet, *Dictionnaire étymologique de la langue latine: Histoire des mots*, fourth edition (Klincksieck, Paris 1959).

Erskine, Andrew, ed., *A Companion to Ancient History* (Blackwell Companions to the Ancient World) (Wiley-Blackwell, Malden, MA/Oxford 2009).

Evans, James, *The History and Practice of Ancient Astronomy* (Oxford University Press, Oxford 1998).

Evans, Thomas L. and Patrick Daly, eds., *Digital Archaeology: Bridging Method and Theory* (Routledge, London/New York 2006).

Fagan, Brian M., *The Oxford Companion to Archaeology* (Oxford University Press, Oxford/New York 1996).

Fassbender, Andreas, *Index numerorum* (Corpus Inscriptionum Latinarum Auctarium Series Nova 1) (de Gruyter, Berlin/New York 2003).

Field, Frederick, ed., *Origenis Hexapla Quae Supersunt* (Clarendon Press, Oxford 1875).

Fink, Bob, "Neanderthal Flute: Oldest Musical Instrument's 4 Notes Matches 4 of Do, Re, Mi Scale," at http://www.greenwych.ca/fl-compl.htm, access date 29 March 2009.

Finley, Moses I., *The Ancient Economy*, second edition (Hogarth, London 1985).

id., "Aristotle and Economic Analysis," *Past and Present* 47 (1970), 3–25, reprinted in id., *Studies in Ancient Society* (Routledge & Kegan Paul, London, 1974), 26–52.

id., ed., *The Bücher–Meyer Controversy* (Arno Press, New York 1979).

id., ed., *The Legacy of Greece* (Clarendon Press, Oxford 1981).

id., "Technological Innovation and Economic Progress in the Ancient World," *Economic History Review* (N.S.) 18 (1965), 29–45.

id., *The World of Odysseus*, second edition (Viking, New York 1978).

Flashar, Hellmut, ed., *Philosophie der Antike* (Grundriss der Geschichte der Philosophie) (Schwabe, Basel/Stuttgart 1983–).

Flemming, Rebecca, *Medicine and the Making of Roman Women* (Oxford University Press, Oxford/New York 2000).

Florance, A., *Geographic Lexicon of Greek Coin Inscriptions* (Argonaut, Chicago 1966).

Foraboschi, Daniele, *P. Mil Vogliano 301–308: La contabilità di un'azienda agricola nel II sec. d.C.* (Papiri della Università degli studi di Milano, Vol. 7) (Istituto Editoriale Cisalpino, Milano 1981).

Forbes, R. J., *Studies in Ancient Technology* (Brill, Leiden 1955–64).

Forcellini, Egidio et al., *Lexicon Totius Latinitatis*, fourth edition (Typis Seminarii, Padua 1864–1926).

Forte, Maurizio and Alberto Siliotti, *Virtual Archaeology: Great Discoveries Brought to Life through Virtual Reality* (Thames & Hudson, London/New York 1997).

Fortenbaugh, W. W. et al., eds., *Theophrastus of Eresus, Sources for His Life, Writings, Thought and Influence* (Brill, Leiden 1992).

Fortenbaugh, W. W. and E. Schütrumpf, eds., *Demetrius of Phalerum: Text, Translation and Discussion* (Rutgers University Studies in Classical Humanities 9) (Transaction, Piscataway, NJ 2000).

id., eds., *Dicaearchus of Messana* (Rutgers University Studies in Classical Humanities 10) (Transaction, Piscataway, NJ 2001).

Fortenbaugh, W. W. and S. A. White, eds., *Aristo of Ceos* (Rutgers University Studies in Classical Humanities 13) (Transaction, Piscataway, NJ 2006).

id., eds., *Lyco of Troas and Hieronymus of Rhodes* (Rutgers University Studies in Classical Humanities 11) (Transaction, Piscataway, NJ 2004).

Fortson, Benjamin W., IV, *Indo-European Language and Culture: An Introduction* (Wiley-Blackwell, Malden, MA 2004).

Fowler, D. H., *The Mathematics of Plato's Academy: A New Reconstruction* (Clarendon Press, Oxford 1987).

Fraenkel, Eduard, *Plautine Elements in Plautus* (Oxford University Press, Oxford/New York 2007).

Frank, Tenney, ed., *An Economic Survey of Ancient Rome* (Johns Hopkins Press, Baltimore 1933–40).

Fraser, P. M. and E. Matthews, *A Lexicon of Greek Personal Names* (Clarendon Press, Oxford 1987–).

Frassinetti, Paolo, *Atellanae Fabulae* (Poetarum Latinorum Reliquae) (Edizioni dell'Ateneo, Rome 1967).

Frazer, James George, Sir, *The Golden Bough*, third edition (Macmillan, London 1913, reprinted 1980). There is also an abridged version, *The New Golden Bough* (Criterion Books, New York 1959).

Frede, Dorothea, "Die wundersame Wandelbarkeit der antiken Philosophie in der Gegenwart," in Ernst-Richard Schwinge, ed., *Die Wissenschaften vom Altertum am Ende des 2. Jahrtausends n. Chr.* (Teubner, Stuttgart/Leipzig 1995), 9–40.

Freeman, Kathleen, *Ancilla to the Pre-Socratic Philosophers* (Harvard University Press, Cambridge, MA 1948).

French, Roger, *Ancient Natural History: Histories of Nature* (Routledge, London/New York 1994).

Freund, Wilhelm, *Wörterbuch der lateinischen Sprache: Nach historisch-genetischen Principien, mit steter Berücksichtigung der Grammatik, Synonymik und Alterthumskunde* (Teubner, Leipzig 1834–40).

Frisk, Hjalmar, *Griechisches etymologisches Wörterbuch* (Winter, Heidelberg 1960).

Fuchs, J. W. et al., *Lexicon Latinitatis Nederlandicae Medii Aevi* (*Woordenboek van het Middeleeuws Latijn van de Noordelijke Nederlanden*) (Hakkert, Amsterdam 1970–2005).

Fuendling, Joerg, review of Werner Eck, Matthäus Heil and Johannes Heinrichs, eds., *Prosopographia Imperii Romani Saec. I. II. III. Pars viii, Fasciculus 1*, BMCR 2009.12.15.

Funaioli, Gino (Hyginus), *Grammaticae Romanae Fragmenta* (Teubner, Leipzig 1907).

Fustel de Coulanges, Numa Denis, *The Ancient City: A Study on the Religion, Laws, and Institutions of Greece and Rome* (Johns Hopkins University Press, Baltimore 1980).

Gaffiot, Félix, *Dictionnaire illustré Latin–Français* (Hachette, Paris 1934).

Gagarin, Michael, "The Unity of Greek Law," in Michael Gagarin and David Cohen, eds., *The Cambridge Companion to Ancient Greek Law* (Cambridge University Press, Cambridge 2005), 29–40.

Gagarin, Michael and David Cohen, eds., *The Cambridge Companion to Ancient Greek Law* (Cambridge University Press, Cambridge 2005).

Gardner, Martin, *Aha! Insight* (Scientific American, New York 1978).

Garelli, M.-H., *Danser le mythe: La pantomime et sa réception dans la culture antique* (Bibliothèque d'Études Classiques 51) (Peeters, Louvain 2007).

Gärtner, Hans and Albert Wünsch, eds., *Paulys Real-Encyclopädie der klassischen Altertumswissenschaft: Register der Nachträge und Supplemente* (Druckenmüller, München 1980).

Gerber, Douglas E., *Greek Elegiac Poetry from the Seventh to the Fifth Centuries B.C.* (Loeb Classical Library) (Heinemann/Harvard University Press, London/Cambridge, MA 1999).

Gere, Cathy, *Knossos and the Prophets of Modernism* (University of Chicago Press, Chicago/London 2009).

Gernet, Louis, *Droit et société dans la Grèce ancienne* (Recueil Sirey, Paris 1956).

Gerson, Lloyd P., *Aristotle and Other Platonists* (Cornell University Press, Ithaca, NY 2005).

id., ed., *The Cambridge Companion to Plotinus* (Cambridge University Press, Cambridge 1996).

Gibbon, Edward, *The Decline and Fall of the Roman Empire* (Modern Library) (Random House, New York 1940).

Gignac, Francis Thomas, *A Grammar of the Greek Papyri of the Roman and Byzantine Periods* (Testi e documenti per lo studio dell'antichità) (Cisalpino-La Goliardica, Milano 1976–81).

Gildersleeve, B. L. and G. Lodge, *Gildersleeve's Latin Grammar*, third edition (Macmillan, New York 1895), available on web at http://www.archive.org/details/gildersleeveslat00gilduoft, access date 26 May 2009.

Gildersleeve, Basil Lanneau, *Syntax of Classical Greek from Homer to Demosthenes* (American Book Company, New York/Cincinnati/Chicago 1900–11), reprinted Bouma's Boekhuis B. V., Groningen 1980.

Glare, P. G. W., ed., *Greek–English Lexicon: Revised Supplement* (Clarendon Press, Oxford 1996).

Glare, P. G. W. et al., eds., *Oxford Latin Dictionary* (Clarendon Press, Oxford 1982).

Glock, Hans-Johann, "Analytic Philosophy and History: A Mismatch?," *Mind* 117 (2008), 867–97.

Glucker, John, *Antiochus and the Late Academy* (Hypomnemata 56) (Vandenhoeck & Ruprecht, Göttingen 1978).

Goffer, Z., ed., *Elsevier's Dictionary of Archaeological Materials and Archaeometry* (Elsevier, Amsterdam 1996).

Gomme, A. W., A. Andrewes and Kenneth J. Dover, *A Historical Commentary on Thucydides* (Clarendon Press, Oxford 1959–81).

Goodwin, William Watson, *Syntax of the Moods and Tenses of the Greek Verb*, rewritten and enlarged (Macmillan, London 1897).

Goodyear, F. R. D., *The Annals of Tacitus: Books 1–6* (Cambridge Classical Texts and Commentaries 15, 23) (Cambridge University Press, Cambridge 1972–81) (only two volumes were published, covering Books 1 and 2).

Gordon, Arthur E., *Illustrated Introduction to Latin Epigraphy* (University of California Press, Berkeley/Los Angeles/London 1983).

Gordon, W. M. and O. F. Robinson, eds., *The Institutes of Gaius* (Cornell University Press, Ithaca, NY 1988).

Gotthelf, Allan, "Darwin on Aristotle," *Journal of the History of Biology* 32 (1999), 3–30.

Gourevitch, Danielle, *Le Mal d'être femme* (Les Belles Lettres, Paris 1984).

ead., *Le Triangle hippocratique dans le monde gréco-romain: Le Malade, sa maladie et son médecin* (B.E.F.A.R. 251) (École française de Rome, Rome 1984).

Gove, Philip Babcock, *Webster's Third New International Dictionary of the English Language Unabridged* (G. & C. Merriam, Springfield, MA 1968).

Grafton, Anthony, *Joseph Scaliger: A Study in the History of Classical Scholarship* (Clarendon Press/Oxford University Press, Oxford/New York 1983–93).

Graham, John A., Robert F. Heizer and Thomas R. Hester, *A Bibliography of Replicative Experiments in Archaeology* (Archaeological Research Facility, Department of Archaeology, University of California, Berkeley 1972).

Grant, Michael, *Roman Myths* (Penguin, Harmondsworth 1971).

Grasby, Richard, "Latin Inscriptions: Studies in Measurement and Making," *Papers of the British School at Rome* 70 (2002), 151–76.

Gratz, Timothy, *Early Greek Myth: A Guide to Literary and Artistic Sources* (Johns Hopkins University Press, Baltimore 1993).

Graves, Robert, "Dr Syntax and Mr Pound," *Punch* 255 (1953), 498.

id., *The Greek Myths* (Penguin, Harmondsworth 1992).

Greene, Kevin, "Technological Innovation and Economic Progress in the Ancient World: M. I. Finley Re-considered," *Economic History Review* 53 (2000), 29–59.

Grenfell, Bernard P. and Arthur S. Hunt, eds., *The Oxyrhynchus Papyri, Part I* (Egypt Exploration Fund: Graeco-Roman Branch, London 1898).

Grimal, Pierre, *The Dictionary of Classical Mythology* (Blackwell, Oxford 1996).

Grmek, Mirko Drazen, *Diseases in the Ancient Greek World* (Johns Hopkins University Press, Baltimore/London 1989).

id., ed., *Western Medical Thought from Antiquity to the Middle Ages* (Harvard University Press, Cambridge, MA 1998).

Groag, Edmund et al., *Prosopographia Imperii Romani*, second edition (de Gruyter, Berlin/Leipzig/New York 1933–).

Guarducci, Margherita, *Epigrafia Greca* (Libreria dello Stato, Roma 1967–78).

ead., *L'epigrafia greca dalle origini al tardo Impero* (Libreria dello Stato, Rome 1987).

ead., *Inscriptiones Creticae* (Libreria dello Stato, Rome 1935–50).

Gutas, Dimitri, *Greek Thought, Arabic Culture: The Graeco-Arabic Translation Movement in Baghdad and Early 'Abbāsid Society (2nd–4th/8th–10th Centuries)* (Routledge, London 1998).

Habinek, Thomas, *Ancient Rhetoric and Oratory* (Blackwell Introductions to the Classical World) (Blackwell, Oxford 2005).

Hall, Edith, *Inventing the Barbarian: Greek Self-Definition through Tragedy* (Clarendon Press, Oxford 1989).

Hall, Edith and Rosie Wyles, eds., *New Directions in Ancient Pantomime* (Oxford University Press, Oxford/New York 2008).

Halm, Karl, ed., *Rhetores Latini Minores* (Teubner, Leipzig 1863).

Halporn, James W., Martin Ostwald and Thomas G. Rosenmeyer, *The Meters of Greek and Latin Poetry* (Methuen, London 1963).

Halstead, Paul, "The Mycenaean Palatial Economy: Making the Most of the Gaps in the Evidence," *Proceedings of the Cambridge Philological Society* 38 (N.S.) (1992), 57–86.

Halton, Thomas P. and Stella O'Leary, *Classical Scholarship: An Annotated Bibliography* (Kraus International Publications, White Plains, NY 1986).

Hamilton, Edith, *Mythology* (Back Bay Books, Boston 1998).

Hammond, N. G. L., ed., *Atlas of the Greek and Roman World in Antiquity* (Noyes Press, Park Ridge, NJ 1981).

Hammond, N. G. L. and H. H. Scullard, eds., *The Oxford Classical Dictionary*, second edition (Clarendon Press, Oxford 1970).

Handley, E. W., *Menander and Plautus: A Study in Comparison. An Inaugural Lecture Delivered at University College London 5 February 1968* (H. K. Lewis, London 1968).

Hannah, Robert, *Greek and Roman Calendars: Constructions of Time in the Classical World* (Duckworth, London 2005).

Hansen, Mogens Herman and Thomas Heine Nielsen, *An Inventory of Archaic and Classical Poleis* (Oxford University Press, Oxford 2004).

Hansen, Peter Allan, *Carmina Epigraphica Graeca* (Texte und Kommentare 12, 15) (de Gruyter, Berlin/New York 1983–89).

Hard, Robin, *The Routledge Handbook of Greek Mythology: Based on H. J. Rose's Handbook of Greek Mythology* (Routledge, London/New York 2004).

Harder, Annette, *Euripides' Kresphontes and Archelaos: Introduction, Text and Commentary* (Mnemosyne Supplement 87) (Brill, Leiden 1985).

Hardie, Philip R., *Virgil* (Greece and Rome: New Surveys in the Classics 28) (Oxford University Press, Oxford 1998).

Hardwick, Lorna, *Reception Studies* (Greece and Rome: New Surveys in the Classics 33) (Oxford University Press, Oxford 2003).

Hardwick, Lorna and Christopher Stray, eds., *A Companion to Classical Receptions* (Blackwell Companions to the Ancient World) (Blackwell, Oxford 2008).

Harley, J. B. and David Woodward, eds., *The History of Cartography*, Vol. 1: *Cartography in Prehistoric, Ancient and Medieval Europe and the Mediterranean* (University of Chicago Press, Chicago/London 1987).

Harris, Edward M., "Antigone the Lawyer, or the Ambiguities of Nomos," in id., *Democracy and the Rule of Law in Classical Athens: Essays on Law, Society, and Politics* (Cambridge University Press, Cambridge 2006), 41–80.

Harrison, A. R. W., *The Law of Athens* (Clarendon Press, Oxford 1968).

Harrison, Jane Ellen, *Themis*, second edition (Cambridge University Press, Cambridge 1927).

Harvey, F. David, "The Wicked Wife of Ischomachos," *Échos du Monde Classique/Classical Views* 3 (N.S.) (1984), 68–70.

Hatch, Edwin and Henry A. Redpath, eds., *A Concordance to the Septuagint and the Other Greek Versions of the Old Testament (including the Apocryphal Books)* (Akademische Druck und Verlaganstalt, Graz 1954).

Havelock, Christine Mitchell, *The Aphrodite of Knidos and Her Successors: A Historical Review of the Female Nude in Greek Art* (University of Michigan Press, Ann Arbor 1995).

Head, Barclay V., *Historia Numorum*, second edition (Clarendon Press, Oxford 1910).

Heath, Malcolm, *Hermogenes on Issues: Strategies of Argument in Later Greek Rhetoric* (Clarendon Press, Oxford 1995).

id., *Interpreting Classical Texts* (Duckworth Classical Essays) (Duckworth, London 2002).

Heath, Thomas Little, Sir, ed., *Greek Astronomy* (Dent, London/Toronto 1932).

id., ed., *A History of Greek Mathematics* (Oxford University Press, Oxford 1921).

Henderson, Jeffrey, ed., *Aristophanes V (Fragments)* (Loeb Classical Library, Harvard University Press, Cambridge, MA/London 2007).

id., *The Maculate Muse: Obscene Language in Attic Comedy*, second edition (Oxford University Press, New York 1991).

Henig, Martin, ed., *A Handbook of Roman Art* (Phaidon, Oxford 1983).

Heubeck, Alfred et al., eds., *A Commentary on Homer's Odyssey* (Clarendon Press, Oxford 1988–92).

Heyerdahl, Thor, *The Kon-Tiki Expedition*, tr. F. H. Lyon (Transworld, London 1957).

Hicks, E. L. et al., eds., *The Collection of Ancient Greek Inscriptions in the British Museum* (Trustees of the British Museum, London 1874–1916).

Highet, Gilbert, *The Classical Tradition: Greek and Roman Influences on Western Literature* (Oxford University Press, New York/London 1949).

Hofmann, Walter and Gunther Wartenberg, *Der Bramarbas in der antiken Komödie* (Abhandlungen der Akademie der Wissenschaften der DDR) (Akademie-Verlag, Berlin 1973).

Hollis, Adrian S., ed., *Fragments of Roman Poetry c. 60 BC–AD 20* (Oxford University Press, Oxford 2007).

Honderich, Ted, ed., *The Oxford Companion to Philosophy*, second edition (Oxford University Press, Oxford/New York 2005).

Hooker, J. T., *Linear B: An Introduction* (Bristol Classical Press, Bristol 1980).

Horden, Peregrine and Nicholas Purcell, *The Corrupting Sea: A Study of Mediterranean History* (Blackwell, Oxford/Malden, MA 2000).

Hornblower, Simon, *A Commentary on Thucydides* (Clarendon Press, Oxford 1991–2008).

Hornblower, Simon and Antony Spawforth, eds., *The Oxford Classical Dictionary*, third edition (Oxford University Press, Oxford/New York 1996).

Horrocks, Geoffrey C., *Greek: A History of the Language and Its Speakers* (Longman, London/New York 1997).

Housman, A. E., "The Application of Thought to Textual Criticism," *Proceedings of the Classical Association* 18 (1921), 67–84.

How, W. W. and J. Wells, *A Commentary on Herodotus* (Clarendon Press, Oxford 1912).

Howgego, Christopher J., *Ancient History from Coins* (Routledge, London 1995).

Hübner, Wolfgang, ed., *Geographie und verwandte Wissenschaften* (Georg Wöhrle, ed., *Geschichte der Mathematik und der Naturwissenschaften in der Antike* 2) (Franz Steiner Verlag, Stuttgart 2000).

Humphrey, John W., *Ancient Technology* (Greenwood Guides to Historical Events of the Ancient World) (Greenwood Press, Westport, CT/London 2006).

Humphrey, John W., John P. Oleson and Andrew N. Sherwood, eds., *Greek and Roman Technology: A Sourcebook* (Routledge, London/New York 1998).

Humphreys, S. C., *Anthropology and the Greeks* (International Library of Anthropology) (Routledge & Kegan Paul, London/Henley/Boston 1978).

Icard, Séverin, *Dictionary of Greek Coin Inscriptions: Identification des monnaies par la nouvelle méthode des légendes fragmentées: Application de la méthode aux monnaies grecques et aux monnaies gauloises* (Argonaut, Chicago 1968).

Institut Fernand-Courby, *Nouveau choix d'inscriptions grecques* (Epigraphica 2) (Les Belles Lettres, Paris 2005).

Irby-Massie, Georgia L. and Paul T. Keyser, eds., *Greek Science of the Hellenistic Era: A Sourcebook* (Routledge, London/New York 2002).

Irving, Washington, *A History of the Life and Voyages of Christopher Columbus* (G. & C. Carvill, New York 1828).

Jacoby, Felix, ed., *Die Fragmente der griechischen Historiker* (Weidmann, Berlin 1923–58).

Jakobson, Roman, "On Linguistic Aspects of Translation," in R. A. Brower, ed., *On Translation* (Harvard University Press, Cambridge, MA 1959), 232–9, reprinted in id., *Selected Writings* (Mouton, The Hague 1962–87), II 260–6.

Jauss, Hans Robert, *Toward an Aesthetic of Reception* (Theory and History of Literature 2) (University of Minnesota Press, Minneapolis 1982).

Jeffery, L. H., *The Local Scripts of Archaic Greece*, second edition (Clarendon Press, Oxford 1990).

Jeffreys, Elizabeth, ed., *The Oxford Handbook of Byzantine Studies* (Oxford University Press, Oxford 2008).

Jenkins, Fred W., *Classical Studies: A Guide to the Reference Literature*, second edition (Reference Sources in the Humanities) (Libraries Unlimited, Westport, CT/London 2006).

Jenkyns, Richard, ed., *The Legacy of Rome: A New Appraisal* (Oxford University Press, Oxford 1992).

id., *The Victorians and Ancient Greece* (Blackwell, Oxford 1980).

Johnston, Sarah Iles, ed., *Religions of the Ancient World: A Guide* (Harvard University Press, Cambridge, MA/London 2004).

Jolowicz, H. F. and Barry Nicholas, *Historical Introduction to the Study of Roman Law*, third edition (Cambridge University Press, Cambridge 1972).

Jones, A. H. M., J. R. Martindale and J. Morris, *The Prosopography of the Later Roman Empire* (Cambridge University Press, Cambridge 1971–92).

Juvenal, *D. Ivnii Ivvenalis Satvrae editorvm in vsvm edidit A. E. Hovsman* (E. Grant Richards, London 1905).

Kallendorf, Craig W., ed., *A Companion to the Classical Tradition* (Blackwell Companions to the Ancient World) (Blackwell, Oxford 2007).

Kapparis, Konstantinos, *Abortion in the Ancient World* (Duckworth, London 2002).

Karamanolis, George E., *Plato and Aristotle in Agreement? Platonists on Aristotle from Antiochus to Porphyry* (Clarendon Press, Oxford 2006).

Kaser, Max, *Roman Private Law: A Translation*, fourth edition (University of South Africa, Pretoria 1984).

id., *Das römische Privatrecht* (Handbuch der Altertumswissenschaft) (C. H. Beck, München 1955–59).

Kaser, Max and Karl Hackl, *Das römische Zivilprozessrecht*, second edition (Handbuch der Altertumswissenschaft 10 Abt., 3. T., 4. Bd.) (C. H. Beck, München 1996).

Kassel, Rudolf and Colin Austin, eds., *Poetae Comici Graeci* (de Gruyter, Berlin/New York 1983–).

Katzoff, Ranon and David Schaps, eds., *Law in the Documents of the Judaean Desert* (Supplements to the Journal for the Study of Judaism 96) (Brill, Leiden/Boston 2005).

Kazazis, J. N., "Atticism," in Anastassios-Fivos Christidis, ed., *A History of Ancient Greek: From the Beginnings to Late Antiquity* (Cambridge University Press, Cambridge 2007), 1200–12.

Keil, Heinrich, *Grammatici Latini* (Teubner, Leipzig 1855–80).

Kelly, Michael, ed., *Encyclopedia of Aesthetics* (Oxford University Press, Oxford/New York 1998).

Kennedy, George A., *The Art of Persuasion in Greece* (Princeton University Press, Princeton, NJ 1963).

id., *The Art of Rhetoric in the Roman World* (Princeton University Press, Princeton, NJ 1972).

id., *Greek Rhetoric under Christian Emperors* (Princeton University Press, Princeton, NJ 1983).

id., *Invention and Method: Two Rhetorical Treatises from the Hermogenic Corpus* (Society of Biblical Literature, Atlanta, GA 2005).

id., *Later Greek Rhetoric* (Fort Collins, CO 2000).

id., *A New History of Classical Rhetoric* (Princeton University Press, Princeton, NJ 1994).

id., *Progymnasmata: Greek Textbooks of Prose Composition and Rhetoric* (Society of Biblical Literature, Atlanta, GA 2003).

Kent, J. P. C., *Roman Coins* (Thames & Hudson, London 1978).

Kenyon, F. G., "Two Greek School-Tablets," *JHS* 29 (1909), 29–40.

Keppie, Lawrence, *Understanding Roman Inscriptions* (Johns Hopkins University Press, Baltimore 1991).

Ketterer, Robert C., *Ancient Rome in Early Opera* (University of Illinois Press, Champaign 2008).

Kevers, Laurent and Bastien Kindt, "Vers un concordanceur-lemmatiseur en ligne du grec ancien," *L'Antiquité classique* 73 (2004), 203–13.

Keyser, Paul T. and Georgia L. Irby-Massie, eds., *The Encyclopedia of Ancient Natural Scientists: The Greek Tradition and Its Many Heirs* (Routledge, London/New York 2008).

Kienast, Dietmar, *Römische Kaisertabelle: Grundzüge einer römischen Kaiserchronologie* (Wissenschaftliche Buchgesellschaft, Darmstadt 1996).

Killebrew, Ann E., *Biblical Peoples and Ethnicity: An Archaeological Study of Egyptians, Canaanites, Philistines, and Early Israel, 1300–1100 B.C.E.* (Archaeology and Biblical Studies) (Society of Biblical Literature, Atlanta, GA 2005).

Killen, John T. and Jean-Pierre Olivier, *The Knossos Tablets: A Transliteration*, fifth edition (Ediciones Universidad de Salamanca, Salamanca 1989).

King, Helen, *Hippocrates' Woman: Reading the Female Body in Ancient Greece* (Routledge, London/New York 1998).

Kirchner, Johannes, *Prosopographia Attica*, second edition (de Gruyter, Berlin 1966).

Kirk, G. S., J. E. Raven and Malcolm Schofield, *The Presocratic Philosophers*, second edition (Cambridge University Press, Cambridge/New York 1983).

Klauser, Theodor et al., *Reallexikon für Antike und Christentum: Sachwörterbuch zur Auseinandersetzung des Christentums mit der Antiken Welt* (Hiersemann, Stuttgart 1950–).

Klebs, Elimar, Paul von Rohden and Hermann Dessau, *Prosopographia Imperii Romani Saec. I. II. III.*, first edition (Reimer, Berlin 1897–98).

Kleiner, Diana E. E., *Roman Sculpture* (Yale Publications in the History of Art) (Yale University Press, New Haven, CT 1992).

Kleiner, Fred S., *A History of Roman Art* (Thomson Wadsworth, Belmont, CA 2007).

Klotz, Alfred, ed., *Tragicorum Fragmenta* (Oldenbourg, München 1953).

Knox, Bernard, *Essays Ancient and Modern* (Johns Hopkins University Press, Baltimore 1989).

Knox, Peter E., ed., *A Companion to Ovid* (Blackwell Companions to the Ancient World) (Wiley-Blackwell, Chichester/Malden, MA 2009).

Koestermann, Erich, *C. Sallustius Crispus: Bellum Iugurthinum* (Carl Winter/ Universitätsverlag, Heidelberg 1971).

Korda, Michael, *Ike: An American Hero* (Harper, New York 2007).

Kovacs, David, "A Cautionary Tale," *Transactions of the American Philological Association* 123 (1993), 405–10.

Kraay, Colin M., *Archaic and Classical Greek Coins* (Methuen, London 1976).

id., *Greek Coins* (Thames & Hudson, London 1966).

Krämer, Sigrid and Birgit Christine Arensmann, *Ergänzungsband zu Latin Manuscript Books* (Monumenta Germaniae Historica, Hilfsmittel 23) (Hahnsche Buchhandlung, Hannover 2007).

Krebs, Johann Philipp, *Antibarbarus der lateinischen Sprache* (Schwabe, Basel 1905–07), available on web at http://www.archive.org/details/krebs, access date 26 May 2009.

Krestchmer, Paul and Ernst Locker, *Rückläufiges Wörterbuch der griechischen Sprache* (Vandenhoeck & Ruprecht, Göttingen 1944).

Kreyszig, E., "Archimedes and the Invention of Burning Mirrors: An Investigation of Work by Buffon," in John Michael Rassias, ed., *Geometry, Analysis and Mechanics* (World Scientific, River Edge, NJ 1994), 139–48.

Kristeller, Paul Oskar and Sigrid Krämer, *Latin Manuscript Books before 1600: A List of the Printed Catalogues and Unpublished Inventories of Extant Collections*, fourth edition (Monumenta Germaniae Historica, München 1993).

Krueger, Paul and Wilhelm Studemund, *Gai Institutiones ad Codicis veronensis apographum Studemundianum novis curis auctum*, seventh edition (Weidmann, Berlin 1923).

Krüger, Karl Wilhelm, *Griechische Sprachlehre für Schulen* (Neu-Ruppin, Leipzig 1871–79).

Krumeich, Ralf, Nikolaus Pechstein and Bernd Seidensticker, eds., *Das griechische Satyrspiel* (Texte zur Forschung 72) (Wissenschaftliche Buchgesellschaft, Darmstadt 1999).

Krummrey, Hans and Silvio Panciera, "Criteri di edizione e segni diacritici," *Tituli* 2 (1980), 205–15.

Kuhn, Thomas S., *The Structure of Scientific Revolutions*, second edition (International Encyclopedia of Unified Science) (Chicago University Press, Chicago 1970).

Kühner, Raphael and Bernhard Gerth, *Ausführliche Grammatik der griechischen Sprache*, third edition (Hahn, Hannover 1898–1904), available on web at http://www.perseus.tufts.edu/hopper/text?doc=Perseus%3Atext%3A1999.04.0019 (Parts I and II; for the two halves of Part III replace the last two digits by "19" or "20"), access date 17 June 2010.

Kühner, Raphael and Carl Stegmann, *Ausführliche Grammatik der lateinischen Sprache* (Hahn, Hannover 1912), available on web at http://www.archive.org/details/ausfhrlichegra01khuoft, access date 26 May 2009.

Kunej, Drago and Ivan Turk, "New Perspectives on the Beginnings of Music: Archaeological and Museological Analysis of a Middle Paleolithic Bone 'Flute,'" in Nils L. Wallin, Björn Merker and Steven Brown, eds., *The Origins of Music* (MIT Press, Cambridge, MA/London 2000), 235–68.

Lachmann, Karl, ed., *Novum Testamentum Graece et Latine* (Reimer, Berlin 1842–50).

LaFleur, Richard A., *Latin for the 21st Century: From Concept to Classroom* (Scott, Foresman, Glenview, IL 1998).

Lajtar, Adam, ed., *Catalogue of the Greek Inscriptions in the Sudan National Museum at Khartoum* (Orientalia Lovaniensia Analecta 122) (Peeters, Louvain 2003).

Lakatos, Imre and Alan Musgrave, eds., *Criticism and the Growth of Knowledge: Proceedings of the International Colloquium in the Philosophy of Science, London, 1965*, second edition (Cambridge University Press, Cambridge 1970).

Lake, Kirsopp and Silva Lake, eds., *Dated Greek Minuscule Manuscripts to the Year 1200* (Monumenta Palaeographica Vetera, first series) (American Academy of Arts and Sciences, Boston 1934–39).

Lakoff, George and Mark Johnson, *Metaphors We Live By* (University of Chicago Press, Chicago/London 1980).

Lakoff, George and Mark Turner, *More than Cool Reason: A Field Guide to Poetic Metaphor* (University of Chicago Press, Chicago 1989).

Lallot, Jean, ed., *Apollonius Dyscole, De la construction* (J. Vrin, Paris 1997).

Lampe, G. W. H., *A Patristic Greek Lexicon* (Clarendon Press, Oxford 1961–68).

Landfester, Manfred, in collaboration with Brigitte Egger, *Dictionary of Greek and Latin Authors and Texts* (Brill's New Pauly, Supplement 2) (Brill, Leiden/Boston 2009).

Langslow, D. R., *Medical Latin in the Roman Empire* (Oxford University Press, Oxford/New York 2000).

Larfeld, Wilhelm, *Griechische Epigraphik* (Handbuch der Klassischen Altertumswissenschaft) (C. H. Beck, München 1914).

id., *Handbuch der griechischen Epigraphik* (O. R. Reisland, Leipzig 1898–1907).

Latham, R. E., *Dictionary of Medieval Latin from British Sources* (Oxford University Press for the British Academy, London, 1975–).

Lausberg, Heinrich, *Handbook of Literary Rhetoric: A Foundation for Literary Study* (Brill, Leiden/Boston/Köln 1998).

Lawler, Lillian B., *The Dance in Ancient Greece* (Adam & Charles Black, London 1964).

Lawrence, A. W., *Greek Architecture*, fifth edition (Yale University Press Pelican History of Art) (Yale University Press, New Haven, CT 1996).

Lefkowitz, Mary R., *Not Out of Africa: How Afrocentrism Became an Excuse to Teach Myth as History* (Basic Books, New York 1996).

Lehoux, Daryn, *Astronomy, Weather, and Calendars in the Ancient World: Parapegmata and Related Texts in Classical and Near-Eastern Societies* (Cambridge University Press, Cambridge 2007).

Lejeune, Michel, *Précis d'accentuation grecque* (Hachette, Paris 1945).

Lennox, James G., *Aristotle's Philosophy of Biology: Studies in the Origins of Life Science* (Cambridge University Press, Cambridge/New York 2001).

Leonard, Miriam, *Athens in Paris: Ancient Greece and the Political in Post-War French Thought* (Oxford University Press, Oxford 2005).

Levine, Molly Myerowitz and John Peradotto, eds., *The Challenge of Black Athena* (Arethusa 22.1 [special issue]) (1989).

Lewis, Charlton T. and Charles Short, *A Latin Dictionary* (Clarendon Press, Oxford 1879). Available on web: see *Glossa* and *Perseus*.

Lewis, Naphtali, *Papyrus in Classical Antiquity* (Clarendon Press, Oxford 1974).

id., *Papyrus in Classical Antiquity: A Supplement* (Fondation Égyptologique Reine Élisabeth, Brussels 1989).

Liakos, Antonis, "'From Greek into Our Common Language': Language and History in the Making of Modern Greece," in A.-F. Christidis, ed., *A History of Ancient Greek: From the Beginnings to Late Antiquity* (Cambridge University Press, Cambridge 2007), 1287–95.

Liddell, Henry George and Robert Scott, *An Intermediate Greek–English Lexicon* (Clarendon Press, Oxford 1889).

id., *A Lexicon Abridged from the Greek–English Lexicon* (Clarendon Press, Oxford 1891).

Liddell, Henry George, Robert Scott and Sir Henry Stuart Jones, *A Greek–English Lexicon*, ninth edition (Clarendon Press, Oxford 1940).

Lindsay, W. M., *Notae Latinae: An Account of Abbreviation in Latin MSS. of the Early Minuscule Period* (c. 700–850) (Cambridge University Press, Cambridge 1915), available on web at http://www.archive.org/details/notaelatinae00linduoft, access date 11 May 2009.

Ling, Roger, *Roman Painting* (Cambridge University Press, Cambridge 1991).

Linke, Konstanze and Walter Haas, eds., *Die Fragmente des Grammatikers Dionysios Thrax; Die Fragmente der Grammatiker Tyrannion und Diokles* (Sammlung griechischer und lateinischer Grammatiker 3) (de Gruyter, Berlin/New York 1977).

Lipsius, Justus Hermann, *Das attische Recht und Rechtsverfahren* (O. R. Reisland, Leipzig 1905–15).

Lloyd, Alan B., *Herodotus: Book II* (Études preliminaires aux religions orientales dans l'empire romain) (Brill, Leiden 1975–88).

Lloyd, G. E. R., *Early Greek Science: Thales to Aristotle* (Ancient Culture and Society) (Norton, New York 1970).

id., *Greek Science after Aristotle* (Ancient Culture and Society) (Norton, New York 1973).

id., *Methods and Problems in Greek Science* (Cambridge University Press, Cambridge/New York 1991).

Lloyd-Jones, Hugh, ed., *Sophocles* (Loeb Classical Library) (Harvard University Press/Heinemann, Cambridge, MA/London 1994–97).

Lobel, Edgar and Denys Page, *Poetarum Lesbiorum Fragmenta* (Clarendon Press, Oxford 1955).

Lodge, Gonzalez, *Lexicon Plautinum* (Teubner, Leipzig 1904–33).

Lomanto, Valeria and Nino Marinone, eds., *Index Grammaticus: An Index to Latin Grammar Texts* (Alpha-Omega, Reihe A: Lexika, Indizes, Konkordanzen zur Klassischen Philologie) (Olms-Weidmann, Hildesheim/Zürich/New York 1990).

Long, A. A., ed., *The Cambridge Companion to Early Greek Philosophy* (Cambridge University Press, Cambridge 1999).

Long, A. A. and D. N. Sedley, *The Hellenistic Philosophers* (Cambridge University Press, Cambridge 1987).

Longrigg, James, *Greek Medicine from the Heroic to the Hellenistic Age: A Source Book* (Routledge, London/New York 1998).

Loomis, William T., *Wages, Welfare Costs and Inflation in Classical Athens* (University of Michigan Press, Ann Arbor 1998).

Loraux, Nicole, *The Experiences of Tiresias: The Feminine and the Greek Man* (Princeton University Press, Princeton, NJ 1995).

Lowe, E. A., *Codices Latini Antiquiores: A Palaeographical Guide to Latin Manuscripts prior to the Ninth Century* (Clarendon Press, Oxford 1934–71).

Lübker, Friedrich, J. Geffcken and E. Ziebarth, eds., *Friedrich Lübkers Reallexikon des klassischen Altertums*, eighth edition (Teubner, Leipzig/Berlin 1914).

Lucan, M. *Annaei Lvcani Belli civilis libri decem: Editorvm in vsvm edidit A.E. Hovsman* (Blackwell, Oxford 1926).

Luce, T. J., "Ancient Views on the Causes of Bias in Historical Writing," CP 84 (1989), 16–31.

Luck, Georg, *Arcana Mundi: Magic and the Occult in the Greek and Roman Worlds: A Collection of Ancient Texts*, second edition (Johns Hopkins University Press, Baltimore 2006).

Lucretius, *De rerum natura libri sex*, ed. Karl Lachmann (Reimer, Berlin 1850).

Lupu, Eran, *Greek Sacred Law: A Collection of New Documents (NGSL)* (Religions in the Graeco-Roman World, Vol. 152) (Brill, Leiden/Boston 2005).

Luraghi, Silvia, *On the Meaning of Prepositions and Cases: The Expression of Semantic Roles in Ancient Greek* (Studies in Language Companion Series 67) (J. Benjamins, Amsterdam/Philadelphia 2003).

Maas, Martha and Jane McIntosh Snyder, *Stringed Instruments of Ancient Greece* (Yale University Press, New Haven, CT/London 1989).

Maas, Paul, *Textual Criticism* (Clarendon Press, Oxford 1958).

MacDowell, Douglas M., ed., *Andokides, On the Mysteries* (Clarendon Press, Oxford 1962).

id., *The Law in Classical Athens* (Thames & Hudson, London 1978).

Macran, Henry S., ed., *The Harmonics of Aristoxenus* (Clarendon Press, Oxford 1902).

Maidment, K. J. and J. O. Burtt, *Minor Attic Orators* (Loeb Classical Library) (Harvard University Press, Cambridge, MA 1953–54).

Maier, Franz Georg, *Griechische Mauerbauinschriften* (Vestigia) (Quelle & Meyer, Heidelberg 1959–61).

Malcovati, Enrica, ed., *Oratorum Romanorum Fragmenta Liberae Rei Publicae*, fourth edition (Corpus Scriptorum Latiorum Paravianum) (G. B. Paravia, Turin 1976–79).

Malmkjær, Kirsten, *The Linguistics Encyclopedia*, second edition (Routledge, London/New York 2002).

Maltese, Enrico V., ed., *Ichneutae / Sofocle: Introduzione, testo critico, interpretazione e commento* (Gonnelli, Firenze 1982).

Mandouze, André, Charles Pietri, Luce Pietri and Sylvain Destephen, eds., *Prosopographie chrétienne du Bas-Empire* (Éditions du CNRS/École française de Rome/Association des amis du centre d'histoire et civilization de Byzance, Paris/Rome 1982–).

Manuwald, Gesine, *Fabulae praetextae: Spuren einer literarischen Gattung der Römer* (Zetemata 108) (C. H. Beck, München 2001).

Marinone, Nino and F. Guala, *All the Greek Verbs* (Duckworth, London 1985).

Marsden, Richard, *The Cambridge Old English Reader* (Cambridge University Press, Cambridge 2004).

Martin, Jean, "Un faux Ménandre," *Bulletin de l'Association Guillaume Budé* (1962), 120–1.

Martindale, Charles, ed., *The Cambridge Companion to Virgil* (Cambridge University Press, Cambridge 1997).

Martindale, Charles and Richard F. Thomas., eds., *Classics and the Uses of Reception* (Blackwell, Oxford/Malden, MA 2006).

Marx, Karl and Frederick Engels, *Collected Works* (International Press/Lawrence & Wishart, New York/London 1975–2004).

Marzullo, B., "Il Cairense di Menandro agli infrarossi," *Rheinisches Museum für Philologie* 104 (1961), 224–9.

Mathiesen, Thomas J., *Apollo's Lyre: Greek Music and Music Theory in Antiquity and the Middle Ages* (Publications of the Center for the History of Music Theory and Literature 11) (University of Nebraska Press, Lincoln/London 1999).

Mathieu, James R., ed., *Experimental Archaeology: Replicating Past Objects, Behaviors, and Processes* (BAR International Series 1035) (Archaeopress, Oxford 2002).

Mattingly, Harold et al., *Roman Imperial Coinage* (Spink, London 1923–).

Maurice, Lisa, *The Teacher in Ancient Rome*, unpub. Ph.D. thesis (Bar-Ilan University, 2001).

Mautner, John, *A Dictionary of Philosophy* (Blackwell, Oxford 1996).

Mayser, Edwin, *Grammatik der griechischen Papyri aus der Ptolemaërzeit: Mit Einschluss der gleichzeitigen Ostraka und der in Ägypten verfassten Inschriften* (de Gruyter, Berlin 1923–34).

McGuire, Martin R. P., *Introduction to Classical Scholarship: A Syllabus and Bibliographical Guide*, second edition (Catholic University of America Press, Washington, DC 1961).

McLean, B. Hudson, *An Introduction to Greek Epigraphy of the Hellenistic and Roman Periods from Alexander the Great down to the Reign of Constantine (323 B.C.–A.D. 337)* (University of Michigan Press, Ann Arbor 2002).

McTighe, Thomas P., "Galileo's Platonism," in Ernan McMullin, ed., *Galileo: Man of Science* (Basic Books, New York 1967), 365–87.

Meiggs, Russell and David M. Lewis, *A Selection of Greek Historical Inscriptions to the End of the Fifth Century B.C.* (Clarendon Press, Oxford 1969).

Meillet, A., *Aperçu d'une histoire de la langue grecque*, third edition (Hachette, Paris 1930).

id., *Introduction à l'étude comparative des langues indo-européennes* (Hachette, Paris 1937).

Meillet, A. and J. Vendryes, *Traité de grammaire comparée des langues classiques*, fourth edition (Champion, Paris 1968).

Meineke, August, ed., *Poetarum comicorum Graecorum fragmenta* (Didot, Paris 1855).

Meißner, Burkhard, *Die technologische Fachliteratur der Antike: Struktur, Überlieferung und Wirkung technischen Wissens in der Antike (ca. 400 v. Chr.–ca. 500 n. Chr.)* (Akademie Verlag, Berlin 1999).

Melena, José L. and Jean-Pierre Olivier, *Tithemy: The Tablets and Nodules in Linear B from Tiryns, Thebes and Mycenae: A Revised Transliteration* (Ediciones Universidad de Salamanca, Salamanca 1991).

Melville Jones, John, *A Dictionary of Ancient Greek Coins* (Seaby, London 1986).

id., *A Dictionary of Ancient Roman Coins* (Seaby, London 1990).

Menge, Hermann, Thorsten Burkard and Markus Schauer, *Lehrbuch der lateinischen Syntax und Semantik* (Wissenschaftliche Buchgesellschaft, Darmstadt 2000).

Merkelbach, Reinhold, ed., *Inschriften griechischer Städte aus Kleinasien* (Rudolf Habelt, Bonn 1972–).

Merkelbach, Reinhold and Josef Stauber, *Steinepigramme aus dem griechischen Osten* (Teubner/K. G. Saur, Stuttgart/Leipzig 1998–2004).

Michaelides, Solon, *The Music of Ancient Greece: An Encyclopaedia* (Faber and Faber, London 1978).

Migne, Jacques-Paul, *Patrologiae Cursus Completus* (J.-P. Migne, Paris 1844–58), consisting of:

id., *Patrologia Graeca* (J.-P. Migne, Paris 1857–58), and

id., *Patrologia Latina* (J.-P. Migne, Paris 1844–45).

Miller, Paul Allen, *Postmodern Spiritual Practices: The Construction of the Subject and the Reception of Plato in Lacan, Derrida, and Foucault* (Ohio State University Press, Columbus 2007).

Mills, A. A. and R. Clift, "Reflections of the 'Burning Mirrors of Archimedes.' With a Consideration of the Geometry and Intensity of Sunlight Reflected from Plane Mirrors," *European Journal of Physics* 13 (1992), 268–79.

Mitteis, Ludwig and Ulrich Wilcken, *Grundzüge und Chrestomathie der Papyruskunde* (Teubner, Leipzig 1912).

Modiano, Mario S., "How Archimedes Stole Sun to Burn Foe's Fleet; Far Better Conditions, Large Number of Mirrors," *New York Times*, 11 November 1973, Section GN, p. 16, available on web at http://select.nytimes.com/gst/abstract.html?res=FA0E14FE3E5D127A93C3A8178AD95F478785F9&scp=2&sq=archimedes%201973&st=cse, access date 25 June 2009.

Momigliano, Arnaldo, *Contributo alla Storia degli Studi Classici* (Edizioni di Storia e Letteratura, Rome 1955).

id., *Nono Contributo alla Storia degli Studi Classici e del Mondo Antico* (Storia e Letteratura: Raccolta di Studi e Testi 180) (Edizioni di Storia e Letteratura, Rome 1992).

id., *Secondo Contributo alla Storia degli Studi Classici* (Storia e Letteratura: Raccolta di Studi e Testi 77) (Edizioni di Storia e Letteratura, Rome 1964).

id., *Studies in Historiography* (Weidenfeld & Nicolson, London 1966).

id., *Terzo Contributo alla Storia degli Studi Classici e del Mondo Antico* (Storia e Letteratura: Raccolta di Studi e Testi 108–109) (Edizioni di Storia e Letteratura, Rome 1966).

Mommsen, Theodor et al., eds., *Corpus Iuris Civilis* (Weidmann, Berlin 1872–95).

Mommsen, Theodor, Paul Krueger and Alan Watson, *The Digest of Justinian* (University of Pennsylvania Press, Philadelphia 1985).

Mommsen, Theodor and Paul Meyer, eds., *Theodosiani Libri xvi* (Weidmann, Berlin 1905).

Montanari, Franco, ed., *I frammenti dei grammatici Agathokles, Hellanikos Ptolemaios Epithetes: In appendice i grammatici Theophilos, Anaxagoras, Xenon* (Sammlung griechischer und lateinischer Grammatiker 7) (de Gruyter, Berlin/New York 1988).

Moore, Timothy, "When Did the Tibicen Play? Meter and Musical Accompaniment in Roman Comedy," *Transactions of the American Philological Association* 138 (2008), 3–46.

Morel, W., Karl Büchner and Jürgen Blänsdorf, *Fragmenta Poetarum Latinorum Epicorum et Lyricorum praeter Ennium et Lucilium*, third edition (Bibliotheca Scriptorum Graecorum et Romanorum Teubneriana) (Teubner, Stuttgart/Leipzig 1995).

Morris, Errol, "The Most Curious Thing," *New York Times*, 19 May 2008, available on web at http://morris.blogs.nytimes.com/2008/05/19/the-most-curious-thing, access date 25 June 2009.

Morris, Ian, "Classical Archaeology," in John Bintliff, ed., *A Companion to Archaeology* (Blackwell, Oxford 2004), 253–71.

Morrison, John S., J. F. Coates and N. B. Rankov, *The Athenian Trireme: The History and Reconstruction of an Ancient Greek Warship*, second edition (Cambridge University Press, Cambridge 2000).

Morwood, James, ed., *Pocket Oxford Latin Dictionary*, third edition (Oxford University Press, Oxford/New York, 2005).

Mossner, Ernest Campbell, *The Life of David Hume*, second edition (Clarendon Press, Oxford 1980).

Muhs, Brian P., ed., *Tax Receipts, Taxpayers, and Taxes in Early Ptolemaic Thebes* (Oriental Institute Publications 126) (Oriental Institute of the University of Chicago, Chicago 2005).

Müller, Carl Werner, *Euripides: Philoktet: Testimonien und Fragmente* (Texte und Kommentare 21) (de Gruyter, Berlin/New York 2000).

Müller, Karl Wilhelm Ludwig, ed., *Fragmenta Historicorum Graecorum* (Firmin-Didot, Paris 1841–1938).

id., *Geographi Graeci Minores* (Didot, Paris 1855–61).

Murray, James A. H., ed., *A New English Dictionary on Historical Principles: Founded Mainly on the Materials Collected by the Philological Society* (Clarendon Press, Oxford 1884–1928).

Murray, K. M. Elisabeth, *Caught in the Web of Words: James A. H. Murray and the Oxford English Dictionary* (Yale University Press, New Haven, CT 1977).

Murray, Tim, ed., *Encyclopedia of Archaeology* (ABC-CLIO, Santa Barbara, CA 1999–2001).

Mylonas, George E., *Mycenae and the Mycenaean Age* (Princeton University Press, Princeton, NJ 1966).

Naerebout, F. G., *Attractive Performances: Ancient Greek Dance: Three Preliminary Studies* (J. C. Gieben, Amsterdam 1997).

Nauck, Augustus, ed., *Tragicorum Graecorum fragmenta*, second edition (Teubner, Leipzig 1889).

Nelis, Jan, "Constructing Fascist Identity: Benito Mussolini and the Myth of *Romanità*," *CW* 100 (2007), 391–415.

Nestle, Eberhard and Erwin, Barbara and Kurt Aland et al., eds., *Novum Testamentum Graece*, twenty-seventh edition (Deutsche Bibelgesellschaft, Stuttgart 1993).

Netz, Reviel, *From Problems to Equations: A Study in the Transformation of Early Mediterranean Mathematics* (Cambridge University Press, Cambridge 2004).

id., *Ludic Proof: Greek Mathematics and the Alexandrian Aesthetic* (Cambridge University Press, Cambridge 2008).

id., *The Shaping of Deduction in Greek Mathematics: A Study in Cognitive History* (Ideas in Context 51) (Cambridge University Press, Cambridge 1999).

Neugebauer, Otto, *The Exact Sciences in Antiquity* (Brown University Press, Providence, RI 1957).

id., *A History of Ancient Mathematical Astronomy* (Studies in the History of Mathematics and Physical Sciences) (Springer-Verlag, New York/Heidelberg/Berlin 1975).

Nicholas, Barry, *An Introduction to Roman Law* (Clarendon Press, Oxford 1962).

Nicholas, Barry and Ernest Metzger, *An Introduction to Roman Law* (Clarendon Press, Oxford 2008).

Nickel, Rainer, *Lexikon der antiken Literatur* (Artemis & Winkler, Düsseldorf/Zürich 1999).

Nicolet-Pierre, Hélène, *Numismatique grecque* (Les outils de l'histoire) (Armand Colin, Paris 2002).

Niermeyer, Jan Frederik and J. W. J. Burgers, *Mediae Latinitatis Lexicon Minus* (Brill, Leiden 2002).

Nisbet, R. G. M., "The Speeches," in T. A. Dorey, ed., *Cicero* (Routledge & Kegan Paul, London 1965), 47–79.

North, John A., *Roman Religion* (Greece and Rome: New Surveys in the Classics 30) (Oxford University Press, Oxford 2000).

Nünlist, René, *The Ancient Critic at Work: Terms and Concepts of Literary Criticism in Greek Scholia* (Cambridge University Press, Cambridge 2009).

Nutton, Vivian, *Ancient Medicine* (Sciences of Antiquity) (Routledge, London/New York 2004).

id., ed., *The Unknown Galen* (BICS Supplement 77) (Institute of Classical Studies, London 2002).

Oakley, S. P., *A Commentary on Livy, Books VI–X* (Clarendon Press, Oxford/New York 1997–2005).

Oates, John F. et al., eds., *Checklist of Editions of Greek, Latin, Demotic, and Coptic Papyri, Ostraca and Tablets*, fifth edition (Bulletin of the American Society of Papyrologists Supplement 9) (American Society of Papyrologists, Oakville, CT 2001).

Ogilvie, R. M., *A Commentary on Livy, Books I–V* (Clarendon Press, Oxford 1965).

Oikonomides, Al. N., *Abbreviations in Greek Inscriptions, Papyri, Manuscripts and Early Printed Books* (Ares, Chicago 1974).

Oleson, John P., *Bronze Age, Greek and Roman Technology: A Select, Annotated Bibliography* (Garland, New York 1986).

id., ed., *The Oxford Handbook of Engineering and Technology in the Classical World* (Oxford University Press, Oxford/New York 2008).

Olson, S. Douglas, *Broken Laughter: Select Fragments of Greek Comedy* (Oxford University Press, Oxford 2007).

Oniga, Renato, *Il Latino: Breve introduzione linguistica*, second edition (FrancoAngeli, Milano 2007).

Orser, Charles E., Jr., ed., *Encyclopedia of Historical Archaeology* (Routledge, London/New York 2002).

Österreichische Akademie der Wissenschaften, *Corpus Scriptorum Ecclesiasticorum Latinorum* (Verlag der Österreichische Akademie der Wissenschaften, Vienna 1866–).

Österreichische Akademie der Wissenschaften, *Tituli Asiae Minoris* (Hoelder-Pichler-Tempsky, Vienna 1901–).

Oxford Handbooks, see under Bagnall; Boys-Stones; Jeffreys; Oleson.

Page, D. L., *Lyrica Graeca Selecta* (Clarendon Press, Oxford 1968).

id., *Poetae Melici Graeci* (Clarendon Press, Oxford 1962).

Palmer, L. R., *The Greek Language* (The Great Languages) (Faber and Faber, London/Boston 1980).

id., *The Latin Language* (The Great Languages) (Faber and Faber, London 1954).

Palmer, L. R. and John Boardman, *On the Knossos Tablets* (Clarendon Press, Oxford 1963).

Panciera, Silvio, "Struttura dei supplementi e segni diacritici dieci anni dopo," *Supplementa Italica* 8 (1991), 2–9.

Panessa, Giangiacomo, *Fonti greche e latine per la storia dell'ambiente e del clima nel mondo greco* (Pubblicazioni della classe di lettere e filosofia 8) (Scuola Normale Superiore, Pisa 1991).

Parker, William Riley, "Where Do English Departments Come From?," *College English* 28 (1966/67), 339–51.

Pasquali, Giorgio, *Storia della tradizione e critica del testo*, second edition (Le Monnier, Firenze 1962).

Passow, Franz, *Handwörterbuch der griechischen Sprache*, fifth edition (F. C. W. Vogel, Leipzig 1841–57).

Patai, Daphne and Will H. Corral, eds., *Theory's Empire: An Anthology of Dissent* (Columbia University Press, New York 2005).

Patillon, Michel, ed., *Corpus rhetoricum* (Collection des universités de France [Budé]) (Les Belles Lettres, Paris 2008–).

Pauly, A., G. Wissowa and W. Kroll, eds., *Real-Encyclopädie der klassischen Altertumswissenschaft* (Druckenmüller, Stuttgart 1893–1980).

Pauly, August Friedrich von, Christian Walz and Wilhelm Sigismund Teuffel, *Pauly's Real-Encyclopädie der classischen Alterthumswissenschaft*, second edition (J. B. Metzler, Stuttgart 1842–66).

Peacock, Sandra J., *Jane Ellen Harrison: The Mask and the Self* (Yale University Press, New Haven, CT 1988).

Pearson, Lionel, ed., *Aristoxenus Elementa Rhythmica* (Clarendon Press, Oxford 1990).

Pellegrin, Pierre, *Aristotle's Classification of Animals: Biology and the Conceptual Unity of the Aristotelian Corpus*, revised edition, tr. Anthony Preus (University of California Press, Berkeley 1986).

Pelzer, Auguste, *Abréviations latines médiévales: Supplément au Dizionario di abbreviature latine ed italiane de Adriano Cappelli* (Publications universitaires/Béatrice-Nauwelaerts, Louvain/Paris 1964).

Pestman, P. W., *New Papyrological Primer* (Brill, Leiden 1990).

Peter, Hermann Wilhelm Gottlob, ed., *Historicorum Romanorum Reliquiae*, second edition (Bibliotheca Scriptorum Graecorum et Romanorum Teubneriana) (Teubner, Leipzig 1906–14).

Peters, Francis E., *Greek Philosophical Terms: A Historical Lexicon* (New York University Press, New York 1967).

Petzl, Georg, "Epigraphik," in Heinz-Günther Nesselrath, ed., *Einleitung in die griechische Philologie* (Teubner, Stuttgart/Leipzig 1997), 72–83.

Pfeiffer, Rudolf, *History of Classical Scholarship* (Clarendon Press, Oxford 1968–76).

Pharr, Clyde, Theresa Sherrer Davidson and Mary Brown Pharr, *The Theodosian Code and Novels, and the Sirmondian Constitutions* (The Corpus of Roman Law [Corpus Juris Romani] v. 1) (Princeton University Press, Princeton, NJ 1952).

Phillips, E. D., *Greek Medicine* (Thames & Hudson, London/New York 1973).

Pinkster, Harm, *Latin Syntax and Semantics* (Romance Linguistics) (Routledge, London/New York 1990).

Plant, Richard, *Greek Coin Types and Their Identification* (Seaby, London 1979).

Platnauer, Maurice, ed., *Fifty Years (and Twelve) of Classical Scholarship* (Blackwell, Oxford 1968).

Pöhlmann, Egert and Martin L. West, *Documents of Ancient Greek Music* (Clarendon Press, Oxford 2001).

Pollard, A. M. et al., *Analytical Chemistry in Archaeology* (Cambridge Manuals in Archaeology) (Cambridge University Press, Cambridge 2007).

Popper, Karl Raimund, Sir, *The Open Society and Its Enemies*, fifth edition (Princeton University Press, Princeton, NJ 1966).

Portal, Jane, ed., *The First Emperor: China's Terracotta Army* (British Museum Press, London 2007).

Porter, Stanley E., ed., *Handbook of Classical Rhetoric in the Hellenistic Period (300 B.C.–A.D. 400)* (Brill, Leiden/New York/Köln 1997).

Powell, J. Enoch, *A Lexicon to Herodotus* (Cambridge University Press, London 1938).

Preiser, Claudia, *Euripides: Telephos: Einleitung, Text, Kommentar* (Spudasmata 78) (Georg Olms Verlag, Hildesheim/Zürich/New York 2000).

Preisigke, Friedrich, *Namenbuch* (Heidelberg 1922).

id., *Wörterbuch der griechischen Papyrusurkunden* (Selbstverlag der Erben, Berlin 1925–71).

Preisigke, Friedrich et al., eds., *Berichtungsliste der griechischen Papyrusurkunden aus Ägypten* (Brill, Leiden/Boston/Köln 1922–).

id., eds., *Sammelbuch griechischer Urkunden aus Ägypten* (Trübner, Strassburg 1915–).

Preston, Laura, "Late Minoan II to III B Crete," in Cynthia W. Shelmerdine, ed., *The Cambridge Companion to the Aegean Bronze Age* (Cambridge University Press, Cambridge 2008), 310–26.

Preuss, Siegmund, *Index Demosthenicus* (Teubner, Leipzig 1892).

Price, Simon and Emily Kearns, *The Oxford Dictionary of Classical Myth and Religion* (Oxford University Press, Oxford/New York 2003).

Probert, Philomen, *A New Short Guide to the Accentuation of Ancient Greek* (Bristol Classical Press, Bristol 2003).

Prott, Hans Theodor Anton and Ludwig Ziehen, *Leges Graecorum Sacrae e titulis collectae* (Teubner, Leipzig 1896–1906).

Prudhommeau, Germaine, *La Danse grecque antique* (Centre national de la recherche scientifique, Paris 1965).

Quicherat, Louis and Émile Chatelain, *Thesaurus Poeticus Linguae Latinae* (Hachette, Paris 1922).

Rabe, Hugo, ed., *Aphtonii Progymnasmata* (Rhetores Graeci 10) (Teubner, Leipzig 1926).

id., ed., *Hermogenis Opera* (Rhetores Graeci 6) (Teubner, Leipzig 1913).

id., ed., *Ioannis Sardiani Commentarium in Aphthonii Progymnasmata* (Rhetores Graeci 15) (Teubner, Leipzig 1928).

id., ed., *Prolegomenon sylloge; accedit Maximi libellus De obiectionibus insolubilibus* (Rhetores Graeci 14) (Teubner, Leipzig 1931).

Rabinowitz, Mario, "Falling Bodies: The Obvious, the Subtle, and the Wrong," *IEEE Power Engineering Review* 10 (1990), 27–31.

Rahlfs, Alfred, ed., *Septuaginta* (Bibelanstalt, Stuttgart 1935).

Ramsauer, G., *Aristotelis Ethica Nicomachea* (Teubner, Leipzig 1878).

Raven, D. S., *Greek Metre: An Introduction* (Faber and Faber, London 1962).

id., *Latin Metre: An Introduction* (Faber and Faber, London 1965).

Reece, Richard and Simon James, *Identifying Roman Coins: A Practical Guide to the Identification of Site Finds in Britain* (Seaby, London 1986).

Reid, Jane Davidson, *The Oxford Guide to Classical Mythology in the Arts, 1300–1990s* (Oxford University Press, New York 1993).

Reinhold, Meyer, *Classica Americana: The Greek and Roman Heritage in the United States* (Wayne State University Press, Detroit 1984).

Rémy, Bernard and François Kayser, *Initiation à l'épigraphie grecque et latine* (Universités/ Histoire) (Ellipses, Paris 1999).

Renehan, Robert, *Greek Textual Criticism: A Reader* (Loeb Classical Monographs) (Harvard University Press, Cambridge, MA 1970).

Renfrew, Colin, "The Great Tradition versus the Great Divide: Archeology as Anthropology?," *AJA* 84 (1980), 287–98.

Rengakos, Antonios and Antonis Tsakmakis, eds., *Brill's Companion to Thucydides* (Brill's Companions in Classical Studies) (Brill, Leiden/New York/Köln 2006).

Reynolds, L. D., ed., *Texts and Transmission: A Survey of the Latin Classics* (Clarendon Press, Oxford 1983).

Reynolds, L. D. and N. G. Wilson, *Scribes and Scholars: A Guide to the Transmission of Greek and Latin Literature*, third edition (Oxford University Press, Oxford 1991).

Rhodes, P. J., "The Cambridge Ancient History," *Histos* 3 (1999), available on web at http://www.dur.ac.uk/Classics/histos/1999/rhodes.html, access date 26 May 2009.

Rhodes, P. J. and David M. Lewis, *The Decrees of the Greek States* (Clarendon Press, Oxford 1997).

Rhodes, P. J. and Robin Osborne, *Greek Historical Inscriptions 404–323 BC* (Oxford University Press, Oxford 2003).

Ribbeck, Otto, *Scaenicae Romanorum Poesis Fragmenta*, third edition (Teubner, Leipzig 1897–98), consisting of id., *Comicorum Romanorum Fragmenta*, and id., *Tragicorum Romanorum Fragmenta*.

Riccobono, Salvatore et al., *Fontes Iuris Romani Antejustiniani* (S. A. G. Barbèra, Firenze 1941–43, 1969).

Rice, Prudence M., *Pottery Analysis: A Sourcebook* (University of Chicago Press, Chicago/London 1987).

Richter, Gisela M. A., *A Handbook of Greek Art*, ninth edition (Phaidon, London 1987).

Rickenbacker, William F., *Wooden Nickels: Or, the Decline and Fall of Silver Coins* (Arlington House, New Rochelle, NY 1966).

Riddle, John M., *Contraception and Abortion from the Ancient World to the Renaissance* (Harvard University Press, Cambridge, MA 1992).

Ridley, R. T., "To Be Taken with a Pinch of Salt: The Destruction of Carthage," *CP* 81 (1986), 140–6.

Riese, Alexander, *Geographi Latini Minores* (Henninger, Heilbronn 1878).

Rihll, T. E., *Greek Science* (Greece and Rome: New Surveys in the Classics 29) (Oxford University Press, Oxford 1999).

Rijksbaron, Albert, ed., *New Approaches to Greek Particles* (Amsterdam Studies in Classical Philology 7) (J. C. Gieben, Amsterdam 1997).

id., *The Syntax and Semantics of the Verb in Classical Greek: An Introduction* (J. C. Gieben, Amsterdam 2002).

Robert, J. and L. et al., *Bulletin épigraphique* (Les Belles Lettres, Paris 1938–).

Robinson, Andrew, *The Man Who Deciphered Linear B: The Story of Michael Ventris* (Thames & Hudson, London/New York 2002).

Robinson, Annabel, *The Life and Work of Jane Ellen Harrison* (Oxford University Press, Oxford 2002).

Robinson, O. F., *Ancient Rome: City Planning and Administration* (Routledge, London/New York 1992).

ead., *The Sources of Roman Law: Problems and Methods for Ancient Historians* (Routledge, London/New York 1997).

Rochelle, Mercedes, *Mythological and Classical World Art Index: A Locator of Paintings, Sculptures, Frescoes, Manuscript Illuminations, Sketches, Woodcuts, and Engravings Executed 1200 B.C. to A.D. 1900, with a Directory of the Institutions Holding Them* (McFarland, Jefferson, NC 1991).

Roisman, Joseph, ed., *Brill's Companion to Alexander the Great* (Brill, Leiden/New York/Köln 2003).

Roscher, W. H., ed., *Ausfürliches Lexikon der griechischen und römischen Mythologie* (Teubner, Leipzig 1884–1937).

Rose, H. J., *A Handbook of Greek Mythology: Including Its Extension to Rome*, sixth edition (Methuen, London 1958).

Rostovtzeff, M. I., *The Social and Economic History of the Hellenistic World* (Clarendon Press, Oxford 1941).

Rouse, W. H. D., *Iliad: The Story of Achilles* (New American Library, New York 1954).

Rowe, Christopher and Malcolm Schofield, eds., *The Cambridge History of Greek and Roman Political Thought* (Cambridge University Press, Cambridge 2000).

Rowe, Galen O., "Style," in Stanley E. Porter, ed., *Handbook of Classical Rhetoric in the Hellenistic Period (300 B.C.–A.D. 400)* (Brill, Leiden/New York/Köln 1997), 121–57.

Ruggiero, Ettore de, *Dizionario epigrafico di antichità romane* (L. Pasqualucci, Rome 1895).

Runes, Dagobert D., ed., *Dictionary of Philosophy* (Philosophical Library, New York 1983), available on web at http://www.ditext.com/runes/index.html, access date 28 April 2009.

Rüpke, Jörg, *Fasti Sacerdotum: A Prosopography of Pagan, Jewish, and Christian Religious Officials in the City of Rome, 300 BC to AD 499* (Oxford University Press, Oxford 2008).

Ruschenbusch, Eberhard, ed., *Solonos Nomoi: Die Fragmente des Solonischen Gesetzeswerkes, mit einer Text- und Überlieferungsgeschichte* (F. Steiner, Wiesbaden 1966).

Rushforth, G. McN., *Latin Historical Inscriptions Illustrating the History of the Early Empire*, second edition (Oxford University Press, London 1930).

Russo, Lucio, *The Forgotten Revolution: How Science Was Born in 300 BC and Why It Had to Be Reborn* (Springer, Berlin 2004).

Russu, Ioan I., *Inscripţiile Daciei romane* (Editura Academiei Republicii Socialiste România, Bucureşti 1975–).

Rychlewska, Ludwika, ed., *Turpilii Comici Fragmenta* (Teubner, Leipzig 1971).

Sallares, Robert, *The Ecology of the Ancient Greek World* (Duckworth, London 1991).

Samama, Évelyne, *Les médecins dans le monde grec: Sources épigraphiques sur la naissance d'un corps médical* (Droz, Geneva 2003).

Sambursky, S., *The Physical World of the Greeks* (Routledge & Kegan Paul, London 1956).

Samuel, Alan E., *Greek and Roman Chronology* (Handbuch der Altertumswissenschaft) (C. H. Beck, München 1972).

Sandbach, F. H., *Menandri Reliquiae Selectae* (Oxford Classical Texts) (Clarendon Press, Oxford 1990).

Sandys, John Edwin, Sir, *A History of Classical Scholarship*, third edition (Cambridge University Press, Cambridge 1921).

id., *Latin Epigraphy: An Introduction to the Study of Latin Inscriptions*, second edition (Cambridge University Press, London 1927).

Saussure, Ferdinand de, *Course in General Linguistics*, ed. Charles Bally and Albert Sechehaye, tr. Roy Harris (Duckworth, London 1983).

Schad, Samantha, *A Lexicon of Latin Grammatical Terminology* (Studia Erudita 6) (Fabrizio Serra, Pisa/Rome 2007).

Schaps, David M., "The Found and Lost Manuscripts of Tacitus' Agricola," CP 74 (1979), 28–42.

id., *The Invention of Coinage and the Monetization of Ancient Greece* (University of Michigan Press, Ann Arbor 2004).

Scheidel, Walter, Ian Morris and Richard Saller, eds., *The Cambridge Economic History of the Greco-Roman World* (Cambridge University Press, Cambridge 2007).

Scheltema, H.-J., "Das Kommentarverbot Justinians," *Tijdschrift voor Rechtsgeschiedenis* 45 (1977), 307–31.

Schepens, Guido, "Jacoby's FGrHist: Problems, Methods, Prospects," in Glenn W. Most, ed., *Collecting Fragments—Fragmente sammeln* (Vandenhoeck & Ruprecht, Göttingen 1997), 1–33.

Schiavone, Aldo, ed., *Storia di Roma* (Einaudi, Turin 1988–93).

Schlam, Carl and Ellen Finkelpearl, "A Review of Scholarship on Apuleius' 'Metamorphoses' 1970–1998," Lustrum 42 (2000), 7–224.

Schlesinger, Kathleen, *The Greek Aulos: A Study of Its Mechanism and of Its Relation to the Modal System of Ancient Greek Music* (Methuen, London 1939).

Schliemann, Heinrich, *Ilios, the City and Country of the Trojans: The Results of Researches and Discoveries on the Site of Troy and throughout the Troad in the Years 1871, 72, 73, 78, 79* (J. Murray, London 1880).

id., *Mycenae: A Narrative of Researches and Discoveries at Mycenae and Tiryns* (J. Murray, London 1878).

id., *Tiryns: The Prehistoric Palace of the Kings of Tiryns, the Results of the Latest Excavations* (C. Scribner's Sons, New York 1885).

id., *Troja: Results of the Latest Researches and Discoveries on the Site of Homer's Troy and in the Heroic Tumuli and the Other Sites, Made in the Year 1882* (J. Murray, London 1884).

id., *Troy and Its Remains: A Narrative of Researches and Discoveries Made on the Site of Ilium, and in the Trojan Plain* (J. Murray, London 1875).

Schmidt, Dennis J., *On Germans and Other Greeks: Tragedy and Ethical Life* (Studies in Continental Thought) (Indiana University Press, Bloomington/Indianapolis 2001).

Schneider, Johann Gottlob, *Griechisch–Deutsches Wörterbuch beym Lesen der griechischen profanen Scribenten zu Gebrauchen*, third edition (Hahn, Leipzig 1819).

Schneider, R. and G. Uhlig, eds., *Grammatici Graeci* (Teubner, Leipzig 1878–1910).

Schreiber, Toby, *Athenian Vase Construction: A Potter's Analysis* (J. Paul Getty Museum, Malibu 1999).

Schubart, Wilhelm, *Griechische Palaeographie* (Handbuch der Altertumswissenschaft) (C. H. Beck, München 1925).

Schürmann, Astrid, ed., *Physik/Mechanik* (Georg Wöhrle, ed., *Geschichte der Mathematik und der Naturwissenschaften in der Antike* 3) (Franz Steiner Verlag, Stuttgart 2005).

Schütrumpf, E., ed., *Heraclides of Pontus* (Rutgers University Studies in Classical Humanities 14) (Transaction, Piscataway, NJ 2008).

Schwinge, Ernst-Richard, ed., *Die Wissenschaften vom Altertum am Ende des 2. Jahrtausends n. Chr.* (Teubner, Stuttgart/Leipzig 1995).

Schwyzer, Eduard and Albert Debrunner, *Griechische Grammatik auf der Grundlage von Karl Brugmanns griechischer Grammatik*, second edition (Handbuch der Altertumswissenschaft) (C. H. Beck'sche Verlagsbuchhandlung, München 1939–53).

Scott, S. P., *The Civil Law, including the Twelve Tables, the Institutes of Gaius, the Rules of Ulpian, the Opinions of Paulus, the Enactments of Justinian, and the Constitutions of Leo* (Central Trust Company, Cincinnati 1932).

Sealey, Raphael, *The Justice of the Greeks* (University of Michigan Press, Ann Arbor 1994).

Sear, David R., *Greek Coins and Their Values* (Seaby, London 1978–79).

id., *Greek Imperial Coins and Their Values: The Local Coinages of the Roman Empire* (Seaby, London 1982).

id., *Roman Coins and Their Values* (Spink, London 2000–).

Sear, Frank, *Roman Architecture*, second edition (Routledge, London/New York 1998).

Séchan, Louis, *La Danse grecque antique* (De Boccard, Paris 1930).

Seckel, E. and B. Kuebler, eds., *Gaius: Institutiones* (Teubner, Leipzig 1935).

Sedley, David, ed., *The Cambridge Companion to Greek and Roman Philosophy* (Cambridge University Press, Cambridge 2003).

Seider, Richard, *Paläographie der griechischen Papyri* (Anton Hiersemann, Stuttgart 1967–90).

Seidl, Erwin, *Ptolemäische Rechtsgeschichte*, second edition (Ägyptologische Forschungen) (J. J. Augustin, Glückstadt/Hamburg/New York 1962).

id., *Rechtsgeschichte Ägyptens als römischer Provinz (Die Behauptung des ägyptischen Rechts neben dem römischen)* (Hans Richarz, Sankt Augustin 1973).

Semple, Clara, *A Silver Legend: The Story of the Maria Theresa Thaler* (Barzan, Manchester 2005).

Serbat, Guy, *Grammaire fondamentale du latin* (Bibliothèque d'Études Classiques) (Peeters, Louvain/Paris 1996–).

Settis, Salvatore, ed., *I Greci: Storia Cultura Arte Società* (Einaudi, Turin 1996–2002).

Shaw, Ian and Robert Jameson, eds., *A Dictionary of Archaeology* (Blackwell, Oxford 1999).

Shay, Jonathan, *Achilles in Vietnam: Combat Trauma and the Undoing of Character* (Atheneum, New York 1994).

Shelmerdine, Cynthia W., ed., *The Cambridge Companion to the Aegean Bronze Age* (Cambridge University Press, Cambridge 2008).

Sherk, Robert K., *Roman Documents from the Greek East: Senatus Consulta and Epistulae to the Age of Augustus* (Johns Hopkins University Press, Baltimore 1969).

Sherratt, Andrew, ed., *The Cambridge Encyclopedia of Archaeology* (Cambridge University Press, Cambridge 1980).

Sihler, Andrew L., *New Comparative Grammar of Greek and Latin* (Oxford University Press, New York/Oxford 1995).

Simon, Erika, *Die griechischen Vasen*, second edition (Hirmer Verlag, München 1981).

Simpson, D. P., *Cassell's Latin–English English–Latin Dictionary*, fifth edition (Cassell, London 1968).

Simpson, D. P. and Philip Vellacott, *Writing in Latin: Style and Idiom for Advanced Latin Prose* (Longman, London 1970).

Simpson, J. A. and E. S. C. Weiner, *The Oxford English Dictionary*, second edition (Clarendon Press, Oxford 1989).

Singer, Suzanne F., "Rising Again: Hi-Tech Tools Reconstruct Umm el-Kanatir," *Biblical Archaeology Review* 33 (2007)/6, 52–60, 86.

Singh, J. A. L., Reverend and Robert M. Zingg, *Wolf-Children and Feral Man* (Harper & Brothers, New York/London 1942).

Skutsch, Otto, ed., *The Annals of Q. Ennius* (Clarendon Press, Oxford 1985).

Slater, Philip E., *The Glory of Hera: Greek Mythology and the Greek Family* (Beacon Press, Boston 1968).

Smith, R. R. R., *Hellenistic Sculpture: A Handbook* (The World of Art Library) (Thames & Hudson, London 1991).

Smith, William, Sir, *A Dictionary of Greek and Roman Antiquities*, third edition (J. Murray, London 1901).

id., *A Dictionary of Greek and Roman Biography and Mythology* (J. Murray, London 1902).

id., *Dictionary of Greek and Roman Geography* (J. Murray, London 1878).

Smith, William, Sir and Theophilus D. Hall, *A Copious and Critical English–Latin Dictionary* (Harper, New York 1871), available on web at http://www.grexlat.com/biblio/smith, access date 26 May 2009.

Smyth, Herbert Weir, *Greek Grammar* (Harvard University Press, Cambridge, MA 1920).

Snell, Bruno, Richard Kannicht and S. Radt, eds., *Tragicorum Graecorum fragmenta* (Vandenhoeck & Ruprecht, Göttingen 1971–2004).

Snell, Bruno and Hans Joachim Mette, *Lexikon des frühgriechischen Epos* (Vandenhoeck & Ruprecht, Göttingen 1955–).

Snodgrass, Anthony M., *An Archaeology of Greece* (University of California Press, Berkeley 1987).

id., "The New Archaeology and the Classical Archaeologist," *AJA* 89 (1985), 31–7.

Sokolowski, Franciszek, *Lois sacrées de l'Asie mineure* (Travaux et mémoires des anciens membres étrangers de l'école et de divers savants, fasc. ix) (École française d'Athènes [De Boccard], Paris 1955).

id., *Lois sacrées des cités grecques* (Travaux et mémoires des anciens membres étrangers de l'école et de divers savants, fasc. xviii) (École française d'Athènes [De Boccard], Paris 1968).

id., *Lois sacrées des cités grecques: Supplément* (Travaux et mémoires des anciens membres étrangers de l'école et de divers savants, fasc. xi) (École française d'Athènes [De Boccard], Paris 1962).

Sommerstein, Alan, ed., *Aeschylus* (Loeb Classical Library) (Harvard University Press, Cambridge, MA/London 2008).

id., *The Sound Pattern of Ancient Greek* (Publications of the Philological Society 23) (Blackwell, Oxford 1973).

Sommerstein, Alan H., David Fitzpatrick and Thomas Talboy, *Sophocles: Selected Fragmentary Plays* (Aris & Phillips, Oxford 2006–).

Sophocles, Evangelinus Apostolides, *Greek Lexicon of the Roman and Byzantine Periods* (From B. C. 146 to A. D. 1100) (Scribner, New York 1887).

Sorabji, Richard, "Ideas Leap Barriers: The Value of Historical Studies to Philosophy," in Dominic Scott, ed., *Maieusis: Essays in Ancient Philosophy in Honour of Myles Burnyeat* (Oxford University Press, Oxford/New York 2007), 374–90.

id., *The Philosophy of the Commentators, 200–600 AD: A Sourcebook* (Cornell University Press, Ithaca, NY 2005).

id., "The Transformation of Plato and Aristotle," in Harold Tarrant and Dirk Baltzly, eds., *Reading Plato in Antiquity* (Duckworth, London 2006).

Souter, Alexander, *A Glossary of Later Latin* (Clarendon Press, Oxford 1949).

Sparrow, John Hanbury Angus, *Mark Pattison and the Idea of a University* (Cambridge University Press, Cambridge 1967).

Spengel, Leonhard von, *Rhetores Graeci* (Teubner, Leipzig 1853–56); Vol. 1, Part 2 was re-edited and expanded by Caspar Hammer (Teubner, Leipzig 1894).

Spolsky, Ellen, *Satisfying Skepticism: Embodied Knowledge in the Early Modern World* (Ashgate, Aldershot 2001).

Stärk, Ekkehard, *Die Menaechmi des Plautus und kein griechisches Original* (Gunter Narr Verlag, Tübingen 1989).

Stein, Peter, *Roman Law in European History* (Cambridge University Press, Cambridge/New York 1999).

Steinby, Eva Margareta, ed., *Lexicon Topographicum Urbis Romae* (Quasar, Rome 1993–2000).

Steiner, George, *Antigones* (Clarendon Press, Oxford 1984).

Stephanus, Henricus, "Excerpta ex H. Stephani Epistola a. 1569 Edita Qua ad multas multorum Amicorum respondet, de suae Typographiae Statu, nominatimque de suo Thesauro Linguae Graecae," in Henricus Stephanus, ed., *Thesaurus Graecae Linguae* (A. J. Valpy, London 1816–28), xxix–xxxvi (in the appendix to the Paris edition, Vol. 8, XXXVII–L).

id., *Thesaurus Graecae Linguae*, second edition (H. Stephani oliva, Geneva 1582); revised editions A. J. Valpy, London 1816–28 and Ambroise Firmin-Didot, Paris 1831–65.

Stephanus, Robertus, *Dictionarium seu Latinae Linguae Thesaurus* (Robertus Stephanus, Paris 1536).

Stern, Ephraim, ed., *New Encyclopedia of Archaeological Excavations in the Holy Land* (Clarendon Press, Oxford 1993–2008).

Stevenson, Seth William, C. Roach Smith and Frederic W. Madden, *A Dictionary of Roman Coins, Republican and Imperial* (George Bell and Sons, London 1889).

Stiebing, W. H., *Uncovering the Past: A History of Archaeology* (Oxford University Press, Oxford 1993).

Stillwell, Richard, William L. MacDonald and Marian Holland McAllister, eds., *The Princeton Encyclopedia of Classical Sites* (Princeton University Press, Princeton, NJ 1976).

Sullivan, J. P., *Ezra Pound and Sextus Propertius: A Study in Creative Translation* (University of Texas Press, Austin 1964).

Sundwall, J., *Nachträge zur Prosopographia Attica* (Finska Vetenskaps-Societetens Förhandlingar 52) (Akademiska Bokhandeln, Helsinki 1910).

Susini, Giancarlo, *The Roman Stonecutter: An Introduction to Latin Epigraphy* (Blackwell, Oxford 1973).

Syme, Ronald, Sir, *The Roman Revolution* (Oxford University Press, Oxford 1939).

Szemerényi, O. J. L., *Introduction to Indo-European Linguistics* (Clarendon Press, Oxford 1999).

Talbert, Richard J. A., *Barrington Atlas of the Greek and Roman World* (Princeton University Press, Princeton, NJ/Oxford 2000).

id., "Greek and Roman Mapping: Twenty-First Century Perspectives," in Richard J. A. Talbert and Richard W. Unger, eds., *Cartography in Antiquity and the Middle Ages: Fresh Perspectives, New Methods* (Brill, Leiden/Boston 2008), 9–27.

id., *The Senate of Imperial Rome* (Princeton University Press, Princeton, NJ 1984).

Tarn, W. W., *The Greeks in Bactria and India*, second edition (Cambridge University Press, Cambridge 1951).

Taub, Liba, *Ancient Meteorology* (Sciences of Antiquity) (Routledge, London 2003).

Taubenschlag, Rafal, *The Law of Greco-Roman Egypt in the Light of the Papyri 332 B.C.–640 A.D.*, second edition (Państwowe Wydawnictwo Naukowe, Warsaw 1955).

Taylor, Michael W., *The Tyrant Slayers: The Heroic Image in Fifth Century BC Athenian Art and Politics* (Arno Press, New York 1981).

Temporini, Hildegard and Wolfgang Haase, eds., *Aufstieg und Niedergang der römischen Welt: Geschichte und Kultur Roms im Spiegel der neueren Forschung* (de Gruyter, Berlin 1972–).

Theodoridis, Christos, ed., *Die Fragmente des Grammatikers Philoxenos* (Sammlung griechischer und lateinischer Grammatiker 7) (de Gruyter, Berlin 1976).

Thomas, J. A. C., *Textbook of Roman Law* (North-Holland Publishing Co., Amsterdam/New York 1976).

Thompson, D'Arcy Wentworth, Sir, *A Glossary of Greek Birds*, new edition (Oxford University Press, London 1936).

id., *A Glossary of Greek Fishes* (Oxford University Press, London 1947).

Thompson, Edward Maunde, Sir, *A Handbook of Greek and Latin Palaeography* (International Scientific Series) (Kegan Paul, Trench, Trubner & Co., London 1893).

id., *An Introduction to Greek and Latin Palaeography* (Clarendon Press, Oxford 1912), available on web at http://www.archive.org/details/greeklatin00thomuoft, access date 11 May 2009.

Thomson, George Derwent, *Aeschylus and Athens*, fourth edition (Lawrence & Wishart, London 1973).

Thomson, J. O., *History of Ancient Geography* (Cambridge University Press, Cambridge 1948).

Threatte, Leslie, *The Grammar of Attic Inscriptions* (de Gruyter, Berlin/New York 1980–96).

Thurmond, David L., *A Handbook of Food Processing in Classical Rome: For Her Bounty No Winter* (Technology and Change in History 9) (Brill, Leiden/Boston/Köln 2006).

Timpanaro, Sebastiano, *The Genesis of Lachmann's Method* (University of Chicago Press, Chicago 2005).

Tintori, Giampiero, *La musica di Roma antica: Ricerca iconografica a cura di Thea Tibiletti* (Akademos, Lucca 1996).

Tod, Marcus Neibuhr, *A Selection of Greek Historical Inscriptions* (Clarendon Press, Oxford 1933–48).

Todd, Robert B., ed., *Dictionary of British Classicists* (Thoemmes Press, Bristol 2004).

Todd, S. C., *A Commentary on Lysias, Speeches 1–11* (Oxford University Press, Oxford 2007).

id., *The Shape of Athenian Law* (Clarendon Press, Oxford 1993).

Tönnies, Ferdinand, *Community and Civil Society* (Cambridge Texts in the History of Political Thought) (Cambridge University Press, Cambridge/New York 2001).

Touloumakos, Johannes, "Aristoteles' 'Politik' 1925–1985," *Lustrum* 32 (1990), 177–282; 35 (1993), 181–289; 39 (1997), 7–305; 40 (2001), 7–197, 261–78; with "Addenda et Corrigenda" in 43 (2001), 7–9.

Tracy, Stephen V., *Athenian Democracy in Transition: Attic Letter-Cutters of 340 to 290 B.C.* (Hellenistic Culture and Society 20) (University of California Press, Berkeley/Los Angeles/Oxford 1995).

id., *Athens and Macedon: Attic Letter-Cutters of 300 to 229 B.C.* (Hellenistic Culture and Society 38) (University of California Press, Berkeley/Los Angeles/Oxford 2003).

id., *Attic Letter-Cutters of 229 to 86 B.C.* (Hellenistic Culture and Society 6) (University of California Press, Berkeley/Los Angeles/Oxford 1990).

id., *The Lettering of an Athenian Mason* (Hesperia Supplement 15) (American School of Classical Studies at Athens, Princeton, NJ 1975).

Traill, David A., *Schliemann of Troy: Treasure and Deceit* (St. Martin's Press, New York 1995).

Traill, John S., *Persons of Ancient Athens* (Athenians, Toronto 1994–).

Trask, R. L. and Robert McCall Millar, ed., *Trask's Historical Linguistics*, second edition (Hodder Arnold, London 2007).

Trauptman, John C., *The Bantam New College Latin and English Dictionary*, revised and enlarged edition (Bantam, New York 1995).

Triantaphyllopoulos, Johannes, *Das Rechtsdenken der Griechen* (Münchener Beiträge zur Papyrusforschung und antiken Rechtsgeschichte 78) (C. H. Beck, München 1985).

Triki, Irini, Οι Φιλοσοφικές Σχολές της Αρχαιότητας και η Δομή του Σύγχρονου Ελληνικού Πανεπιστημίου: Συγκριτική Θεώρηση, in Socrates L. Skartsis, ed., *Ancient Greece and the Modern World: 2nd World Congress, Ancient Olympia, 12–17 July 2002* (University of Patras, Patras 2003), 305–23.

Tuominen, Miira, *The Ancient Commentators on Plato and Aristotle* (University of California Press, Berkeley 2009).

Tuplin, C. J. and T. E. Rihll, eds., *Science and Mathematics in Ancient Greek Culture* (Oxford University Press, Oxford/New York 2002).

Turner, E. G., *Greek Manuscripts of the Ancient World* (Princeton University Press, Princeton, NJ 1971).

id., *Greek Papyri: An Introduction* (Clarendon Press, Oxford/New York 1980).

Ueding, Gert, ed., *Historisches Wörterbuch der Rhetorik* (M. Niemeyer, Tübingen 1992–).

Union Académique Internationale, *Novum Glossarium Mediae Latinitatis ab Anno DCCC ad Annum MCC* (Ejnar Muksgaard/U.A.I., Copenhagen/Brussels 1957–).

Unione Accademica Nazionale, *Inscriptiones Italiae* (Libreria dello Stato, Rome 1931–).

Urmson, J. O., *The Greek Philosophical Vocabulary* (Duckworth, London 1990).

Usher, Stephen, *Greek Oratory: Tradition and Originality* (Oxford University Press, Oxford 1999).

van Effenterre, Henri and Françoise Ruzé, eds., *Nomima: Recueil d'inscriptions politiques et juridiques de l'archaïsme grec* (Collection de l'école française de Rome 188) (École française de Rome, Palais Farnèse 1994–95).

van Minnen, Peter, "An Official Act of Cleopatra (with a Subscription in Her Own Hand)," *Ancient Society* 30 (2000), 29–34.

Ventris, Michael and John Chadwick, *Documents in Mycenaean Greek* (Cambridge University Press, Cambridge 1956).

id., *Documents in Mycenaean Greek*, second edition (Cambridge University Press, Cambridge 1973).

Vermeer, H., "Skopos and Commission in Translational Action," in Andrew Chesterman, ed., *Readings in Translation Theory* (Oy Finn Lectura Ab, Helsinki 1989), 173–87.

Vlastos, Gregory, *Socrates, Ironist and Moral Philosopher* (Cornell University Press, Ithaca, NY 1991).

id., *Socratic Studies* (Cambridge University Press, Cambridge 1994).

Vollkommer, Rainer, *Künstlerlexikon der Antike* (K. G. Saur, München/Leipzig 2001–04).

von Jan, Carl, ed., *Musici Scriptores Graeci* (Bibliotheca Scriptorum Graecorum et Romanorum Teubneriana) (Teubner, Leipzig 1895).

von Ranke, Leopold, *Geschichten der romanischen und germanischen Völker von 1494 bis 1514*, second edition (Leopold von Ranke's Sämmtliche Werke 33–34) (Duncker und Humblot, Leipzig 1874).

von Staden, Heinrich, *Herophilus: The Art of Medicine in Early Alexandria* (Cambridge University Press, Cambridge 1989).

Vretska, Karl, *C. Sallustius Crispus: De Catilinae Coniuratione* (Carl Winter/ Universitätsverlag, Heidelberg 1976).

Wacht, Manfred, *Concordantia Vergiliana* (Alpha-Omega, Reihe A: Lexika-Indizes-Konkordanzen zur klassischen Philologie 154) (Olms-Weidmann, Hildesheim/Zürich/New York 1996).

Walbank, F. W., *A Historical Commentary on Polybius* (Clarendon Press, Oxford 1957–79).

Walde, A. and J. B. Hofmann, *Lateinisches Etymologisches Wörterbuch*, third edition (Carl Winter, Heidelberg 1938–56).

Wallis, John, *Claudii Ptolemaei Harmonicorum Libri Tres* (E Theatro Sheldoniano, Oxford 1682).

Walsh, E. H. C., *Punch-Marked Coins from Taxila* (Memoirs of the Archaeological Survey of India 59) (Manager of Publications, Delhi 1939).

Walz, Christian, ed., *Rhetores Graeci* (J. G. Cotta, Stuttgart 1832–36).

Waquet, Françoise, *Latin, or, The Empire of a Sign: From the Sixteenth to the Twentieth Century* (Verso, London/New York 2001).

Ward-Perkins, J. B., *Roman Imperial Architecture*, second edition (Yale University Press Pelican History of Art) (Yale University Press, New Haven, CT 1981).

Watkin, Thomas Glyn, *An Historical Introduction to Modern Civil Law* (Ashgate-Dartmouth, Aldershot/Brookfield, NH/Singapore/Sydney 1999).

Watkins, Calvert, *The American Heritage Dictionary of Indo-European Roots*, fourth edition (Houghton Mifflin, Boston 2000).

Watson, Alan, ed., *The Digest of Justinian* (University of Pennsylvania Press, Philadelphia 1998).

id., *The Law of Persons in the Later Roman Republic* (Clarendon Press, Oxford 1967).

id., *The Law of Succession in the Later Roman Republic* (Clarendon Press, Oxford 1971).

Webb, Ruth, *Demons and Dancers: Performance in Late Antiquity* (Harvard University Press, Cambridge, MA 2008).

Weber, Marianne, *Max Weber: A Biography* (Wiley, New York 1975).

Weber, Max, *Roman Agrarian History*, tr. Richard I. Frank (Gorgias Press, Pisacataway, NJ 2008).

Wehrli, Fritz, *Die Schule des Aristoteles*, second edition (Schwabe, Basel 1967–69).

id., *Die Schule des Aristoteles: Supplementband I, II* (Schwabe, Basel 1974, 1978).

Wellington, Jean Susorney, *Dictionary of Bibliographic Abbreviations Found in the Scholarship of Classical Studies and Related Disciplines*, second edition (Praeger, Westport, CT/London 2003).

Werre-de Haas, M., *Aeschylus' Dictyulci: An Attempt at Reconstruction of a Satyric Drama* (Papyrologica Lugduno-Batava 10) (Brill, Leiden 1961).

West, David, *Cast Out Theory: Horace Odes 1.4 and 4.7* (Classical Association, London 1995).

West, Martin L., review of H. Lloyd-Jones and N. G. Wilson, *Sophoclis Fabulae*, and idem, *Sophoclea*, CR 41 (N.S.) (1991), 299–301.

id., *Ancient Greek Music* (Clarendon Press, Oxford 1994).

id., *Delectus ex Iambis et Elegis Graecis* (Clarendon Press, Oxford 1980).

id., *The East Face of Helicon: West Asiatic Elements in Greek Poetry and Myth* (Clarendon Press, Oxford 1997).

id., *Greek Metre* (Clarendon Press, Oxford 1982).

id., *Iambi et Elegi Graeci ante Alexandrum Cantati* (Clarendon Press, Oxford 1971–72, 1989).

id., *Textual Criticism and Editorial Technique Applicable to Greek and Latin Texts* (Teubner, Stuttgart 1973).

White, Hayden, *Metahistory: The Historical Imagination in Nineteenth-Century Europe* (Johns Hopkins University Press, Baltimore/London 1973).

White, K. D., *Greek and Roman Technology* (Cornell University Press, Ithaca, NY 1984).

Whitehead, Alfred North, *Process and Reality: An Essay in Cosmology. Gifford Lectures Delivered in the University of Edinburgh during the Session 1927–28* (Macmillan, New York 1929).

Whitehead, David, *Hypereides: The Forensic Speeches* (Oxford University Press, Oxford 2000).

Whitehouse, Ruth D., ed., *The Macmillan Dictionary of Archaeology* (Macmillan Reference Books) (Macmillan, London 1983).

Whitley, James, *The Archaeology of Ancient Greece* (Cambridge World Archaeology) (Cambridge University Press, Cambridge 2001).

Wieacker, Franz, *Römische Rechtsgeschichte: Quellenkunde, Rechtsbildung, Jurisprudenz und Rechtsliteratur* (C. H. Beck, München 1988).

Wikander, Örjan, ed., *Handbook of Ancient Water Technology* (Technology and Change in History 2) (Brill, Leiden/Boston/Köln 2000).

Wilamowitz-Möllendorff, Ulrich von, review of Felix Jacoby, *Die Fragmente der griechischen Historiker*, T.2, *Deutsche Literaturzeitung* 22 (1926), 1044–7.

id., *History of Classical Scholarship* (Duckworth, London 1982).

Wilcken, Ulrich, *Griechische Ostraka aus Ägypten und Nubien* (von Giesecke & Devrient, Leipzig/Berlin 1899).

Wille, Günther, *Musica Romana: Die Bedeutung der Musik im Leben der Römer* (P. Schippers, Amsterdam 1967).

id., *Schriften zur Geschichte der antiken Musik, mit einer Bibliographie zur antiken Musik 1957–1987* (Quellen und Studien zur Musikgeschichte von der Antike bis in die Gegenwart 26) (Peter Lang, Frankfurt am Main 1997).

Willis, James, *Latin Textual Criticism* (Illinois Studies in Language and Literature 61) (University of Illinois Press, Urbana/Chicago/London 1972).

Wilson, N. G., *From Byzantium to Italy: Greek Studies in the Italian Renaissance* (Johns Hopkins University Press, Baltimore 1992).

id., *Scholars of Byzantium* (Duckworth, London 1983).

Wilson Jones, Mark, *Principles of Roman Architecture* (Yale University Press, New Haven, CT 2000).

Wimsatt, W. K. and Monroe C. Beardsley, *The Verbal Icon* (University of Kentucky Press, Lexington 1954).

Winckelmann, Johann Joachim, *History of Ancient Art* (Frederick Ungar, New York 1968).

Winnington-Ingram, R. P., ed., *Aristidis Quintiliani de Musica Libri Tres* (Bibliotheca Scriptorum Graecorum et Romanorum Teubneriana) (Teubner, Leipzig 1963).

Wiseman, T. P., *The Myths of Rome* (University of Exeter Press, Exeter 2004).

Wittgenstein, Ludwig, *Tractatus Logico-Philosophicus* (Kegan Paul, Trench, Trubner & Co., London 1922).

Wittke, Anne-Maria, Eckart Olshausen and Richard Szydlak, *Historischer Atlas der antiken Welt* (*Der Neue Pauly* Supplemente Band 3) (J. B. Metzler, Stuttgart/Weimar 2004).

Wöhrle, Georg, ed., *Biologie* (id., ed., *Geschichte der Mathematik und der Naturwissenschaften in der Antike* 3) (Franz Steiner Verlag, Stuttgart 1999).

Wolf, Erik, *Griechisches Rechtsdenken* (Klostermann, Frankfurt am Main 1950–70).

Wolf, Friedrich August, *Prolegomena ad Homerum* (Princeton University Press, Princeton, NJ 1985).

Wolff, Hans Julius and Hans-Albert Rupprecht, ed., *Das Recht der griechischen Papyri Ägyptens in der Zeit der Ptolemaeer und des Prinzipats* (Handbuch der Altertumswissenschaft) (C. H. Beck, München 1978–2002).

Woodhead, A. G., *The Study of Greek Inscriptions*, second edition (Cambridge University Press, Cambridge 1981).

Woodhouse, Sidney Chawner, *English–Greek Dictionary: A Vocabulary of the Attic Language* (Routledge, London 1910), available on web at http://www.lib.uchicago.edu/efts/Woodhouse, access date 26 May 2009.

id., *The Englishman's Pocket Latin–English and English–Latin Dictionary* (Routledge & Kegan Paul, London 1913).

Woodman, A. J. and R. H. Martin, *The Annals of Tacitus: Book 3* (Cambridge Classical Texts and Commentaries 32) (Cambridge University Press, Cambridge 1996).

Wooten, Cecil W., *Hermogenes' On Types of Style* (University of North Carolina Press, Chapel Hill 1987).

Worthington, Ian, ed., *Brill's New Jacoby* (Brill, Leiden/Boston/Köln, forthcoming); access to an online version is available for purchase at http://www.brill.nl/default.aspx?partid=64&cid=854, access date 25 May 2009.

Wright, G. R. H., *Ancient Building Technology* (Technology and Change in History, Vols. 4 and 7) (Brill, Leiden/Boston/Köln 2000–05).

Wuensch, Richard, *Defixionum Tabellae* (IG[1] 3 Appendix) (Reimer, Berlin 1897).

Wyse, William, *The Speeches of Isaeus* (Cambridge University Press, Cambridge 1904).

Yiftach-Firanko, Uri, *Marriage and Marital Arrangements: A History of the Greek Marriage Document in Egypt 4th Century BCE–4th Century CE* (Münchener Beiträge zur Papyrusforschung und antiken Rechtsgeschichte 93) (C. H. Beck, München 2003).

Zalta, Edward N., *Stanford Encyclopedia of Philosophy*, at http://plato.stanford.edu, access date 27 May 2009.

Zeyl, Donald J., ed., *Encyclopedia of Classical Philosophy* (Greenwood Press, Westport, CT 1997).

Ziegler, Konrat and Walther Sontheimer, eds., *Der Kleine Pauly: Lexikon der Antike* (Alfred Druckenmüller, Stuttgart 1964–75).

Zimmermann, Reinhard, *The Law of Obligations: Roman Foundations of the Civilian Tradition* (Juta, Cape Town 1990).

id., *Roman Law, Contemporary Law, European Law: The Civilian Tradition Today* (Oxford University Press, Oxford/New York 2001).

Zimmern, Alfred E., Sir, "Was Greek Civilization Based on Slave Labor?," *Sociological Review* (1909)/2, 1–19, 159–67, reprinted in Sir Alfred E. Zimmern, *Solon and Croesus* (Oxford University Press, H. Milford, London 1928).

Ziolkowski, Theodore, *Varieties of Literary Thematics* (Princeton University Press, Princeton, NJ 1983).

Zukofsky, Celia and Louis Zukofsky, *Catullus (Gai Valeri Catulli Veronensis Liber)* (Cape Goliard Press, London 1969).

Zumpt, Karl Gottlob, *Ueber den Bestand der philosophischen Schulen in Athen und die Succession der Scholarchen* (F. Dümmler, Berlin 1843).

INDEX

The items in this index represent concepts, not individual words. Since, for example, the study of codices is discussed on pages 254–5, that passage appears under the heading "codicology" despite the fact that the word "codicology" does not appear on those pages; on the other hand, although Richard III and Henry VII of England are mentioned by way of example on page 3, they do not appear in the index. I have tried to err on the side of inclusiveness, but limitations of space have restricted many items, and removed from the index many modern scholars who deserve to be there. Numbers in **boldface** indicate page ranges where the subject indicated is the main topic treated.